CAMBRIDGE LATIN AMERICAN STUDIES

10

MINERS AND MERCHANTS IN BOURBON MEXICO 1763–1810

THE SERIES

1 SIMON COLLIER. *Ideas and Politics of Chilean Independence, 1808–1833*

2 M. P. COSTELOE. *Church Wealth in Mexico: A Study of the Juzgado de Capellanias in the Archbishopric of Mexico, 1800–1856*

3 PETER CALVERT. *The Mexican Revolution, 1910–1914: The Diplomacy of Anglo-American Conflict*

4 RICHARD GRAHAM. *Britain and the Onset of Modernization in Brazil, 1850–1914*

5 HERBERT S. KLEIN. *Parties and Political Change in Bolivia, 1880–1952*

6 LESLIE BETHELL. *The abolition of the Brazilian slave trade: Britain, Brazil and the slave trade question, 1807–1869*

7 DAVID BARKIN AND TIMOTHY KING. *Regional Economic Development: The River Basin Approach in Mexico*

8 CELSO FURTADO. *Economic Development of Latin America: A Survey from Colonial Times to the Cuban Revolution*

9 WILLIAM PAUL MCGREEVEY. *An Economic History of Colombia, 1845–1930*

10 D. A. BRADING. *Miners and Merchants in Bourbon Mexico, 1763–1810*

11 JAN BAZANT. *Alienation of Church Wealth in Mexico. Social and Economic Aspects of Liberal Revolution, 1856–1875*

12 BRIAN HAMNETT. *Politics and Trade in Southern Mexico*

MINERS AND MERCHANTS IN BOURBON MEXICO 1763–1810

BY

D. A. BRADING

Assistant Professor of History
University of California
Berkeley

CAMBRIDGE
AT THE UNIVERSITY PRESS
1971

Published by the Syndics of the Cambridge University Press
Bentley House, 200 Euston Road, London N.W.1
American Branch: 32 East 57th Street, New York, N.Y.10022

Library of Congress Catalogue Card Number: 74-123666

ISBN 0 521 07874 1

Printed in Great Britain
at the Aberdeen University Press

FOR MY MOTHER

CONTENTS

PLATES

TABLES AND FIGURES

TABLES

FIGURES

PREFACE

Eight years have passed since, after a summer's wandering through Mexico, I came to Guanajuato, Valenciana and San Miguel Allende and there, almost by chance, found what I wanted to study. With the place chosen, the time could only be the eighteenth century, the period when these towns assumed their present form. By inclination, I was, anyway, a student of colonialism. But if the scholar chooses his theme it is the availability of source material which disposes the lines he must pursue. Very little of much value has been written about eighteenth-century New Spain. To this very day the best account is still Alexander von Humboldt's *Essai politique sur le Royaume de la Nouvelle-Espagne*, first published in 1811. During the struggle for Independence and the decades which followed Juan López de Cancelada, Fray Servando Teresa de Mier, Manuel Abad y Queipo, Lorenzo de Zavala, Sir Henry Ward, José María Luis Mora and Lucas Alamán all provided valuable descriptions of the colony and its society. At much the same time an effort was made to print such informative compilations as the *Informe general* of Viceroy the Count of Revillagigedo and the *Historia general de Real Hacienda* of Fabián de Fonseca and Carlos de Urrutia. But then, during the latter half of the nineteenth century, the interests of most Mexican scholars shifted towards the early periods of their national history. In particular many set about the great work of rediscovering the Indian past. Others, of whom in our own days Silvio Zavala is the most distinguished, concentrated their researches upon the sixteenth century. Foreign scholars also followed this tendency to study the formation rather than the florescence of colonial society. Here the names of François Chevalier, Robert Ricard, J. H. Parry, George Kubler, Charles Gibson and José Miranda immediately come to mind. Then again, that remarkable series of monographs produced by the Berkeley 'school' of Carl O. Sauer, Lesley Byrd Simpson, Sherburne F. Cook and Woodrow Borah has been largely devoted to the Indian and his fate subsequent to the Conquest. Only H. I. Priestley in his *José de Gálvez, Visitor-General of New Spain*, published as long ago as 1916, selected a theme which was, like my own, concerned with Spaniards and the eighteenth century. All this has meant that I have had to serve my historical apprenticeship in an unmapped field of study with few more guides to lead me than Humboldt, Ward, Revillagigedo, Alamán and Padre Mier. These are the men who have helped me most in my research.

The three studies into which this book is divided are mainly based, however, not on any printed sources but on archival material. They follow the trajectory of my own research. 'The Revolution in Goverment' is almost entirely built upon notes taken in the *Archivo de Indias* at Seville, whereas 'Guanajuato' depends upon an extensive use of the local notarial records; the intervening piece 'Merchants and Miners' has a more variegated base, with the section *Minería* of the *Archivo General de la Nación* in Mexico City supplying the weightiest bricks. It should be emphasised that all three studies are designed to stand as autonomous approaches to late eighteenth-century Mexico; there is no logical progression from one to another. Nevertheless, 'Guanajuato' will probably not yield its full meaning to a reader unacquainted with the preceding study of 'Miners and Merchants'. My purpose in writing this book has been first to define a historical period, which I name Bourbon Mexico, and then to describe its salient features.

Naturally in the course of seven years' research and composition I have incurred many intellectual and other debts. David Joslin, my undergraduate supervisor at Pembroke College, Cambridge, gave me good counsel when I started and much needed encouragement when I sent him the first draft of my book. Frederick Bowser, from our days together in Seville until the present, has been a patient listener, a sceptical reader and a kindly critic. Many other persons, each in his own way, have assisted me. I wish to thank, at London, my dissertation supervisors, R. A. Humphreys and John Lynch, my fellow students, Nancy M. Farriss and Juan Maiguashca; at Seville, Enrique Otte, Miguel Maticorena, Pierre Ponsot, Günter Vollmer; and, on visit, J. H. Parry; in Mexico City, Ignacio Rubio Mañé and Gonzalo Obregón, Jr; in Guanajuato, Manuel Leal, Tiburcio Alvarez and Jesús Fraustro Rodríguez; in San Miguel Allende, Miguel Malo Zozaya; at Berkeley, William P. McGreevey, José Antonio Matesanz, Peter Mathias, Raymond K. Kent, and—not least—Woodrow Borah. Several institutions have rendered me financial assistance. In the first place, without an award of a Henry Fellowship to Yale College I would never have visited Latin America. Later, the central research fund of London University gave me a supplementary grant for my months at Seville and the Astor Foundation made it possible for me to undertake research in Mexico. At Berkeley, the Center of Latin American Studies has generously provided me with sufficient funds to devote no less than three summers to complete this book. Finally, I wish to thank my wife Celia Wu; she alone knows how much I have relied upon her help.

Guanajuato-Berkeley D.A.B.
1966–9

ARCHIVAL ABBREVIATIONS

ACM	Archivo Casa Morelos (Morelia)
AGI	Archivo General de Indias (Seville)
AGN	Archivo General de la Nación (Mexico City)
AGS	Archivo General de Simancas
AHG	Archivo Histórico de Guanajuato
AHGP	Archivo Histórico de Guanajuato, Protocolos
AHH	Archivo Histórico de Hacienda (Mexico City)
AHN	Archivo Histórico Nacional (Madrid)
AMM	Archivo Municipal de Morelia
AHL	Archivo Histórico de León
AMZ	Archivo Municipal de Zacatecas
APS	Archivo Provincial de Santander
BN (Madrid)	Biblioteca Nacional (Madrid)
BN (Mexico)	Biblioteca Nacional (Mexico City)
BM	British Museum (London)
BRP	Biblioteca del Real Palacio (Madrid)
CV	Cancillería de Valladolid
FV	Fundación Valenciana (Mexico City)

MEASURES AND MONEY

Some explanation of the units of measurement and value used in the text may prove helpful.

All yards are Castilian yards (*varas*) which comprise 33 English inches or 0·835 metres.

The term 'hundredweight' translates the Spanish unit *quintal* which was composed of 4 *arrobas* or 100 *libras*. It weighed about 101½ English pounds. All pounds and ounces are of the Castilian variety.

The *fanega* approximately equalled 1·5 English bushels.

The silver peso of Mexico, sometimes referred to as the *peso fuerte* or *duro* was equal in value to the American dollar of that epoch. It divided into 8 silver reales and 20 *reales de vellón*, the unit of account then used in Spain. 8½ pesos were cut from each Castilian mark of silver. The following table should clarify these equivalents.

1 mark = 8½ pesos
1 mark = 8 ounces
1 peso = 8 reales de plata
1 peso = 20 reales de vellón
1 real = 12 granos
1 real = 34 maravedis

GLOSSARY

Note on Spanish Words in Text

Where possible common English forms of Spanish place-names have been used, e.g. Biscay and Seville instead of Vizcaya and Sevilla, Mexico rather than México. To avoid an unsightly text most Spanish terms have not been italicised especially those which occur frequently or are more familiar.

Acuerdo: an agreement or decision, a resolution of the audiencia
agente fiscal: a lawyer who assisted the Crown's attorneys
alcabala: sales tax
alcalde del barrio: ward magistrate
alcalde del crimen: junior judge in audiencia, a member of the sala del crimen
alcalde mayor: district magistrate
alcalde ordinario: municipal magistrate
alcaldía mayor: district governed by alcalde mayor
alférez real: senior member of town council
alhóndiga: municipal granary
almacén: store, warehouse
almacenero: merchant of Mexico City, usually the owner of an import house
arrastre: crush mill
asesor general: the viceroy's legal advisor
audiencia: high court of justice
aviador: financial backer
avíos: supplies and cash advanced on credit by aviador
ayuntamiento: town council
azoguero: supervisor of amalgamation process

Barrenadores: mine-workers, blasters
barreteros: mine-workers, pick-men
buscones: mine-workers, who received half the ore produced in lieu of wage

Cabildo: town council
cacique: Indian chief
caja real: provincial treasury
cajero: apprentice merchant
castas: half-breeds
catastro: register of property, census

Glossary

cédula: royal decree
consulado: merchant guild and its court
consulta: recommendation, resolution of Council of the Indies
contaduría: audit department
corregidor: district magistrate
corregidor de letras: district magistrate who was a lawyer

Depositario general: town councillor
dinero: measure of silver quality, 24 grains

Encomienda: a grant of Indians
encomendero: possessor of an encomienda
expediente: file, case

Fanega: measure of dry weight, about 1·5 bushels
fiel ejecutor: town councillor charged with inspection of municipal market, etc.
fiscal de lo civil: Crown attorney attached to audiencia, handling all non-exchequer and non-criminal matters
fiscal de real hacienda: Crown attorney, attached to audiencia, handling all exchequer cases
fuero: exemption from royal jurisdiction, right to trial by members of same profession

Gañán: peón
gachupín: Spaniard, born in Europe, resident in New Spain
gente de razón: lit. people of reason, in effect, all non-Indians
gente decente: the respectable, persons of quality
granos: grains

Hacienda: large landed estate
hacienda de beneficio: a refining mill
hacendado: owner of an hacienda
hidalgo: a person of gentle birth

Junta de real hacienda: chief financial committee of viceroyalty
junta superior de real hacienda: chief finance committee after creation of intendencies

Legajo: a bundle of documents
leyes de partida: medieval code of Spanish law
libranza: promissory note, Mexican variant of bill of exchange

Malacate: whim
Malagueño: native of Malaga
maravedí: coin, 34 to a real

Glossary

media annata: half year's income paid as taxation by officials during first term of office
mercader: merchant
Montañés: native of province of Santander

Obraje: large textile workshop
ordenanzas: ordinances
oidor: judge in audiencia

Partido: share of ore taken by mine-workers
policía: administrative functions of government, especially public works
polizón: unlicensed immigrant
procurador general del común: town councillor charged with representing the interests of the public, especially of the poor
pueblo: Indian village
pulque: alcoholic beverage made from the juice of the maguey plant
pulquería: tavern, a bar

Rancho: small estate, a hamlet of farmers
real: coin, if of silver worth one eighth of a peso
real orden: a ministerial decree
regidor: town councillor
repartimientos de comercio: public distribution (usually enforced) of merchandise and stock by district magistrate
rescatador: independent refiner
residencia: judicial review of an official's record

Sala del crimen: lower court of audiencia which heard all criminal cases
superintendente subdelegado de real hacienda: superintendent of the exchequer

Temporalidades: government department which administered the ex-Jesuit estates
tenateros: mine-workers, porters
tratante: dealer, petty trader
tribunal de cuentas: the court of audit
tribunal de minería: the mining court

Vagos: vagabonds, migrant labourers unattached to either haciendas or Indian pueblos

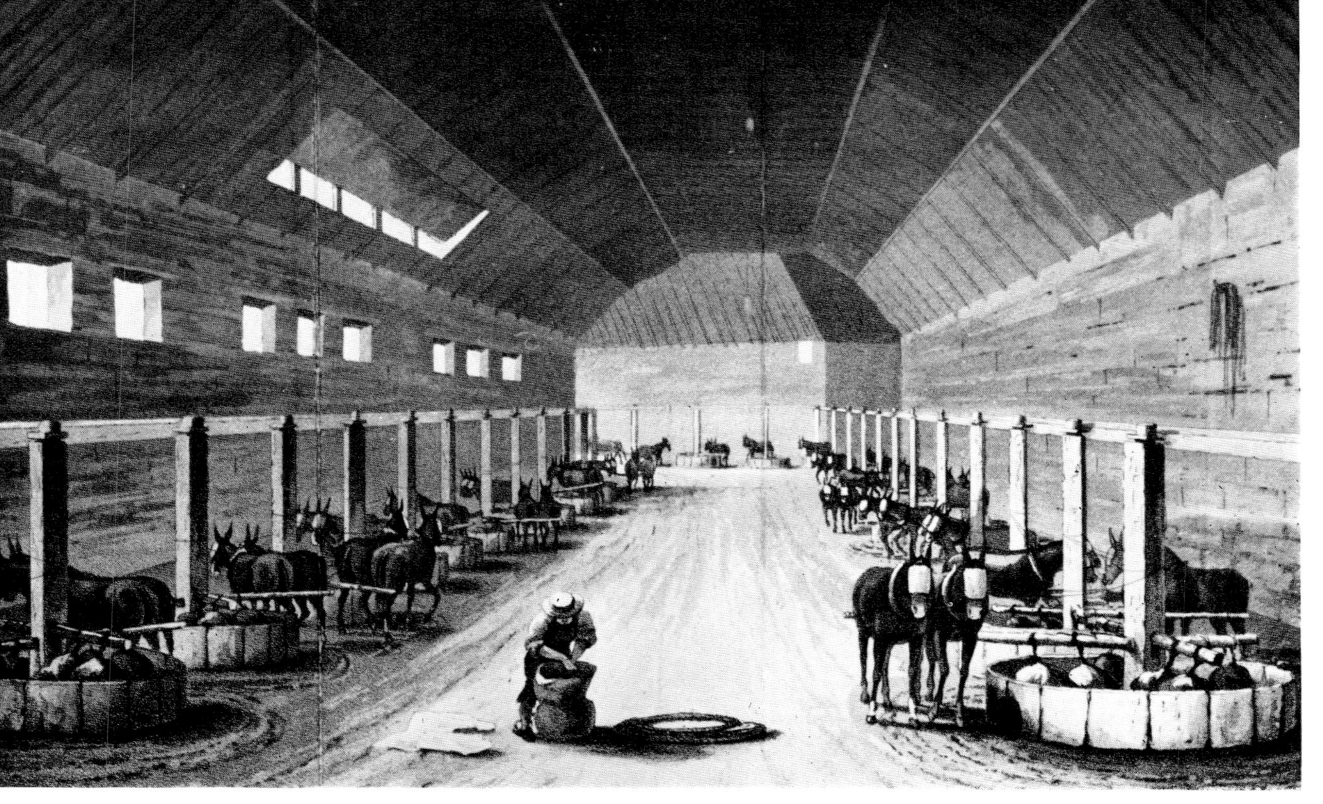

1 *An arrastre gallery* [*Salgado, Guanajuato*]

2 *Patio of refining mill* [*Salgado, Guanajuato*]

INTRODUCTION

'I and my companions suffer from a disease of the heart which can be cured only by gold', Hernán Cortés told Montezuma's ambassador.[1] Yet once the emperor's hoard was divided among the conquerors gold and silver were not found in any great quantity within the confines of the Aztec Empire. As Bernal Díaz del Castillo, himself a participant in the Conquest, later recalled: 'and since we saw that the villages around Mexico did not have any gold, cotton or mines, but only a good deal of maize and maguey plants from which they make their wine, for this reason we held it to be a poor country, and went to settle other provinces'.[2] And indeed for the first thirty years of settlement after 1521 New Spain offered little in the way of mineral production. If the early conquerors were a restless race, endlessly seeking El Dorado, it was because the Conquest, once the initial flush of plunder was exhausted, brought them little fortune and opened up few sources of acceptable employment.

Central Mexico was rich in Indians, not gold. According to recent estimates the coastlands and plateau of central and southern Mexico supported a population that numbered anywhere between twelve and twenty-five million.[3] The splendours of Tenochtitlan, the empire's wealth and culture, all rested upon the small marginal surplus created by the muscle-power and energy of a peasantry unassisted by either the wheel or by draught animals. Labour, in these circumstances, constituted both wealth and power; taxes were largely paid in personal service; and the ownership of land usually carried with it a right to peasant labour. Surplus produce went to the local chiefs, the temples, and the Triple Alliance which had created the empire. The imperial tribute comprised large amounts of maize, beans and cloth, and luxury items, such as feather-shields, head-dresses, gold and amber.[4]

1 Francisco López de Gómara, *Cortés, The Life of the Conqueror by His Secretary*, trans. and ed. Lesley Byrd Simpson (Berkeley and Los Angeles, 1966), p. 58.

2 Bernal Díaz del Castillo, *Historia verdadera de la conquista de la Nueva España*, introducción y notas de Joaquín Ramírez Cabañas (Mexico, 1960), p. 349.

3 Sherburne F. Cook and Lesley Byrd Simpson, *The Population of Central Mexico in the Sixteenth Century* (Berkeley and Los Angeles, 1948), p. 38. Woodrow Borah and Sherburne F. Cook, *The Aboriginal Population of Central Mexico on the Eve of the Spanish Conquest* (Berkeley and Los Angeles, 1963), pp. 88, 157. For a hostile view of these calculations, see Angel Rosenblat, *La población de América en 1492: viejos y nuevos cálculos* (Mexico, 1967), pp. 23–80.

4 For a list of imperial tribute, see Borah and Cook, *Aboriginal Population*, pp. 109–49.

To maintain and feed his soldiers Cortés took advantage of this system and distributed large encomiendas to his principal followers. The encomenderos each received an allocation of Indians—in some cases as many as 20,000—who were obliged to pay their new masters tribute in both goods and service. These grants did not confer any civil jurisdiction or title to land.[1] In practice the Mexican encomienda replaced the former imperial tribute, and hence did not entail any immediate disruption of the local Indian society which continued to be governed by its own nobles and chieftains.

But this distribution of Indians did not content the Spaniards whose quest for fortune in the New World was not to be satisfied by the maize, cotton and feathers offered them by their tributaries. A frantic search began, therefore, not merely for precious metals, but for any product of commercial value. Encomenderos imported livestock from Europe and seized land for the cultivation of wheat. Cortés, the greatest of the encomenderos, hunted for pearls in the Gulf of California, traded with Peru, initiated gold placer-mining in the south, and opened the first silver mines at Taxco.[2] On his vast estates he also raised great herds of cattle, sheep and pigs. In all these enterprises he and his fellow encomenderos did not hesitate to summon their Indian tributaries to work for them free of charge. Their Spanish dependents and their negro slaves were fed and clothed from tribute. The encomienda thus gave an initial impetus to the creation of a European economy in New Spain: the free labour it provided alone made possible many of the first Spanish ventures.

But this phase of wageless labour was legally terminated by the New Laws of 1542. Many encomenderos had grossly mistreated their Indian subjects, over whom, contrary to the terms of their grant, they had exercised a quasi-absolute authority.[3] To prevent further exploitation and to safeguard its jurisdiction, the Crown decreed that henceforth all encomienda tribute should be paid either in money or goods, but never by service. The encomenderos thus lost contact with the Indians and became a mere rentier class, subject to a declining income. In any case, the superabundant labour supply of the 1520s was soon to be replaced by relative scarcity as the Indian population rapidly dwindled in number. Recent computations state that, by 1568, only two and a half million persons

[1] Charles Gibson, *The Aztecs under Spanish Rule* (Stanford, 1964), pp. 58–81.

[2] Woodrow Borah, *Early Colonial Trade and Navigation between Mexico and Peru* (Berkeley and Los Angeles, 1954), pp. 8–16. Jean Pierre Berthe, 'Las minas de oro del Marqués del Valle en Tehuantepec 1540–47', *Historia Mexicana*, 7 (1958), pp. 122–31.

[3] Gibson, *The Aztecs*, pp. 78–80.

survived in the area of New Spain.[1] The curve of this decline, sharp at the outset, slowly flattened out as the century progressed, to reach a horizontal in the first decades of the seventeenth century, when little more than a million Indians remained.

The causes of this demographic catastrophe were several. In the first place, the very density of population had brought Indian society close to the margin of subsistence. Already—in 1454–7 and 1504–6—two great famines had killed thousands.[2] So, when the Spaniards made unreasonable demands upon the labour capacity of their new subjects, it was small wonder than many should have died. But, more importantly, the Conquest destroyed the continental immunity that had permitted the growth of such a dense population. America fell prey to European and Asian disease, and even while Cortés besieged Tenochtitlan its defenders lay stricken under an attack of smallpox. In part, Mexico received a transatlantic overflow of the epidemics which in many areas of fourteenth-century Europe had reduced the population by a third or more, and which continued to haunt the cities of the Old World. But the Spaniards also brought with them tropical diseases, acquired in Africa and Asia, which flourished with great violence in the coastal regions of America.[3] It appears that these tropical scourges were more lethal than their European counterparts, since while the Indians of the plateau suffered decimation, along the Veracruz coast and in the islands of the Caribbean they virtually disappeared. As an English traveller of the time observed: 'In this towne of Veracruz within twenty yeres, when women were brought to bed, the children new borne incontinently died.'[4]

The effect of this demographic crisis upon Indian society was all-pervasive. In the early decades of Spanish rule the tribal chieftains and nobles retained their authority. They organised labour drafts for the encomenderos and the Church; they collected the royal tribute levied on their communities; they still enjoyed the exclusive service of an extensive class of serfs who were exempted from other tribute payment.

[1] Sherburne F. Cook and Woodrow Borah, *The Indian Population of Central Mexico 1531–1610* (Berkeley and Los Angeles, 1960), p. 48.

[2] Sherburne F. Cook, 'The Incidence and Significance of Disease among the Aztecs and Related Tribes', *Hispanic American Historical Review*, 26 (1946), pp. 320–31.

[3] *The Cambridge Economic History of Europe*, I. *The Agrarian Life of the Middle Ages* (2nd ed., ed. M. M. Postan, Cambridge, 1966), pp. 562–70, 673–7.

[4] Woodrow Borah, 'America as Model: The Demographic Impact of European Expansion upon the Non-European World', *Congreso Internacional de Americanistas* (Mexico, 1962), pp. 379–87. Richard Hakluyt, *Voyages* (8 vols.; London: Everyman, 1962), VI. 'A Relation of the Commodities of Nova Hispania, and the Manners of the Inhabitants, written by Henry Hawks merchant, 1572', p. 280.

But, during the 1560s, the Spanish Crown shattered this sytem of indirect rule. Labour had become scarce and tributes exiguous. The Crown, therefore, demanded that free peasant and private serf alike should pay tribute collected on a strict capitation basis. Chiefs remained exempt, but they were deprived of the tribute, expressed either in goods or service, formerly paid by their serfs.[1] By the close of the century Indian society had been reshuffled into a series of small villages governed by elected magistrates, recruited from the peasantry. The wider relations of tribe or empire were eliminated; the internal hierarchy was simplified and reduced. The few Indian noble families that retained their wealth were soon absorbed into the Hispanic community.

The continuous reduction of the Indian work force also redefined the pattern of Spanish colonisation. The encomendero class, its source of income drying up, suffered a loss in social position. More importantly, the Spaniards were obliged to enter the realm of agrarian production to obtain an adequate supply of food and clothing for the colony's urban population. For it must be emphasised that the Spaniard, both from reasons of safety and general cultural preference, was a town-dweller, so that throughout the New World the empire rested upon a network of towns which dominated the surrounding countryside.[2] These urban centres soon attracted large numbers of Indian and negro domestics, and mestizo and mulatto artisans, and so formed a considerable market for the produce of the rural economy.

Since the diminishing number of Indians proved incapable of supplying the towns, the Spaniards, authorised by viceregal grants, appropriated the land left vacant. The tide of land transfer mounted rapidly after 1550 to reach a peak in the years 1570–1600: in all, some 30,000 square miles were legally ceded.[3] Each town came to be encircled by a group of relatively small estates devoted to the cultivation of wheat, maize and fruit. Further afield, great tracts of land were thrown open to livestock, which in the new environment multiplied with remarkable rapidity. Cattle and sheep, in effect, competed with the Indian for living space, and at times pastured

[1] Sherburne F. Cook and Woodrow Borah, 'Quelle fut la stratification sociale au Centre du Mexique durant la première moitié du XVIe siècle?', *Annales*, 18 (March–April 1963), pp. 23–35.

[2] Fernand Braudel, *El mediterráneo y el mundo mediterráneo en la época de Felipe II* (2 vols.; Mexico City and Buenos Aires, 1953), I, 258. J. H. Parry, *The Spanish Seaborne Empire* (London, 1966), p. 112. Richard M. Morse, 'Some Characteristics of Latin American Urban History,' *The American Historical Review*, 63 (January 1962), pp. 317–38.

[3] Lesley Byrd Simpson, *Exploitation of Land in Central Mexico in the Sixteenth Century* (Berkeley and Los Angeles, 1952), pp. 19–21.

off his crops.[1] In large sections of central Mexico, European livestock virtually replaced the indigenous population. On the open ranges of the north huge herds roamed unhindered. Hispanic society outside the towns was highly pastoral, almost nomadic, and depended heavily upon the rapid increase of these imported animals. Horses and mules for transport, sheep and cattle for wool, leather and meat—these as much as wheat or maize were indispensable, and, unlike the cereals, could be produced without much effort.

But although the partial disappearance of the former population permitted both the creation of the Mexican hacienda and the proliferation of livestock, the Indian was still required for the cultivation of the soil. The Crown, therefore, organised a system of draft labour to supply the cereal-producing haciendas with workers. In addition, the Indian villagers were called upon to build churches, to construct roads and to serve in the silver mines. Then, in the first decades of the seventeenth century, the Crown recruited thousands of Indians from the central valleys to cut the great drainage trench of Huehuetoca.[2] Small wonder that, faced with such heavy demands upon their labour, many Indians abandoned their villages. They fled to the towns to become servants or artisans; to the north to work in the mines; and more commonly, they enrolled as peons on the nearest hacienda. Landowners welcomed these refugees. They protected their peons from the labour levies of Crown and village alike; they paid their tribute; they gave them small plots of land; and, by the grant of loans which were never to be repaid, they bound them for life to the hacienda. The Indians who opted permanently to join the Spanish economy—in the town, hacienda or mining camp—slowly became hispanised in dress, custom and language. Their daughters slept with, or married, the mestizo and mulatto hired hands, the negro slaves, and the Spanish overseers. Their descendants formed part of that mestizo class in which lay Mexico's future. But the present, numerically speaking, still belonged to the Indian who remained in his village and who, despite often excessive labour demands, cultivated his own property. Many villages, it is true, especially in the central valleys, soon lost their land, but they still formed autonomous communities, which, in return for seasonal assistance, rented land from the neighbouring hacienda. They thus still dwelt within a relatively self-sufficient agrarian economy.

In general the countryside did not attract much Spanish settlement.

[1] François Chevalier, *La formación de los grandes latifundios en México* (Mexico, 1956), pp. 71–90; see also map, p. 252.

[2] Gibson, *The Aztecs*, pp. 248–9.

Hacendados found it difficult to obtain managers. In 1599 Gonzalo Gómez de Cervantes stated: 'Those who have rural estates let them go to ruin because they are unable to find anyone to entrust them to . . . no one can be found who wishes to go to the country.'[1] Instead, he asserted, Spaniards would rather sell wine in the streets of a town. Yet the local economy could not satisfy all the needs of the Spanish society resident within the colony. Mexico, as much as early New England, depended upon its metropolis for both iron and cloth.[2] It required weapons, iron and steel for implements, brandy and wine, paper, and, above all else, textiles. Indians could dress in cotton, and the populace might be satisfied with the coarse, locally woven woollens, but the well-to-do demanded cloth of European manufacture. But for what could these imports be exchanged? As Luis de Castilla wrote, 'there was no use sending cotton cloth or cacao, or maize to Castile, nor would ships come from Spain to pick up such products'.[3] Similarly, wool and wheat were so many coals to Newcastle. Apart from a few hides, the Mexican hacienda existed to supply an internal market, it did not produce anything worth exporting.

This balance of payments problem was solved by the export of bullion, furnished first from the windfall confiscation of Aztec treasure, then by the scanty yields of gold placer-mining, and finally, after 1550, by the large-scale production of silver. At the close of the century bullion comprised over 80 per cent of NewSpain's total exports.[4] Cochineal was the only other item of much worth. The curve of silver production determined the rhythm of transatlantic commerce, which in terms of preponderant value, resolved itself into an exchange of American silver for European cloth.

The internal economy was equally affected by the rise of silver mining. The discovery of this metal drove the Spaniards far beyond the boundaries of the Aztec empire into the vast northern area, then called the Great Chichimeca, after the savage, nomad Indians whose hunting ground it was. For although rich deposits of silver were to be found near Mexico City —in Pachuca, Sultepec, Tlalpujahua and Taxco—the mining camps which

[1] Gonzalo Gómez de Cervantes, *La vida económica y social de Nueva España al finalizar el siglo XVI*, prólogo y notas de Alberto María Carreño (Mexico, 1944), pp. 117–18.

[2] Bernard Bailyn, *The New England Merchants in the Seventeenth Century* (2nd ed.; New York, 1964), p. 61.

[3] Quoted in Borah, *Early Colonial Trade*, p. 8.

[4] Parry, *The Spanish Seaborne Empire*, pp. 242–3: 'At no time in the late sixteenth and early seventeenth centuries did the proportion of gold and silver in the recorded eastbound cargoes amount to less than 80 per cent, computed by value.' In the peak year of 1595, gold and silver comprised 95·6 per cent of the total value, cochineal amounted to 2·8 per cent and hides 1·4 per cent.

produced most ore lay in the north, interspersed upon the outflung ridges of the Sierra Madre that cut across the northern plateau, and located for the most part along an axis that stretched from Pachuca to Sonora. Effective production began during the 1550s following the discovery of Zacatecas (1546), Real del Monte (1552), Pachuca (1552), Guanajuato (1550) and a string of smaller camps in the north.[1] If the upward curve in output did not continue beyond the 1590s, a serious decline did not occur until after 1630. Thus the rise in silver production coincided with the end of the encomienda system, and reached its peak at a time when the major effects of the demographic crisis had already made their mark.

Information as to which camps produced most silver is hard to find. But, in 1632, two-thirds of the mercury required by the industry was distributed in the north, including Guanajuato in that term; and a full third of that was consumed by the mines subject to the Zacatecas treasury.[2] This northern preponderance of mineral deposits initiated the effective settlement of that region, since each mining camp was soon surrounded by a dependent group of haciendas. Most of these estates were developed by mine-owners in search of grain for their mules and workers, as well as wood, leather, and other raw materials for their mines. The northern hacienda's prosperity was closely subordinated to the progress of the mining industry.

Mining profits paid for the conquest of entire provinces. Francisco de Ibarra, for example, financed the colonisation of Nueva Vizcaya (modern Durango) out of the fortune made by his uncle in Zacatecas.[3] Similarly the conqueror of New Mexico, Juan de Oñate, inherited a fortune from his uncle—another miner of Zacatecas.[4] Then again, the great estates of Francisco de Urdiñola in Coahuila, which later formed the basis of the marquisate of San Miguel de Aguayo, were largely supported by his silver mines.

The northern mines attracted a small but persistent flow of Indian workers, who, since the Chichimecas proved intractable employees even as slaves, must have emigrated from Michoacán or the central valleys. Towards the end of the sixteenth century, the mines of the centre, Guanajuato and Zacatecas employed the following categories of men.[5]

1 Modesto Bargalló, *La minería y la metalurgia en la América española durante la época colonial* (Mexico City and Buenos Aires, 1955), pp. 61–3.

2 A. Matilla Tascón, *Historia de las minas de Almadén* (Madrid, 1958), p. 223.

3 See J. Lloyd Mecham, *Francisco de Ibarra and Nueva Vizcaya* (Durham, N.C., 1927), and George P. Hammond, *Juan de Oñate and the Founding of New Mexico* (Santa Fe, N.M., 1927).

4 Vito Alessio Robles, *Coahuila y Texas en la época colonial* (Mexico, 1938), p. 148.

5 Woodrow Borah, *New Spain's Century of Depression* (Berkeley and Los Angeles, 1951), pp. 37–8.

Negro slaves	1,022
Free Indians	4,606
Drafted Indians	1,619
	7,247

Nearly all the drafted labour worked in mines relatively close to Mexico City—in Taxco and Pachuca—whereas in Zacatecas the Indians were almost all free wage-earners. Negro slaves, it should be noted, were used in the refining phase of the industry; they could not endure the rigours of deep-shaft mining, given the altitude of the Mexican plateau.

If we use the mercury distribution scale of 1632 as a rough guide, then it appears that these 7,247 men accounted for about two-thirds of New Spain's silver production. The industry, therefore, probably did not require more than 11,000 men. A labour force of such dimension could easily escape the effects of Indian population decline, the more especially since mine-owners paid high wages and granted their workers a share of the ore they cut.[1] To the tougher and more spirited Indians, oppressed by communal obligations, the mines presented an attractive road of escape. Once in the mining camps, they doubtless soon mixed with the Spaniards, mestizos, mulattoes and negroes for whom the industry also offered the prospect of high earnings and a possible fortune. The northern miners formed a labour aristocracy among the workers of Mexico, characterised by freedom, mobility and lavish spending.

Two distinct processes were at work in New Spain during the sixteenth century. In the area formerly governed by the Aztecs the Indian economy was either entirely replaced or subordinated to the growth of the hacienda and the new Spanish towns. In the north a frontier mining economy was created. But by the first decades of the seventeenth century both these movements slowed down or went into reverse. The causes and stages, however, of this economic depression remain obscure.

For the central valleys, it is true, the continuing erosion of the labour force can serve as an explanation. We may reasonably postulate that the expansion in agrarian production implied by the wholsesale seizure of land during the years 1570–1600 soon reached a high-water mark, only to recede as it conflicted with the declining curve of labour supply. Much land, temporarily brought under cultivation by the new hacendado class, was abandoned particularly after the 1620s when the Crown's demand for

[1] Alonso de la Mota y Escobar, *Descripción geográfica de los reynos de Nueva Galicia, Nueva Vizcaya y Nuevo León*, introducción por Joaquín Ramírez Cabañas (Mexico, 1940), pp. 151–2. The monthly wage for a pickman was 5–8 ps.

Indian levies to cut the drainage trench of Huehuetoca terminated the already waning system of draft labour.[1] From then on, Spanish farmers were obliged to rely upon free wage-earners and a small group of peons who resided permanently on their estates. During this critical decade many hacendados entirely abandoned production. These were experimental years, so to speak, and if the price of maize be accepted as a measure, then the relation between supply and demand—between haciendas and towns—did not attain equilibrium until the 1620s. A *fanega* of maize, which in 1573 sold for 4·8 rls. (*reales*), by 1627 cost 9 rls., a level beyond which it was not to rise, drought years apart, for more than a century.[2]

If in the central valleys little more than a 'shaking down' process occurred, in the north, by contrast, the mining industry experienced a severe depression. Earl J. Hamilton's estimates of American bullion exports to Spain clearly demonstrate that during the 1630s production declined precipitously, reaching a trough in the 1650s that barely equalled the output of the 1550s.[3] The curve of transatlantic trade drawn up by M. Chaunu corroborates Hamilton's figures.[4] Similarly, Fausto de Elhuyar, an eighteenth-century mining expert, who was granted access to mint records, declared that in 1632 some 5,109,000 pesos were coined by the Mexican mint, a figure which was not surpassed until the years 1689–92, and not permanently bettered until after 1706.[5]

Any explanation of this fall in silver production must be tentative. The 'labour crisis', however, cannot be easily invoked, since the mines enjoyed a boom as the population declined, and fell into decay only after the population had reached a point of stability.[6] The two movements cannot be synchronised. Possibly camps such as Pachuca and Taxco, which relied upon drafted labour, experienced competition from Huehuetoca. But most viceroys gave first priority to the mines; in any case, these camps near Mexico City only accounted for a third of total production. Moreover, the number of men employed in the industry was sufficiently small

1 Gibson, *The Aztecs*, pp. 236–42.

2 Woodrow Borah and Sherburne F. Cook, *Price Trends of Some Basic Commodities in Central Mexico, 1531–1570* (Berkeley and Los Angeles, 1958), p. 18. See also C. Chester L. Guthrie, 'Colonial Economy Trade, Industry and Labor in the Seventeenth Century', *Revista de Historia de América*, 7 (December 1939), pp. 103–34. For a critique of these studies see Enrique Florescano, *Precios del maíz y crisis agrícolas en México 1708–1810* (Mexico, 1969), pp. 21–8.

3 Earl J. Hamilton, *American Treasure and the Price Revolution in Spain 1501–1650* (Cambridge, Mass., 1939), pp. 34, 43.

4 H. and P. Chaunu, *Séville et l'Atlantique (1504–1650)* (8 vols.; Paris, 1955–9), VII, 54–5. See also John Lynch, *Spain under the Hapsburgs* (Oxford, 1964), pp. 163–6.

5 Fausto de Elhuyar, *Indagaciones sobre la amonedación en la Nueva España* (Madrid, 1818), p. 12.

6 Borah, *New Spain's Century of Depression*, pp. 43–4.

and the wages they received sufficiently high for silver mining to escape the effects of labour scarcity.

What, then, caused New Spain's mines to decay? Poor technique, exhausted lodes, exorbitant taxation—did these familiar threats haunt the industry? To begin with, mere discovery of mineral deposits did not of itself create the late sixteenth-century mining boom. For the average quality of Mexican ore was not high enough to permit much profit from the simple smelting method in vogue at the time of the Conquest. Only during the 1550s was a German technique introduced in which silver was separated from base metal by a lengthy amalgamation with mercury.[1] It was this process that liberated the industry from its former dependence upon lucky strikes of rich metals. Furthermore, in 1548, the Crown reduced the tax it levied upon silver production from a fifth to a tenth.[2] This concession, extended only to miners and not to mere refiners or merchants who bought silver, when combined with the amalgamation technique, established the new discoveries of the 1550s upon a durable economic basis.

But in the years that followed the industry experienced a steady rise in general costs as the world-wide inflation in which New Spain participated drove up both the price of raw materials and the cost of labour. At the same time the value of silver relative to gold fell from 12:1 to 14:1.[3] Then again, since most silver was coined, its market price remained stable, and hence its value, expressed in commodities, steadily declined. However, althought this upward curve of prices may well have reduced profits, it did not hinder production, since the mines boomed when inflation was most pronounced, and only decayed after the inflationary movement had been halted. Nor can poor technique carry the burden of explanation. For example, during the years 1612–20, the zealous royal magistrate of San Luis Potosí distributed 60,000 ps. (pesos) in credit to the local industry, and, equally important, organised the construction of a drainage tunnel below the lode some 250 yards long. The result was to increase production by a third.[4] Technique, it appears, although primitive, was still adequate to the needs of the time.

[1] Modesto Bargalló, *La minería*, pp. 115–33. See also Alan Probert, 'Bartolomé de Medina: The Patio Process and the Sixteenth Century Silver Crisis', *Journal of the West*, 8 (January 1969), pp. 90–124.

[2] Fabián de Fonseca and Carlos de Urrutia, *Historia general de Real Hacienda escrita por orden del virrey, conde de Revillagigedo* (6 vols.; Mexico, 1845–53), I, 15.

[3] Hamilton, *American Treasure*, p. 71.

[4] Woodrow Borah, 'Un gobierno provincial de frontera en San Luis Potosí, 1612–20', *Historia Mexicana*, 13 (April–June 1964), pp. 532–50.

Instead, contemporaries blamed the high cost and inadequate supply of mercury for the crisis within the industry. This indispensable catalyst was produced in three great mines, located at Almadén in Spain, at Huancavelica in Peru, and in the Istrian Peninsula. Although Almadén was leased to the Fugger Banking House, the sale and distribution of mercury was managed by the royal treasuries and authorised magistrates. At first the Crown exacted exorbitant profit from the monopoly. During the 1560s the cost price at Mexico City averaged 117–125 ps. a hundredweight, but auction prices ranged from 132 to 236 ps., with quotations between 170 and 187 ps. being the most frequent. But then, in deference to local protest, the Crown steadily reduced the price—from 113 ps. in 1590 to 96½ ps. in 1602—until by 1627 the level which was to be standard for over a century of 82½ ps. a hundredweight was finally reached.[1] Contrary, therefore, to general trends, the sale price of mercury, the major individual cost in refining, actually fell in these years.

But plentiful supply was as important as a reasonable price, and during the 1630s shipments from Almadén to Veracruz were cut or directed to Peru. The scheme shown in table 1 demonstrates the dimension of the change.[2]

Without mercury much medium quality ore could not be refined since, for this range of mineral, smelting did not separate sufficient silver to pay for its cost. It can be calculated—in rough terms—that during these years prior to 1632 at least two-thirds of Mexican silver was produced by the amalgamation process.[3] Hence the sudden reduction by half in mercury shipments inevitably brought ruin to many a mine.

[1] A. Matilla Tascón, *Minas de Almadén*, pp. 214–15, and p. 213; Fonseca and Urrutia, *Historia general de Real Hacienda*, I, 302, 310; and AGI, Mexico 2235, *Real Cédula*, 7 February 1602.

[2] A. Matilla Tascón, *Minas de Almadén*, pp. 291–2.

Table 1 *Shipments of mercury to Veracruz, 1610–45.*

In quinquennia		In decades	
1611–15	19,048 cwt.	1611–20	43,359 cwt.
1616–20	24,311 cwt.	1621–30	46,685 cwt.
1621–5	24,045 cwt.	1631–40	20,274 cwt.
1626–30	22,640 cwt.		
1631–5	11,033 cwt.		
1636–40	9,241 cwt.		
1641–5	14,579 cwt.		

[3] To arrive at this percentage I made the following calculation. The average annual import of mercury, 1626–30, was 4,528 cwt. Multiplied by a hundred, this gives the approximate production by amalgamation measured in marks, i.e. 452,800. Total mintage for 1630 was

In later years recourse was had to Peru and Germany to supplement the inadequate supply from Almadén. In 1670, for example, some 3,000 cwt. arrived from Peru. Even China was called upon to help. But all these sources shared a common fault: their prices were too high, ranging from 110 to 120 ps. as against the 82½ ps. charged for Spanish mercury.[1] Nor were they able to furnish the 4,000–5,000 cwt. of mercury a year that the Mexican mining industry required if it was to return to the production level of the 1620s. An anonymous correspondent to the Crown, writing in the 1690s, declared apropos of Zacatecas: 'the only way to obtain more silver is to send this kingdom sufficient mercury'.[2] The same correspondent singled out a subsidiary cause of the industry's decay—lack of capital. In Zacatecas the royal magistrate attempted to monopolise credit operations so that merchants were unwilling or unable to invest in, or advance credit to, the industry. In consequence, local miners frequently lacked cash to meet even their operating costs. Only an extensive entrance of mercantile capital, he asserted, could redeem the mines.

In general, the sparse evidence so far assembled suggests that many of the great mining and landed families established during the late sixteenth-century boom experienced the same fate as the former encomendero class. Bankruptcy and the abandonment of estates were not uncommon. Already, in 1599, Gómez de Cervantes lamented: 'those who but yesterday served in shops, taverns and other low jobs are today in possession of the best and the most honourable positions in the country, whereas the gentlemen and the descendants of those who conquered and settled it are poor, humiliated, disfavoured and cast down'.[3] Seventy years later, in 1673, the viceroy, the Marquis of Mancera, commented upon 'the straightened circumstances and decay at which the patrimonies and entails of the nobility have arrived'.[4] Clearly, in New Spain neither silver mines nor great landed estates provided a stable economic foundation for a hereditary aristocracy.

Too much should not be made of this mid-seventeenth-century depression. It mainly sprang from the mining crisis and the subsequent

---

601,065 marks. For mercury imports, see A. Matilla Tascón, *Minas de Almadén*, pp. 291–2. For the mercury-silver ratio see Fonseca and Urrutia, *Historia general de Real Hacienda:* I, 306–83. For 1630 mintage see Elhuyar, *Indagaciones*, p. 12.

1 Francisco Javier de Gamboa, *Comentarios a las ordenanzas de minas dedicados al cathólico rey, nuestro señor Don Carlos III* (Madrid, 1761), p. 46.

2 BRP, MSS Miscelánea de Ayala, 45, f. 304.

3 Gómez de Cervantes, *La vida económica*, pp. 94, 132.

4 *Instrucciones que los virreyes de Nueva España dejaron a sus sucesores* (Mexico, 1867), p. 258.

reduction in transatlantic commerce. It terminated an overconfident cycle of landgrabbing and silver mining. It possibly ruined or reduced to more modest circumstances many wealthy families. Yet even in the very eye of this economic storm, during the 1650s, the diarist Gregorio de Guijo recorded mercantile fortunes of 416,000 pesos 'in plate and coin alone'; of 800,000 in cash without counting houses, gardens and furniture; and of 900,000 pesos.[1] Only the Church could compete with these great merchants. A departing archbishop of Mexico took with him to Europe some 800,000 pesos in jewels and specie. The crisis, such as it was, obviously did not affect everyone with equal violence. Nor were all the consequences injurious. Any reduction in the importation of European cloth naturally favoured the production of the domestic industry. Moreover, by 1650 the hispanic community—which comprised mestizos, mulattoes and negroes as well as Spaniards—may well have numbered three hundred thousand persons compared to an Indian population of just over a million.[2] Then again, certain figures for the Bajío indicate that the northward ripple of settlement did not cease. Between 1644 and 1688 the register of Indian tributaries in Querétaro rose from 600 to 2,000, and in the neighbouring town of Celaya from 2,184 to 6,419 between the years 1657 and 1698.[3]

Now M. Chevalier, it is true, has argued that during this period the Mexican haciendas together with their owners and peons retreated into a rural isolation and self-sufficiency reminiscent of the great estates of Europe during the Dark Ages.[4] But his argument and its proofs essentially apply to the north. There, undoubtedly, the closure of mines caused some haciendas to be deserted completely and others to be left to vegetate in mere self-subsistence. But we must distinguish between the north and the centre. Equally important, we must distinguish between haciendas that grew cereals and sugar and haciendas that raised livestock. Only the latter class could easily adapt to a regime of self-sufficiency; the former with a production governed by the demand of their markets were more likely to be abandoned. As M. Berthe observes: 'the sugar refinery was thus a specialised enterprise which concentrated all its resources on the production of one commodity, sugar, destined for sale. It was bound to a market economy and hence exposed to all its fluctuations'.[5]

[1] Gregorio M. Guijo, *Diario 1648–1684* (2 vols.; Mexico, 1953), I, 184; II, 40, 61, 147.

[2] Borah, *New Spain's Century of Depression*, p. 3.

[3] José Miranda, 'La población indígena de México en el siglo XVII', *Historia Mexicana*, 12 (1963), pp. 182–9.

[4] Chevalier, *Los grandes latifundios*, pp. 226–33.

[5] Jean Pierre Berthe, 'Xochimancas, les travaux et les jours dans une hacienda sucrière de Nouvelle-Espagne au XVIII siècle', *Jahrbuch für Geschichte . . . Lateinamerikas*, Band 3 (Köln, 1966), p. 102.

In the central regions of New Spain, therefore, the continuous expansion of the hispanic community with its relatively high concentration in towns promoted a corresponding advance in the domestic economy. But contemporary evidence for the growth of this internal circle of exchange, both for industrial and agrarian produce, is still largely unavailable. Viceroys and diarists alike were too fascinated by the glitter of transatlantic commerce and the silver mines. Indeed it is only towards the close of the colonial period that information becomes abundant.

II

During the eighteenth century New Spain experienced a profound economic recovery based both upon the revival of silver mining and the persistent increase of its population. Since, in many ways, the silver boom depended upon the growth of the domestic economy, the latter movement warrants a closer examination. In broad terms the Mexican population grew from an estimated 3,336,000 persons in 1742 to some 6,122,000 persons in 1810.[1] Nearly all the races which inhabited the colony multiplied at much the same rate. In both the cited years Indians comprised some 60 per cent of the population. The breakdown of the remainder varied somewhat. 'Spaniards' amounted to 11 per cent in 1742 and 18 per cent in 1810. Mestizos and mulattoes, grouped together as *castas*, accounted for the other 22 per cent.[2] These racial proportions represented national, not regional, averages. The further south one went the more Indians were to be found, whereas in the north the hispanic group easily predominated. In the intendency of Oaxaca, Indians constituted over 88 per cent of the population whereas the inhabitants of the Guadalajara intendency divided into three approximately equal groups of Indians, Spaniards and *castas*. The central Mexican intendency more closely followed the general average with Indians forming 66 per cent of the total number. This provincial diversity becomes equally manifest if the rate of overall increase is considered. For whereas in 1742 the northern dioceses, including Michoacán in that definition, supported 26 per cent of New Spain's inhabitants, by 1810 their share had grown to 38 per cent. The greater part of this expansion occurred in that area which can be defined as the near north. In 1742 the diocese of Michoacán contained 11 per cent of the population; in 1810 the inhabitants of the same area, by

[1] For these population figures see Peter Gerhard, *México en 1742* (Mexico, 1962); Alexander von Humboldt, *Ensayo político sobre el reino de la Nueva España*, ed. Juan A. Ortega y Medina (Mexico, 1966), pp. 37–9. Fernando Navarro y Noriega, *Memoria sobre la población del reino de la Nueva España* (Mexico, 1954).

[2] Gerhard, *México en 1742*, pp. 17–18; Navarro, *Memoria*, p. 30.

then split into the three provinces of Guanajuato, Michoacán and San Luis Potosí, comprised 19 per cent of the total number.[1]

These statistics, crude and approximate as they are, serve to demonstrate that by the close of the eighteenth century the different regions of New Spain each possessed remarkably distinctive characteristics. Here, geography conspired with history. For although the heart of the country was composed of broad fertile valleys, all relatively accessible, in the south the two mountain ridges which skirted the plateau converged to break the landscape into a series of hills and valleys. To the north travel was easier, despite the flanks of the Sierra Madre which bisected the plateau, but the distances were much greater. Moreover, the further north one went the more barren and arid the land became. Climate was a function of altitude, so that the temperate areas all adjoined more tropical zones. But the descent to the coastlands was sharp and arduous. The sea did not, as in Europe, offer a convenient or a cheap form of communication between regions. Apart from the lake of Mexico itself and its few miles of canal leading to Chalco, New Spain did not possess any navigable rivers or inland waterways. Travel, therefore, was difficult, being conducted entirely upon horses, mules and a few horse-drawn carriages. In commercial transport the mule train reigned supreme.[2] But since the average mule carried only three hundred pounds on its back and plodded but twelve miles a day, very effective costs limits were placed upon the long-distance carriage of cheap, bulky goods.[3] New Spain's physical environment thus accentuated regional diversity and isolation.

Nevertheless, the residents of nearly all regions could produce at a fairly short distance all the usual Mexican staple crops. Maize and beans could be grown almost everywhere and most country dwellers cultivated their own plot of land—their *milpas*. Wheat, of course, was restricted to the more temperate zones. But cattle, pigs and poultry could be raised throughout the colony. Sheep, like wheat, however, did not fare so well in the tropics. Some regional specialisation occurred. The north possessed the greatest quantity of livestock. In 1807 the intendant of Durango estimated that his province contained over two million sheep and some 324,000 cattle.[4] Coahuila and New León were also celebrated for their great

[1] My own calculations on the basis of the figures supplied by Gerhard and Navarro.

[2] Robert C. West, *The Mining Community in Northern New Spain: The Parral Mining District* (Berkeley and Los Angeles, 1949), pp. 86–7.

[3] H. G. Ward, *Mexico in 1827* (2 vols.; London, 1828), II, 216.

[4] Jesús Silva Herzog, *Colección de documentos*, III, *Relaciones estadísticas de Nueva España a principios del siglo XIX* (Mexico, 1944), p. 96.

flocks of sheep. By contrast, in 1807 Michoacán had but 150,000 head of cattle and 237,000 sheep.[1] Tropical crops, principally cotton and sugar, could usually be obtained from an adjoining stretch of *tierra caliente*. Mexico City acquired its sugar from plantations situated near Cuernavaca in the modern state of Morelos. The Bajío procured raw cotton and sugar from Michoacán. Jalisco despatched its crude sugar cakes to Sinaloa and Durango.[2] Veracruz supplied the eastern districts of the plateau.

This trend towards racial diversity and regional self-sufficiency promoted quite distinct patterns of land tenure and agricultural production. In the province of Oaxaca very few haciendas could be found: in 1810 no more than 83 were listed compared to 928 Indian villages and 264 ranchos. On the other hand, in the province of Guadalajara in addition to 370 haciendas and 326 villages, there were 1,155 ranchos, an ill-defined term which covered both small estates and hamlets of homestead farmers who either owned or rented their land. Once again the central intendancy of Mexico approximated to a middle position with 1,228 villages, 824 haciendas and 871 ranchos.[3] The contrast here lay between the Indian south and the mestizo north, between an agricultural system largely characterised by self-subsistence and one which existed to supply a market.

But the effective demand for rural produce was mainly governed by the costs of transport and the extent of the urban markets. H. G. Ward, the first British minister to Mexico, made an accurate assessment of the situation: 'But in New Spain, the want of roads, and the consequent difficulty of intercourse between the corn-growing states, excludes from competition, in each market, all those who are situated beyond a very circumscribed circle in its immediate vicinity; and thus maintains a sort of fictitious price.'[4] He found the price of maize in Mexico City to be over double that which prevailed 180 miles away. The cause of these differences lay in the cost of transport. In 1785 Juan Antonio de Yermo, a wealthy merchant and landowner, reckoned that to convey maize to Mexico City over land for a distance of more than 60 miles cost $5\frac{1}{3}$ rls. a fanega, a sum which amounted to 50 per cent of the current sale price of $10\frac{2}{3}$ rls.[5] Bulky, inexpensive goods such as cereals had to be grown and consumed locally or not at all. Yet the available markets were remarkably limited in size compared to the production capacity of the great estates. The demand

[1] For Michoacán see BM Add. MSS 17557, ff. 140–2.
[2] West, *The Mining Community*, pp. 78–9.
[3] Navarro y Noriega, *Memoria*, foldpaper, p. 30.
[4] Ward, *Mexico in 1827*, I, 42, 50.
[5] BN (Mexico) MSS 1535, f. 129.

for maize in Mexico City could be almost entirely satisfied by the haciendas of the one district of Chalco.[1]

This picture of a merely local circle of exchange should not be overdrawn. For industrial goods commanded markets that lay far beyond the immediate locality. And for the most part colonial industry simply processed agricultural and pastoral produce. Cotton, wool, leather, soap and candle tallow: these were the commodities which figured prominently in the intendants' reports. In Jalisco, for example, soap production was valued at 288,000 ps. and candle tallow at 271,000 ps. The province of Puebla, so its intendant stated, produced five million pounds of soap a year.[2] In textiles there was manifested a certain division of labour between regions. The south, and more particularly the city of Puebla, specialised in the manufacture of cotton cloth, the Bajío in woollens and Jalisco in leather and suede. But these preferences, determined in part by climate and in part by proximity to the source of the raw materials, by no means proved invariable. Puebla also cured leather, the Bajío spun cotton. Moreover, although Querétaro and Puebla figured as the great textile cities, smaller towns such as Oaxaca and Celaya and many villages also manufactured great quantities of cloth.[3]

The scale of this colonial textile industry was often surprisingly large. At the close of the century the intendant of Puebla estimated that at least half the town's population (some 52,000 persons in 1793) were engaged in spinning and weaving cotton cloth.[4] The source of supply lay in Veracruz and Oaxaca, from whence the raw cotton was transported by mule to Puebla. Purchase and distribution both of the raw material and the manufactured commodity were handled by a group of some 28 merchant houses.[5] Precise figures of production are not available; but in the years 1790–1805 Puebla annually despatched to Mexico City over a million pounds of cloth.[6]

The most profitable and extensive markets for domestic cloth lay in the north. In 1804 the intendant of Guadalajara calculated that his province imported Mexican textile products valued at 462,000 ps. True, this figure did not compare favourably with the 1,299,000 ps paid for European cloth, but then the domestic product was a coarse, low-priced article:

[1] Enrique Florescano, *Precios del maíz*, p. 95.

[2] Silva Herzog, *Documentos*, pp. 54, 101.

[3] In Oaxaca over 10,000 persons were engaged in spinning and weaving cloth. See BM Add. MSS 17557, f. 31.

[4] Silva Herzog, *Documentos*, p. 54.

[5] Jan Bazant, 'Evolución de la industria textil poblana (1554–1845)', *Historia Mexicana*, 13 (1964), pp. 473–516.

[6] Robert A. Potash, *El banco de avío de México, 1821–1846* (Mexico, 1959), pp. 17–25.

in bulk it may well have surpassed its foreign rival; moreover, the intendancy possessed its own, albeit small, industry.[1] Further north, however, not even cottage looms existed, so that the vast provinces of Durango, Sonora and Coahuila were entirely dependent upon the textile industries of Puebla, San Miguel el Grande and Querétaro to supply them with cheap cloth, blankets and ponchos.[2]

In many ways the north, sparse in population, rich in mines and livestock, backward in industry and agriculture, constituted a colonial dependency of the central provinces.[3] It supplied them with many raw materials, with leather, wool, some cotton, mules, horses and bulls, and with silver. In return it bought manufactured goods, especially cloth, ceramics, fine silverware, and tropical foodstuffs, such as sugar. Here, then, was the most profitable and probably the most extensive example of inter-regional exchange of domestic produce in New Spain. What Upper Peru was to Quito, Cuzco, Arequipa and Buenos Aires, so was the north to central Mexico and the Bajío. In both cases, of course, it was the purchasing power of the mining industry and its workers which generated this long-distance commerce of the interior.

But how important was this domestic, as distinct from the export economy? After all, did not New Spain, as a colony, exist to satisfy the needs of the mother country? Now the response to such questions must of necessity be statistical. Fortunately, we can refer to the contemporary calculations of José María Quirós, secretary of the Veracruz Consulado. His estimates, recently subjected to detailed revision, are presented below.[4]

Value of New Spain's annual production, c. *1810*

Agriculture	106,285,000 ps.	(56%)
Manufactures	55,386,000 ps.	(29%)
Mining	28,451,000 ps.	(15%)
	190,122,000 ps.	(100%)

[1] Silva Herzog, *Documentos*, p. 103.

[2] *Ibid.*, pp. 96, 137.

[3] The northerners complained about their dependency upon the centre. See Miguel Ramos Arizpe, *Memoria sobre el estado de las provincias internas de oriente presentada a las Cortes de Cádiz*. Noticia biográfica y notas por Vito Alessio Robles (Mexico, 1932).

[4] José María Quirós, *Memoria de estatuto. Idea de la riqueza que daban la masa circulante de Nueva España sus naturales producciones* (Veracruz, 1817). This pamphlet had been reprinted in *Colección de documentos para la historia del comercio exterior de México* (Mexico, 1959), VI. Fernando Rosenzweig Hernández, 'La economía novo-hispánica al comenzar el siglo XIX', *Ciencias Políticas y Sociales*, 9 (1963), pp. 455–93.

Naturally these figures must be handled with caution; essentially they are rough approximations based upon extrapolations from the assumed minimum consumption of the Mexican population. In no sense do they represent the values of goods actually sold. Nevertheless, despite their obvious crudity, the estimates of Quirós demonstrate that the domestic economy both in the value of its production and, more importantly, in the value of its commercial exchange (for most industrial goods were sold) clearly exceeded the export sector of the colonial economy. It also employed the overwhelming majority of the population since mining, even in 1803, probably did not occupy more than 50,000 workers.[1]

At the same time, however, we must not underestimate the decisive role of overseas commerce and mining. Mexican agriculture and industry dealt mainly in low-priced produce which yielded but small opportunities for profit. True, at least two-thirds of the population were clothed by local manufactures; similarly the colony largely fed itself.[2] But it was European and Oriental imports—textiles, brandy and wine—which commanded high prices and provided equally high profits. Then again, silver mining was probably the only activity which permitted a few lucky individuals to become millionaires overnight. The importance of the export sector, therefore, lay not so much in the number of persons it employed; nor even in the absolute value of its product; but precisely in its profitability: only there, in foreign trade and mining, could great fortunes be readily assembled. It constituted the one area within a lethargic spectrum of economic activity in which large-scale surplus capital could be accumulated.

III

New Spain's society was as unbalanced, distinctive and colonial as its economy. The contemporary European class distinctions of noble, gentle, bourgeois, free commoner and serf cannot be applied in Mexico without violent distortion. True, a species of titled aristocracy existed, but for the most part of such recent creation and transitory florescence as to excite derision among a European nobility.[3] Moreover, we seek in vain for any middle class, any bourgeoisie, mercantile or professional, conscious of a middle rank in society. Nor does the distinction between free and unfree commoners invite employment: apart from a handful of slaves, everyone in New Spain was free, in the sense that all subjects of the

[1] Humboldt, *Ensayo político*, p. 48.

[2] Juan López de Cancelada, *Ruina de la Nueva España* (Cadiz, 1811), pp. 11–12.

[3] Mariano Otero, *Obras* (2 vols.; ed. Jesús Reyes Heroles, Mexico, 1967), I, 28–9.

Crown enjoyed access to royal justice; no man at law was bound to a landowner for life. In effect, Mexico did not possess any clearly defined class system.

Yet a harsh, sharply divided social hierarchy did, of course, exist, which made nonsense of any claim to common citizenship, and which forbade any major degree of upward mobility. In New Spain race as much as class determined a person's position in society. The population separated into three broad categories—Spaniards, both European and American; *castas*, i.e. mestizos, mulattoes and other permutations; and Indians. These categories, into which individuals were enrolled at baptism, described civic and fiscal status rather than genetic formation. Most 'Spaniards' were mestizos; many *castas* were acculturated Indians; and 'Indians', especially their caciques, could often be mestizos.[1] Each group, it should be emphasised, possessed distinct civic rights and fiscal obligations. Quite commonly, however, a simple contrast was drawn between the *gente de razón*, the hispanic community, and the Indians, a dichotomy which stressed the sharp division which still existed between the two great communities which inhabited New Spain.

Another equally simple distinction was drawn between the *gente decente*, the respectable classes, and *la plebe*, the populace. This ill-defined colonial upper class was entirely composed of Spaniards. Its members were easily recognised by reason of their wealth, occupation, legal privileges, Spanish blood, education and costume. But in no sense did it act as a fixed caste, rather it constituted a somewhat unstable élite group. Lucas Alamán wrote that it formed

> a nobility which was distinguished from the remainder of the Spanish caste only by its wealth, and when this disappeared its members fell back into the populace. This class, which was joined by all who acquired riches—since everyone pretended to pass as Spaniards and nobles—differed from the rest of the population in its costume, being more or less well-dressed when in general the populace were not, and was known by the name of the *gente decente*—and this far more than birth formed its distinctive character.[2]

No single criterion, therefore, such as the ownership of land, a certain form of education, or hereditary birthright, governed entrance into this heterogeneous colonial élite. It formed not so much a class as rather an aggregation of those privileged orders which had *fueros*—the right to trial by

[1] Gonzalo Aguirre Beltrán, *La población negra de México, 1519–1810. Estudio etno-histórico* (Mexico, 1946), pp. 154, 174–5, 274–80. See Woodrow Borah, 'Race and Class in Mexico', *The Pacific Historical Review*, 22 (1954), No. 4, pp. 331–42.

[2] Lucas Alamán, *Historia de Méjico* (5 vols.; 1942), I, 19.

their peers. In this sense all clergymen, with their total immunity from the jurisdiction of the royal courts, were members of the élite. The bureaucracy, merchants, the army and, after 1783, the miners also had fueros. In addition we may presume that the great landowners, although not legally privileged, were recognised as members of the *gente decente*. Similarly, most peninsular Spaniards resident in the colony entered the group as of birthright.

This Colonial élite differed from most of its European counterparts in that merchants enjoyed a prestige in society equal to landowners. This was especially true of the great import merchants, the *almaceneros* of Mexico City, among whom were to be found some of the richest men in the colony. Status and social acceptance followed wealth. As early as 1673 the viceroy, the Marquis of Mancera, declared: 'The merchants and traders, who in the Indies comprise a good part of the Spanish nation, approach the nobility very much, affecting their carriage and style. ... It can be generally reckoned that for the most part in these provinces the gentleman is a merchant and the merchant is a gentleman.'[1] In recognition of this fact the Crown granted several merchants titles of nobility and rewarded many more with entrance into the chivalrous orders of Santiago, Alcántara and Calatrava.[2] During the last century Latin American social thinkers such as the Argentinian Domingo de Sarmiento used to emphasise the contrast between the puritans of New England and the conquistadores of Peru and Mexico; they failed to take note, however, that in both colonies by the beginning of the eighteenth century merchants had emerged as dominant figures in society.[3]

Certain minimum prerequisites existed, however, for entrance into the ranks of the *gente decente*. Apart from a handful of hispanised caciques no Indians were admitted; similarly the *castas*, mestizos and mulattoes alike were rejected. Only Spaniards were recognised as possible members. A peculiar racial sliding scale, therefore, governed social advancement in colonial Mexico. Not all whites belonged to the respectable classes, but all the respectable were white. More explicitly, not all the group designated as Spaniards were wealthy, educated or respectable, but all the wealthy and educated were Spaniards.[4] It was this scale which virtually debarred upward social mobility to anyone who did not count as a Spaniard.

1 *Instrucciones que los virreyes ... dejaron*, p. 258.

2 See below, Part Two, chapter 1, 'Merchants'.

3 Domingo de Sarmiento, *Conflicto y armonía de las razas en América* (2 vols.; Buenos Aires, 1953), I, 197–211, 240–6. Bailyn, *The New England Merchants*, pp. 192–7.

4 See 'Los escritos de Manuel Abad y Queipo', printed in José María Luis de Mora, *Obras sueltas* (Mexico, 1963), p. 205.

Naturally, a certain hyprocrisy and pretence prevailed; many upper-class creoles possessed some Indian blood. But social prejudice determined marriage patterns; the more mestizo creoles strove to marry spouses who appeared to be more European. Wealthy creole women married peninsular Spaniards.

Among the populace, on the other hand, we encounter a certain confusion of race and occupation. Men of different races worked in much the same jobs, yet they still possessed a distinct social and legal status. In the first place Indians paid a distinctive capitation tax, the tribute, assessed at just over two pesos a year, and collected by their local magistrates. They were therefore enrolled in a permanent register of tributaries kept for each village.[1] In partial compensation for this tax burden, they were exempted from the payment of excise duties; nor did they pay the ecclesiastical tithe. Equally distinctive was the Indian form of land tenure: ownership was vested in the village community so that the individual cultivator did not possess any right to sell or alienate his property. The Crown guaranteed each village an area of six hundred yards extending in radius from the perimeter of the settlement.[2] Naturally these laws were not always fulfilled, but in theory at least all Indian subjects were entitled to a share of communal land. Furthermore, the Crown surrounded Indians with a legislative code, which, designed to protect, virtually defined them as minors in the eyes of the law. The Inquisition, for example, did not consider Indians as fair game for its surveillance, since they were considered too ignorant to be capable of true heresy as distinct from childish superstition. Then again, Indians were forbidden to contract debts of more than five pesos. True, this law received universal neglect, but it reflected the official opinion of Indian capacity.[3] A special court, the *juzgado de indios*, entrusted to the care of the viceroy, dealt with all Indian problems and appeals. Other institutions, such as hospitals and colleges, were also devoted to their exclusive use. Finally, we must consider that many Indians retained the use of their own language, separate tribal costume and, in some cases, tribal superstitions. By 1810 some 60 per cent of the population still remained caught in a peculiar legal and social category for which no European equivalent could be found. Free subjects of the Crown, they were nevertheless treated at law as children, and after three centuries of colonial rule formed a separate community, oppressed and despised by

[1] Gibson, *The Aztecs*, pp. 207–9; Alamán, *Historia*, I, 24.

[2] Mora, *Obras sueltas*, 'Escritos de Manuel Abad y Queipo', p. 205.

[3] Alamán, *Historia*, I, 22–4. Silvio Zavala, 'Orígenes coloniales del peonaje en México', *El Trimestre Económico*, 10 (1943–4), pp. 711–48.

the rest of the population, to whom, in turn, they manifested both fear and hostility.

The three categories—Spaniards, mestizos and mulattoes—that largely comprised the lower class *gente de razón* were much less closely defined or socially separated than the Indians. The mestizos, for example, enjoyed much the same rights and obligations as the Spaniards, with the exception that many Crown and clerical appointments stipulated that their holders must be Spaniards. And between a Spaniard of the élite and a Spaniard of the populace—and by 1810 the latter amounted to 13 per cent of the population—few if any legal barriers existed except the tendency of élite members to possess private fueros. On the other hand, mulattoes, to whom may be added the few surviving negroes, were clearly marked out as a distinct group. Alone among the *gente de razón*, they paid tribute, assessed at three pesos on a capitation basis; like the Indian, therefore, they were enrolled on permanent tributary lists and separate baptismal registers.[1] African blood still carried with it the stigma of former slavery; mulattoes could not hope to obtain municipal office; the priesthood was theoretically barred to them. Moreover, the general social prejudice from which they suffered made the fiscal obligation all the more odious since it alone prevented them from merging with the mestizos.

In general, if we compare the condition of the lower-class hispanic community to that of the Indian the balance is not always struck in favour of the former. As *gente de razón* they paid excise duties and clerical tithes; they had no guaranteed rights to land. Unlike the Indian they could be drafted into the regular soldiery and were always liable for militia service. Similarly, in mining camps mestizos and mulattoes, if found unoccupied, could be press-ganged and thrust down a mine, whereas Indians were safeguarded by the law which only permitted a draft of 4 per cent of their village work force.[2] A landless mulatto labourer might well envy the relative security of the Indians, who enjoyed more rights and bore less burdens.

The tendency to identify mestizos and mulattoes as a middle stratum of society situated between a Spanish élite and an Indian mass must be avoided. Possibly the south and Oaxaca in particular approximated to that image of society. But elsewhere, especially in what were once Chichimeca areas, lower-class Spaniards, mulattoes and mestizos worked alongside

[1] Mora, *Obras sueltas*, pp. 205–6; Alamán, *Historia*, I, 25.

[2] Eusebio Buenaventura Beleña, *Recopilación sumaria de todos los autos acordados de la real audiencia y sala de crimen de esta Nueva España* (2 vols.; Mexico, 1787). Vol. II contains the *1783 ordenanzas de minería*: see II, 258–61.

Indians in much the same jobs; they acted as direct competitors for land and for wages, rather than as an emergent middle stratum. If the two communities are to be contrasted, the distinctions lie in their geographical distribution between north and south; between an urban proletariat and a peasantry; and in the countryside between the peons of haciendas or the farmers of the ranchos and the peasants who still dwelt in villages that owned land in communal tenure. Among the *gente de razón* themselves, however, the chief social difference lay quite simply in the possession or lack of wealth. But in New Spain the cut of the economic cake was remarkably uneven. When Humboldt visited the colony in 1803, he noted that 'unfortunately . . . great riches . . . are distributed with even greater inequality in Mexico than in the captaincy-general of Caracas, Havana and Lima'.[1] His opinion was shared by the enlightened bishop-elect of Michoacán, Manuel Abad y Queipo, who wrote: 'In America . . . there are no graduations or middle ranges: everyone is either rich or miserable, noble or contemned.'[2]

In no sense, of course, did this assorted mixture of races and privileged orders form a nation. True, they were all subjects of the King of Spain, yet even in this respect the colony was not notable for its devotion to the royal service. The viceroy, the Duke of Linares, complained that during the War of the Spanish Succession only three persons had offered pecuniary assistance to the Crown. 'The aim of everyone,' he wrote, 'is to live in absolute freedom.'[3] José de Gálvez later commented: 'Until now reward for good service has been as unknown and remote as punishment for bad conduct.'[4] Despite this lack of public spirit the Crown did not maintain any regular troops in the colony apart from locally recruited garrisons stationed along the northern frontier and at Veracruz. The viceroy only possessed a minute guard barely sufficient to defend him from popular assault.[5]

It was the Church rather than any military force which kept the peace in New Spain and which united the colony's diverse races into a single flock of believers. Indians looked to their parish priest to protect them from the rapacity of the royal magistrates. The populace of the towns and the mining camps could expect the religious and the secular clergy to administer them the sacraments which celebrated their marriages, the birth

[1] Humboldt, *Ensayo político*, p. 83.

[2] Printed in Mora, *Obras sueltas*, p. 205.

[3] BN (Madrid) MSS 2929, 'Instrucciones del Duque de Linares', f. 135. The Instrucción printed in *Las instrucciones que dejaron los virreyes* (Mexico, 1867) is incomplete and omits much of the detail found in the Madrid MSS.

[4] AGI, Mexico 2256, José de Gálvez to Marquis of Grimaldi, 23 December 1765.

[5] Alamán, *Historia*, I, 57.

of their children, their illnesses and their deaths. The Church, through its multiple institutions, administered all the colony's hospitals, asylums, orphanages and colleges. In many respects, therefore, it provided that range of social services, the responsibility for which in later centuries was assumed by the civil state. As a result of this intimate contact with both the masses and élite alike, the priesthood was able to intervene to prevent class conflict. In colonial Mexico when the populace burst into riot it was the clergy, and not the military, who sallied into the streets to remonstrate with, and to pacify, the mob.

IV

The structure of colonial society and economy sketched in the preceding pages mainly applies to that dark age of Mexican historiography which stretches from 1640 to 1750. This was the period in which the control exercised by the great merchants over the economy was most pronounced, and when the clergy's influence over society was most manifest. It was also the century in which the Spanish Crown paid least attention to its vast American possessions and during which in consequence it probably obtained from them the least profit. The statesmen of the new Bourbon dynasty did not seriously attempt to reform the disorderly and antiquated Habsburg patrimony until the middle decades of the eighteenth century. Then, in the name of fiscal and strategic necessity, they launched a fierce attack upon the privileged bodies and private institutions which sustained the old order.

The reformers' bible, the definitive text which inspired this Bourbon revolution in government, was José del Campillo y Cosío's *Nuevo sistema de gobierno económico para la América*. Written in 1743, the book circulated in manuscript until 1762 when it was incorporated virtually intact in Bernardo Wall's *Proyecto económico*.[1] Campillo started his analysis by a simple comparison of the great profits gained by both the French and English from their Caribbean islands with the derisory returns of Spain's continental empire. To remedy this sorry state of affairs he advocated the introduction of *gobierno económico*, by which term he meant the methods of government characteristic of Colbertian mercantilism. He demanded the termination of the commercial monopoly of Cadiz, the distribution of land to the Indians, and the encouragement of silver mining. Above all else, Campillo viewed the American colonies as an untapped market for

[1] José del Campillo y Cosío, *Nuevo sistema de gobierno económico para la América* (Madrid, 1789), p. 32. Bernardo Wall, *Proyecto económico* (Madrid, 1779). See Miguel Artola, 'Campillo y las reformas de Carlos III', *Revista de Indias*, 50 (1952), pp. 685–714.

Spanish manufacturers. But that market could only increase its power of consumption if its system of government was reformed, its economy released from malign monopolies and impediments to trade and if the great mass of its population, the Indians, were incorporated into society. To implement this programme of reform Campillo proposed to subject the colonies to a general inspection, to be then followed by the establishment of permanent intendancies.

Foreign methods might not have appeared so attractive had not foreign power become so threatening. As it was, Spain suffered a humiliating defeat during the Seven Years War. Havana was captured by the British.[1] Moreover, the Peace of Paris, which virtually terminated French influence in the New World, left Spain alone, confronted with an enemy more powerful and aggressive than before. At about this time José de Gálvez, then a ministerial lawyer, wrote: 'Each day Spanish America is more exposed to the insatiable ambition of certain European powers. . . . England especially aspires to dominate the entire commerce of both hemispheres.'[2] As much as the Austria of Maria Theresa after the seizure of Silesia, the Spain of Charles III after the Seven Years War had to 'modernise' its methods of government or go to the wall.[3] And to modernise in the colonial context meant higher taxation and militarisation. It entailed what can only be defined as a revolution in government. Equally important, its success depended upon a transformation of the economy and a profound re-ordering of status within colonial society.

As early as 1764 Mexico experienced the first impact of the new policies. In that year two regiments of Spanish troops, led by the inspector-general, Juan de Villalba, arrived for permanent duty in the colony. The Crown also directed Villalba to organise a small army of militia regiments. His efforts to levy recruits for these volunteer forces soon provoked riots in Michoacán, Puebla and Guanajuato.[4] Moreover, in Mexico City the Spanish regulars soon quarrelled with the populace; some years later the viceroy, the Marquis of Croix, commented on the almost nightly brawls that still occurred.[5]

At much the same time, José de Gálvez, visitor-general to New Spain

1 See John Lynch, *Spanish Colonial Administration* (London, 1958), pp. 12–18.

2 BRP, MSS 2816, Miscelánea de Ayala, 278, ff. 110, 117.

3 See R. R. Palmer, *The Age of the Democratic Revolution* (Princeton, 1959), pp. 103–7. In general see Richard Herr, *The Eighteenth-Century Revolution in Spain* (Princeton, 1958).

4 María del Carmen Velásquez, *El estado de guerra en Nueva España 1760–1800* (Mexico, 1958), pp. 80–5.

5 Marqués de Croix, *Instrucción . . . que deja a su sucesor Antonio María de Bucareli*, prólogo y notas de Norman F. Martin (Mexico, 1960), p. 53.

(1765–71) and Minister of the Indies (1776–87), devoted his considerable energies to the great task of raising more revenue.[1] As a first step he converted the manufacture and sale of tobacco into a royal monopoly. To prevent contraband its cultivation was restricted to a group of licensed districts. All consumers henceforth had to purchase their cigars, often badly made, from royal officials. In addition, Gálvez demanded increased sums of money from the provincial merchants who farmed the excise duties of their district. Naturally it was the consumers who paid for all this.

The popular riots against the militia, the new taxes and the Crown monopolies changed into rebellion when in 1767 the Crown ordered the arrest and exile of all Jesuits. The Indians of Pátzcuaro and Uruapan, and the mine-workers of San Luis Potosí and Guanajuato rose up in revolt, seized control of their town and threatened the lives and property of the European Spaniards. Gálvez, supported by Villalba's regular troops and by apprehensive creole miners and landowners, suppressed this challenge with unprecedented harshness. He hanged 85 persons, flogged 73, banished 117, and sentenced 674 to various terms of imprisonment.[2] These events, taken together, marked a sharp turning-point in Mexico's colonial history. Peninsular soldiers and tax collectors arrived, Mexican-born Jesuits—over four hundred—were expelled.[3] The populace, which did not appreciate the exchange, was subjected to an unaccustomed and brutal exercise of military force. An entire intellectual generation was driven into exile and the children of the élite lost their best teachers. The new Bourbon state began, as it was to end, in violence and bloodshed.

The events of the 1760s set the pattern for the next 40 years. Ruled by regalist theories of government, the ministers of Charles III launched a pin-pricking series of attacks against clerical jurisdiction and legal immunity, a campaign which culminated in the unprecedented imprisonment in civil gaols of several priests accused of criminal offences.[4] Where the Habsburgs used priests the Bourbons employed soldiers. For although the clerical fuero was attacked, the military fuero was strengthened and its application extended.[5] By the close of the eighteenth century New Spain possessed its own small army of 32,000 men, composed of 9,917 regulars and 22,277

[1] For Gálvez see Herbert Ingram Priestley, *José de Gálvez, Visitor-General of New Spain (1765–71)* (Berkeley, 1916).

[2] Priestley, *José de Gálvez*, p. 228.

[3] Birthplaces of expelled Jesuits can be found in Mariano Cuevas, ed., *Tesoros documentales de México siglo XVIII: Priego, Zelis, Clavijero* (Mexico, 1944), pp. 234–93.

[4] See N. M. Farriss, *Crown and Clergy in Colonial Mexico 1759–1821* (London, 1968), pp. 99–100, 173–96. Mora, *Obras sueltas*, 'Escritos de Abad y Queipo: sobre la inmunidad personal del clero', pp. 195–8.

[5] See Lyle N. Macalister, *The fuero militar in New Spain 1764–1800* (Gainesville, Fla., 1957).

militia.[1] The wealthy classes enrolled in the militia forces established in the principal towns of the colony. All officers enjoyed the military fuero, the right to trial by regimental superiors rather than in the royal courts. The army, therefore, replaced the Church as the Crown's favoured instrument for securing the loyalty of its colonial subjects. It was the inspector-general of Infantry who wrote in 1804: 'In America the essential part of a youth's education ought to be the inculcation of principles of love and obedience to the Sovereign.'[2]

In the economic sphere much the same policy prevailed. The visitor-general, José de Gálvez, declared: 'Since mining is the origin and unique source of the metals which give spirit and movement to all human occupations and to the universal commerce of this globe, in justice it demands the principal attention of the government.'[3] He therefore organised the miners into a guild which possessed its own courts and exercised jurisdiction over all mining litigation. To the concession of this new fuero was added the entire battery of current economic policy.[4] His object, apart from increasing silver production, was to liberate the mining industry from mercantile control. For Gálvez, following Campillo, was determined to destroy the economic dominance of the great Mexico City import houses. In 1778 the famous decree of *comercio libre* terminated the old Cadiz monopoly: henceforth all the chief ports of the Peninsula could trade freely with the American colonies. Somewhat later, new independent merchant guilds were established at Veracruz and Guadalajara. This attack upon the old monopolists proved largely successful: both the silver miners and the provincial merchants obtained financial independence. More importantly, silver production, as measured by annual mintage, augmented from under twelve million pesos in 1762 to a peak of over twenty-seven million pesos in 1804.[5] The less complete figures for transatlantic commerce indicate an equally dramatic expansion.

If Gálvez devoted much energy and thought to the restructuring and expansion of the export economy, he paid little attention to Mexican industry and agriculture. Landowners did not have any legal privilege, nor did they receive much encouragement, fiscal or otherwise, from the new regime. As for native manufacturers, their very existence was con-

[1] Humboldt, *Ensayo político*, pp. 554–7.

[2] AGS, Guerra Moderna 7299, Count of Alcaraz, 24 September 1804.

[3] José de Gálvez, *Informe general . . . al excelentísimo señor virrey d. frey Antonio Bucareli y Ursúa* (Mexico, 1867), p. 40.

[4] See Walter Howe, *The Mining Guild of New Spain and Its Tribunal General 1770–1821* (Cambridge, Mass., 1949).

[5] Miguel Lerdo de Tejada, *El comercio esterior de México* (Mexico, 1853), App. 54.

demned. Gálvez asserted that colonial industries damaged Spain, 'whose interest consists in that the inhabitants of the Indies do not become accustomed to live independently of this monarchy for the supply of necessities'.[1] Years later that enlightened viceroy, the second Count of Revillagigedo, reiterated this opinion: 'It must not be forgotten that this [country] is a colony which ought to depend upon its origin, Spain, and to yield some profit in return from the benefits of protection. But great prudence is required to arrange the dependency and to make the interest mutual and reciprocal, for this relation would cease the moment European manufactures and produce are no longer needed here.'[2]

The 'profit' to which Revillagigedo referred was by no means small. Whereas in 1712 royal revenue from Mexico amounted to no more than three million pesos, by the last decade of the century annual tax and monopoly receipts averaged over twenty million pesos.[3] This revenue can be divided into four broad categories. First, there were the various taxes raised from the mining industry—the tithe on production and the monopoly profits on mercury, gunpowder and mintage. The vast tobacco monopoly formed a class in itself. Then there was a variegated range of customs and excise duties levied on all produce sold on the open market, including under this head taxes charged on pulque and salt. The final category was formed by the capitation tribute paid by Indians and mulattoes, by this time far less important than the other types of taxation. The principal innovation introduced by the Bourbons consisted in the establishment of Crown monoplies in tobacco, playing cards and gunpowder and in the utilisation of salaried officials to administer these monopolies and to collect excise duties. After 1776 the Habsburg practice of farming out revenue collection to private individuals or institutions was terminated. A small army of officials, clerks and guards, stationed in all the chief towns of New Spain, administered these taxes, new and old, with unparalleled vigour and efficiency. The drive to revitalise and expand the bureaucracy was crowned in 1786 with the appointment of some twelve intendants.

This revolution in government undoubtedly paid off. In all the Crown obtained nearly fourteen million pesos a year from New Spain. Of this sum four million were required to support the civil administration, the law courts, the fiscal bureaucracy, the military, and to protect the northern frontiers. The remainder, some ten million pesos, were shipped out of

[1] BRP, MSS 2816, Miscelánea de Ayala, 278, f. 118.

[2] Conde de Revillagigedo, *Instrucción reservadísima que ... dió al ... Marqués de Branciforte* (Mexico, 1831), p. 91.

[3] Humboldt, *Ensayo político*, p. 540.

Mexico. Four million went to subsidise a wide circle of forts and garrisons that stretched from Trinidad to Louisiana, from California to the Philippines. The other six million—the monopoly profits—went straight to the royal chest in Madrid. For the monarchy only raised thirty-five million pesos in taxes from the Peninsula. It therefore relied upon its American possessions to finance their own administration and defence. In addition, the Crown received from America a surplus of eight million pesos, of which three-quarters came from Mexico.[1] Clearly, by the close of the century New Spain had emerged as a source of revenue second only to the metropolis itself.

For Mexico, as for most of Spanish America, the decades following the Seven Years War constituted a distinct epoch in its colonial history. Far from being the culmination of two hundred years' settlement, however, this so-called golden age of the late eighteenth century sprang from a profound regeneration of the New World's hispanic society. In some sense, the Bourbon dynasty reconquered America. It entirely transformed the system of government, the structure of the economy and the order of society which had prevailed in the colonies since the days of the Habsburgs. At the same time, a more numerous Spanish immigration invaded the continent. Many arrived to occupy the newly created posts in government and the army, but the great majority entered commerce to profit from the great economic expansion of these years. Whereas in 1689 only 1,182 peninsular Spaniards resided in Mexico City, by 1792 that number had just about doubled.[2] Bourbon Mexico, if such we may style the period 1763–1810, took its origin from the successful collaboration of a despotic but enlightened administration with a vigorous group of merchant-capitalists and silver millionaires. The success of the government's economic reforms in large measure depended upon the enterprise and capital of these businessmen. Here, then, we encounter the theme of our subsequent discussion.

1 Humboldt, *Ensayo político*, pp. 546–52.

2 See Ignacio Rubio Mañé, *Gente de España en la ciudad de México año de 1689* (Mexico, 1966), p. 13.

PART ONE

THE REVOLUTION IN GOVERNMENT

All other Errors but disturb a State;
But Innovation is the Blow of Fate.

JOHN DRYDEN

When in August 1789 Viceroy Manuel Antonio Flores compiled his final report for the benefit of his successor, the second Count of Revillagigedo, he went out of his way to praise an equivalent *instrucción* written by the Count's father, Viceroy of New Spain in the years 1746–55. At the same time, he indicated its complete inapplicability to the present. 'It treats and explains all the most important parts of New Spain's great government, showing the happiness of a more innocent age. But in our days the system [of government] has varied to such a degree that that wise report, a true witness to the talent, zeal and insight of its author, can assist Your Excellency solely to compare the changes brought about during the course of thirty-five years.'[1]

The most notable of these changes in New Spain's administration to which Flores referred was the establishment of intendancies in 1786. The viceroy took a remarkably gloomy view about this great reform: 'Until now all we hear are deafening complaints prophesying the ruin of the kingdom and the immediate destruction of all branches of the royal exchequer.' In this judgment Flores gave vent not merely to his own opinion, but rather to the sentiments of a large party within colonial officialdom. In the very same year, Teodore de Croix, Viceroy of Peru, issued a strident condemnation of the entire system.[2] In Madrid itself voices were raised in favour of outright abolition.[3]

Now why should the intendants have raised such controversy? What powers or quality did they possess to provoke such enmity? After all, the Bourbons had employed intendants in Spain itself for more than two decades before introducing them into the Americas.[4] Any answer to this question, of course, must return to that context of thirty-five years of almost continuous change already mentioned by Flores. For in this period the entire structure of colonial government was transformed. Old institutions of Habsburg provenance found the limits of their jurisdiction sharply reduced by the creation of new officials and departments. Their members, often quite aged, often of American birth, came to resent bitterly the sudden influx of young men from the Peninsula, chosen by Gálvez to manage the new monopolies and other offices of state. At the

[1] AGI, Mexico 1525, Flores to Revillagigedo, 26 April 1789; the Elder Revillagigedo's report can be found in AGI, Estado 42, 28 November 1754.

[2] Lillian Estelle Fisher, *The Intendant System in Spanish America* (Berkeley, 1929), pp. 83–6.

[3] Luis Navarro García, *Intendencias de Indias* (Seville, 1959), pp. 115–23.

[4] John Lynch, *Spanish Colonial Administration*, pp. 46–61.

same time the organisation of a fairly rapid, efficient royal postal service throughout the empire put an end to that former freedom of action conferred by distance and bad communications. For these men the intendancies represented the culmination, the capstone, so to speak, of the new Bourbon state. Here, in part, they accepted the propaganda of their opponents. Had not Campillo written up the intendancies as the very quintessence of his cherished *gobierno económico*? For Gálvez they constituted the indispensable instruments of his reform programme.[1] In consequence, the entire project became the object of an essentially political controversy, both a rallying cry and a whipping boy for reformers and conservatives alike. At the same time the wide range of duties with which these magistrates were endowed offered a potential challenge to virtually all other government institutions. Small wonder, then, that from the outset their authority was contested, their ordinances abrogated, and their very existence brought into question. Our interest in all this, it must be emphasised, is more with the structure than with the operation of the revolution in government.

I

The story must start, as always, with the Gálvez Visitation (1765–71). For the colonial bureaucracy came to resent bitterly the measures of the 1760s. The revolt of the populace against the Jesuit expulsion and the introduction of the militia, the quarrels of the Marquis of Cruillas, viceroy 1760–6, with both the visitor-general and the head of the military mission, Juan de Villalba, the opposition of the viceroy and the fiscal, Juan Antonio Velarde, to Gálvez's energetic reorganisation of the tobacco monopoly, the alarm of the Council of the Indies at the sudden bypassing of the usual procedures of consultation—all this is known to every student of Mexican history.[2] What has been less emphasised is the degree to which the Visitation and the Expulsion marked a turning-point in the relations between the Spanish monarchy and that small colonial establishment which had hitherto governed Mexico. Some of its members were peninsulars who had spent most of their official lives in the New World, the majority were probably creoles; moreover, either they themselves or their children were formed at the Jesuit College of San Ildefonso in Mexico City, concerning which a historian of the Company, Francisco Javier Clavijero, made boast: 'It suffices to say that several educated and disinterested persons who have travelled through Italy, France and Spain confess that they have

[1] Campillo y Cosío, *Nuevo sistema*, pp. 70–8, 93–101.
[2] See Priestley, *José de Gálvez, passim.*

not seen in Europe anything to compare to the San Ildefonso of Mexico. There, distinguished men were trained—bishops, judges, canons, and professors in all the faculties.'[1] It was against these men that Gálvez's faithful ally, the Marquis of Croix, viceroy 1766–71, warned Madrid: 'I shall not hide from Your Excellency that all the clergy and lawyers, since they belong entirely to them [the Jesuits] are also the most resentful.'[2]

The situation was all the more dangerous because both the audiencia and the cathedral chapter of Mexico City were dominated by American Spaniards. This creole predominance needs to be stressed. Later advocates of Independence wasted much ink compiling lists of viceroys and bishops to prove that American Spaniards were excluded from high office in the colonies.[3] What they failed to notice was that many *oidores* and probably most canons, deans and archdeacons were in fact recruited from among the natives of the New World. Now, this omission sprang not merely from the demands of political rhetoric, but also from that profound change in imperial policy wrought during the middle years of the preceding century. For whereas the first kings of the Bourbon dynasty had promoted creoles on a liberal scale to all offices in colonial government, apart from those of viceroy and bishop, the enlightened ministers of Charles III, intent upon a deep-reaching reform of the old order, for the most part relied upon soldiers and bureaucrats brought in from Europe. The revolution in government entailed not just the creation of new institutions, it also meant the importation of new men.

The chief proponent of this policy was, of course, José de Gálvez, that once poor Malagueño lawyer with a French wife, who succeeded as few men before him in arousing the hatred of the colonial élite. Already in an official memorandum written several years before his journey to Mexico, Gálvez had criticised the then apparently common practice of choosing creoles for important posts in American government. In his own words: 'Lately, in all the American audiencias many natives of the province or city in which these courts are situated have been appointed.' And again: 'Many presidences, governorships and captaincies-general—after the three viceroyalties the most important posts into which America is divided—have been occupied by creoles.' This policy he condemned on the grounds that the creoles were too bound by 'the ties of family and faction in the New World to provide a disinterested impartial government'.[4] His

[1] Cuevas, ed., *Tesoros documentales*, p. 307. See also Félix Osores, *Noticias bio-bibliográficas de alumnos distinguidos de San Pedro y San Pablo y San Ildefonso de México* (2 vols.; Mexico, 1908), *passim*.

[2] AGI, Mexico 1365, Croix to Arriaga, 26 August 1767.

[3] See José Miguel Guridi Alcocer, *Censor extraordinario* (Cadiz, 1812), pp. 22–7.

[4] BRP, MSS 2816, Miscelánea de Ayala, 278, ff. 129–30.

worst apprehensions were confirmed when he went to Mexico and found that in the audiencia, contrary to legislation, 'the majority of its members were natives of the country'.[1] Nor was this situation limited to New Spain. For the Visitor-General of Peru, José Antonio de Areche, discovered that five of the eight oidores of the Lima audiencia were American-born.[2] Just when such appointments became common is difficult to say; in Lima, as early as the turn of the century, the creoles predominated in that audiencia; for Mexico, evidence is wanting.[3]

Now while Gálvez was in New Spain, in 1768, an extraordinary council of state was summoned in Madrid to discuss the best methods of reconciling the colonies to the monarchy after the shock of the Jesuit expulsion. The two fiscals, Pedro Rodríguez de Campomanes and José de Moñino, the future Count of Floridablanca, declared that it was advisable to attract creoles to the Peninsula, both as children for education and as adults by giving them administrative and military positions there. It was equally necessary, they declared, 'to maintain the policy of always sending Spaniards to the Indies for the principal offices, bishoprics and prebendaries, giving the creoles the equivalent places in Spain'.[4] The conclusions of the junta soon became public; moreover, the actual practice of Gálvez gave clear proof of his own sentiments in this respect. In 1771, therefore, the ayuntamiento, the council of Mexico City, always a creole stronghold, issued its famous representation to the Crown. In the first place it roundly condemned a secret report of Archbishop Francisco Antonio Lorenzana in which that regalist prelate was alleged to have asserted that 'the spirit of the Americans is submissive and yielding; they are well-suited for an inferior condition, but once raised to power or position they become exposed to the greatest errors'. The ayuntamiento, naturally enough, defended both the nature and capacity of their nation. More significantly, they then proceeded to dismiss European Spaniards as foreigners who simply did not understand Mexico or the New World. They then appealed to the laws of Castile insisting, as of right, that all government posts in New Spain should be given to natives of that country.[5] In a word, Mexico for the Mexicans.

[1] Gálvez, *Informe general*, p. 3.

[2] Vicente Palacio Atard, *Areche y Guirior, observaciones sobre el fracaso de una visita* (Seville, 1946), p. 21.

[3] Jorge Tovar Velarde, 'La audiencia de Lima 1705–1707. Dos años de gobierno criollo en el Perú', *Revista de Historia*, 23 (Lima, 1957–8), pp. 338–448.

[4] Jaime Eyzaguirre, *Ideario y ruta de la emancipación chilena* (Santiago de Chile, 1957), p. 53.

[5] Printed in Juan Hernández y Dávalos, *Colección de documentos para la historia de la guerra de independencia de México de 1808 a 1821* (6 vols.; Mexico, 1877–82), I, 427–55.

Such impolitic declarations, though qualified by many protestations of loyalty to the Crown, could only confirm the apprehensions already entertained in Madrid. So in 1776, the year in which Gálvez became Minister of the Indies, decrees were issued inviting creoles to compete for clerical and judicial positions in the Peninsula; henceforth only a third of all posts in the American audiencias and cathedral chapters were to be reserved for creoles; the rest were to be thrown open to candidates from Europe.[1] Upon receipt of these royal orders, agitated meetings were held in Mexico City, plans were formed for a public protest, and the city council once more presented an anguished memorial to the Crown in which they asseverated that their children, denied access to clerical or judicial promotion, would have no incentive for further study.[2] Gálvez wrote quickly to allay their fears. He explained that the decree merely set aside a third of all these places for Americans, but 'it does not exclude [the possibility] that there might be many more, as there always had been, there is and there will be'.[3]

In fact, Gálvez soon became renowned not merely for his preference for European Spaniards but for his persistent favouritism towards his compatriots, the Malagueños, and for his implacable nepotism. During his ministry (1776–87) as hundreds of administrative places were created in the great fiscal departments of the excise service and the tobacco monopoly and among the intendants, Gálvez gave full rein to his prejudices. In the older institutions, such as the treasuries, the audiencias, the cathedral chapters and the courts of audit, the change, although quite perceptible, was less pronounced. Naturally, this drastic re-ordering of imperial policy did not escape contemporary notice. Melchor Paz, the Peruvian chronicler of the Tupac Amaru revolt, cited an anonymous letter, written *c.* 1781, which lamented, 'thus we see regents and an increased number of the members of the audiencias [who are] all relatives, favourites and dependents of Gálvez'.[4] And Dean Gregorio Funes of Córdoba in the Argentine, later commented:

For all American clerics the gate was shut, not merely for bishoprics but even for appointment to the seats of the cathedral chapters . . . never were the remaining civil and military positions distributed with such a one-sided prepossession in favour of the

[1] Eyzaguirre, *Ideario y ruta*, pp. 53–4; AGI, Mexico 1863, Mexico City Ayuntamiento to Gálvez, 22 May 1778.

[2] Rómulo Velasco Ceballos, ed., *La administración de d. Frey Antonio María de Bucareli y Ursúa* (2 vols.; Mexico, 1936), II, 314–20.

[3] AGI, Mexico 1863, Gálvez to Ayuntamiento, 2 January 1778.

[4] Melchor Paz, *Guerra separatista, rebeliones de indios en Sur América, la sublevación de Tupac Amaru*, ed. Luis Antonio Eguiguren (2 vols.; Lima, 1952), II, 131.

European Spaniards ... to the point where every Spaniard, especially if he were Andaluz or Malagueño, simply for being so, was accredited with merit and capacity.[1]

Now Funes laid the blame of this policy directly at the door of Gálvez, whom he characterised as 'a man as daring in his schemes as he was diligent in carrying them out; as eager to increase the royal revenues as he was unscrupulous in his means; in short, so prejudiced in favour of the rights of the metropolis as he was disposed to outrage those of the colonies'.[2] This view should not be dismissed as so much propaganda. For there exists in the *Archivo de Indias* at Seville an anonymous document, *Apuntes suscintos y prácticas de la América Española*, composed in the years 1775–6 by a person whom internal evidence suggests to have been a high peninsular official resident in Madrid.[3] The author bluntly described Gálvez as a man 'without experience, without prudence and without wisdom'. He pictured him as 'a minister who completely despises the habits and people' of America. Jobs in colonial government had been multiplied but all vacancies went to new men, directly recruited from Spain, thus ignoring 'the due order of promotion' for Americans. The creoles resented their exclusion from the additional range of positions opened up by the recent reforms. The author noted that peninsular officials of long service in the colonies had become concerned as to the fate of their children in this new system. But why should creoles be denied access to government employment, since 'lacking these rewards for study, will not the Americans experience the same fate as the Greeks subject to the Ottoman Empire?' Now lest these accusations be thought too strong, they should be compared with those extraordinary secret instructions sent by Gálvez to his favourite, Areche, in Peru, in which he dismissed the inhabitants of Lima as being 'of a quick humour and understanding, but superficial and unreliable in judgement, even though remarkably presumptuous ... they are of little spirit, being timid and submissive'. Clearly, if Gálvez gave vent to such contemptuous expressions in a confidential state paper, no doubt in conversation he voiced his opinions in an even franker fashion. Small wonder, then, that our anonymous critic should aver that New Spain 'shall never cease to abominate the rule of the Marquis of Croix during the period of the last Visitation'. The colony was dismayed to learn that 'the same destructive agent ... should be now placed with greater power to whet his ambition to throw into uproar both hemi-

[1] Gregorio Funes, *Ensayo de la historia civil de Buenos Aires, Tucumán y Paraguay* (2 vols.; Buenos Aires, 1856), II, 211.

[2] *Ibid.*, II, 210; see also Paz, *Guerra separatista*, II, 131: 'promoted to the ministry for the misfortune of these Indies, Gálvez has made it his object to destroy them'.

[3] AGI, Estado 42/3, unfoliated, undated. See *Apuntes*, 324–53.

spheres'. He concluded on a prophetic note: 'Gálvez has destroyed more than he has built . . . his destructive hand is going to prepare the greatest revolution in the American Empire.'[1]

The effects of this revolution, launched from without and from above, can be best observed in the history of the Mexican audiencia. During the years of the Visitation this body protested to Madrid that the viceroy, Croix, refused to accord its members the traditional ceremonies of respect and that he ignored the customary procedures of consultation.[2] At the same time at least one of its judges, Francisco Javier de Gamboa, the well-known author of the *Comentarios a las ordenanzas de minas*, and a recently appointed alcalde del crimen, actively conspired with the fiscal Juan Antonio de Velarde against the pretensions of the visitor-general. He went so far as to slander Gálvez's character, alleging that he held 'strange' disorderly entertainments in his house. In return, however, both he and Velarde, 'being inseparable companions', were accused by the viceroy, Croix, of being the leaders of an 'anti-government party'.[3] The case became more serious when rumour associated Gamboa with the canon Antonio López Portillo, a cleric then famous for his erudition, as being the joint authors of a pamphlet written in favour of the Jesuits against the Archbishop Lorenzana.[4] Although proofs were lacking, Croix was sufficiently convinced to recommend to Madrid that Velarde, Gamboa, López Portillo and his cousin, the archdeacon Ignacio Ceballos, should all be removed from New Spain. Sure enough, in 1768, the four men received promotion: Gamboa to the audiencia of Barcelona, Velarde to the court at Granada, López Portillo to the Cathedral of Valencia, and Ceballos to yet another place in the Peninsula. Croix also despatched a list of other members of this 'party' on whom he advised no immediate action. Those were the prebendary Francisco Vives; the audiencia judge, Diego Antonio Fernández de Madrid; the chief accountant of tributes, José Rafael Rodríguez Gallardo; the chief accountant of the *tribunal de cuentas*—the court of audit—Ignacio Negreiros; the chief official of the viceregal secretariat, Martín de Aspiroz; and the superintendent of the mint, Pedro Villavicencio. Some of these men had attacked the Visitation, others supported the Jesuits, the remainder were close friends of the banished.[5]

1 AGI, Estado 42/3, unfoliated, undated. See *Apuntes*, 310.

2 AGI, Mexico 1127, Audiencia to Council of the Indies, 26 May 1769.

3 AGI, Mexico 1369, Croix to Arriaga, 27 August 1769.

4 José Mariano Beristáin de Sousa, *Biblioteca hispano-americana septentrional* (3rd ed., 5 vols.; Mexico, 1947), II, 334–5; III, 155–8.

5 AGI, Mexico 1369, Croix to Arriaga, 27 August 1769.

An intriguing aspect of this 'party' is the extent to which it embodied a creole, as distinct from a conservative, resistance to the enforced Italian exile of over four hundred Mexican-born Jesuits. For both Gamboa and López Portillo were American Spaniards, educated at the San Ildefonso. How far their respective institutions supported their stand is difficult to say. But the audiencia, at least, was mainly composed of men of much the same origin and formation (see table 2).

Table 2 *Mexican audiencia membership* c. *1769.*

Dean	
Domingo Valcárcel y Baquerizo	Peninsular
Oidores	
Francisco Antonio Echevarri	Peninsular
José Rodríguez de Toro	Creole
Félix Venancio Malo de Villavicencio	Creole
Antonio Joaquín de Rivadeneira	Creole
Antonio de Villaurrutia	Creole
Ambrosio Eugenio Melgarejo y Santaella	Creole
Francisco López Portillo	Creole
Alcaldes del Crimen	
Francisco Javier de Gamboa	Creole
Diego Antonio Fernández de Madrid	Creole
Francisco Leandro de Viana	Peninsular
Antonio Rojas y Abreu	?

Many of these men came from families with long records of government service. The most distinguished was the dean, Domingo Valcárcel y Baquerizo whose father and grandfather had served on the council of Castile. He himself had spent his entire official life in New Spain, arriving in 1721 as an alcalde del crimen. Contrary to the theoretical rules governing his office, he married locally, to a daughter of the Count of Santiago, a descendant of Mexico's second viceroy, Luis de Velasco.[1] In addition to his judicial duties Valcárcel also, from 1761 until his death in 1783, directed the important mercury monopoly. His career thus spanned 62 years. The other members could not boast such long service, but several had extensive connexions with the audiencia. Both Fernández de Madrid and Melgarejo Santaella were sons of former *oidores*.[2] Similarly, Villaur-

[1] A description of his career is to be found in AGI, Mexico 1317, Bucareli to Arriaga, 26 November 1773.

[2] For Melgarejo see AGI, 1856, relation of services, 4 March 1761. For Fernández de Madrid, see Alberto and Arturo García Caraffa, *Enciclopedia heráldica y genealógica hispanoamericana*, XXXIV (Madrid, 1919–?), p. 74.

rutia's father had been governor of Tlaxcala.[1] Rodríguez de Toro belonged to a prominent family of Caracas, his father being the first Marquis of Toro.[2] Then again, Rivadeneira was closely related to the counts of Santiago; he could trace his ancestry in New Spain back to the sixteenth century.[3] The same was true of López Portillo, a native of Guadalajara who numbered several conquistadores in his genealogy; he was cousin to the exiled canon and the father of a Jesuit.[4] Malo de Villavicencio was related to, possibly the son of, the superintendent of the mint, Pedro Malo de Villavicencio.[5] Even the newly appointed peninsular alcalde del crimen, Francisco Leandro de Viana, soon found an acceptable Mexican bride in the Marchioness of Prado Alegre, the granddaughter of the wealthy immigrant merchant, the Count of San Bartolomé de Jala.[6] It was, of course, precisely this circle of Jesuit-trained interrelated creole judges whom Gálvez wished to dislodge from their commanding role in colonial administration. Naturally, granted their connexions both in the New World and Madrid, he had to move cautiously and slowly.

Even by the end of the 1770s, however, a decided change had occurred in the composition of the audiencia, as table 3 indicates.

Here the contrast between the creole senior judges and the peninsular alcaldes del crimen is especially striking; the normal sequence of promotion would soon destroy the old creole majority. As it was, Gamboa had utilised his contacts in Madrid to effect his return to Mexico in 1774. In 1778 another outstanding creole lawyer, Baltazar Ladrón de Guevara, at last received his promotion to the bench, the reward of over thirty years' legal practice, during the greater part of which he had been engaged in administrative tasks. In 1773 he had become assessor-general to the viceroy, Antonio María de Bucareli. He and Gamboa probably had the best legal brains in the colony. According to José Mariano Beristáin de Sousa, the bibliographer, Gálvez had once called him 'the American Ulpian'.[7] He was about the only creole to win the favour of the great minister, since all the other new judges were peninsular Spaniards. Francisco Roma

[1] Rafael Nieto y Caravellas, *Los Villaurrutias* (Habana, 1952), *passim*.

[2] Guillermo Lohman Villena, *Los americanos en las órdenes nobiliarias 1529–1900* (2 vols.; 1947), II, 361.

[3] Beristáin, *Biblioteca*, III, 210, 211.

[4] Osores, *Noticias bio-bibliográficas*, II, 46.

[5] *Ibid.*, II, 66.

[6] AGI, Mexico 1762, Viana to Crown, 7 February 1777; see also José Antonio Calderón Quijano, *El banco de San Carlos y las comunidades de indios de Nueva España* (Seville, 1963), footnote, p. 18.

[7] Beristáin, *Biblioteca*, II, 393–34; see also AGI, Mexico 1139, Ladrón de Guevara to Council of the Indies, 12 November 1798.

Rossel, nominated to occupy the recently created post of regent or head of the audiencia, was a Catalan with no previous experience of the Indies.[1] In part the continued creole predominance among the senior men sprang from the promotion of Viana, by this time the Count of Tepa, to the Council of the Indies and of Vicente Herrera Rivero to be regent of the Guatemalan audiencia. In 1777 the new archbishop of Mexico, Alonso de

Table 3 *Mexican audiencia membership* c. *1779*.

Regent	
Francisco Roma Rossel	Peninsular
Dean	
Domingo Valcárcel	Peninsular
Oidores	
Antonio de Villaurrutia	Creole
Diego Antonio Fernández de Madrid	Creole
Francisco Javier de Gamboa	Creole
Baltazar Ladrón de Guevara	Creole
Francisco Gómez Algarín	Peninsular
Ruperto Vicente de Luyando	Peninsular
Miguel Calixto de Acedo	Peninsular
Domingo de Arangoiti	Peninsular (?)
Juan Antonio Uruñela	Peninsular (?)
Alcaldes del Crimen	
Ramón González Becerra	Peninsular
Cosme Antonio Mier y Trespalacios	Peninsular
Eusebio Ventura de Beleña	Peninsular
Simón Antonio de Mirafuentes	Peninsular
Juan Francisco Anda	Peninsular

Haro, no friend of the creoles, warned Gálvez that if Valcárcel and Herrera left the court then the next three judges in order of seniority were Villaurrutia, Fernández de Madrid and Gamboa, 'all three Americans, and certainly this is not convenient'.[2] Gálvez took the hint. He later arranged for Gamboa and Villaurrutia to serve as regents of the Santo Domingo and Guadalajara audiencias, and recalled Herrera Rivero to New Spain to succeed Roma Rossel as regent. By the late 1780s, the Mexican court was easily dominated by peninsular Spaniards with no more than three creoles among the eleven judges of the upper court. Gálvez had thus fulfilled to the letter the terms of the 1776 decree.

[1] AGI, Mexico 1930, Mayorga to Gálvez, 25 July 1781.

[2] AGI, Mexico 1862, Archbishop to Gálvez, 27 February 1777.

At the same time the new Bourbon reliance upon military men and fiscal officers tended to diminish the prestige of the oidores and their court. Moreover, Gálvez stripped the audiencia of a good part of its former power when he created a series of fueros, or private jurisdictions. As was to be expected peninsular judges as much as creole resented this displacement from that central role in colonial administration which they had hitherto enjoyed. In 1782 Vicente Herrera Rivero, the newly appointed regent of the Mexican court, despatched a long memorandum to Gálvez in which he proposed the establishment of two new audiencias in New Spain and an increase in the membership of all four. He then continued:

> With the audiencias augmented and reorganised in this fashion, it will then be desirable to restore to them their original authority which has been notably diminished by the fueros, the immunities conceded to all branches of exchequer—to the postal service, the excise, the tobacco, playing cards and gunpowder monopolies, and to all the offices, secretaries and the court of audit—to the point where the *jurisdicción ordinaria*, the regular royal justice, only takes cognisance of the lesser part of the privileged community, and will soon be left with the lowest, since the former is already gaining exemption with the expansion of the militia.

He then condemned the policy of multiplying fueros as inimical to the normal exercise of justice. Herrera also sharply criticised the employment of military men in civil administration: 'Soldiers in general understand nothing about civil affairs.' Their training did not fit them to govern anywhere and still less in colonies. Now although the ostensible target here was the use of the military to act as presidents of audiencia, his attack applied equally well to the intendants, many of whom were recruited directly from the armed forces.[1] In effect, therefore, Herrera took exception to almost every feature of the new regime introduced by Gálvez.

In the upshot, however, the Minister of the Indies paid little attention to those proposals. To the contrary: in 1783 he created an entirely new fuero when he established a mining guild and courts to handle all litigation arising out of that contentious industry. Similarly under the intendant ordinances of 1786 all authority over Indian tributes and community funds, previously vested in the audiencia, was transferred to the finance committee. Moreover, far from the military fuero being restricted in later years, it was amplified and extended. Nearly every major administrative reform of the period thus entailed a diminution in some area of the audiencia's jurisdiction.

At the same time, the individual judges no longer enjoyed the unique

[1] AGI, Mexico 1645, Herrera to Gálvez, 10 November 1782. The best study of an audiencia is J. H. Parry, *The Audiencia of New Galicia in the Sixteenth Century* (Cambridge, 1948).

status of their predecessors. In the first decades of the century the Crown had chosen members of the court to manage both the mercury monopoly and the mint. Apparently the audiencia formed the only pool of reliable public servants then available in New Spain. But after 1763 a different kind of trained intellect appeared on the scene, a new breed of fiscal officials, men without legal formation who yet proved quite capable of directing the great departments of state. In consequence, the judges found themselves thrown back upon their judicial function. Furthermore, if salary be taken as a measure of status, then even with the fees of their various commissions the oidores barely attained the 6,000 ps. paid to both the intendants and the fiscal directors-general. Herrera Rivero expressed this sense of personal diminishment when he asserted that once, in former years, women had positively fallen over themselves to marry the oidores, whereas nowadays, 'judges are the persons whom they least seek after and esteem'. Now the case must not be overstated. Herrera himself in fact won the hand of an heiress, the daughter of the wealthy miner, the Count of Regla.[1] The audiencia still continued to wield considerable power but the official landscape, in which it operated, had indeed become more variegated and autonomous, and less susceptible to its influence.

II

Chief among the institutions inherited from the Habsburgs which Gálvez wished to strip of its power, if not abolish outright, was the viceroyalty. When he first arrived in New Spain he quarrelled violently with the Marquis of Cruillas, and although his successor, the Marquis of Croix, proved to be a faithful ally, Gálvez never reneged upon his prejudice against the office. In 1765 he wrote to the Marquis of Squillace: 'If the ruinous government of the viceroys lasts much longer then this kingdom will run rapidly to its ultimate extinction.' He wished to replace the viceroys by 'the system which I have proposed of commandants-general and intendants'. Such a change, especially if he himself were appointed superintendent-general, would permit the colony 'to remit from the second year on over three million pesos'. More concretely he proposed 'to divide ... this rich country which should be the source of Spain's felicity ... into three commandants-general and in seven intendancies subject to their superintendent-general'.[2] Now although Gálvez was never able to carry out these suggestions he certainly infected his subordinates with the same kind of sentiments. At the end of the 1770s, Areche, the

[1] García Caraffa, *Enciclopedia*, XLIII, 148.

[2] AGI, Mexico 2256, Gálvez to Squillace, 24 December 1765.

Visitor-General of Peru, confided to him: 'My judgement will always be that it is never right to have so powerful a chief within provinces so distant as these.'[1] As it was, Gálvez later transferred all control over revenue affairs to a new, independent official, the *superintendente subdelegado de real hacienda*, who was to supervise and lead the work of the intendants. Then again, he created regents to act as the heads of the audiencias, giving them the ceremonial right to sit in public when the viceroy was present. Now his aim was clearly to create a troika arrangement whereby the viceroy, the superintendent, and the regent would be viewed as being relatively equal, with the viceroy thus reduced to his political and military functions. Naturally, this attempt to divide power provoked a rash of acerbic disputes over jurisdiction of such proportions that within a year of Gálvez's death the superintendency was reunited to the viceroyalty. Colonial institutions, addicted as they were to almost perpetual conflicts over the limit of their powers, obviously needed an omnicompetent governor endowed with the traditional prestige and authority of the viceroys.

The chosen instrument in this dethronement of the viceroys and the audiencias was of course the intendancy. In 1768 Gálvez and the viceroy, Croix, presented a plan to establish eleven intendancies in New Spain. In deference to Croix, the viceroy was to retain the superintendency general. Three arguments in support of the proposal were adduced.[2] In the first place, Spain itself owed its economic and fiscal rejuvenation to the intendants—an office created by the Bourbon dynasty. Spanish America, 'which has arrived at the point of decadence which threatens its total and immediate ruin', urgently needed such officials to reform its economy and government. Equally important, the introduction of intendants would render colonial administration uniform with that of the Peninsula, and hence facilitate the transference of officials between the two systems. The second point simply indicated that the viceroy, if he were to govern effectively, required the assistance of trained provincial governors. In the third and most significant argument, Gálvez and Croix denounced the existing district magistrates, the alcaldes mayores, as 'a ruinous plague of more than 150 men', whose only aim was self-enrichment, who maintained an enforced distribution of over-priced merchandise, and who defrauded the Crown of more than half a million pesos of tribute a year.[3]

Since they wished to replace the alcaldes mayores by intendants, Gálvez and Croix devoted little space to the problems of local government. They

[1] Cited in Palacio Atard, *Areche y Guirior*, p. 32.

[2] Printed in Navarro García, *Intendencias*, pp. 164–76.

[3] *Ibid.*, p. 166.

merely suggested that the collection of Indian tribute should be handled by alcaldes ordinarios, the elected magistrates of all Spanish towns. In those areas where such officials were absent the intendant could name subdelegates to gather the tributes or commission the local managers of the tobacco monopoly and excise officers for this task. In a letter of support for the proposals, the Bishop of Puebla immediately fixed upon this glaring weakness of the plan: eleven intendants could not hope to replace 150 alcaldes mayores; moreover, he estimated that the entire Puebla diocese did not contain more than five alcaldes ordinarios.[1] It would be dangerous, he added, to leave the Indians without a district magistrate to govern them.

In Madrid the Gálvez-Croix project was accepted in principle, and in 1769 Gálvez appointed an intendant for Sonora. But doubts soon arose as to the best method of implementing such an important reform, especially since the initial plan was so sketchy. The new viceroy, Antonio María Bucareli y Ursúa, was therefore commissioned to formulate more detailed proposals. Instead, however, Bucareli, who as captain-general of Cuba had already quarrelled with the island's new intendant, issued an extensive condemnation of the entire scheme.

Bucareli, a skilful but conservative administrator, was opposed to the spirit of radical innovation which characterised Gálvez's approach to government. He wrote: 'The evil has been not in the system or method of government prescribed by the laws, but in the quality of officials in those obscure times.'[2] Elsewhere he asserted that it was 'one of the chief principles of good government not to change old customs when they are not corrupt'.[3] Supported by an extensive memorandum submitted by the oidor, the Count of Tepa, Bucareli then attacked the central articles of Gálvez's scheme.[4] To begin with, New Spain, both in geography and society, was quite different from the Peninsula: some of its haciendas equalled the area of entire Spanish provinces; it possessed barely twenty-five towns worthy of the name; the bulk of its inhabitants were impoverished Indians who lived scattered in isolated settlements. In no sense, therefore, would the introduction of eleven intendants into this vast, underpopulated territory effect much improvement. As it was, New Spain was gaining in prosperity; the flow of revenue was rising and the system of collection was more honest. The viceroy relied for assistance not upon the alcaldes mayores, but rather upon the treasury officials and upon the

1 Printed in Navarro García, *Intendencias*, pp. 176–9.

2 Velasco Ceballos, *Administración de . . . Bucareli*, II, 186–204.

3 AGI, Mexico 1129, Bucareli to Crown, 24 December 1771.

4 AGI, Mexico 1973, Count of Tepa report, 1 July 1775.

directors of the new departments of the tobacco monopoly and the excise duties (alcabalas). These fiscal officials 'are nothing else than so many intendants subject to the viceroy as superintendent'. The establishment of intendants would only confuse what was already a satisfactory system of revenue collection.

Bucareli and Tepa were at pains to protect the alcaldes mayores from the blanket condemnation of Gálvez and Croix. They did not embezzle royal tributes; no increase in that tax could be expected from their abolition. Moreover, since New Spain had so few municipal magistrates (alcaldes ordinarios) the intendants would have to appoint subdelegates to fill the vacuum left by the alcaldes mayores. If these were forbidden to engage in trade, then they would need a wage of at least 2,000 ps. The total cost of local government would rise to about 300,000 ps. Tepa defended the practice called *repartimientos de comercio*, whereby the alcaldes mayores distributed merchandise and domestic animals to the Indians on credit, and cash in advance for products such as cotton and cochineal. The Indians themselves begged for credit and their poverty required these advances. He stated: 'The repartimientos are a sort of company between the alcaldes mayores and the Indians, in which the former put money and the latter labour.'[1]

For the most part, Bucareli defended the *status quo* in local government. He merely suggested that judges from the audiencia should be despatched in regular circuits of inspection to check the district magistrates. Furthermore, a system of promotion from alcalde mayor to revenue official should be initiated. His arguments carried great weight in Madrid, the more particularly since his term of government was marked by greater revenue remittance to the Peninsula. The 1770s was the decade in which silver production leapt to unprecedented heights. Then again, Bucareli's cautious but conscientious style of administration attracted favourable comment from the colonial bureaucracy. The Mexican audiencia praised the viceroy's 'industry, intelligence, huge talent, kindness and moderation', and prophesied that 'posterity will remember the epoch of this prudent, judicious and admirable viceroy'.[2] In effect, Bucareli's critique delayed the establishment of intendancies in New Spain for more than a decade.[3]

Gálvez, however, refused to be deterred. In 1777, taking his cue from the viceroy of Peru, Manuel de Amat, who in his final report had denounced the violence and commerce of the corregidores as leading to the

[1] AGI, Mexico 1973, Count of Tepa report, 1 July 1775, f. 181.

[2] AGI, Mexico 1509, Audiencia to Crown, 8 July 1774, signed by Valcárcel, Villaurrutia, Viana, Herrera and Fernández de Madrid.

[3] Navarro García, *Intendencias*, pp. 28–31.

total destruction of the Indians, he directed a circular to the bishops of New Spain.[1] He inquired: should *repartimientos de comercio* be permitted to continue, or should Indian tributes be increased in order to provide the alcaldes mayores with an adequate salary? Now clearly, Gálvez hoped to elicit a thoroughgoing condemnation of the entire system. If so, he could then justify the intendancy project by appeal to the social malignity of the repartimientos. In this way he did not have to rebut Bucareli's administrative arguments. Instead, he just had to point to the misery and oppression of the Indians. The intendancy reform thus became inextricably bound to the old, weary question about the condition and nature of the Indian. Yet, of course, it was quite possible to have both intendants and alcaldes mayores, with or without repartimientos. The issues in question were quite distinct.

To separate these issues is not to deny that the structure of local government required reform. The Bourbon dynasty had abandoned in New Spain all attempt to pay the alcaldes mayores a salary. After 1718 only the magistrates of Zacatecas and Tabasco received the customary stipend fixed under the Habsburgs; elsewhere all payments were suspended.[2] The alcaldes mayores were therefore obliged to engage in trade in order to subsist. In 1751 the Crown finally recognised their plight, and granted a general permission for the district magistrates of the Indies to make *repartimientos de comercio*, a practice hitherto current but illegal. In New Spain a plan to fix a tariff of prices was soon revoked.[3] In effect, the alcalde mayor became a merchant, or, more accurately, a merchant's agent. Most of these magistrates were impoverished military men who obtained their capital and supplies from the merchants of Mexico City or Oaxaca and in return accepted their backer's *cajero* as their chief lieutenant of justice. Judicial authority was thus exercised, not to say prostituted, in the pursuit of commercial profit. The natural victims of this system were the Indians who had to accept merchandise and mules at high prices, and who got lower than market prices for their produce. Defaults in payments frequently resulted in whipping and imprisonment.

Profits varied from district to district. In 1779 the fiscal Martín Merino estimated that only 13 out of the 143 alcaldías mayores subject to the Mexican audiencia yielded a high return. Nearly all these were districts in the Indian south which produced cochineal, New Spain's second export,

[1] Manuel de Amat y Junient, *Memoria de gobierno*, edición y estudio preliminar de Vicente Rodríguez Casado y Florentino Pérez Embid (Seville, 1947), p. 820.

[2] AGI, Mexico 1367, Croix to Arriaga, 18 June 1768.

[3] AGI, Lima 1119, report of accountants-general, 30 December 1800.

and hence attracted heavy mercantile investment. But elsewhere many magistrates barely made a living. Merino stated: 'In general the guild of alcaldes mayores is composed of the needy who live off their offices while they have them, without any gain for the future.'[1] An earlier report made much the same point: 'Others who find themselves employed in those kingdoms, live in misery lamenting the deceit which brought them to a place where they can barely feed themselves.'[2] Not all alcaldes mayores proved to be adept traders.

Gálvez preferred to base his case upon the effects of repartimientos in the south. For the Bishop of Oaxaca, in response to his inquiry, had pronounced a striking censure of the current system of government. He had recently returned from a general inspection of his diocese; he was appalled at the condition of the Indians and the degree to which they were oppressed by the alcaldes mayores. All his parish priests had condemned the *repartimientos de comercio*. The bishop then opened up a problem which was to haunt nearly all later debate about the value of intendancies. What kind of man was the Indian? He admitted the Indian's vices—his drunkenness, lust and sloth, and above all 'his implacable hatred of the Spaniards'. Some observers, he noted, especially those with vested interests, 'wish to attribute to the very nature of the Indian himself the cause and origin of his vices'. But anyone who has dealt with them 'clearly sees that they were of the same character and inclination as other men, open to all the virtues and vices in the political, moral and Christian spheres of life, as those born in Castile, and consequently the origin of their disorder and lack of application is to be found in the humiliation and abjection in which they were reared and live'. If the Indians were left to live in their natural liberty, in which they could enjoy the fruits of their labour, then they would soon work hard, prosper and become both good citizens and good Christians.[3] If the *repartimientos de comercio* were abolished, other merchants would trade with them and this 'will restore to the Indian his natural freedom to treat and deal with whoever brings him more return'. Obviously the bishop, in these optimistic declarations, was inspired by a typical enlightenment belief in the uniformity of man's nature: it was tyrannical institutions which degraded the Indian, it was liberty which would make him an industrious citizen.

In 1783, Gálvez used this episcopal report to issue a public condemnation of the abuses and injustices committed by Oaxaca's alcaldes mayores.

[1] AGI, Mexico 1868, Merino to Gálvez, 10 March 1779.

[2] AGI, Mexico 1513, fiscal to Aranda, 4 May 1763.

[3] AGI, Mexico 1872, Bishop of Oaxaca to Gálvez, 20 July 1778.

Each magistrate then serving in the diocese was personally informed of the royal displeasure. All attempts to establish local monopolies in trade were denounced. Most magistrates reacted strongly to this decree: they presented evidence and testimony of their impeccable honesty and low profits. The corregidor of Oaxaca, for example, stated that he had brought a thousand cattle from Guatemala; on the journey 150 died, and the remainder required two months' pasture before sale. He purchased them at 14 ps. a head and sold them for 18 ps., making a profit of 5 per cent. He noted that other merchants had shops in all the villages of his jurisdiction. Similarly the alcalde mayor of Zimatlán claimed that he bought mules for 16 ps. and sold them at 25 ps. on the basis of a year's credit. Cochineal he acquired for 12 rls. a pound and sold for 14 rls. He reckoned his rate of return at 12 per cent.[1] Nearly all the reports followed similar lines: profits were moderate and other merchants engaged in trade within their jurisdictions. Little mention was made of the Indian, however, either of his misery or his nature. But then, already in 1779, the fiscal, Martín Merino, had defended the necessity of repartimientos on the ground that 'indolence and abandon [are] co-natural to the Indian'. Without the alcaldes mayores' supply of cash and goods the agriculture of Oaxaca, and especially the cochineal trade, would collapse.[2]

Gálvez paid little heed to these protestations: he was determined to replace the alcaldes mayores by intendants. We may distinguish three arguments to account for his attitude. In the first place, the Bourbon dynasty increasingly relied upon salaried officials; it had largely terminated the Habsburg system of farming out to private individuals tax collection and other state functions. Yet here, in the very centre of local administration, stood the alcalde mayor, an unpaid magistrate who farmed from the Crown the collection of Indian tribute in return for the right to employ judicial authority for commercial profit. This could no longer be tolerated by the reformers. Secondly, the alcalde mayor frequently exercised a monopoly of trade within his jurisdiction. Here again the Bourbon reformers were scandalised: they were opposed to all commercial monopolies (except the Crown's); they had introduced the decree of *comercio libre*; yet in the localities they encountered a deleterious monopoly. In addition to these administrative and economic criticisms, they adduced a social argument: the repartimientos formed the major cause of the Indians' degradation. All eighteenth-century observers were agreed that the Indian lived in

[1] These statements are included in AGI, Mexico 1461, Audiencia Gobernadora to Gálvez, 28 March 1785.

[2] AGI, Mexico 1868, Merino to Gálvez, 10 March 1779.

a state of utmost squalor; they only differed as to the causes of his misery. The reformers ascribed it to the oppression of tyrannical institutions and looked to a reform in administration to improve the Indian's condition. The conservatives declared that it was the Indian's nature to be lazy and improvident, that he had to be forced to work, that he required repartimientos to maintain his agriculture. Thus at times this third argument verged on the metaphysical: the controversy awoke memories of older disputes and hovered close to cherished 'enlightened' beliefs concerning the uniformity of man's nature and the power of the state to create economic progress. What encomiendas were to the missionaries of the sixteenth century, repartimientos became for the eighteenth-century reformers.

III

Little of the preceding debate had much to do with what was, after all, the intendant's primary function—the increase of revenue. Bucareli's administrative critique went unanswered. But then both sides in the controversy saw the intendants as part of a much wider battle between reformers and conservatives. Many older institutions of government had already suffered a certain displacement, if not a loss in prestige and power, and feared that the intendants would weaken them still further. The transformation of the fiscal bureaucracy demonstrated clearly enough the forces at work within colonial government. Here, until the middle years of the century, the treasuries dominated the scene, each being staffed, generally speaking, with an accountant, a treasurer, at times a factor, and a varying number of clerks. By 1770 New Spain possessed at least fifteen of these institutions all subordinate to the central treasury in Mexico City.[1] It was only the latter, however, which received the full range of taxes. The remainder divided into two classes—those at the ports which collected customs and excise duties, and those in the mining camps which managed the mercury monopoly and levied the silver tithe. No other tax of importance was handled by such *cajas* as Guanajuato, Zacatecas and Pachuca. Instead, both excise duties and tributes, farmed from the Crown by groups of merchants and by alcaldes mayores, were remitted directly to the central treasury in the form of bills of exchange, *libranzas*, as they were called, drawn upon the great trading houses of Mexico City. In the capital itself the merchant guild, the consulado, traditionally leased the excise, contracting with the Crown to pay a fixed sum each year.

The first major change in this system occurred in 1754 when the Crown finally terminated the agreement with the consulado and installed royal

[1] Gálvez, *Informe general*, p. 16.

officials to administer the excise duties of Mexico City and its environs.[1] Then in 1776, after a certain amount of experiment during the Gálvez Visitation, salaried excise directors were appointed in the 24 leading towns of New Spain. Each of these men, assisted by an accountant, clerks and guards, collected the normal 6 per cent duty on all sales and the special charge levied on pulque, the favourite alcoholic beverage of the populace. In outlying districts local citizens continued to farm these taxes, taking a 14 per cent commission for their work.[2] This small army of excise men was governed by a director-general resident in Mexico City. Local directors were paid wages that ranged from 1,000 ps. to 2,500 ps.; their chief received a minimum of 6,000 ps. The system was never fully unified since Veracruz remained independent and Mexico City had its own customs superintendent equal both in rank and salary to the director-general.[3]

The new organisation soon demonstrated its value. Total receipts rose from 1,488,690 ps. in 1775 to 2,360,252 ps. in 1779 and in later decades amounted to about three million pesos. Similarly, the returns on the pulque duty expanded from 468,888 ps. in 1775 to 814,755 by 1779, a figure not much less than the later average of 900,000 ps.[4] In part, of course, some of this increase can be ascribed to the effects of the *comercio libre* decree of 1778 which freed transatlantic trade from former impediments. But as the pulque receipts show, official efficiency also played an effective role. Naturally both the merchants and populace who paid for this additional royal revenue must have resented the new breed of customs and excise men, anxious to win promotion by charging duties wherever they could. Most of their directors were peninsular Spaniards. At this period the superintendent of Mexico City customs was Miguel Páez de la Cadena, a native of San Lucas de Barrameda in Andalusia.[5] His colleague, the director-general Juan Navarro y Madrid, came from Málaga.[6] Both of these men, we may note, acted as independent heads of department being subject only to the viceroy in his capacity as general superintendent of the royal exchequer.

1 Robert S. Smith, 'Sales Taxes in New Spain, 1575–1770', *Hispanic American Historical Review*, 28 (1948), pp. 2–37.
2 Fonseca and Urrutia, *Historia general de Real Hacienda*, II, 101–18.
3 *Ibid.*, II, 101–5.
4 *Ibid.*, II, 93, 423–4.
5 García Caraffa, *Enciclopedia*, LXVII, 127; AGI, Mexico 1426, Flores to Porlier, 26 February 1789.
6 AGI, Mexico 1420, Count of Gálvez to Gálvez, 30 June 1786; AGI, Mexico 1448, list of services, 25 February 1799.

Equally autonomous and even more numerous in its personnel was the tobacco monopoly established by Gálvez during his Visitation. The new department of state purchased tobacco from contracted growers in the districts of Orizaba, Córdoba and Zongolica (cultivation elsewhere being forbidden), manufactured the leaf into cigars in factories situated at Puebla, Mexico City, Querétaro, Orizaba and Guadalajara, and then sold the finished article to the public. The scale of operation was remarkable. In all, including directors, accountants, guards, clerks, salesmen, and factory workers, the monopoly employed over 17,000 persons, whose total earnings by 1801 amounted to 789,000 ps. In that same year the gross receipts came to 7,825,000 ps., a sum which yielded a net profit of nearly four million pesos. The Crown regarded this great enterprise as its own private property; all net returns went straight to Madrid; they could not be used for normal state expenditures.[1] Its employees were placed under the sole supervision of the viceroy. As was the case with the excise service, most of its administrators were recruited from the Peninsula. The first director-general in Mexico was Felipe del Hierro, a native of Madrid, who received a salary of 6,000 ps.[2]

In the early 1790s Viceroy Revillagigedo attempted to consolidate these two branches of the exchequer at the provincial level, appointing but one official to administer both the excise and the sale of tobacco. He set up a committee of the directors to implement this plan but his successor, the Marquis of Branciforte, did not pursue the scheme.[3] As it was, despite certain bureaucratic conflicts, the new structure proved remarkably efficient in raising revenue. Whereas in 1765 New Spain yielded the Crown only 6,130,314 ps. in revenue, by 1782 that amount had tripled to 19,594,490 ps., including monopoly costs in the sum. This great expansion sprang from an advance on all fronts. Tributes, for example, which averaged 596,220 ps. during the 1760s reached 955,813 ps. in 1779.[4] Similarly, the various taxes and monopoly profits deriving from mining all rose as silver production surged forward. The key decade in all this was the 1770s; during the remainder of the century, indeed until 1810, all further increase was relatively marginal.[5] We can now assess the force of Bucareli's objection to the intendancy system. What was the point of introducing yet another set of fiscal officials, if the current group were

1 Humboldt, *Ensayo político*, p. 453; Joaquín Maniau Torquemada, *Compendio de la historia de la Real Hacienda, escrita en el año de 1794* (Mexico, 1914), pp. 50–1.

2 García Caraffa, *Enciclopedia*, XLIII, 235.

3 AGI, Mexico 2356, Revillagigedo to Gardoqui, 30 September 1792.

4 Fonseca and Urrutia, *Historia general de Real Hacienda*, I, 450.

5 Humboldt, *Ensayo político*, p. 540.

doing so well? His objection proved to be prophetic: the intendants were destined to be an irrelevance as far as revenue collection was concerned. Their significance, if any, lay in their political and executive functions.

The relations of the new revenue departments with the older fiscal institutions were never clearly defined. Until 1786 no fixed system of payments in the treasuries existed; at times excise duties and tobacco monies were remitted directly to Mexico City; on other occasions they were deposited in the local treasury. More importantly, the executive independence conferred upon these departments freed them from the necessity of presenting their accounts for scrutiny to the court of audit. This exemption lasted until at least the 1790s, with the result that the court, hitherto the central revenue institution, suffered a certain loss of rank within the official hierarchy, a loss similar to that experienced by its parent body, the audiencia.

Prior to its creation in 1605 the court's three accountants had served as the fiscal members of the audiencia, in much the same way as the *contaduría* always formed part of the Council of the Indies. The new court was entitled *el tribunal mayor y real audiencia de cuentas*. Its accountants reminded Bucareli in 1776: 'This royal court ... was dismembered from the audiencia, but conserves its name and inherent authority. ... For this reason it has the regalian right to despatch orders with the royal seal in the august name of His Majesty.'[1] Despite the institution's illustrious origin and persistent pretensions, its chief accountants never obtained the formal appellation of *vuestro señor*, an honour enjoyed by the judges of the audiencia, the intendants, full colonels of the army and the directors of the new revenue departments.[2] It was especially galling to them that these directors should be granted the nominal honour of membership in the council of the royal exchequer. The court of audit desired to establish itself as the central exchequer institution, with a status in fiscal affairs equal to that exercised by the audiencia in matters of justice. Its pretensions, however, although cherished from 1605 until Independence, were never recognised by the Council of the Indies.

The court's original function was the audit of treasury accounts, a task it was rarely able to perform with much despatch. It acted as court of first instance in the examination of all errors detected: but if error reached criminal proportions then it was reconstituted to comprise three oidores of the audiencia and the two chief accountants. In regard to treasury officials, the court issued recommendations as to promotion based upon

[1] AGI, Mexico 1380, Bucareli to Gálvez, 27 October 1777.
[2] AGI, Mexico 1752, Azanza to Soler, 28 February 1799.

its knowledge of performance in office. More importantly, as its chief accountants stated: 'This court of audit is a veritable archive in which record is kept of all the matters which have arisen in the vast department of the royal exchequer.' In consequence: 'All [viceroys] have applied to it without stop, asking for reports, statistics and other documents which require weeks and months on end to supply.'[1] This claim was corroborated by the comments of Viceroy José de Iturrigaray. He protested that the court had been converted into 'an office of government' so that 'almost all the year its tables are occupied in drawing up reports, to the ruin of its primitive obligation of scrutiny and audit'.[2] Moreover, when the court submitted a statement, it always included the reports of the subordinate accountants, a custom which produced bulky files. His complaints led the accountant-general attached to the Council of the Indies to declare—no doubt inspired by professional pride: 'The court of audit is the vital axle on which rests or round which revolves the branches [of revenue] of the vast Mexican empire; in short it is the firm bulwark of the royal exchequer.'[3]

In point of fact, nearly all viceroys echoed Iturrigaray's criticism: almost from its inception the court suffered from a great backlog of unchecked accounts. Its personnel constantly increased in number, but its backlog was never conquered. At the beginning of the eighteenth century the institution comprised a regent, three chief accountants, four accountants of the second rank, and six of the third rank; in addition some 16 supernumeraries were then employed divided among the three classes. In 1753 the regent obtained permission to appoint five temporary accountants since the court by then had a backlog of 2,272 accounts to audit.[4] The number of these supernumeraries varied according to need; they did not enjoy tenure in office. The court was subjected to at least two reorganisations in our period, in 1776 and 1793. The office of regent was abolished in 1776, a decree which took effect five years later upon the death of the incumbent. In 1790 the court, headed by its three chief accountants, possessed 27 permanent members of all ranks. Salaries had risen considerably. By 1790 the senior accountants received 4,000 ps. compared to the 2,757 ps. paid to them prior to the Gálvez Visitation. The accountants of the second and third rank also benefited; they were awarded 2,500 ps. and 1,800 ps. a year respectively, which put them on a scale equal to the

[1] AGI, Mexico 2018, court of audit to Valdés, 26 March 1790.
[2] AGI, Mexico 1623, Iturrigaray to Soler, 26 November 1804.
[3] AGI, Mexico 1960, Report of accountant-general Pedro de Aparici, 8 May 1807.
[4] AGI, Mexico 1394, Cossío to Viceroy, 26 March 1782.

provincial excise directors.[1] It should be noted that the court still required the services of many temporary clerks, and that the number of its fixed personnel altered considerably.

Viceroy Revillagigedo singled out the chief cause of the court's inefficiency. 'The origin of the backlog of accounts lies in the fact that its chief men are too old and very tired.'[2] Not that they were expected to do a full day's work. In 1741 the Crown exempted the court from afternoon attendance and in 1765 laid down that its schedule should only extend from 7.30 until 11.30 each morning, on the grounds that auditing was such an arduous labour.[3] Certainly, since colonial accountants never retired, even if blind or ill, four hours of arithmetic must have been too much for the court's septuagenarians.

Although earlier viceroys complained bitterly about the court's lentitude, it was Revillagigedo who obtained some action. In 1789 the court had yet to begin the audit of the excise departments' accounts. The viceroy first installed a trusted accountant, Ramón Gutiérrez del Mazo, to examine the excise accounts at Puebla. A fraud of over 164,000 ps. was immediately discovered.[4] Backed by this revelation, Revillagigedo received permission to hire a temporary staff of ten accountants to audit the entire mass of excise accounts, aided by another ten clerks; they took up to 1803 to complete this vast task.[5]

In 1792 the Crown, no doubt impressed by Revillagigedo's revelations, ordered the court to check the tobacco monopoly's accounts, since that department hitherto had maintained a complete independence from the established exchequer institutions. The court summarily demanded the presentation of accounts. But the monopoly's director, Silvestre Díaz de la Vega, requested that the court should approach him via the viceroy acting as the *superintendente subdelegado de real hacienda*.[6] He protested that the court was attempting to convert its simple function of audit into the status of executive authority. In 1802 the court was granted four new accountants to begin the great audit: with what success we do not know. The quarrel, however, illustrates the uneasy, ill-defined relation that existed between the old Habsburg fiscal institutions and the new Bourbon departments of revenue.

A brief description of the family background of the three chief account-

1 AGI, Mexico 1382, Bucareli to Gálvez, 26 June 1777; Revillagigedo, *Informe general*, p. 201.
2 AGI, Mexico 1394, Cossío to viceroy, 26 March 1782.
3 AGI, Mexico 1531, Revillagigedo to Valdés, 30 November 1789.
4 AGI, Mexico 1542, Revillagigedo to Lerena, 7 May 1791.
5 AGI, Mexico 1960, report of accountant-general, 8 May 1807.
6 AGI, Mexico 1619, Iturrigaray to Soler, 26 November 1803.

ants of 1795 will reveal the continuity in the recruitment to the court. The senior member, Fernando de Herrera, aged fifty-three, after a short period in the contaduría general in Madrid, had served in the Americas since 1761. Presumably he was the usual type of peninsular colonial official.[1] The two remaining chief accountants, however, both came from families long connected with the court of audit. Juan de la Fuente, aged seventy-five, first entered the court in 1741; his son, Juan Ignacio, followed his example in 1767. But de la Fuente had also married into bureaucracy; his father-in-law, Juan de Ureña, served in the court for 34 years and his brother-in-law, Juan José de Ureña for 45 years. When de la Fuente finally died, in 1798, his son stood ready to succeed him, but promotion was refused on the grounds that he was insubordinate, epileptic and already too old.[2] The third chief accountant, Pedro María de Monterde y Antillón, aged forty-eight, was the grandson of a wealthy peninsular merchant resident in Mexico City at the beginning of the eighteenth century. His father joined the court in 1744, and he followed suit in 1766, so that his entire career was confined to one institution, of which he later became dean.[3] The presence of such long-tenured official families gave the court a continuity in policy and pretension that more than spanned the entire period of Bourbon reform.

In 1780, to act as a watchdog over this rapidly growing bureaucratic empire, the Crown appointed a *fiscal de real hacienda*, a royal attorney for exchequer affairs. Like the two existing fiscals charged with the protection of the royal interest in civil and criminal matters, the new official received a salary of 4,500 ps.[4] The lawyer chosen to occupy this new post, Ramón de Posada y Soto, was an Asturian, a nephew by marriage of Gálvez's brother, Matías.[5] A remarkably intelligent and enlightened public servant, Posada was warmly praised by Viceroy Revillagigedo—in general so little given to eulogy—as 'outstanding in integrity, disinterest, zeal and talent'.[6] He remained in Mexico until 1794 when he became fiscal of the Council of the Indies. While in Madrid he had occasion to assist the Mexican patriot, Fray Servando Teresa de Mier, who praised him for his rectitude, a rare quality in the venal government of Charles IV.[7]

[1] AGI, Mexico 1568, see service sheets of court, *c.* 1795.

[2] AGI, Mexico 1867, Mayorga to Gálvez, 7 September 1780; AGI, Mexico 1587, Azanza to Saavedra, 26 September 1798. [3] AGI, Mexico 2379, Iturrigaray to Soler, 26 February 1804.

[4] A select list of salaries and other stipends can be found in BN (Mexico) MSS 1380, ff. 77–9. In fact Posada earned 8,500 ps.

[5] AGI, Mexico 1138, Posada's wife was the sister of Francisco Fernández de Córdova, the superintendent of the Mint. Council of the Indies, 21 August 1797.

[6] AGI, Mexico 1540, Revillagigedo to Lerena, 27 July 1791.

[7] Fray Servando Teresa de Mier, *Memorias* (2 vols.; Mexico, 1946), I, 235, 259, 275.

Some notion of Posada's industry and the range of his work can be obtained from a petition he presented to the Crown. Apparently during the 1780s he also in part discharged the duties of *fiscal de lo civil*. Posada classified his work by *expedientes*, briefs or files, that entered and left his office[1] (see table 4).

Table 4 *Fiscal de Real Hacienda's expedientes (files) January 1781–8.*

Expedientes arising from:	No. of Expedientes
Fiscalía de Real Hacienda	20,160
Fiscalía Civil	6,743
Fiscalía Criminal	504
Protectoría de Indios	977
Pedimientos fiscales	745
Total	29,129
Fiscalía de Real Hacienda	
Viceregal secretariat	11,016
Government notary offices	4,231
Audiencia	919
Jesuit properties	2,000
Customs and excise	423
Tobacco monopoly	162
Gunpowder monopoly	161
Mint	7
Royal Treasuries	54
Court of Audit	153
Secretariat of Superintendency and Junta Superior of Real Hacienda	812
Indian court	222
Total	20,160
Fiscalía Civil	
Viceregal secretariat	2,279
Government notary offices	2,778
Audiencia	1,025
Miscellaneous	661
Total	6,743

Precisely what these grand totals signify is difficult to know: Posada handled between three and four hundred briefs a month; no doubt some merely required a signature, but others must have needed more thought. In a letter of November 1782, he claimed that in ten months he had written in his own hand over six hundred *pedimientos*—formal pleas for action—

1 AGI, Mexico 1515, Posada to Flores, 21 February 1788.

and answers. Presumably for more routine business he dictated his opinion to copyists. All three fiscals, faced with a great burden of work, employed lawyers, called *agentes fiscales*, to despatch the less important briefs. Up to 1780 these assistants varied in number; only one had a fixed salary, the remainder lived off fees arising from suits contested between parties. But in that year the Crown ordered the appointment of six permanent *agentes fiscales*, each with a fixed stipend of 1,800 ps.; it was estimated, however, that their fees would yield together with stipend a total of up to 3,500 ps. At first, two agents were allocated to each fiscal, but in 1783, one was transferred from the criminal to the exchequer attorney.[1] Even with this staff Posada's task must have been wearisome in the extreme.

Final responsibility for all fiscal affairs was vested in the viceroy, who since 1749 had enjoyed the title and power of *superintendente subdelegado de real hacienda*. The simultaneous expansion of the revenue and military establishments multiplied his duties, since nearly all the important innovations, such as the monopolies and the excise, were placed under his direct supervision. In consequence, it became necessary for the viceroys to employ a numerous secretariat upon a scale unknown in earlier years.

In 1723 the viceroy, the Duke of Linares, wrote: 'The only two organs where the viceroy gives effect to all the affairs of the kingdom, be they political, military, ecclesiastical, or fiscal, are the offices of government.'[2] These offices were managed by the two grand notaries of government who purchased them from the Crown and who gained a handsome profit from the fees charged on all the documents they drew up. They were responsible for the legal authentication of all official documents—appointments, decrees, the actuation of lawsuits arising out of government measures, and the general preparation of expedientes and despatches. Viceregal reliance upon notarial assistance reflected the traditional, adjudicatory nature of Habsburg administration.

Most viceroys also made use of a private secretary to deal with the more secret aspects of government, for whom the Crown fixed a stipend of 300 ps. By the 1740s, however, the Marquis of Casafuerte paid another 1,400 ps. out of his own pocket to maintain a secretary and three clerks to assist him. It was only in 1756 that the Crown appointed three officials, paid respectively 1,500, 1,000, and 500 ps. to form a permanent secretariat, not dependent upon viceregal whim.[3] In 1761, to meet the protests of the grand notaries, the Crown decreed that 'the secretariat should only deal with executive affairs which do not require legal sanction or ratification',

[1] BN (Mexico) MSS 1380, ff. 58–65.

[2] BN (Madrid) MSS 2929, f. 90.

[3] BRP, MSS Miscelánea de Ayala, x, ff. 234–41.

and again: 'the duties of the secretariat should extend only to the comprehension of affairs, their formation and initiation, leaving the decrees, the titles and other judicial measures for the notaries to authenticate'.[1] But the notaries, like the audiencia, found that their sphere of work increasingly was restricted.

In the years following the Gálvez Visitation, the secretariat, however, experienced an almost continuous expansion in numbers. By 1778 it comprised 15 persons led by the chief secretary who received a salary of 4,000 ps. The remuneration of the other clerks ranged from 450 ps. to 2,000 ps. Even then, Viceroy Bucareli was obliged to hire another six supernumeraries, unpaid assistants, who worked in hopes of subsequent appointment.[2] A decade later, the number of officials employed in the secretariat rose to 30. Viceroy Revillagigedo complained, however, that since salaries remained so low, there was a constant flux of personnel, as officials left the secretariat for more remunerative posts. The many supernumerary clerks were usually peninsular officials awaiting vacancies in other departments of government. He declared that although 'the viceregal secretariat is the axle, the workshop, the direction of all which manages the government and happiness of the empire of New Spain', its staff 'suffer from the almost universal epidemic of ineptitude'.[3] He protested against the disorder of its archive. As always, Revillagigedo drew up an elaborate scheme to reorganise the office, which Madrid ignored.

It appears that each official was charged with matters arising from different departments of government, such as the tobacco monopoly, alcabalas, temporalidades, California, the army, and the ports of San Blas and Veracruz. A great part of their duties dealt with fiscal matters—a labour which the creation of intendancies helped to augment. During Revillagigedo's administration, from 1789 to 1794, the secretary Antonio Bonilla estimated that about 30,000 different expedientes or files had entered his office some 100,771 times. In addition, 4,505 reports had been despatched to the ministries in Madrid. All this had been handled by himself, eight permanent officials, eight supernumeraries and ten copyists.[4] To keep this enormous weight of paper moving through the government offices the secretariat had to work long hours—up to ten, even fourteen hours a day, especially when the correspondence for Madrid needed to be hastily prepared for the mail-boats.

[1] AGI, Mexico 1973, Cossío to Gálvez, 20 October 1781.
[2] AGN, Historia 44/6, Revillagigedo to Valdés, 11 January 1790.
[3] AGN, Intendencias 25, Revillagigedo to Valdés, 11 January 1790.
[4] AGI, Mexico 1555, Bonilla to Crown, 15 September 1790.

By the early 1780s New Spain's fiscal bureaucracy had become both numerous and disunited. No single institution, office or minister, existed which possessed sufficient powers to govern the vast unwieldy machine. The viceroy himself, although greatly assisted by the enlarged secretariat, was too much burdened by the political, military and clerical responsibilities of his position to assume such a role. Clearly some unifying measure was called for: the tobacco monopoly and the customs and excise service formed virtually independent baronies. Yet to guide and govern this proliferating, often quarrelling officialdom, all the viceroy could do was to summon the *junta de real hacienda*, a consultative body without executive power. It then comprised, in order of precedence, the viceroy, the regent and the two senior judges of the audiencia, the superintendent of the mint, the fiscal of the exchequer, the two senior accountants of the court of audit, the superintendent and the director-general of customs and excise, the accountant-general of tributes and the two officials of the central treasury.[1] Here at least Greek met Greek. But the duties of this unmanageable body were occasional and consultative: the viceroy's signature was required to give a decree the force of law.

It was to provide a centralised direction to this medley of revenue departments that Gálvez, as Minister of the Indies, favoured the appointment of a superintendent for all exchequer affairs, independent of the viceroy. He expected to introduce this feature of the intendancy system once he could install his brother Matías as viceroy of New Spain. But Bucareli's sudden death in office brought Martín de Mayorga, the President of the Guatemalan audiencia, automatically to the viceregal throne. Gálvez, in a display of contempt for both the man and his office, then indulged in a strange experiment. He chose Pedro Antonio de Cossío to be both the viceroy's secretary and an intendant with supervisory powers over all revenue affairs. Mayorga was stripped of all responsibility in this sphere save for the humiliating task of affixing his signature to the decrees and documents drawn up by the intendant.[2] Now Cossío, a former Montañés merchant, whose assistance to Gálvez during the creation of the tobacco monopoly had earned him the post of director of customs at Veracruz, was a peculiarly tactless fellow. His letters to the great Minister, cast almost in diary form and written in a colloquial style, were full of wild denunciations of other officials and groans of self-pity. But they contained very little analysis or comprehension of his peculiar situation. For in fact

[1] AGI, Mexico 1870, Herrera to Gálvez, 27 February 1804.

[2] AGI, Mexico 1510, *real orden* of appointment, 14 August 1779. See also Navarro García, *Intendencias*, pp. 56–9.

his appointment was a temporary device; and no clear definition of his powers was to be found in any decree.

Yet Cossío, supported by the Viceroy Mayorga, ventured to sharply criticise the directors of customs and excise. Their accounts had never been subjected to independent audit; the excise department still lacked 245,000 ps. from the year 1777. Their officials, owing to inadequate supervision, frequently received exorbitant returns; the manager of the tobacco monopoly at Zamora, for example, obtained 6,000 ps. a year from his commissions and stipend. More importantly, the directors did not accept the nominations to office made by Mayorga and Cossío, and complained to Madrid when Cossío tried to appoint a local excise official. He bitterly stated that 'each one [of the directors] wishes to have under his absolute command an army of men and many posts for appointment'. He openly accused both Miguel Páez and Juan Navarro, the two directors of customs and excise, of corruption.[1] Furthermore, Páez had refused to implement the decision to impose an extra 2 per cent excise to meet the expenses of the current war with Britain, so that Cossío himself was obliged to form the tariff of duties. Cossío proposed the appointment of one director-general of revenue to whom all the heads of department would be directly subordinate.[2] His attempt to establish himself as such an official failed miserably; he was sharply reprimanded by Madrid for his attacks upon the directors.

Cossío also quarrelled with several judges of the audiencia. He wished to set up a bank of deposit in the Mexico City mint, for both private capital and, more importantly, for the vast funds managed by the Church. The details of this interesting scheme remain obscure. But such a central matter required the audiencia's approval, which was by no means forthcoming. Cossío wrote: 'The regent tells me that the other judges, with Gamboa as standard-bearer, are reporting against my project for deposits at the mint . . . especially those such as Gamboa and Ladrón de Guevara, who are accustomed to work in secretariat affairs.'[3] Again the opposition proved successful; nothing more was heard of this scheme.

Cossío's plans to create a central secretariat for exchequer affairs also came to grief. He had brought four officials with him from Veracruz to supplement the permanent eight officials of the viceregal secretariat; in addition he hired 20 copyists. With this greatly augmented staff he then decreed that all exchequer business should be confined to the secretariat;

1 AGI, Mexico 2504, Mayorga to Gálvez, 4 January 1782.

2 AGI, Mexico 1391, Mayorga to Gálvez, 28 September 1781.

3 AGI, Mexico 1511, Cossío to Gálvez, 20 October 1781.

he forbade the two offices of government managed by the grand notaries to admit any fiscal suits; they were to restrict their operations to the simple legal authentication of government decrees. Cossío complained: 'It costs me drops of blood to get the declarations of official briefs from these accursed government notaries, and some they have confused and lost.' Hitherto all petitions, claims and suits dealing with fiscal affairs had been initiated with the notaries; now, Cossío ordered, they were to be filed immediately with the secretariat. As in other instances, Cossío's actions were not upheld in Madrid. The notaries protested that his decree robbed the offices of half their business; they appealed to previous laws which laid down that all exchequer matters affecting private parties must be initiated with them. Madrid concurred with their claim; Cossío was summarily told to return to the old system; the 20 copyists he had hired to deal with the additional paper work were to be dismissed.[1]

Cossío's attempt to impose a centralised direction upon New Spain's fiscal system lasted less than three years, from August 1779 to March 1782. Clearly as a mere intendant, he did not possess sufficient authority to succeed; nor did the viceregal secretariat provide an adequate power base for such a scheme. Moreover, his impolite treatment of the upper bureaucracy threw officialdom into uproar. His order of dismissal took note of the 'infinite clamour from all classes of persons about the despotism, hardness and bad treatment' of his term of government.[2] If we remember that José Antonio de Areche, Visitor-General of Peru, provoked much the same storm of protest, then we may conclude that Gálvez's judgment of men or choice in policy was by no means infallible.

IV

The opposition of Bucareli, the failure of Cossío, the death in office of the next two viceroys, Matías and Bernardo de Gálvez—all these factors impeded the establishment of the intendencies. It was not until December 1786 that the *ordenanzas de intendentes* for New Spain were finally promulgated. Gálvez himself did not for long survive this crowning achievement of his long ministry; he died in June 1787. In consequence, his enemies soon moved to modify the more innovative sections of the intendants' code. The ordinances—which in broad outline adhered to the scheme proposed by Croix and Gálvez in 1767—reformed the entire range of colonial administration, changing its structure at three distinct levels—district, provincial and central. The project's most glaring failure occurred

[1] AGI, Mexico 1405, Matías Gálvez to Gálvez, 30 May 1783.

[2] AGI, Mexico 1878, Cossío to Valdés, 20 October 1787.

in the sphere of local government, a failure which will be extensively treated below. But a brief word is required to characterise the general nature of the reform.

To begin with, twelve intendancies were set up in Yucatán, Oaxaca, Puebla, Mexico, Veracruz, Valladolid, Guanajuato, Guadalajara, Zacatecas, Durango, San Luis Potosí and Sonora. Each magistrate was granted a legal advisor and lieutenant: all were subject to the authority of the *superintendente subdelegado de real hacienda*, who also governed the central Mexican province. As always, Gálvez followed his usual policy. He chose but one creole, Antonio de Villaurrutia, whom he installed as regent, president, and intendant of Guadalajara. For the rest he turned to his family, to Malaga and to his dependents. Fernando Mangino, a favourite protegé since the days of the Visitation, became superintendent. Manuel de Flon and Juan Antonio de Riaño, the brothers-in-law of the former viceroy, Bernardo de Gálvez, the minister's nephew, received appointments to Puebla and Valladolid. And so on. Among the twelve men, five came from a military background, four were former revenue officials, and at least four were related to Gálvez.[1] Among their legal advisors the same pattern prevailed. Only three creoles were selected; the rest were peninsular lawyers without experience of the New World.

The intendant, as conceived in the ordinances, acted as a virtually omnicompetent provincial governor, whose tasks were defined under the four heads of Justice, War, Exchequer and *Policía*.[2] Hitherto New Spain had lacked any civil magistrates of the intermediary level: the lines of authority—be they judicial, executive or fiscal—had stretched directly from the districts and towns to the authorities in Mexico City. Only the Church, in the persons of its bishops, offered provincial centres of authority. After 1786 they were joined by intendants, in several cases, in Mérida, Oaxaca, Puebla, Valladolid, Guadalajara and Durango—resident in the same towns. The result was to constitute true local capitals, interposed between the districts and Mexico City, through which the flow of government action had to move. The intendancies, therefore, based in some cases upon the old diocesan boundaries, were the ancestors of the modern Mexican states.

The intendant differed markedly from the alcalde mayor, in that his office represented an active view of government. Under the head of

[1] A list of intendants can be found in Navarro García, *Intendencias*, pp. 60–1.

[2] The best discussion of the intendants' duties is given by John Lynch, *Spanish Colonial Administration, passim*; the governing ordinances are printed and translated in Fisher, *The Intendant System*, pp. 97–344.

policía, for example, he was expected to encourage local industry and agriculture, to compile statistics, to inspect the subordinate districts, and to construct public works such as bridges, roads and public lighting. The range of his authority was very broad: he served as the chief executive officer in provincial government, implementing all royal decrees and viceregal edicts. He also exercised the *patronato*, the royal right of appointment to clerical benefices. Under the head of Justice his powers were more restricted: his legal advisor only possessed jurisdiction over the capital city and its district: appeals from the first instance judicial decisions of the subdelegates were heard by the audiencia, not by any intendancy court. By contrast, in all fiscal affairs the intendant acted as the chief provincial officer. All complaints, crimes, or suits arising out of any local branch of revenue and its officers went to the intendant for adjudication. In addition all tax receipts had to be paid into the intendancy treasury; they could no longer be remitted directly to Mexico City. Three new treasuries—at Valladolid, Puebla and Oaxaca—were created for this purpose, and the old mining *cajas*, such as Guanajuato and Zacatecas, now handled the receipts from the tributes, the excise and the sale of tobacco as well as the silver tithe. Thus, in the fiscal sphere, in contrast to the judicial, the intendancy served as a true intermediary authority. For this reason the directors of the excise and the tobacco monopoly resented and attacked the powers of the intendants even more than the audiencia. Finally, it should be noted that unlike all past governors the intendants were permanent officials; no limit was set upon their term of office, and several remained at their post from 1786 until 1810. In salary—6,000 ps. a year—they were superior to the judges of the audiencias and the treasury officials and equal to heads of the new fiscal departments.

At the central level of administration, Gálvez tenaciously adhered to his old desire to diminish viceregal authority. He therefore appointed a *superintendente subdelegado de real hacienda* to assume all responsibility for exchequer affairs. It was to him that the intendants were directly subordinate in their more distinctive duties. In New Spain, the first and only independent superintendent was Fernando Mangino, who in reward for his services during the Visitation had been given the superintendency of the mint and the direction of the mercury monopoly. By this time a trained bureaucrat, Mangino immediately, at the first meeting of the new central finance committee, obtained the services of the four officials whom Cossío had brought from Veracruz. The committee also ordered that all exchequer suits should be initiated in this secretariat and not in the offices of the grand notaries of government. Mangino then named his own notary, aided by an official and a copyist, to deal with the legal authentication of titles of office and decrees, etc.[1] In addition, he appointed a second legal lieutenant and advisor, José Ignacio Ruiz Calado, a creole lawyer who had worked under him in the mercury monopoly, to handle the work of the Mexican intendancy as distinct from the superintendency. In all, Mangino rapidly created three offices: his secretariat, and two notaries, one for the superintendency and the other for the Mexican intendancy; furthermore, he had two legal advisors.[2]

As was only to be expected, Mangino soon quarrelled with the viceroy, Archbishop Haro, over the limits of their respective authority. The disputes were all relatively minor. To whom was the mint superintendent subordinate—Mangino or the viceroy? Which of the two should possess the keys to the funds of the Indian communities of Mexico City? Did the viceroy or the superintendent have the power to authorise the despatch to Yucatán of 120,000 ps. needed for military purposes?[3] Such conflicts in jurisdiction sprang inevitably from the basic plan to separate the direction of revenue from the political command. Far more serious disputes had already occurred in the Buenos Aires viceroyalty. The system, however, did not for long survive Gálvez. The new minister, Frey Antonio Valdés y Bazán, acting on the advice of the Count of Tepa—Bucareli's former counsellor and by this time an influential member of the Council of the Indies—reunited the office of *superintendente subdelegado* to the viceroy. In October 1787, Mangino was promoted to the Council of the Indies; his secretariat was returned to the viceroy and his notary offices disbanded; the grand notaries of government regained their lost business. The experiment in divided command had lasted for only nine months.[4]

With the superintendent removed from the scene, the *junta superior de real hacienda* emerged as the central authority in exchequer and intendancy affairs. This committee differed markedly from its predecessor, the *junta de real hacienda*, in its duties and its membership. Whereas the former junta had merely acted as a consultative council for the viceroy, the new committee had power 'to command, implement and execute its decisions'. The viceroy only served as its chairman; all matters were determined by majority vote; nor was his counter-signature required to validate this vote.[5] Besides this executive function, the junta also con-

[1] AGI, Mexico 1973, Mangino to Gálvez, 27 May 1787.
[2] AGI, Mexico 1879, Mangino to Gálvez, 25 June 1787.
[3] AGI, Mexico 1974, Mangino to Gálvez, 8 August 1787.
[4] García Navarro, *Intendencias*, pp. 114–16.
[5] AGI, Mexico 1973, Mangino to Gálvez, 15 July 1787.

stituted a court of appeal for all judgments and measures taken by the intendants in the exchequer affairs. Furthermore, it replaced the audiencia as the final authority over Indian tributes and community funds and the revenues of Spanish towns. To ensure that the junta dealt effectively with its wide range of responsibilities, the two chief clerks of the grand notaries were appointed as secretaries. The task of these men, both qualified lawyers, was to receive and to draw up all the cases handled by the committee. They carefully recorded its decisions and despatched the official orders for their execution.[1] The employment of the government notaries prevented confusion and conflict with the viceroy's office and conferred immediate legal warrant to the junta's resolutions.

In composition the junta also differed from its predecessor. Its membership was restricted to the *superintendente subdelegado*, the regent of the audiencia, the fiscal for exchequer affairs, the chief accountant of the court of audit, and the senior official of the central treasury. The directors of the fiscal departments were excluded. As designed by Gálvez, the junta was to be led by the superintendent, backed by the regent, and the fiscal, all three officials being carefully chosen by the great minister himself to safeguard the efficacy of the intendancy reform. But after his death the balance of power within the committee moved in the opposite direction. An already heavily burdened viceroy assumed the duties of the superintendent while the regency was then awarded to the senior member of the audiencia. Paradoxically enough, therefore, the central authority charged with the direction of the great Bourbon revolution in government came to be largely composed of officials drawn from the older institutions which regarded the entire scheme with grave suspicion, if not enmity. Several of these men, moreover, were creoles or peninsulars of such long residence that they identified more with the interests of the colony than with those of Madrid. Yet the very extensive powers granted to the junta permitted these often aged lawyers and bureaucrats to cancel or suspend the central articles of the code which governed the new system. Viceroy Revillagigedo, after taking note of the situation, roundly denounced the junta as 'the source of all the evils of New Spain', since hours were wasted in debate with 'some members, addicted to the customs, style and abuses of the old way striving to maintain them and others with better reasons to abolish them'.[2] Somewhat later, he recommended that, in deference to its multiple functions, the junta should be divided into two bodies meeting separately. The first section, to be mainly formed of oidores,

[1] AGI, Mexico 1461, Revillagigedo to Porlier, 26 November 1790.
[2] AGI, Mexico 1532, Revillagigedo to Lerena, 26 September 1790.

should handle the essentially judicial work of review; the second, should comprise all the fiscal directors of department and other chief officials and should govern policy and executive decisions.[1] The trend of this proposal was to prevent members of the older institutions such as the court of audit from dominating the intendancies. As it was, his suggestion was ignored.

The junta met regularly twice a week. Its business varied greatly: it could include, for example, an exemption from the silver tithe, a contraband case, approval of expenses for the construction of a municipal granary, criminal proceedings against fraudulent officials, a reduction in Indian tithes for villages harmed by famine, and so on. Their business could be generated by private individuals as in the case of the silver miner or by the intendants and other revenue officials. In general, since the junta members had other work to do, it was left to the *fiscal de real hacienda* to present pleas (pedimientos) for laws to be observed or for the royal interests to be better protected. In routine affairs, by the usual process of bureaucratic default, his voice was the most influential. In addition, the junta relied upon reports submitted upon request by the court of audit, the treasury and other concerned departments. The fiscal himself, since he lacked a secretariat, depended upon the same sources for his evidence. The system was slow, and dependent upon multiple reports, but it was reasonably efficient and permitted a far greater degree of executive independence than is usually imagined. Let us suppose, for instance, a miner asked for an exemption from the silver tithe. He would initiate the appeal in the offices of the grand notaries of government. He might accompany his petitions with supporting statements already obtained from the local treasury officials. If the appeal went to the junta further information would be obtained from the mining court. Possibly at this stage the fiscal would oppose the concession: he might raise the issue of how many exemptions had already been granted. Recourse would then be had to the court of audit; an accountant of the second rank might prepare an exhaustive report, the court itself would submit their recommendation based upon his research. The central treasury might record its view of the matter. The intendant of the province in which the mine was located might also weigh in with an opinion. The viceroy would probably then ask his general legal advisor to examine the case; his vote would follow the counsel he received. The junta would then decide the matter by majority vote, at times rejecting the fiscal's plea.

To understand the junta's policy on certain issues, therefore, an analysis of its membership is all-important. And here we encounter a striking

[1] Fisher, *The Intendant System*, pp. 79–80.

revelation of the degree to which old enmities, both personal and political, could succeed in reversing entire sections of the 'revolution in government'. This was especially the case during the first months since from April 1788 until the arrival of Viceroy Revillagigedo in October 1789 the Mexican *junta superior de real hacienda* was entirely dominated by Francisco Javier de Gamboa, the newly appointed regent of the audiencia.[1] And during this short period of time several leading articles of the intendant code were abrogated. How did Gálvez's old enemy contrive to secure a position of such influence over the great minister's cherished reform? To begin with, it must be remembered that the accusations made against him by Croix and Gálvez were not accepted in Madrid: in 1772 he was reinstated in office and in 1774 promoted to be an oidor in the Mexican audiencia. There he remained until 1783. In addition to his regular judicial work he undertook several commissions: he reformed the administration of the Indian College of St Gregory; he inspected the Crown's management of the former Jesuit haciendas of Jalpa; he investigated frauds in the royal lottery and served as the judge of intestate inheritances.[2] Gamboa had also attacked Cossío's plans to establish a bank of deposit at the mint.

Gálvez, possibly apprehensive that the famous jurist might one day become regent of the Mexican audiencia, or annoyed at his opposition to Cossío, decided to remove him from New Spain. In 1781 he made him regent of the audiencia of Santo Domingo. As was to be expected, Gamboa strongly resisted this transfer, obtaining letters of support from both the viceroy and the archbishop. He himself wrote a long letter of protest. He was almost sixty-four and for the last three years had been sick: 'According to my public aspect I am more ready for the grave than for a journey by land and sea.' His previous enforced voyage to Spain had cost him over 40,000 ps., he claimed, so that 'I have little more fortune than my library, one of the most complete in this kingdom, assembled at the cost of patience of forty years.'[3] Other judges and even Gálvez himself when in Mexico had used it. In a word, Gamboa was too old, too ill, and too poor to travel to Santo Domingo.

His condition, however, had not prevented him from acting as executor of the vast inheritance of his old friend, and fellow student, the Marquis of Jaral, one of the greatest landowners in New Spain. He and the widow, the Countess of San Mateo Valparaíso, had the task of implementing a

[1] AGI, Mexico 1879, Gamboa to Porlier, 27 May 1788; he took possession of office 29 April 1788. Porlier was clearly a friend.

[2] AGI, Mexico 1404, Matías Gálvez to Gálvez, 31 July 1783.

[3] AGI, Mexico 1876, Mayorga to Gálvez, 16 March 1781.

last will and testament which had been carefully designed—presumably by Gamboa himself—to stop the only heir, the young Marchioness of Moncada, from selling her property. She wrote furiously to Gálvez to complain of 'the impiety, the avarice and self-interest of the author of my misfortune, Señor don Francisco Javier de Gamboa'.[1] But then she and her Sicilian husband were notorious for their public quarrels, their separation, their probable infidelities and their hunger to spend the vast inheritance which awaited them. Somewhat later Gálvez's nephew by marriage, Cristóbal Fernández de Córdova, later the superintendent of the mint, succeeded in carrying off Moncada's eldest daughter.[2]

Gálvez did not accept Gamboa's pleas. So two years after he had received the first *real orden* appointing him regent—in October 1783—Gamboa finally left for Santo Domingo, leaving his wife and three daughters in Mexico under the care of his son, Juan José, recently returned from Europe, who had become a prebendary of the Mexican cathedral chapter. In Santo Domingo the new regent, with the help of the oidor Agustín Emparán, drew up a new code for the treatment of negro slaves. It was, he claimed, more humane than that applied by the French in their adjoining colony. Needless to say, he longed to escape from 'this miserable island'.[3] And within six months of Gálvez's death, the new Minister of Government and Justice for the Indies, Antonio Porlier, appointed him regent of the Mexican audiencia. He took possession in April 1788. The reaction in Madrid against the grand project of Gálvez now also became manifest in New Spain.

It was Revillagigedo in a letter to the Minister of State, Floridablanca, who remarked Gamboa's peculiar career. As the Madrid agent for the Mexican consulado he had advanced many of the monopolistic pretensions of that body. Later, he had been expelled from New Spain, first for his backing of the Jesuits, and then because of his opposition to Cossío.

> Nothing in his entire story can be recommended since it shows him to be ungovernable, petulant, in no sense a supporter of the king's interest and consequently extraordinarily prejudicial in these kingdoms, for which reason he was made to leave, and he would not have returned if Porlier had not favoured him.... This opinion of his bad character I find confirmed from my experience in all the meetings of the audiencia and the junta... his colleagues... give him the name of the defender of bad causes.[4]

And all this from a septuagenarian ripe for the grave! In effect, Gamboa, born in Guadalajara and educated by the Jesuits in Mexico City, attacked

1 AGI, Mexico 1403, Mayorga to Gálvez, 7 February 1783.
2 AGI, Mexico 1893, Revillagigedo to Godoy, 30 June 1794.
3 BM, MSS Egerton 517, Gamboa to Bernardo de Iriarte, 25 March 1785, f. 156.
4 AGI, Estado 20, Revillagigedo to Floridablanca, 29 August 1790.

nearly all the major Bourbon reforms introduced by Gálvez, yet by reason of his talent and his excellent connexions in Madrid and Mexico City, he reached the highest judicial post in New Spain. He was now able to modify policy in a significant fashion. Small wonder that his nineteenth-century biographer, Mariano de Otero, wrote: 'If one day the literary and social history of Mexico is written, this personage [Gamboa] shall play a great role since his was a great epoch and because he was great in it.'[1]

By the time Gamboa arrived in Mexico, the superintendent Mangino had been recalled to Spain leaving Viceroy Flores as chairman of the junta superior, but since the viceroy, on account of his illness, was usually represented by his legal advisor, the new regent became the committee's effective chairman. He used this position to great effect. For example, the fiscal, Ramón de Posada, pressed for several years for an audit and general examination of the accounts of the Indian tributes. The accountant-general of the responsible department, Juan de la Riva Agüero, had not submitted his accounts to the court of audit for several years; moreover, it was well known that receipts for 1787 had fallen disastrously. But Riva Agüero, a scion of an important official family with one brother on the Council of the Indies, and another the director of the tobacco monopoly in Peru, successfully secured delays from Madrid. Moreover, in the junta superior, Posada charged, 'The regent, D. Francisco de Gamboa, who always presides, is with others the declared protector of Riva.' At one meeting, in May 1789, when Posada reiterated his demands for immediate action, Gamboa co-opted the dean of the audiencia, Ladrón de Guevara, onto the committee, and in this way obtained a majority vote to give Riva Agüero another four months in which to settle the matter. Posada indignantly but without avail denounced this tactic.[2] The dispute was later resolved by Riva Agüero's death; the subsequent audit revealed that he had indeed mismanaged his department.

Further conflict between the regent and the fiscal occurred when the junta superior decided to abrogate article 137 of the intendancy ordinances. This article declared that henceforth all Indian men, aged eighteen to fifty-five, married or unmarried, should pay an annual tribute of two pesos; mulattoes and negroes were charged three pesos. Previously tributes varied from province to province, but in general a married couple had

[1] Otero, 'Apuntes para la biografía de Don Francisco Javier de Gamboa', in *Obras*, II, 438–62. See also Toribio Esquivel Obregón, *Biografía de d. Francisco Javier de Gamboa* (Mexico, 1941). The two contemporary printed sources are: José Antonio Alzate Ramírez, *Gacetas de literatura de México* (4 vols.; Puebla, 1831), III, 373–84, and Beristáin, *Biblioteca*, II, 334–6.

[2] AGI, Mexico 1799, Posada to Valdés, 25 March 1789 and 22 May 1789.

paid two and a half pesos, and a bachelor or widower half this amount. To implement the reform the intendants were obliged to compile new registers of tributaries. But in 1787, New Spain had barely recovered from the successive harvest failures of the two previous years when thousands of Indians died from famine.[1] The intendants therefore refrained from introducing the new system, the more especially since many Indians had left their villages in search of food.

In the spring of 1788, however, the fiscal, Posada, demanded compliance with article 137 of the ordinances. But at the junta superior called to discuss his plea, it was argued that the new system of payment would raise the total amount of tribute collected, and in view of the current Indian suffering it would be contrary to divine and human law to augment their burdens. 'No time could be less appropriate [than the present] either to make new registers or to increase the tributes.'[2] In September 1788 the junta therefore suspended the operation of article 137. It also ordered the intendants of New Galicia and Valladolid to continue to collect the tribute on an annual basis and not every four months as prescribed in the ordinances.[3] The junta's decision, inspired by considerations that were both practical and humanitarian, nevertheless abrogated without reference to Madrid an important section of the intendancy reform.

But who were the men responsible for the junta's decision? On that occasion its members were the regent, Gamboa, the fiscal, Posada, two chief accountants from the court of audit, Martín José de Alegría and Manuel Campo Marín, and the accountant of the central treasury, Francisco Sales Carrillo. Presumably one of the chief accountants acted as the viceroy's representative. Gamboa and Posada we know. Alegría, a Basque, had come to New Spain during the Gálvez Visitation. He was then appointed as administrator-general of the exchequer in Veracruz, and interim secretary of the viceroyalty. But for some reason he eventually incurred the displeasure of Gálvez and Croix, and in 1770 was ordered to join his wife in Havana.[4] He was succeeded in his Veracruz office by Pedro Antonio de Cossío. Alegría, however, stayed in New Spain and obtained various official positions among them an alcaldía mayor, before be became a senior accountant in the court of audit. Revillagigedo later described Alegría as being 'always opposed to the establishment of the intendancies, without other cause than his own will; tenacious in his caprice, and now

[1] See Gibson, *The Aztecs*, p. 312; Florescano, *Precios del maíz*, pp. 148–59.

[2] AGI, Mexico 1521, junta decree, 9 September 1788, in Flores to Valdés, 28 October 1788.

[3] AGI, Mexico 1522, Flores to Valdés, 24 November 1788.

[4] AGI, Mexico 1724, Bucareli to Arriaga, 26 November 1772.

full of impertinence'.[1] Clearly he belonged to the anti-Gálvez party; his nephew, the future Viceroy Miguel José de Azanza, had been arrested by Gálvez during the Visitation for describing the future minister's fit of madness in Sonora.[2]

We know less about the two remaining members of the junta: both, it appears, were creoles. Manuel de Campo Marín, by this time ill and aged, had helped Gamboa form the inventory of the estates of the Marquis of Jaral.[3] He had studied at the old Jesuit College of San Ildefonso. Francisco Sales Carrillo had occupied his office at the central treasury since 1779. One of his brothers, Joaquín José, was a parish priest at Guanajuato; another, Ignacio, became a historian, well known in his day, if now forgotten.[4] Thus the junta comprised three creoles and one old enemy of Gálvez. Small wonder that the fiscal, Posada, felt isolated and bitterly complained to Madrid that his 'pedimientos', or pleas, for compliance with the law, were ignored or rejected by the junta. The situation changed when Viceroy Revillagigedo arrived: that vigorous and enlightened viceroy later wrote that he was always zealous 'to support and hasten forward the pleas of the most upright *fiscal de real hacienda*, which without my assistance would have been made for the greater part in vain'.[5]

The junta's freedom of action in this matter stemmed from the absence in Madrid of a minister strong enough to impose his will. After Gálvez's death the old ministry of the Indies was separated into two departments, responsible respectively for war and the exchequer, each subject to a different head. At the same time the Council of the Indies, and its audit section, the *contaduría*, appears to have been overwhelmed by the ever-mounting tide of official letters and reports flooding in from America. Thus it was only during the late 1790s, almost by chance, that the Council discussed the junta's decision on Indian tributes. Viceroy Flores' letters about the case were mislaid in their passage from the ministry of the exchequer to the *contaduría* of the Council. The accountant-general only got wind of the affair in 1795 and then took more than a year to find the correspondence. The upshot was a series of *consultas* issued by the Council in 1796 and 1797 demanding the full implementation of the intendant's ordinances.[6] Clearly, a colonial institution such as the junta

1 AGI, Mexico 1540, Revillagigedo to Lerena, 1 May 1790.
2 Priestley, *José de Gálvez*, p. 281.
3 AGI, Mexico 1403, Mayorga to Gálvez, 7 February 1783; Beristáin, *Biblioteca*, II, 31.
4 AGI, Mexico 1866, Sales Carrillo to Gálvez, 6 October 1780; Beristáin, *Biblioteca*, II, 56–7.
5 AGI, Mexico 1540, Revillagigedo to Lerena, 30 November 1790.
6 AGI, Mexico 1799, accountant-general report, 9 May 1796.

superior, when governed by a determined chairman like Gamboa or Revillagigedo, could run a horse and carriage through the entire paper-heavy system.

V

But the most significant attack upon the ordinances of intendants occurred in the sphere of local government. For there, confronted with the impossibility of effective implementation, the junta superior abrogated most of the central features of the new system. As a result the subdelegate soon became an alcalde mayor writ large. The reasons for this reversal to type are several, but first it must be noted that the code created two distinct classes of subdelegates. The first category, appointed in all areas inhabited by Indians, enjoyed much the same range of duties as the intendant, with responsibility for justice, *policía*, war and exchequer. As salary they received 5 per cent of all tributes they collected. The problem here lay in the area of their jurisdiction, for the code stipulated that a subdelegate should be appointed in all districts hitherto presided over by the alcalde mayor and his lieutenants, a provision which therefore demanded the partition of the old alcaldías mayores. The second class of subdelegate, only found in Spanish towns, was merely responsible for the duties falling under the heads of war and exchequer. Unlike the old alcaldes mayores, he did not preside over the town council. More importantly, he did not collect Indian tributes, since this task was entrusted to the alcaldes ordinarios, the elected municipal magistrates. In short, this official had little power and almost no means of financial support. The question of remuneration was important since both classes of subdelegates were strictly forbidden to engage in *repartimientos de comercio*.

Nearly every clause of the new system, however, was controverted and then suspended. The first difficulty arose in September 1787 when the intendant of Puebla, Manuel de Flon, appointed a subdelegate to replace the alcalde mayor of Amozoc and Totomehuacán. The junta, led by the superintendent Mangino, ordered him to install two subdelegates in fulfillment of article 11 of the ordinances. When he then remitted a list of all his nominations, the fiscal, Posada, immediately advised the junta to reject confirmation since he had named subdelegates to collect tributes in districts which possessed Spanish towns. Flon justified his appointments on the grounds that the alcaldes ordinarios of the smaller towns were in no sense trustworthy; they would defraud the exchequer; 'They call *gente de razón* all those who are not Indians, even though they come from the lowest caste.' Furthermore, he claimed that to name subdelegates to every district, *tenientazgos*, would reduce what was already an exiguous wage. It would then be impossible to attract suitable candidates for the office. He complained of the 'chaos of confusion, in which neither the intendant knows what to command nor his subject if he has to obey'. But Mangino and Posada remained adamant that the ordinances should be obeyed.[1]

A similar case in July 1788 occurred over the alcaldía mayor of Chalco, a jurisdiction which comprised the three districts of Tlalmanalco and Chalco. Posada demanded that if the area be not determined as Indian then the alcaldes ordinarios should be charged with tribute collection and justice, and three subdelegates of the second-class with duties for war and exchequer should be appointed. The difficulty, of course, centred upon the trustworthiness of the elected magistrates and the remuneration of the subdelegates, particularly the second class.[2]

In August 1788 the junta superior, upon receipt of further complaints, voted to suspend the operation of articles 11, 12, and 129 of the intendants' ordinances. They ordered the intendants not to appoint alcaldes ordinarios where such magistrates had not previously existed. They enjoined great caution in the selection of subdelegates, the more especially since in view of the low salary, the usual financial guarantees could not be exacted.[3] The members of this junta were Viceroy Flores, Gamboa, Posada, Alegría, and the treasurer of the central treasury, Luis Gutiérrez, a native of Mexico City, the son of the former 'factor' of the same treasury.[4] Posada was once again outnumbered.

The following autumn the intendants wrote back to confirm the wisdom of the junta's decree. Remarkably few alcaldes ordinarios existed and most who did could not be entrusted with tributes. In effect, when the current alcaldes mayores terminated their period of office, they were generally replaced by subdelegates of the first class responsible for the governance and tributes of the entire alcaldía mayor. Naturally, to assist them administer what were frequently large areas, these subdelegates chose lieutenants to manage the subordinate districts. When in 1791 the Mexican audiencia denounced this practice as being contrary to the ordinances of intendants, they pointed out that the subdelegate had become an alcalde mayor with another name.[5] And indeed in most areas this was the case.

1 AGI, Mexico 1521, see Flores to Valdés, 27 October 1788.
2 AGI, Mexico 1579, Posada to junta, 31 July 1788.
3 AGI, Mexico 1521, junta decree 12 August 1788, Flores to Valdés, 27 October 1788.
4 AGI, Mexico 1388, Mayorga to Gálvez, 4 March 1790. His father was Juan Antonio Gutiérrez de Herrera.
5 AGI, Mexico 1750, audiencia to Crown, 29 November 1791.

The junta's decision not to employ alcaldes ordinarios for tribute collection thrust all responsibility upon the subdelegates.

In general, therefore, most intendants maintained the structure of local government as it existed prior to 1786: only a few more extensive alcaldías mayores were divided. The chief exception to this rule lay in Valladolid. There, the intendant Juan Antonio de Riaño fully implemented the ordinances: 'He established subdelegates in all the districts where the corregidores had commissioners (*encargados*) of justice.'[1] In all, apparently, he created at least thirteen new jurisdictions. But this was the only instance in which such a drastic change in local government occurred.

In one respect, however, the old structure had been changed. In those Spanish towns which possessed a municipal council and magistrates, the intendant could only appoint a subdelegate of the second class, responsible for the duties of war and exchequer. This situation provoked considerable controversy between the subdelegates and the local magistrates, so in March 1793 the junta superior, in a vain attempt to settle the conflict, decreed that subdelegates should exercise all four duties—justice, *policía*, exchequer and war—in all areas where no chartered town existed, and, more controversially, in the district (partido) immediately subordinate to such towns, although inside the actual town the alcaldes ordinarios were to continue to be responsible for justice and *policía*. This decision added to the confusion and provoked quarrels and conflicts of jurisdiction in Jalapa, Sombrerete, Catorce, Querétaro and elsewhere. In Jalapa, for example, there were two auctions for the public supply of meat, one organised for the town by the alcaldes ordinarios, the other for the surrounding district organised by the subdelegate.[2]

In Querétaro the town council, citing article 11 of the ordinances, appealed to the audiencia to return to the alcaldes ordinarios full responsibility for justice and *policía* throughout the subordinate district and not merely for the city. The audiencia admitted their appeal and hence ordered the subdelegate to be stripped of these duties of government. But Querétaro, a rich, populous city, required a royal magistrate with more authority than a mere subdelegate of the second class to control its quarrelsome council. In consequence, in 1794 the Council of the Indies commanded that the town should be given a *corregidor de letras*, i.e. a legally qualified corregidor.[3] Although this remained the only office of its kind in New

[1] AGI, Mexico 1890, intendant of Michoacán to Azanza, 20 December 1799; AGN, Intendencias 17, intendant to Revillagigedo, 5 July 1793.

[2] AGI, Mexico 1139, *consulta* of Council of the Indies, 6 February 1800.

[3] AGI, Mexico 1812, Revillagigedo to Crown, 28 February 1792; *real cédula*, 17 July 1794.

Spain, the same need for a royal magistrate with greater authority was met elsewhere by a transformation of the subdelegate. In response to petitions made by the intendants of Mexico City, Veracruz and San Luis Potosí, in March 1797 the junta superior suspended articles 11, 12 and 77 of the ordinances and ordered that the subdelegates should exercise responsibility for all four heads of government within chartered towns. Two years later, in February 1799, the junta further decreed that the subdelegate should preside over rather than merely participate in the meetings of the town councils. And despite vigorous protests from Jalapa and Córdoba, the Council of the Indies confirmed these decisions.[1] That elusive creature, the subdelegate of the second class, was thus finally abolished. The slow reversion to the former system of local government was all but complete.

Open-minded, to say the least, in its approach to the ordinances, the junta superior nevertheless jealously guarded its own prerogatives when dealing with the intendants. The aged lawyers and bureaucrats who staffed the committee dealt harshly with any display of independence from officials but recently arrived from Europe. In some cases they combined with the audiencia to put down the pretensions of their subordinates; in others they stooped to support the subdelegates against them. Manuel de Flon, intendant of Puebla, who had, according to Revillagigedo, 'an effective, if hot-tempered zeal . . . and an average talent' became the especial object of their aversion.[2] As energetic as he was irate, Flon attempted to exercise his authority to its very limit. When in a contraband case, for example, he confiscated a merchant's smuggled goods, the junta superior quashed his judgment and merely condemned the offender to pay double excise duties upon the goods.[3] On another occasion he claimed cognisance of all intestate inheritances in Puebla, demanding that the value of the estate, if auctioned, should be paid into the provincial treasury. Here again the junta found against him, forbidding him to act until the Crown decided upon the matter. In reply, Flon, with the assistance of his legal lieutenant, composed a long diatribe against the court of *bienes difuntos*, which, he asserted, had exercised its jurisdiction over intestate inheritances to the frequent prejudice of the natural heirs.[4] Nevertheless the Council of the Indies ordered that this court and not the intendant should take cognisance of such cases.

[1] AGI, Mexico 1139, *consulta* of Council of the Indies, 6 February 1800.
[2] AGI, Mexico 1532, Revillagigedo to Valdés, 3 July 1790.
[3] AGI, Mexico 1743, Flores to Valdés, 12 March 1788.
[4] AGI, Mexico 1976, Mangino to Porlier, 22 December 1787.

Another occasion for conflict arose when Flon attempted to assert his authority over the town and province of Tlaxcala. As early as October 1787 Tlaxcala's town council had obtained royal confirmation that the intendancy ordinances were not designed to abrogate the traditional privileges still enjoyed by that province for its assistance to the Spaniards during the Conquest.[1] So when Flon ordered the election of alcaldes ordinarios to collect tribute, the governor, Francisco de Lissa, an old soldier who had been governor since 1776, summarily refused to implement the ordinances. He himself acted as magistrate and tribute was collected by four annually elected Indian alcaldes. He complained of Flon's imperious tone. Lissa was supported by the town council which reiterated their traditional privileges and independence.

To counter these protests Flon drew upon the reports of the directors of customs and excise in Tlaxcala. These officials stated that Lissa continued to issue repartimientos. He also rented out the city pastures for his own profit. In general, they claimed, the city was administered for the benefit of the governor and his friends. The town councillors, the regidores, far from being Indians as their names might indicate, were in fact mestizos who helped to oppress the Indian community of Tlaxcala.[2]

The junta superior ignored this testimony and in December 1789 recommended that Tlaxcala should continue to be ruled by a military governor; he was, however, to act as the subdelegate of the Puebla intendant. Later in 1793, in deference to further protests and controversy, entire jurisdictional autonomy was conferred upon Tlaxcala, its governor being subjected to the direct supervision of the viceroy.[3] Lissa remained in office until 1800 when at last he was dismissed following a bitter controversy with a former friend, a wealthy hacendado. The Council of the Indies then fined him 1,000 ps. for making repartimientos, although he alleged that he had only distributed livestock to local merchants and landowners. By then aged seventy-four, Lissa had acted as governor for 25 years.[4]

For Flon, Lissa's successful evasion of his jurisdiction formed but part of a widespread attempt by subordinate judges to resist the authority of the intendant. He directed a vehement protest to Madrid stating that since 'the authority of the intendant over the other judges of his province under the four heads of justice, *policía*, exchequer and war, is found to be

1 AGI, Mexico 1421, Archbishop Haro to Gálvez, 26 June 1787.
2 AGI, Mexico 1976, Flon to Flores, 20 December 1788.
3 AGI, Mexico 1136, *consulta* of Council of the Indies, 16 February 1793.
4 AHN, Consejos 20727, Council of the Indies sentence, 17 December 1803.

so contested, contradicted and resisted by them', it was necessary to issue a royal edict enjoining their total obedience.[1] He cited Lissa, the alcaldes ordinarios of Puebla, and the subdelegates of Tepeaca, Cholula and Atrisco as all being guilty of such insubordination. But the Council of the Indies was not impressed. Its fiscal pointed out that in judicial cases the subdelegates were subordinate not to the intendant but to the audiencia, which alone had power to review their judgments.

At much the same time Flon embroiled himself in a fierce conflict with both the junta superior and the audiencia. He had appointed a notary public, Mariano Zambrano, to serve as the notary for the intendancy; but then, following unproven charges of fraud, he dismissed Zambrano from office and replaced him by a notary royal. Zambrano then appealed to the junta superior alleging that Flon was carrying on a vendetta against him. The junta ordered Flon to reinstate the notary to his office, and reiterated their command when he did not comply. Revillagigedo refused to permit Flon to appeal to him in his capacity as viceroy. Finally, after three refusals, Flon accepted the fiscal's ruling that in exchequer matters he was subject to the junta and hence must obey its decisions.[2]

Flon then wrote a furious letter of protest to the minister, Diego de Gardoqui. He wrote that the authorities in Mexico City were bent upon undermining his authority: they had welcomed and supported all the appeals of his subordinates. He complained of 'the aversion and jealousy in which the establishment of intendancies was always held by those, who, accustomed to despotism, could not suffer other magistrates to share authority with them. . . . Mexico always continues to snatch everything for its own possession'. He attributed the leadership of this campaign to discredit the intendancies to the regent.

> Such a general disorder does not issue at the moment from any other source than the ascendancy enjoyed by the regent, Francisco Javier de Gamboa in both the junta superior and the audiencia. . . . This man, who as a native of this kingdom and by reason of his advanced age, should not govern and much less lead it, is the decisive vote in both courts since his character, fertile in resource, easily attracts the others to his party.[3]

In much the same months as writing this letter, in the summer of 1792, Flon again moved to attack Zambrano. The notary was engaged in litigation over an inheritance at the subdelegate's court in Cholula. Flon ordered the case to be transferred to the alcaldes ordinarios of Puebla since he

1 AGI, Mexico 1751, Flon to Bajamar, 21 May 1792.

2 AGI, Mexico 1548, Revillagigedo to Crown, 30 June 1792.

3 AGI, Mexico 1976, Flon to Gardoqui, 27 June 1792.

claimed that Zambrano was a friend of the subdelegate and was intent upon fraud. Naturally the notary once more appealed to the audiencia, which after an inspection of the writs, returned them to the subdelegate, fining Flon's legal advisor 30 ps. for counselling intervention. The intendant, who previously had communicated his sentiments to Madrid, now directly addressed himself to the audiencia accusing that court of an attempt to destroy the authority of the intendants by encouraging the subdelegates to disobey their decisions. Both fiscals immediately denounced his letter as 'a disrespectful, immodest, insulting and outrageous outburst against the audiencia and its ministers'. The audiencia complained to Madrid, noting that contrary to Flon's allegations this was the first conflict of jurisdiction with an intendant which they had experienced. They asked the Council 'to take the most serious measures against his person, both to reprove and punish his daring, and with this example to restrain the other magistrates of his class'.[1] The Council ordered Flon to present himself before the audiencia, there to be reproved by its president, the viceroy: in addition he had to visit each oidor at home to make a personal apology.[2] Even under the later Bourbons, it was still unwise to quarrel with the audiencia. Flon later attributed his defeat on the matter to Zambrano's wealth and his influence with Gamboa 'who with his intelligence and skill in the management of the kingdom, knew how to attain whatever he undertook'.[3]

VI

After the death of Gálvez in 1787, the Ministry of the Indies was arbitrarily divided into two sections; three years later responsibility for colonial administration was distributed among the Spanish monarchy's five permanent ministries of War, Navy, the Exchequer, Justice and State.[4] Only the Council of the Indies, charged with judicial review, fiscal audit and political consultation, remained solely concerned with the Americas. The single-minded executive energy with which Gálvez transformed the colonial system vanished forever. Moreover his successors seriously questioned the value of his reforms. They waited but a few months to suppress the independent *superintendentes subdelegados*. Soon after, they insisted that the viceroys should act as intendants for the province directly subordinate to their capitals.[5] It was this division of authority in Madrid

1 AGI, Mexico 1753, audiencia to Council of the Indies, 9 January 1793.

2 BN (Mexico) MSS 1405, ff. 267–8, *real cédula*, 27 February 1795.

3 AGN, Intendencias 64, Flon to Iturrigaray, 2 July 1803.

4 C. H. Haring, *The Spanish Empire in America* (New York, 1963), p. 107.

5 García Navarro, *Intendencias*, p. 117.

and the doubts entertained in the ministries as to the value of the new system that permitted the colonial authorities to suspend or cancel so many central articles of the intendants' code.

If the ministers took little direct action against the intendancies it was because they were impressed by the vigorous defence of the new system made in 1791 by the Count of Revillagigedo.[1] The Mexican viceroy emphatically declared: 'The extinction at birth of the intendancies would be the most lamentable blow for New Spain: they rather ought to be sustained and organised in the best possible fashion.'[2] Both the vigour of the defence—his report comprised 186 folios—and the policy which lay behind it, were typical of the man. For Revillagigedo brought to New Spain the style and spirit of enlightened despotism. Unlike the conservative Bucareli, he 'wished to make everything new'.[3] At the same time he asserted viceregal authority to its limits, under the conviction that as the king's image—his favourite expression—he alone should govern New Spain. Admittedly, rather like the intendants he was most successful in transforming his capital: it was Mexico City which benefited most from his administration. Nevertheless most departments of government bore the mark of his scrutiny and reforming energy. It was only natural, therefore, that the principal exponent of an active view of government should support the intendants as the chief instruments of that policy.

Revillagigedo, the greatest of the eighteenth-century Mexican viceroys, was a creole, born in Cuba and educated in Mexico, where his father, the first count, was also viceroy in the years 1746–55.[4] Although Charles III and possibly Gálvez did not trust him, in many ways Revillagigedo, appointed by his friend and protector the Count of Floridablanca, represented the culmination of the Bourbon administrative enlightenment in New Spain. For his successor, the Marquis of Branciforte, the Sicilian brother-in-law of the Queen's favourite, Manuel de Godoy, became notorious for his avarice and venality.

Revillagigedo set the tone of his approach to government when he forbade the guards at the viceregal palace to receive either the archbishop or the audiencia with their traditional honours. He refused to listen to their protests. Furthermore, he complained to Madrid that the ordinances permitted the regent to remain sitting in the viceroy's presence; he took

[1] García Navarro, *Intendencias*, pp. 124–5.
[2] BN (Mexico) MSS 432 (1391), f. 76.
[3] AGI, Mexico 1541, Branciforte to Campo de Alange, 5 October 1794.
[4] See Ignacio J. Rubio Mañé, 'Síntesis histórica de la vida del II Conde de Revillagigedo, virrey de Nueva España', *Anuario de estudios americanos*, VI (Seville, 1949), 451–96.

exception to this practice as being disrespectful of the king's image.[1] The effect of his personality and policy upon the upper bureaucracy was summed up by Archbishop Haro. He noted that he had never quarrelled with a viceroy before, but Revillagigedo had not treated him with the respect his office demanded. The viceroy had ordered the imprisonment of a priest by secular law officers. Only the archbishop's protests stopped a trial. He appealed to the audiencia to prevent the viceroy's arbitrary actions but 'the *oidores*, owing to the panic terror in which they hold the viceroy... did not know what to do'. He noted that Revillagigedo 'treats the oidores with haughtiness and almost with contempt. They fear him and in whatever matter he takes up they act timidly and with much apprehension: and the terror of the other inferior courts is even greater'.

More generally, the archbishop wrote that Revillagigedo 'continually has the most vast projects... without leaving anyone in quiet and without much profit, he keeps the entire kingdom in movement with his impetuosity'. He concluded: 'The heart of the viceroy, as I have noticed in his conversation, is penetrated with all the maxims which the philosophers of this century have scattered abroad in their books about what they call the liberty of men. It becomes clear that in substance he approves of the revolution in France and only deplores the excess with which that action was precipitated.'[2] Obviously Archbishop Haro, when he wished to damn someone, did not pull his punches. Nevertheless, there is little reason to dispute the drift of his description. Enlightened despots and Jacobins shared a common desire to reduce the power of the Church. The contrast between Haro's description of Revillagigedo and the audiencia's earlier eulogy of Bucareli marked the gulf that separated the approach to government of these two viceroys.

Revillagigedo's administrative capacity and policy is best observed in his handling of the problems raised by the abolition of *repartimientos de comercio*. In his 1791 report he roundly condemned the abuses of the alcaldes mayores: 'in general they and their merchant backers have been the locusts of the kingdom'.[3] But he associated this censure with a positive proposal to pay the subdelegates an adequate salary, since in his accompanying letter he declared that if such salaries were not forthcoming, then the subdelegates must be permitted to engage in trade. By 1794 his opinion had changed somewhat. In his final report he concluded that the termination of repartimientos had cut off the Indians' supply of credit and hence

[1] AGI, Estado 20/45, 47, Revillagigedo to Porlier, 10 January 1790.
[2] AGI, Estado 41, Haro to Crown, 27 January 1792.
[3] BN (Mexico) MSS 432 (1391), f. 60.

had injured their agriculture.[1] He then claimed that it was precisely those officials who wished to discredit the intendants who had most vigorously enforced the prohibition. By 1794 Revillagigedo was less convinced of the intendants' worth: 'It is very certain that an establishment which at first sight ought to have been so useful, has in proportion produced very few of the advantages expected from it'.[2]

The cause of his change of heart in part rested upon a greater acquaintance with local reality. Soon after his arrival in October 1789, Revillagigedo inquired whether in fact the intendants had suppressed repartimientos and what was their opinion on the matter. Already Manuel de Flon, the intendant of Puebla, had petitioned the junta superior to permit existing alcaldes mayores to continue to issue merchandise on credit until their term of office expired. For the most part, the intendants, writing in the first months of 1790, attacked the old system. However, the northern officials—in Guadalajara, Sonora, Durango and Zacatecas—pointed out that at no time had repartimientos been common in their provinces. The further north one went the less the system was found; in Sonora it was totally unknown; in San Luis Potosí repartimientos were limited to one district. On the other hand, in both Guanajuato and Valladolid, there used to be a considerable distribution of mules, bulls and cloth; this had now stopped. For Guanajuato, the intendant claimed that the Indians suffered most from their lack of land. In Veracruz and Yucatán, however, the intendants advocated a return to suitably supervised repartimientos since local agriculture had already declined following the termination of the old system.[3]

Bernardo Bonavía, the interim intendant of the central Mexico intendancy, issued a vehement denunciation of those persons with vested interests who defended repartimientos by appeal to the childish nature of the Indians. He exclaimed: 'Why are they [infantile]? And when will they cease to be so? How can we agree to maintain the great part of the nation in a state of infancy . . .? Opportune measures will draw them out of childhood so that they will walk with the firmness and liberty of other men.' The intendant of Oaxaca stated that the elimination of repartimientos had freed the Indians from their former servitude. Agriculture still flourished. He noted that the Indians of his province were 'quite rational'.

It was Flon, however, who struck the most practical note. 'There is no more arduous enterprise than to banish abuses which rest upon avarice.'

1 Revillagigedo, *Informe general*, p. 115.
2 *Ibid.*, p. 210.
3 These reports and those that follow are in a large *expediente* in AGI, Mexico 1974.

Many subdelegates continued to engage in commerce, claiming that the ordinances only prohibited the enforced distribution of merchandise. He himself favoured total suppression in order 'to re-establish for the Indians and the other castes their enjoyment of the rights given to every man by divine and human laws'. He noted that repartimientos could only be eliminated if the subdelegates were given an adequate salary. He therefore suggested the division of the subdelegations into three classes carrying the respective stipends of 1,200 ps., 1,000 ps., and 800 ps. Promotion through these grades would form an incentive for honest government. In all, for Puebla, his scheme would cost 19,200 ps., of which 11,353 ps. were already covered by the 6 per cent of tributes allocated to the subdelegates. The remainder could be obtained from the community funds of the Indians; alternatively the local directors of the excise or the tobacco monopoly could be employed as magistrates.[1] Somewhat later, this plan was embraced by Revillagigedo and indeed was written into the new ordinances of 1803.

Revillagigedo was not satisfied with this first batch of rather uninformative reports, the more especially since he had also received protests from the consulado and individual merchants asserting that the cessation of repartimientos was ruining Mexican agriculture. He therefore issued a circular to all intendants divided into two parts, the first a public order demanding vigorous suppression of repartimientos, and the second a secret directive counselling prudence and leniency in dealing with offenders. He furthermore ordered a detailed inquiry into the former extent of repartimientos and a statement of the current wages and commissions paid to the subdelegates.

The intendants' reports, submitted during 1792, revealed that New Spain's district magistrates had suffered a drastic reduction both in status and income. Since most subdelegates relied upon their commission of 5 per cent of tributes, in those areas where Indians were few in numbers their salaries soon became derisory. The total receipts of Guadalajara's 25 subdelegates only amounted to 3,756 ps.; many were paid less than a mere clerk. Clearly, most of these magistrates were local citizens who accepted the office for reasons of civic prestige or to add to their personal authority. Whatever the case, they had to obtain an income from other sources. By contrast, the receipts of many subdelegates in central and southern Mexico were adequate, and in some instances passed the 1,000 ps. mark. Variations, however, were considerable. Chalco's magistrate received 2,400 ps. whereas Texcoco only yielded 895 ps. to its subdelegate. At best these salaries

[1] Flon to Revillagigedo, 4 January 1790, in AGI, Mexico 1974.

could barely support a district magistrate; at worst they drove him to search for other means of support. In no sense did they equal the returns of the former alcaldes mayores. At Izúcar in the Puebla intandancy the alcalde mayor could hope to make a 15,000 ps. profit, compared to the subdelegate's annual 661 ps.; Tehuacán used to yield its alcalde mayor 80,000 ps. profit over a five-year period; but its subdelegate's wage amounted to an annual 816 ps.[1]

The intendants also reported upon the prior extent of repartimientos. Several reversed their opinions and now favoured the reintroduction of the old system. By 1793, Bonavía supported a limited return to the old system. The new intendant of Valladolid, Felipe Diez de Ortega, declared that several districts urgently required repartimientos of mules. The sugar industry, for example, had suffered, since it could no longer obtain mules either for the haciendas or for transport to its markets in the Bajío. Similarly, the coastal province of Colima needed distribution of cloth and mules to the value of 18,000 ps. In general, therefore, he asserted that the withdrawal of credit had entailed a marked decline in Michoacán's agriculture. Much the same position was taken by the intendant of Veracruz. The coastal cotton growing areas especially required the stimulus of repartimientos.

In Oaxaca, where cochineal production had traditionally rested upon repartimientos, the situation was somewhat different. The intendant confessed that it was most difficult to terminate the old system. He cited a contract signed in 1792 between the subdelegate of Miahuatlán and a merchant of Oaxaca, in which the latter agreed to supply merchandise and cash for repartimientos and the purchase of cochineal. True, he imprisoned the merchant for this infraction of the ordinances, but then in this case the contract had been notarised in Oaxaca itself. No doubt many other, more discreet arrangements persisted.

For Puebla, Flon provided detailed estimates which clearly demonstrated the importance of repartimientos for the Indians of his province.[2] In Huejotzingo the alcalde mayor used to distribute each year 1,500 bulls, 200 mules and 1,000 ps. in cash for the harvest. In Tlaxcala the annual value of these repartimientos was reckoned at over 25,000 ps.; here 1,300 bulls, 350 mules and 150 horses were brought in by the governor. Such figures were by no means uncommon. The magistrate at San Juan de Llanos invested about 20,000 ps. in his district, advancing on credit

[1] These and following reports are in AGI, Mexico 1579, intendant of Guadalajara report, 4 June 1792; Flon report, 3 July 1792.

[2] AGI, Mexico 1579, Flon to Revillagigedo, 23 November 1793.

some 1,500 mules, 1,200 bulls and 700 horses. His profits were quite high. Bulls costing 7 ps. sold for 12 ps., mules acquired for 20 ps. sold at 30 ps. And so on.

This round of reports was submitted in the years 1792–3. The result was to intensify the doubts entertained both by Revillagigedo and the junta superior as to the value of the outright prohibition of repartimientos contained within the ordinances. Fiscal Posada, however, continued to attack the practice as a form of monopoly which destroyed the Indians' freedom to trade with whom he wished. On the other hand, in September 1794 the *fiscal de lo civil*, Lorenzo Hernández de Alba, declared that the passage of seven years had demonstrated that Indian agriculture depended upon a supply of livestock upon credit. Moreover, 'only in this form will the hacendados of the north go back to their old custom of bringing strings of bulls, mules and horses to sell precisely to the distributors'. In other words, the cessation of repartimientos had undermined the structure of internal commerce.

The junta superior then asked Gamboa's successor as regent, Baltazar Ladrón de Guevara, to consider the matter. In a long report the aged creole jurist recommended a return to the past system. He first noted that contrary to the spirit of the ordinances subdelegates had simply replaced alcaldes mayores: the only difference between the two magistrates was that the subdelegate had greater power and more duties than his predecessor, yet received a grossly inadequate remuneration for his services. Intendants found it increasingly difficult to obtain suitable candidates for the office. He then asserted that the Indian required repartimientos, since 'it is necessary to suppose that the chief features of the Indian character are indolence and abandonment'. He concluded, 'if the repartimientos are absolutely necessary for the subsistence of the subdelegates, they are no less necessary for the Indians and the poor, because otherwise ... their misery will increase, lacking the most necessary things to exist such as their poor clothing, and oxen for the cultivation of their fields and mules for the transport of their goods'.[1]

Once again, therefore, the intimate relation between the intendancy reform and the contemporary view of the Indian's nature was developed. The conservatives pointed to the present reality, the reformers to the future. The practical solution, to give the subdelegates an adequate salary, was ruled out of court, since by this time the Spanish Crown needed every penny it could extract from its colonies to avert the impending bankruptcy of the monarchy.

1 AGI, Mexico 1974, statement of Guevara, 8 November 1794.

Convinced by this report, in November 1794, the junta superior decided to suspend the prohibition against repartimientos. The new viceroy, Branciforte, then passed the matter to a specially constituted junta of six judges of the Mexican audiencia, who in June 1795, by majority vote, gave their support to the decision of the junta superior.[1] Henceforward, subdelegates could issue goods on credit to their Indian subjects; they could also advance cash for future crops. The junta was careful to specify that although subdelegates could become merchants, they could not monopolise trade within their districts nor could they enforce this distribution of merchandise. In all transactions they had to act as other merchants, selling and buying goods at normal market prices. To give warrant to these principles the junta encouraged the intendants to make regular inspections of their provinces to supervise the activity of their subordinates. Possibly an oidor could also be despatched on circuit to hear Indian appeals. The junta clearly recognised that the decision might lead to abuses, but pointed out that in fact many subdelegates had continued to make repartimientos, 'even in the very outskirts of Mexico City'. In part, therefore, they simply conferred legal sanction on the *status quo*.

Branciforte accepted the decision of both junta superior and audiencia and declared that all appeals or suits arising out of repartimientos should be remitted to the viceroy alone; all other courts were forbidden to intervene. Although this ruling never obtained the approval of the authorities in Madrid, it was enforced in New Spain. The Council of the Indies continued to fulminate against repartimientos and in 1797 demanded that the viceroy should comply with the ordinances. But the new viceroy, Azanza, refused to meddle with the matter; he merely promised to correct those abuses to which his attention was drawn.[2] After 1795 Indian communities appealed against abuses in repartimientos and if the abuse was serious the viceroy intervened to punish the subdelegates.[3] In 1800 the Council of the Indies obtained another royal decree prohibiting the practice, but, once again, the authorities in Mexico refrained from action. And there the matter stood.

VII

During the years 1801–3 the Council of the Indies sat down to frame a new set of ordinances to govern the American intendancies. An exhaustive documentation concerning the various controversies occasioned by this

[1] AGI, Mexico 1579, Branciforte to Gardoqui, 30 March 1797, The members of the junta were Ladrón de Guevara, Hernández de Alba, Herrera and Monterde.

[2] AGI, Mexico 1890, Azanza to Caballero, 27 July 1799.

[3] AGN, Civil, 161/1. See protest of village of San Raymundo Jalpa.

great reform was gathered together in sixteen voluminous *legajos*. But the opinion to which the members of the Council paid most heed was that of the viceroy, the second Count of Revillagigedo, by then defunct. Most of the significant reforms introduced into the new code of 1803 derived from his long report on this theme written in 1791.[1] At the Council itself, it was Jorge de Escobedo, Areche's successor as visitor-general to Peru, who led the discussion, and who made the most incisive comments. He started the debate with the observation that 'the intendancies have been a simple result of the knowledge of the evils and disorders of America, and the necessity and desire for their reform'. Granted this fact, there could be no question of abolition. Yet he admitted that the new system had in no sense fulfilled the expectations of its proponents. The failure was especially glaring in the sphere of local government, and here he agreed with Revillagigedo upon the absolute necessity of paying the district magistrates an adequate salary. He declared that if the intendants 'have not produced the favourable results which were expected, it was through not having regulated the question of subdelegates and repartimientos', since up till then, 'only in name and the prohibition of repartimientos have the subdelegates differed from the old corregidores or alcaldes mayores'.[2] He therefore adopted Revillagigedo's suggestion (taken originally from Flon) to divide the subdelegations into three classes with graded salaries and a scheme of promotion, thus creating a permanent set of relatively well-paid district administrators. Repartimientos were once more to be vigorously prohibited. In this manner the 1803 ordinances removed the central defect of Gálvez's original plan of government, which Bucareli had already criticised during the 1770s. For the transformation of subdelegates into magistrates who differed only in name from alcaldes mayores sprang directly from Gálvez's attempt to use alcaldes ordinarios and from his failure to provide adequate remuneration for the subdelegates. His inability to formulate a viable structure of local government inevitably provoked, as a logical consequence, the junta superior's decision to permit those officials to engage in trade. Until this omission was rectified the intendancy reform could not hope to penetrate effectively beyond the provincial capitals.

Certainly, as Escobedo himself conceded, very little so far had been done to help the Indians, despite the fact that for Campillo the intendants' prime responsibility was to have been to incorporate them into society. But then, surely Gálvez had merely used the Indian question as a pretext

1 Navarro García, *Intendencias*, pp. 127–34.

2 AGI, Lima 1119, Escobedo's statement, 23 November 1801.

to defame the old order and to advance the cause of his favoured reform. Escobedo, without offering a solution, posed the matter in accurate terms, when he claimed that the problem 'reduces itself to seek and propose means by which to stimulate the Indians to work and to supply them with goods without violence and by hands other than those of their own judges'. It was the fiscal, Ramón de Posada, however, who best expressed the reason why the controversy over repartimientos had aroused so much ire and distress. He frankly admitted that, despite the protection and laws of the Spanish kings, the Indians had been oppressed for nearly three centuries. And now they were subjected to a further indignity: 'Such has been the misfortune of the Indians, that in these times, in which even the monuments of their civilisation, greater than those of the Egyptians, Greeks and Romans in some of their periods, have not disappeared, already it is argued that their incapacity makes them slaves by nature.'[1]

In the upshot, little of this prolonged discussion had much effect. Owing to some unexplained whim of Manuel de Godoy, the leading minister of Charles IV, the new ordinances were never promulgated. We must, therefore, look to Mexico itself for a final assessment of the value of the intendancy system. And there, as before, the junta superior continued to exercise a remarkable freedom of action. In 1801, the Mexican silver miners, their production falling owing to the British naval blockade, clamoured for fiscal relief. The superintendent of the mint, the mining court, the central treasury and the court of audit all advised some measure of assistance. The viceroy, Félix Beranguer de Marquina (1800–2) and the fiscal, Lorenzo Hernández de Alba, opposed any rebate since the Crown, at war with Great Britain, needed every peso it could raise in taxes. Nevertheless, the junta superior, after much pressure had been applied by the mining industry, relented and granted a 50 per cent tax reduction on all silver presented at the treasury, the concession to last until the arrival of mercury at Veracruz. This rebate, which lasted for five months, cost the Crown over half a million ps. in revenue.[2]

The men present at the junta which took this decision were the regent, Baltazar Ladrón de Guevara, the fiscal, Hernández de Alba, two accountants of the court of audit, Fernando de Herrera and Pedro María de Monterde, and the treasurer of the central caja, José de Villosola. The regent and Monterde were, of course, creoles who had spent a lifetime in royal service. An interesting aspect to the junta's composition at this time

[1] AGI, Lima 1119, Posada's statement, 6 March 1801.

[2] See below, chapter on 'The Mining Court'; AGI, Mexico 1608, Marquina to Soler, 26 February 1802.

lay in the absence of the accountant of the treasury, José María Lasso Nacarino, a native of Veracruz. He was Monterde's cousin, and the viceroy, thinking it dangerous to have the court of audit and the central treasury both represented by men of the same family, forbade them to attend the junta at the same time.[1]

As was to be expected, the Minister of the Exchequer issued a strong reprimand to both the viceroy and the junta superior for their invasion of the royal prerogative. He warned them: 'under no circumstances should they grant similar concessions, the dispensation of which is private and peculiar to the sovereign's authority'.[2] Realising, however, the impossibility of regaining the lost taxes, he converted the rebate into an outright gift to the mining industry. The case clearly demonstrated both the wide power of the junta superior, and the confidence with which its members, then as before in good part creole, were prepared to ignore the known views and policies of the Ministries of Madrid.

The final word on the intendancy system is best left to Manuel de Flon, who in 1803 made some blunt reflexions upon the past and some hopeful proposals for the future. His principal achievements, he asserted, related almost entirely to the city of Puebla itself. There, he had eliminated the public disorders and riots hitherto so common. He had built a municipal granary and a prison and had cleaned up the city so that 'the aspect and comfort of the streets . . . and the paving, is all different from what it was like at my arrival'. As for the province, Flon confessed that he had not bothered to make the general inspection demanded by the ordinances, for what use would it serve? All his reports had been invariably filed. 'We have seen nothing done—without doubt, through lack of funds.'[3] Similarly, he did not try to stop his subdelegates from engaging in trade provided they did not force goods upon their subjects. Injustices were far easier to correct, since the Indians could complain to the intendants, whereas before 1786 only the audiencia in Mexico City could offer them redress. Then again, he noted that the subdelegates, 'although they enjoy more substantial formal authority than the alcaldes mayores, do not have the political connexions and support with which the latter were able to suffocate the complaints of the oppressed . . . nor are the Indians now willing to permit themselves to be so oppressed'.[4]

1 AGI, Mexico 1614, Marquina to Soler, 27 December 1802. For Lasso, see AGI, Mexico 1975, Iturrigaray to Soler, 27 April 1808. He later became intendant of Oaxaca. Also see Lohman Villena, *Los americanos*, I, 75.

2 AGI, Mexico 1786, Council of the Indies, 2 July 1803.

3 AGN, Intendencias 64, Flon to Iturrigaray, 2 July 1803.

4 AGN, Civil, 189–1, Flon to Iturrigaray, 6 December 1806.

On the other hand, Flon attacked the power and wealth of the Church, taking strong exception to 'the arrogance of the ecclesiastics and the humble state to which they have reduced royal jurisdiction'.[1] He sharply criticised clerical control of agriculture in Puebla: 'The owners of haciendas are little more than so many contributors to mortmain at 5 per cent a year.' He suggested that the large estates should be divided among the Indians, since then 'the axiom would be verified . . . that a well maintained small property yields more than a badly-cultivated great estate'.[2]

In general, Flon agreed with Escobedo that the intendants, although beneficial to the kingdom, had in no sense justified the hopes aroused by their establishment. The reasons he gave for this failure, however, were quite different from those of the former Visitor-General. Flon lamented that 'the royal ordinances [of 1786] have retained little more than the skeleton or faint shadow of what intendants ought to be'. The authorities resident in Mexico City had united to suspend its central articles and to undermine the intendants' powers, so that these magistrates had become 'nothing more than so many pipes and conduits of the superior courts'. His own battle for autonomy had been long since lost. Among his enemies, Flon included the viceroy. Contrary to the usual viceregal dirge that their office had lost its ancient position, Flon averred: 'Since the superintendency of the exchequer was reunited to the command of their excellencies the viceroys, their authority . . . is much greater than that of their predecessors before the creation of the intendancies and is now almost without limit.' Thus far had Gálvez's plans been defeated.[3] If we further aggregate the vast power exercised by the viceroy as commander-in-chief of the militia and the small regular army, then the truth of Flon's dictum becomes readily apparent. Moreover, since 1787 the viceroy as superintendent had exercised direct supervision over the mercury monopoly, a control which José de Iturrigaray converted into personal profit by making private allocations to individual miners.

To remedy this dangerous concentration of authority, Flon, in terms highly reminiscent of Gálvez's original proposals, counselled a radical decentralisation. He bluntly advocated 'the abolition of the viceroyalty, the creation of captains-general and the establishment of small audiencias in the provincial capitals'. Similarly, each intendancy should possess its own directors of the excise service and the tobacco monopoly and a court of audit. In all, he suggested appointing five captains-general, to be

[1] AGI, Mexico 1976, Flon to Porlier, 18 July 1789.
[2] AGN, Intendencias 48, Flon to Revillagigedo, 12 May 1790.
[3] AGN, Intendencias 64, Flon to Iturrigaray, 2 July 1803.

resident in Oaxaca, Puebla, Mexico City, Valladolid and Guadalajara. (Yucatán and the north, of course, already had these officials.) Only then 'would this capital [Mexico City] cease to be the stepmother [*madrasta*] of all the towns subject to her'. Furthermore, the division of authority would help secure the kingdom from the dangers of revolt. 'Even if Mexico or another of these provinces rebelled, the others, being independent and not subject as at present, would not follow suit.'[1] Clearly, all this represented little more than the pipe-dreams of a provincial governor resentful of the pinpricks of the central bureaucracy. Yet despite this dubious motivation the proposals themselves sound peculiarly like those advanced by the federalists after Independence. Here, then, in an unlikely context, we encounter proof of that basic continuity which existed between the administrative principles of the Bourbon state and its secular heirs, the Mexican liberals of the early nineteenth century.

1 AGI, Indiferente General 1713, Flon to Soler, 21 December 1801.

PART TWO

MINERS AND MERCHANTS

The fining pot is for silver, and the furnace for gold; but the Lord trieth the hearts.

Prov. xvii. 3

CHAPTER I

MERCHANTS

In 1599 Gonzalo Gómez de Cervantes commented that most Spaniards in Mexico preferred to set up small shops and stalls in the streets rather than take up agriculture. The reason for this, he declared, was that 'there is nothing permanent in which capital can be employed, except trade'.[1] A century later, the Viceroy Linares (1711–16) stated that in America everyone desired to be rich 'and to be so, all want to be merchants'.[2] The celebrated travellers, Jorge Juan and Antonio de Ulloa, gave these statements a deeper economic significance: 'In the Indies commerce [is] the only occupation which exists capable of maintaining a fortune without decay.'[3] Now by trade these observers meant the importation of goods across the oceans, from Seville and Manila, rather than the exchange of local produce. The great fortunes to which they referred were founded upon international rather than domestic commerce. For until the close of the colonial period New Spain's wealthy classes continued to demand great quantities of European textiles, iron and steel, paper, Spanish wine, olives and brandy, the cacoa of Caracas, Havana wax, Chinese silks and Indian calicoes. In exchange Mexico exported silver coin, cochineal and, after 1790, some sugar. Precise figures as to the bulk and value of the country's foreign trade are not available until the years 1796–1820 and then they are distorted by a heavy incidence of unrecorded contraband. The scheme in table 5 provides a useful guide.[4]

In contemporary language New Spain's trade was essentially passive: imports were purchased by coin rather than by the sale of native produce. Moreover, its commerce was passive in the sense that transatlantic trade was managed by the mercantile houses of the Peninsula, especially of Cadiz, or, in the case of contraband, by British dealers in Jamaica. The merchants of New Spain acted as receivers of goods, for which they paid cash: their chief function lay in the internal distribution of these imports.

This passivity in large measure sprang from the colonial system of trade imposed by the metropolis. From the 1550s until 1778 all commercial exchange between Spain and Mexico was conducted through the

[1] Gómez de Cervantes, *La vida económica*, pp. 94, 132.

[2] BN (Madrid) MSS 2929, f. 69.

[3] Jorge Juan and Antonio de Ulloa, *Noticias secretas de América* (2 vols.; Madrid, 1918), II, 96.

[4] Lerdo de Tejada, *Comercio esterior*, Appendices 3–7, 54.

despatch of periodic fleets which sailed from a single port in the Peninsula, at first Seville, but later Cadiz. At the outset these fleets left annually, but by the eighteenth century delays of up to four years between departures were not uncommon. And for the years 1739–57 the system was temporarily replaced by individual, licensed shipping from Cadiz.[1] A similar

Table 5 *Composition of New Spain's Exports. (1761–75 via Veracruz)*

Return fleet	Coin (pesos)	Cochineal (pesos)	Misc.	Total (pesos)
1761	5,295,560	1,541,728	622,515	7,459,803
1763	12,532,722	1 892,455	777,619	15,202,796
1766	13,264,518	1,457,943	899,823	15,622,284
1770	13,652,666	1,979,952	459,704	16,092,322
1775	6,392,401	2,997,253	152,612	9,542,266

1796–1820: foreign trade via Veracruz

Annual average imports	10,364,238 ps.
Annual average exports	11,141,372 ps.

1796–1820: composition of exports

Bullion	74·9%
Cochineal	12·4%
Sugar	2·9%
Miscellaneous	9·8%
	100·0%

Quinquennium 1802–6: composition of imports

Textiles	64·2%
Wine and brandy	10·4%
Cacao	5·6%
Paper	5·0%
Iron and steel	4·0%
Miscellaneous	10·8%
	100·0%

arrangement governed trade with the Orient: once a year a single galleon sailed from Manila to Acapulco. The convoy system, initiated to protect the treasure ships of the Indies from English and Dutch attack, was maintained at a later period, by the vested interests of the merchants of Cadiz and Mexico City who profited from the scarcity and consequent high prices that the system created. But if the convoys benefited the middlemen, they proved injurious both to the producers of Spain, who were

[1] For a list of these convoys see Lerdo de Tejada, *Comercio esterior*, Appendix 1–2.

obliged to ship their goods to Cadiz, and to the consumers of America, who received an inadequate and costly supply.

Moreover, by the eighteenth century, it was the merchants resident in Mexico City rather than in Cadiz who made the greatest profits. From 1729 onwards all merchandise upon landing was sent to the trade fair of Jalapa, held in a town situated on the hills overlooking the port of Veracruz. Cadiz merchants were not permitted to travel further inland. At the fair they were approached by the wealthiest dealers of Mexico City and a scattering of traders from the provinces. Clearly this arrangement favoured the local merchants: time was on their side; they did not have to keep a ship in harbour, or pay for the costs of storage; and whereas the Spaniards had to sell, to avoid a loss, the natives did not have to buy. In effect, therefore, as a contemporary observed, the Mexican merchants 'lay down the law in prices'.[1] The Cadiz shipper either accepted these prices or left their goods unsold in a Jalapa warehouse. Their only method of retaliation was to delay the despatch of the next fleet, limit its cargo, and hence force up prices by a contrived scarcity. But such expedients encouraged contraband from Jamaica, so that when the convoy did arrive, the market was likely to be already flooded with smuggled goods.

But although the exchange at Jalapa favoured the merchants resident in the colony, it did so only if they possessed enough specie to buy large consignments of merchandise. For the shippers, apprehensive that their best wares would sell fast, and the remainder slowly or not at all, usually demanded bulk purchase, cash down.[2] Naturally this demand excluded most provincial or lesser dealers from the market, which was hence largely dominated by a small group of wealthy Mexico City merchants, *almaceneros*, as they were called. These men each brought to the fair between two and four hundred thousand pesos in specie—an amount sufficient to acquire enough stock to supply the colony until the arrival of the next fleet. Then, at Jalapa itself, they resold part of this stock to provincial traders, who either lacked cash or required but small consignments, at a credit of two-thirds the value.[3] Somewhat later they distributed another part of their purchases at the northern trade fairs of San Juan de los Lagos and Saltillo. The rest they stored in Mexico City, at intervals issuing it on credit to dealers throughout the colony. It was the same group of men who sent their agents to Acapulco to buy up the cargo of the Manila galleon.

[1] BRP, MSS 2815, Miscelánea de Ayala, 278/1, f. 119.

[2] José Joaquín Real Díaz, *Las ferias de Jalapa* (Seville, 1959), pp. 10–25, 52. *El comercio de España y las Indias* (Mexico, 1958), pp. 22–3.

[3] Eduardo Arcila Farías, *El siglo ilustrado en América, reformas económicas del siglo XVIII en Nueva España* (Caracas, 1955), pp. 75–7.

These great import houses did not restrict themselves to wholesale commerce. The almaceneros of Mexico City each maintained a shop in the capital which dealt directly with the public. As one critical contemporary observed: 'These men besides distributing in bulk from their warehouses all the goods of Europe and China also have shops in which they sell merchandise in small quantities.' Nor did they disdain to own smaller, 'mestizo', stores which sold sugar, cacao, brandy, vegetables, candles and soap.[1] The almaceneros dealt in everything on which they could make a profit.

In their search for direct outlets many Mexico City merchants set up stores in the provinces, especially in the mining camps and towns of the north where the mine workers—a notoriously high-paid and lavish-spending group of men—provided a lucrative market for foreign luxury goods.[2] In addition the industry itself required a great variety of raw materials, including iron and steel. But once established in such a market, the merchant was soon called upon to finance productive enterprise. Few mine owners or refiners could pay for their supplies at once and many lacked ready cash with which to pay their workers' wages. Northern stores, therefore, faced with the threat of losing their entire market through the collapse of the local industry, advanced either cash or goods on credit to at least the refining industry. For example, at Sierra de Pinos, a small town situated in the modern state of San Luis Potosí, the local refining industry depended upon two merchant houses of Mexico City belonging to José de Arizmendi and José Andrés González. Both men owned stores in the town and both issued cash to the refiners to buy ore from the surrounding region. Arizmendi maintained this business for 30 years. By the 1780s he distributed 150,000 ps. every four months in exchange for silver bar. He also farmed the local excise, contracting to pay an annual block sum into the treasury in Mexico City. His profits derived as much from ordinary commerce as from finance: the town, although small, bought foodstuffs and merchandise worth an annual one and a half million pesos.[3] Such dependence upon two or three outside merchants was most common in the lesser mining camps. Towns such as Zacatecas or Guanajuato possessed their own silver merchants.

The Mexico City almaceneros found another outlet for their merchandise in the Indian south. In that region it was customary for the royal

[1] AGI, Mexico 1858, anonymous description.

[2] West, *The Mining Community*, pp. 83–4.

[3] AGI, Mexico 1540, Revillagigedo to Lerena, 30 January 1791; AGI, Mexico 1377, Bucareli to Gálvez, 26 April 1777.

magistrates, the alcaldes mayores, to engage in trade. They distributed on credit great quantities of mules, bulls and cloth, charging their subjects considerably higher prices for their services. Furthermore, they disbursed cash, six months in advance, for the cultivation of cotton, cacao and especially cochineal. To finance these operations the magistrates—for the most part impoverished military men on the reserve list—required both capital and credit. Some applied to the charitable funds of the Church, a few to friends, but most called upon the great merchant houses of Mexico City or the wealthier traders of Oaxaca and Puebla.

Mercantile capital, therefore, largely financed the production of cochineal, New Spain's second export, a commodity which became particularly valuable during the 1770s when its price rose from 15 ps. to over 30 ps. a pound.[1] The scale of operations was at times remarkable. In the three years, 1781–4, the alcalde mayor of Jicayán, a coastal district, distributed 400,000 ps. in cash. He maintained several shops where the mestizos or mulattoes exchanged the cotton they had grown for merchandise. The Indians of the province provided him with cochineal. He sent the cotton to Puebla and the cochineal to Veracruz. Profits on the enterprise, shared between the magistrate and his backer, Pedro Alonso de Alles, a merchant of Mexico City, were rated at 20 per cent. Alles made a similar arrangement with the alcalde mayor of Tabasco, who sent him cacao.[2]

The precise nature of these contracts can be ascertained from the instrument drawn up in 1782 by the alcalde mayor of Chichicapan and Zimatlán, a district near Oaxaca, and Manuel Ramón de Goya, a merchant of Mexico City.[3] Goya agreed to pay the magistrate an annual salary of 1,500 ps.; to supply him with 60,000–70,000 ps. in Oaxaca at once, and another 30,000 in the second year; and to pay into the central treasury an amount equivalent to the Indian tribute collected by the alcalde mayor. In return, Goya appointed the chief lieutenant of justice who was charged with the management of the magistrate's shops. In this way he gained access to a captive market. All cochineal was to be forwarded directly to his agent in Veracruz. Presumably the tribute money was used locally to finance this cochineal production. The profits were to be deposited with the merchant, and at the end of the five years were to be divided equally between the two partners. On the other hand, all judicial affairs and all

1 Lerdo de Tejada, *Comercio esterior*, Appendix 55.

2 Alles appears to have specialised in this type of business. See AGI, Mexico 1769, petition by Alles, 27 September 1778; AGI, Mexico 1416, alcalde mayor, José González de Mesa to viceroy, 20 October 1784; AGI, Mexico 1400, Mayorga to Gálvez, 29 May 1782.

3 BN (Mexico) MSS 1374, ff. 300–7.

commissions arising from them were strictly reserved to the magistrate; the general lieutenant, despite his title, was forbidden to meddle in such matters. But, of course, if Indians defaulted on their payments or production, then the magistrate's authority could be invoked to punish or imprison them: that, indeed, was the point of the arrangement. Goya, we may note, also backed the alcalde mayor of Villa Alta, a rich district in Oaxaca, famous for its cotton cloth.[1]

But although the finance of productive enterprise was to some extent necessary the wise merchant endeavoured to avoid too deep an entanglement in production: he preferred to extend short-term credit rather than to enter upon fixed investment. In a country chronically short of both specie and capital, the merchant's saving strength lay in his liquidity, in his command of ready cash. This was especially true of the wealthy traders of the capital who accumulated vast hoards of silver pesos in order to deal with the next fleet. Naturally this gathering in of currency and its subsequent export accentuated the colony's lack of hard cash. The problem was all the more pressing since New Spain did not possess any bank notes, just silver pesos, reales and half reales. Some gold was coined, but it rarely entered circulation. And, at the other end of the scale, the colony lacked an official copper currency, although traders often issued copper tokens, acceptable however only at their own stores.[2] Mexico, therefore, depended upon a silver coinage which its chief merchants hoarded for export.

The inevitable result of this situation was an almost universal reliance upon credit transactions. An inspection of any merchant's accounts, be he petty dealer or almacenero, at once reveals that the greater part of his trading capital existed in the form of credits advanced—*dependencias activas*—to either fellow merchants or the public. Equally important, the usual method of payment between merchants was by bill of exchange, a preference strengthened, of course, by the bandit-infested nature of New Spain's territory. By 1807, the bishop-elect of Michoacán, Manuel Abad y Queipo, stated that two-thirds of all commercial transactions were paid in bills rather than by cash. The notes drawn by silver miners upon their Mexico City correspondents were especially acceptable, and changed hands ten or twelve times before their final payment three or four months after their issue.[3] Tax collectors as well as merchants used such bills. Both the alcaldes mayores and the excise officials, for example, whenever

[1] AGI, Mexico 1400, Mayorga to Gálvez, 29 May 1782.

[2] AGI, Estado 42/4, report by consulado to viceroy, undated, *c.* 1770.

[3] Mora, *Obras sueltas*, p. 235.

possible obtained notes from local traders made out on Mexico City merchants who then deposited the equivalent sum in the central treasury.[1] In this fashion money collected in taxes re-entered the local circle of exchange.

But what was the nature of the Mexican bill of exchange? In 1796 the Mexico City *consulado*, in a report to the viceroy, discussed its peculiarities. They explained that the *libranza*, as it was called, was only employed in internal trade; it was frequently issued for very small sums; and it often served as a form of currency.[2] It lacked, therefore, the formality of the international instrument. On the other hand, it appears to have been a true bill of exchange, in that it involved three parties—the drawer of the note, called the *librante*; the recipient, the *libritario*; and the payor, the *manditario*. Some bills, like their European counterparts, carried specific time limits within which they had to be paid. But most, the consulado asserted, were governed by no further condition than the amount to be paid by the manditario. The initial recipient, by simple affixture of his signature, often ceded the bills to a fourth party, and the note then circulated as virtual currency until final presentation to an unexpectant payor. Fraud in these circumstances was easy, and the payor frequently refused to pay until he received confirmation from the original drawer.

The use to which these notes were put is illustrated by the following case. In 1801, Diego Rul, a wealthy miner and landowner of Guanajuato, sold 2,000 sheep in Valladolid at 23 rls. a head.[3] He remitted the money to the manager of his Guanajuato refining mill by means of three libranzas he had acquired.

1. For 2,000 ps.: issued on 12 November 1800, no. 32 by Bernabé de Bustamante against Antonio Uscola, endorsed by Francisco Sánchez del Villar.
2. For 3,610 ps.: issued on 22 December 1800, by Miguel de la Parra against Domingo de Ugarte y Acha, endorsed by the tithe judges of Valladolid Diocese (*jueces hacedores*).
3. For 122 ps.: issued on 22 December 1800 by Pedro Telmo Primo against Pedro Andrés Terreyro, endorsed by José Quirino Marmolejo.

TOTAL 5,732 ps.

[1] AGI, Mexico 2811, excise manager of Sierra de Pinos to Zacatecas treasury, 8 October 1796; AGI, Mexico 2255, report by Pedro de Aparici, 2 February 1801; BN (Mexico) MSS 1385, report by Juan de la Riva to viceroy, 29 February 1788, ff. 261–3.

[2] AGN, Consulado 44/4, report of consulado to viceroy, 2 May 1796.

[3] FV, 3, Diego Rul to Alonso Candamo, 5 January 1801.

Rul endorsed these bills in favour of his manager; he wrote from Valladolid on 5 January 1801; hence all three bills were of recent issue. Both Bustamante and Telmo Primo lived in Guanajuato and were known personally to Rul.

In part, the libranza filled the vacuum left by the export of silver specie. But its widespread employment sprang from the peculiarly centralised nature of New Spain's commercial and financial system. From Mexico City flowed merchandise issued on credit and to it flowed all silver to be minted, most taxes, and libranzas for payment of goods. Much silver, once coined, never left the capital, but almost immediately entered the coffers of the almaceneros to await shipment abroad.

But what was the origin of these great merchant houses of Mexico—from where did they obtain their capital—what degree of institutional permanence did they enjoy? In the first place, New Spain did not possess any of the great corporate commercial and financial institutions that had been developed in Europe. Instead the typical figure of its business world was the individual trader. Even partnerships, as distinct from commission arrangements, were rare, and the practice of multi-partnered ventures almost unknown. The merchant of New Spain began his career sitting behind a shop counter, and most continued throughout their life to manage a shop. Mercantile skills were essentially personal, and a man's success largely depended upon the degree of confidence he inspired in his fellow traders. Fortunes were created by the acumen and parsimony of a lifetime and working capital was increased by ploughing back profits and seeking outside credit and deposits. Some clerical institutions, a few rich widows or officials, were willing to entrust their money to merchants, usually at 5 per cent interest. But naturally these deposits only went to well-established merchant houses, and not to young beginners. Moreover, it is our impression that such deposits were less important than current short-term credit granted by fellow traders. Then again, the rate of commercial profit was not sufficiently high as to justify reliance upon deposits at 5 per cent interest.

But if thrift and business talent could together create a fortune, death and a fertile wife could destroy it. New Spain was governed by the inheritance laws of Castile. These laid down that all capital acquired during a marriage belonged equally to the partners, so that at the death of either spouse the survivor was only entitled to half the estate.[1] The deceased

[1] This description is taken from José María Ots de Capdequí, *Historia de América: instituciones* (Barcelona and Madrid, 1959), pp. 311–12, 320, 324. The operative laws were *Leyes de Toro* 18, 28, 7. See also *Novísima recopilación de las leyes de España* (6 vols.; Madrid, 1805–26), Lib. x, tit. 4, 6, 20.

person's share was then divided in equal portions among all his children, male and female alike. The same fate awaited the survivor's half of the estate. This equal distribution among heirs was mitigated by two exceptions. A third of a person's estate, termed the *mejora*, could be separated from the rest, and granted to a favoured child. Similarly, a fifth, the *quinta*, could be freely bequeathed to third parties or to charity. Clearly these inheritance laws favoured a continual dissolution of accumulated capital.

The successful merchant was hence confronted with the good probability that after his death his business would be terminated, its stock auctioned and the proceeds divided between his widow and children.[1] He could not convert his enterprise into a joint stock company; he could not satisfy his heirs with the purchase of interest-paying bonds and stocks. How then could he prevent the destruction of his fortune? The best way was to withdraw from trade altogether and to invest his capital in land. He could then establish an entail, a *mayorazgo*, secured upon his haciendas, which, once bequeathed to a given heir, was exempt from the usual process of division. Such an arrangement coincided with the wealthy merchant's usual ambition to found a noble family. Neither in the Peninsula nor in the New World did Spanish merchants encourage their sons to join them. Instead, if at all successful, they wanted 'to give a career to my children', they educated them for the professions and government service; in a word to be gentlemen.[2]

On the other hand, it often paid to maintain the family firm; any sudden cessation of business or abrupt auction of stock usually entailed financial loss. Many merchants therefore contrived to marry their daughters to the young assistants whom they employed to manage their shops. These men were already virtual partners since they usually earned, on a commission basis, a quarter or a third of the profits; frequently they lived with their employer; in many instances they were relatives, often nephews, of the merchant. What better method to perpetuate a family business than to bring in a poor nephew, train him, make him a partner, and then marry him to one's daughter? Here then was the way in which many trading

1 Compare: 'But the general tendency was for a business to dissolve in every generation, mainly because its assets had to be realised and distributed among a considerable number of children.' W. G. Hoskins, 'The Elizabethan Merchants of Exeter', in *Elizabethan Government and Society: Essays presented to Sir John Neale*, ed. S. T. Bindoff et al. (London, 1961). See also Walter E. Minchinton, 'The Merchants in England in the Eighteenth Century', in *Explorations in Enterprise*, ed. Hugh G. J. Aitken (Cambridge, Mass., 1965).

2 James Clayburn La Force, Jr., *The Development of the Spanish Textile Industry 1750–1800* (Berkeley and Los Angeles, 1965), p. 169. Juan López de Cancelada, *El Telégrafo Americano*, 20, 19 February 1812, p. 248.

houses of Mexico City survived their founder's death. Indeed several of the greatest firms sprang from the acumen and reinvestment of at least two generations of merchants.

II

Colonial commerce cannot be fully understood without a discussion of the unusual sociology upon which much of its structure depended. All our evidence suggests that generation by generation, from the Conquest until Independence, immigrant Spaniards dominated colonial trade. Most almaceneros of Mexico City, many wealthy merchants of provincial towns, and a good sprinkling of lesser traders were all recruited from the Peninsula. The proof for this hypothesis is literary, however, not statistical: it rests upon a compilation of travellers' accounts and historians of the early nineteenth century who had personal experience of the colony. But the striking uniformity of these sources is sufficient to command assent until a more quantitative investigation is undertaken.

At the close of the seventeenth century Gemelli Carreri, an Italian traveller, noted that Simón de Haro, Domingo Lorenzana and Diego del Castillo, merchants who bequeathed fortunes of nearly a million pesos, were all peninsular Spaniards. The churches and convents of Mexico City, he declared, were largely constructed from the benefactions of such men.[1] Half a century later, during the early 1760s, José de Gálvez divided the mercantile community into three classes: the almaceneros who purchased merchandise from the fleets, the merchants of Mexico City who sold it in their shops, and the distributers of cloth who despatched it to the provinces.[2] He then added: 'nearly all those employed in these branches of commerce come from Spain, since generally speaking the creoles do not attempt to enter trade, even though their fathers have lived off it'. Much the same situation prevailed at the end of the century. In 1809 Pedro de Fonte, later Archbishop of Mexico, wrote: 'Commerce in general, the sugar plantations, the best cultivated haciendas, a good part of the mines ... are in the hands of the Europeans.'[3] Similarly, Lorenzo de Zavala, himself a creole from the Yucatán, admitted that the country's commerce was largely dominated by immigrants, men who 'were occupied solely in accumulating riches within the obscurity of their dirty shops'.[4] Finally, we may cite an English observer, Captain

1 Gemelli Carreri, *Viaje a la Nueva España* (2 vols.; Mexico, 1955), II, 171–3.

2 BRP, MSS 2816, Miscelánea de Ayala 278, f. 119.

3 AGI, Mexico 1895, Pedro de Fonte to Benito Hermida, 24 April 1809.

4 Lorenzo de Zavala, *Ensayo histórico de las revoluciones de Nueva España* (2 vols.; Paris and Mexico, 1831), I, 34.

Basil Hall, who visited Mexico in 1822: 'The Spanish merchants, therefore, the great, and almost the only capitalists ... were already sole possessors of the market, by holding in their hands the greater part of the active trading capital.'[1]

One small test can be applied to these generalisations. During the eighteenth century at least ten merchants purchased or were awarded titles of nobility. All of them were peninsulars[2] (see table 6).

Table 6 *New Spain's mercantile nobility 1700–1812 (creations).*

Title	Year of creation	Birthplace
Marquis of Altamira	1704	Santander
Count of San Bartolomé de Jala	1749	Logroño
Marquis of Rivascacho	1764	Santander
Marquis of Castañiza	1772	Biscay
Count of Torre de Cossío	1773	Santander
Count of Rábago	1774	Castile
Marquis of Santa Cruz de Inguanzo	1792	Asturias
Count of Heras Soto	1811	Santander
Count of Agreda	1811	Asturias(?)
Count of Bassoco	1811	Biscay

Trade, it appears, attracted the majority of European immigrants, and even those who later became miners or landowners frequently began work as apprentice merchants or *cajeros*. In 1689 some 628 men out of the total 1,182 peninsular Spaniards then resident in Mexico City were listed as engaged in commerce, by far the largest single group. By contrast, those employed in government service amounted to no more than 124.[3] It was the merchants who constituted the backbone of the hispanic community and who created its distinctive style of life. Justo Sierra, himself the descendant of such a man, wrote: 'It was the shopkeeper ... who formed the substance of the hispano-american mixture ... the shopkeeper, and not the conqueror is the true Spanish father of Mexican society.'[4] We may now recall Viceroy Mancera's statement, written in 1673: 'The traders and dealers who in the Indies comprise a good part of the Spanish nation, approach the nobility very much, affecting their carriage and style. ... It can be generally reckoned that in

[1] Basil Hall, *Extracts from a Journal written on the coasts of Chili, Peru and Mexico in the years 1820, 1821, 1822* (2 vols.; Edinburgh, 1824), II, 189.

[2] This list was calculated from Ricardo Ortega y Pérez Gallardo, *Historia genealógica de las familias más antiquas de México* (3 vols.; Mexico, 1908–10).

[3] Rubio Mañé, *Gente de España*, pp. 357–65.

[4] Justo Sierra, *Evolución política del pueblo mexicano* (Mexico, 1957), pp. 128–9.

these provinces the gentleman is a merchant and the merchant is a gentleman.'[1] In colonial Mexico the peninsular Spaniard was always a gentleman, no matter what his occupation.

What was the origin of this immigration: were they in fact hidalgos? Did they spring from established merchant families in the Peninsula? Our evidence, once more literary rather than statistical, implies that most immigrants came from the mountainous seaboard of northern Spain. This, however, was an eighteenth-century development. As late as 1689 northerners resident in Mexico City only numbered 40 per cent of the immigrant community, the largest provincial group still being the Andalusians who alone comprised 25 per cent of the total.[2] Yet by 1724 Gerónimo de Ustáriz, the mercantilist thinker, declared that the north, as befitted the most densely populated area of Spain, accounted for the greater part of the emigration: 'most Spaniards who go to those kingdoms [the Indies] are from Cantabria, Navarre, Asturias, the mountains of Burgos, and Galicia'.[3] In Mexico two groups emerged with especial prominence: the Basques and the Montañeses, the mountaineers of Santander. Humboldt later contrasted this northern hegemony in Mexico to the situation in Venezuela where Andalusians and Canary Islanders prevailed.[4]

The majority of Mexico's immigrants were northern peasants. They came from a region in which the small family farm was the characteristic form of enterprise. In the Basque provinces most peasants owned their land; in Santander and Asturias tenant farmers enjoyed greater security of tenure than elsewhere in the Peninsula and benefited from the extensive remaining common land.[5] Farmhouses were scattered throughout the mountain valleys rather than being grouped together in villages. Few large estates were to be found, and in general a sense of social equality pervaded the people of the region.

Since the sixteenth century Basques had migrated to Mexico. They settled in Zacatecas, and they conquered the north, as Durango's colonial name of New Biscay bore witness.[6] From the first days of the Conquest,

1 *Instrucciones que los Virreyes, . . . dejaron*, p. 258.

2 Rubio Mañé, *Gente de España*, pp. 349–51.

3 Gerónimo de Ustáriz, *Theórica y práctica de comercio y de marina* (2nd ed.; Madrid, 1755), pp. 21–2. See also V. Aubrey Neasham, 'Spain's Emigrants to the New World', *Hispanic American Historical Review*, 19 (1939), pp. 147–60.

4 Alexander von Humboldt and Aimé Bonpland, *Personal Narrative of Travels to the Equinoctial Regions of America during the years 1799–1804* (3 vols.; London, 1870), I, 395.

5 Raymond Carr, *Spain, 1808–1939* (Oxford, 1966), pp. 6–8.

6 See Mecham, *Francisco de Ibarra and Nueva Vizcaya.*

Basque merchants were to be found in New Spain.[1] Moreover, the New World formed an important market for the iron and steel produced in Biscay. Famous for their industry and independence, the Basques have been held responsible for both the Chilean national character and the economic success of Antioquia in Colombia.[2] For three centuries they played an equally important role in shaping the character and activity of the hispanic community in Mexico.

By contrast it appears that it was only in the eighteenth century that the Montañeses emerged as a dominant group in New Spain. Theirs was a poor province from which seasonal migration to Castile was already frequent.[3] Many went to Andalusia to become tavern-keepers.[4] In 1712 the port of Santander possessed no more than 225 householders. But in the course of the century the province and its capital, partly in response to royal promotion, partly in consequence of an increase in population, experienced a decided growth in prosperity and importance. A road was constructed to connect the port to Castile; a new iron industry was created; and the Crown deliberately fostered the port of Santander as a rival to Bilbao.[5] The opening of free trade with the Indies benefited the entire province. Even so, by 1822, Santander's population only amounted to 175,152.[6]

In 1742 the eighteenth-century predominance of these northern Spaniards within the commercial community received official recognition when the Mexican *consulado*, the merchant guild, was divided into the two parties of Basques and Montañeses, each of whom elected a consul and, on alternate years, the prior. Natives of other provinces and creoles were obliged to abstain or to enrol in these parties.[7] The formation of such provincial groups reflected the immigrant Spaniard's deep sense of *paisanaje*, a loyalty which was further emphasised by communal religious and charitable organisations. Most Basques became members of the

1 Enrique Otte, 'Los mercaderes vizcaínos Sancho Ortiz de Urrutia y Juan de Urrutia', *Boletín Histórico Fundación Boulton*, 6 (1964), pp. 3–32.

2 Alberto Edwards Vives, *La fronda aristocrática* (Santiago de Chile, 1952), pp. 18–19. Benjamín Vicuña Mackenna, *Los orígenes de las familias chilenas* (3 vols.; Santiago de Chile, 1903), I, *Los vizcaínos*. Everett E. Hagen, *On the Theory of Social Change* (Homewood, Ill., 1962), pp. 371–3.

3 In general see Fernando Barreda y Ferrer de la Vega, *Aportación al estudio de la historia económica de la montaña* (Santander, 1957), pp. 481–612.

4 Lady Elizabeth Holland, *The Spanish Journal* (London, 1910), p. 55.

5 Vicente Palacio Atard, *El comercio de Castilla y el puerto de Santander en el siglo XVIII* (Madrid, 1960), pp. 51–70, 144–6, 180–7.

6 Barreda y Ferrer de la Vega, *Aportación*, p. 506. See also Luis María de la Sierra, *Memoría sobre el estado de comercio que publica la real junta de Santander* (Santander, 1833), pp. 90–1.

7 Alamán, *Historia*, I, 45; AGI, Mexico 1775, consulado to Crown, 14 August 1787.

confraternity of Our Lady of Aranzázu, whereas the Montañeses adhered to the confraternity which took the Christ of Burgos for its patron. The many altars in Mexican churches dedicated to these two great cults give clues as to which group was strongest in any particular locality.

The Basques especially supported communal activity. In 1754 the confraternity of Our Lady of Aranzázu completed building a college for orphan girls of Basque origin, a magnificent edifice composed of several courtyards, still known as 'Las Vizcaínas'. The names of the three men chiefly responsible for its construction were carved above the principal stairway of the college. These were Francisco de Echeveste, Manuel de Aldaco and Ambrosio de Meave: all three had served as prior or consul in the Mexican consulado.[1] The college's rules of government were drawn up by Francisco Javier de Gamboa, the famous mining jurist, who was the son and grandson of Basques. Another organisation which interested these men was the Basque economic society or *Amigos del País*, founded in 1764. Meave was especially active. In 1773 he and the judge Leandro de Viana, later Count of Tepa, secured the signatures of 171 new associate members.[2] In the same year the vice-collectors of subscriptions were Antonio Bassoco, Manuel Ramón de Goya and Sebastián de Eguía.[3] Four years later Meave and Viana were able to collect 14,000 ps. from the local society, to support the new Basque college at Vergara where mineralogy and metallurgy figured prominently in the curriculum. In his will Meave left 14,000 ps. for this institution.[4] The Basques, therefore, were highly conscious of their provincial affiliation; their party within the consulado rested upon the communal organisation of their confraternity, their economic society, business partnership and compadrazgo. No doubt, with more evidence available, a similar pattern could be discerned among the Montañeses.

Both groups were famous for their nobiliary pretensions and genealogical passion. Whereas in the Spanish population at large only 10 per cent were entitled to be designated *hidalgos*, or gentlemen, in Guipuzcoa everyone was a hidalgo, in Biscay half the population, and in Asturias one sixth.[5] Montañeses were equally famous for their claims. 'Hidalgo like the king because he was Montañés', wrote Cervantes ironically.[6] Similarly,

1 Gonzalo Obregón, Jr., *El real colegio de San Ignacio de México* (Mexico, 1949), pp. 47–9.

2 Nicolás de Soraluce y Zubizarreta, *Real sociedad bascongada de los Amigos del País* (San Sebastian, 1880), pp. 34, 46–7.

3 Robert Jones Shafer, *The Economic Societies in the Spanish World, 1763–1821* (Syracuse, N.Y., 1958), pp. 45–6.

4 Soraluce y Zubizarreta, *Real sociedad bascongada*, p. 47.

5 Antonio Domínguez Ortiz, *La sociedad española en el siglo XVIII* (Madrid, 1955), pp. 81–99.

6 Miguel de Cervantes y Saavedra, *Don Quijote de la Mancha*, Part II, Chapter 48.

in a seventeenth-century dialogue between a Basque and a Castilian, the former declared: 'Since we Basques are all hidalgos, it is natural that peasants [i.e. Castilians] should hate us.'[1] Yet in fact these northern hidalgos were frequently little more than farmers whose very poverty drove their sons to seek their fortunes abroad.

Once in Mexico, all doubts as to social rank disappeared. There, no matter what their previous status or occupation, all Spaniards were considered to be gentlemen. Father Francisco de Ajofrín, a Capuchin traveller of the 1760s, observed: 'All gachupines [peninsular Spaniards] are addressed as "don" and are treated with great respect, all being taken for nobles, no matter what class they are, since to be European suffices.'[2] In part, of course, the prevalence of hidalgos in the north accounted for this; but, equally important, the Spaniard as member of the conquering nation laid claim to superior status. We should not forget that the Conquest was annually celebrated with great festivity until the end of the colony.[3] Furthermore, in Mexico the colour of skin helped to determine social rank. In 1735 an anonymous observer wrote: 'Among the inhabitants [of this kingdom] no further distinction is made than between the whites and the coloured.'[4] At the close of the century Humboldt confirmed this opinion: 'the most miserable European, without education or cultivation, believes himself superior to the whites born in the New Continent . . . a white, although mounted barefoot on a horse, believes himself to constitute the nobility of the country . . . a barefooted fellow with a white skin is often heard to exclaim: "Does that rich man think himself whiter than I am?"'[5]

But these peasant-hidalgos were still obliged to acquire the wealth which alone could support their pretensions. Most entered trade, starting off as apprentices or cajeros in the house of a relative, frequently an uncle, or a paisano, from their own valley or province. The cajero's training was strict and narrow, and his early years were consumed in the grinding monotony of a shopkeeping existence. Parsimony and sobriety distinguished these men. The result was the creation of a caste rather than a class, a colonial élite who differed in outlook and training both from the Spaniards of the Peninsula and the creoles among whom they lived. Lucas

[1] J. Zaragoza, ed., *Castellanos y vascongados* (Madrid, 1876), p. 32.

[2] Francisco de Ajofrín, *Diario del viaje que hizo a la América en el siglo XVIII* (2 vols.; Mexico, 1964), I, 63. See also Juan and Ulloa, *Noticias secretas*, II, 102–3, and Hipólito Villaroel, *Enfermedades políticas que padecen la capital de esta Nueva España* (Mexico, 1830), p. 131.

[3] In 1794 a splendid new mausoleum for the remains of Hernán Cortés was erected in the Hospital de Jesús. See *Gaceta de México*, VI (1794), 78, pp. 647–8.

[4] BRP, Miscelánea de Ayala 55/14, f. 311.

[5] Humboldt, *Ensayo político*, pp. 76, 90. See also Humboldt and Bonpland, *Personal Narrative of Travels*, I, 44–5.

Alamán observed: 'the employees of each house were held under a system almost monastic in the strictness of its order and regularity, and this kind of Spartan education made the Spaniard resident in America a type of man that did not exist in Spain itself'.[1] The routine that formed this group was the subject of a brilliant if venomous description by Lorenzo de Zavala.[2]

> The majority of those who directed the country's trade were, with few exceptions, *polizones* [unlicensed immigrants or stowaways], a name given to the poor young men who left the provinces of Spain for America, with no more clothing than a pair of trousers, a jacket, a waistcoat and two or three shirts. Many hardly knew how to read or write . . . in their village they had rarely heard more than the priest's sermons and the advice of their mother. . . . They went consigned to some relative who had a business there and entered their novitiate. Early in the morning they dressed to go to hear daily mass. Then they returned home to breakfast on chocolate and open the shop where they sat reading a book of devotion after settling the accounts. They lunched at nine and at twelve shut the shop to eat and take a siesta. At three they said the rosary and opened the shop until seven at night when they again said the rosary, and some praises to the Virgin. . . . The employees generally stayed with their master and rarely left them. Conversation reduced itself to the price of goods, which, however, being subject to the monopoly of Cadiz and Barcelona, did not vary much. . . . How could any idea of reform enter the minds of men grown old in such habits and hardened, so to speak, by a life semi-monastic in its routine?

Spartan, novitiate, semi-monastic: such characterisations point to a training better fitted to create an élite caste rather than a merchant class. Moreover, thrust into an easy-going environment where drunkenness and simple sloth were only too common, the immigrants strengthened their consciousness of superiority by a deep devotion to religion and the consolidation of their fortunes. As much as any Calvinist, their careers were justified by material success; as much as any Victorian, they despised the coloured masses from whom they profited.

An impression of their attitudes to colonial society can be obtained from the famous memorial of 1811, presented by the Mexican consulado to the Cortés of Cadiz. Its tone was somewhat hysterical in reaction to the massacres of the 1810 rebellion; nevertheless, it revealed much of their embattled mentality. They declared: 'New Spain is a region where an indolent and sensual humour prevails; where people live for pleasure and dissipation; where care for the future yields to a confidence in the permanent [supply] of the necessities of life.' The Indians were 'submerged in a perpetual infancy with all the appearances of a vile automaton'.

[1] Alamán, *Historia*, I, 15.

[2] Zavala, *Ensayo histórico*, I, 67.

Indeed, it had required three centuries of Spanish rule 'to transform into domesticity the orangoutang inhabitants of the Americas'.[1] Mestizos and mulattoes were dismissed in equal terms for their low life and vices. The memorial attacked the creoles for their refusal to work, their envy of Europeans, and their desire for independence. By contrast only the peninsular Spaniards worked hard, saved money and sustained society: they constituted 'the soul of the prosperity and opulence of the kingdom by reason of their enterprise in mining, agriculture, industry and commerce, the management of which they enjoy almost exclusively, not so much because of their energy or avarice but through the neglect and lack of application of the creoles'.[2] Here then were prejudices that would have done credit to any Algerian colon.

Naturally the Mexican populace viewed these immigrants in a different light. During the 1767 riots popular clamour accused them of being Jews: 'The gachupines are so many Jews, ambitious and full of avarice, who come only to rob people of their riches, to dispossess them of their lands, to usurp their jobs and positions, and to steal their very daughters and wives.'[3] Justo Sierra later compared the anti-Spanish prejudice so prevalent in Mexico to the anti-semitism of Poland; in both countries the hard-handed petty shopkeepers and estate managers who came into daily contact with the masses became objects of popular hatred.[4]

The gachupín's economic success which he himself attributed to his own industry and the populace to avarice, can in good measure be explained by his command of the two sure avenues to wealth in colonial Mexico—trade and marriage. The emigré Spaniard entered a widespread confraternity of relatives and compatriots all engaged in commerce. His early years spent as a cajero enabled him not merely to learn the elements of his job but also to build up a wide circle of business contacts. Once trained, his employer, so often an uncle or paisano, took him into partnership, or if he set up his own business, supplied him capital and goods on credit. The very nature of colonial trade—its organisation into one-man concerns and its reliance upon credit transactions—imparted a highly personal quality of individual trust to all its operations. And the peninsular merchant trusted, in order of confidence, his relatives, his compatriots, fellow peninsular merchants, and only then, the creoles. By the

[1] The Memorial is printed in Andrés Cavo, *Los tres siglos de México durante el gobierno español hasta la entrada del ejército trigarante. Publicada con notas y suplemento por Carlos María de Bustamante* (3 vols.; Jalapa, 1870), III, 346–76.

[2] *Ibid.*, III, 365.

[3] Fr. José Joaquín Granados y Gálvez, *Tardes americanas* (Mexico, 1778), p. 528.

[4] Justo Sierra, *Juárez, su obra y su tiempo* (Mexico, 1956), p. 243.

eighteenth century attitudes of dislike and distrust had crystallised between creole and gachupín that worked for the exclusion of the American Spaniard from commerce.

Secondly, the immigrants enjoyed preferential rights in the marriage market. Many successful peninsulars summoned their nephews to join them with the expectation that they would marry their cousins and so inherit and continue their uncle's business. Widows, similarly, frequently married their husbands' cajeros. Creole daughters, impelled by their mother's example and advice, and their natural affection for their father, tended to choose men drawn from the same caste. Moreover, traditional stereotypes of the respective characters of creole and gachupín men greatly favoured the latter. In 1697 Gemelli Carreri observed of Mexican women: 'They have a great affection for Europeans . . . whom, even though poor, they prefer to marry rather than wealthy compatriots, who, because of this, consort with mulatto women from whom they have suckled evil customs along with their milk.'[1] Whatever the case, it appears that a startling number of creole heiresses gave their hand to European Spaniards. If we pause to consider that a historian of the English aristocracy has declared that during the late sixteenth century great fortunes were assembled by two great paths—public office and matrimony—then clearly the propensity of creole females to marry peninsulars in part explains the immigrant's frequent economic success.[2] He was able to build upon the capital accumulated by his father-in-law.

This pattern of marriage preference was to be found at all levels of hispanic society in the New World, but it was especially noticeable in the business community. Many commercial houses owed their survival to such endogamy. A striking example is to be found in the Cossío family, Montañeses from the hamlet of Obesso in the valley of Riona. Their trading house in Veracruz was established by Mateo González de Cossío in the middle of the seventeenth century. His firm was continued by immigrant nephews. In the third generation, Pedro Antonio de Cossío, who arrived in Mexico in 1736, married the daughter of his uncle, Juan Domingo de Cossío, and took over the business. This firm was important since it acted as agent for the Duke of Veragua in Santo Domingo and for the Duke of Atrisco in Mexico.[3] Basques followed much the same pattern.

[1] Gemelli Carreri, *Viaje*, I, 45.

[2] Lawrence Stone, *The Crisis of the Aristocracy, 1558–1641* (Oxford, 1965), p. 191. '. . . the really important causes of rise into the peerage were not thrift, the administration of land, trade, or the law. They were precisely the same two factors as had been decisive in the Middle Ages, firstly royal favour, and secondly marriage.'

[3] AGI, 1878, Cossío to Valdés, 20 October 1787.

Two brothers, Juan Antonio and Gabriel Joaquín de Yermo, natives of the hamlet of Sodupe in the valley of Gordejuela in Biscay, first emigrated to Mexico, where by the 1780s they had become wealthy merchants. They then invited three nephews, Gabriel, Juan Antonio and Juan José de Yermo, to join them. Gabriel married his cousin and so acquired his uncle's estates.[1] In the next generation their nephew, Gabriel Patricio de Yermo, also emigrated to New Spain.

The nature of the peculiar sociology which sustained colonial commerce should by now be clear. Generation by generation, new waves of immigration maintained the European economy of New Spain. Far from being pioneers these immigrants entered a semi-hereditary, virtually endogamous mercantile and entrepreneurial élite, a group which dominated the economic life of the colony. In many senses it was these men, rather than the great landowners and miners, who formed New Spain's true aristocracy.

Political and institutional influence, moreover, closely followed the lines of financial power and social prestige. From the epoch of its inception in 1592 the Mexican consulado, the merchant guild and court, constituted a pillar of the established order. As early as 1602 it obtained the farm of the Mexico City excise—the alcabalas—and apart from an occasional lapse continued to collect this tax until 1754 when the Crown finally installed salaried royal officials.[2] The Bourbon dynasty relied upon the consulado to undertake several major public works in Mexico City. It built a hospital, a prison, a lunatic asylum, the central customs house, and several small roads.[3] Between 1767 and 1789 the consulado, led in the first instance by José González Calderón, Ambrosio de Meave and Juan de Castañiza, supervised the completion of the famous drainage trench of Huehuetoca. This vast project cost 800,000 ps.[4] For some of these tasks the guild collected excise duties levied upon local produce; the remainder it financed out of its staple income, the 2 per cent avería charged on all

[1] Alamán, *Historia*, I, 156. See Juan Martín de Juan Martineña, *Verdadero origen, carácter, causas, resortes, fines y progresos de la revolución de Nueva España* (Mexico, 1810), *Documentos*, pp. 54–7. According to the solicitudes for immigration licenses, there were three generations of Yermos in New Spain: two uncles, Juan Antonio and Gabriel Joaquín, their three nephews, Juan José, Antonio and Gabriel, and *their* nephew Gabriel Patricio. On this see AGI, Mexico 1765, solicitude of José de Yermo, 24 March 1775; and AGI, Mexico 1772, solicitude of José de Yermo, 18 May 1784. The elder Juan Antonio de Yermo lived in San Miguel el Grande, AHGP, Presos, 14 May 1755.

[2] Robert Smith, 'The Institution of the Consulado in New Spain', *Hispanic American Historical Review*, 24 (1944), pp. 61–83, also by the same author, 'Sales Taxes in New Spain, 1575–1770', *Hispanic American Historical Review*, 28 (1948), pp. 2–37.

[3] Alamán, *Historia*, I, 45.

[4] Humboldt, *Ensayo político*, p. 146.

imported merchandise, a duty which in the years following 1778 yielded an annual 100,000 ps.[1] If the consulado's revenue was devoted to public works constructed for the benefit of the capital it was because the wealthy almaceneros of Mexico City dominated the court. Despite the large numbers of merchants resident in the capital only 82 attended the general meeting of 1787 which elected the consuls and prior for that year.[2] These officers and the court they composed thus represented and defended the interests of a highly restricted, oligarchical constituency; essentially they acted as the political voice of the great import houses.

III

In the years following the Gálvez Visitation the almaceneros and their guild fell victim to a sustained attack launched from Madrid. José del Campillo first put the case against them when he sharply distinguished 'political trade' from 'mercantile trade'.[3] That is to say, he contrasted a system of commerce governed by the Crown for the common good to a monopolistic system ruled by merchant guilds and their courts for the private profit of their own members. Similarly José de Gálvez, when still ministerial lawyer, condemned the Mexican merchants for their 'exorbitant profits' at the Jalapa fair, claiming that the artificial scarcity induced by the periodic fleets actually encouraged smuggling.[4]

These criticisms received royal approbation when in 1778 by the decree of *comercio libre* the Spanish Crown finally abolished the convoy system of shipment to Veracruz and terminated Cadiz's monopoly of trade with the American colonies. Henceforth all the major ports in the Peninsula could deal directly with New Spain, at first by individual licence, and then, after 1789, without restriction. This measure, of course, represented the tardy application of mercantilist principles to the Spanish Empire. For the old system, with its two staples Cadiz and Jalapa, was more medieval than mercantilist in spirit; and the convoys rested upon military exigencies long since past. As Eli Heckscher has pointed out, mercantilist statesmen generally strove to destroy such local monopolies and barriers in order to promote the free flow of trade within the political realm.[5] José de Gálvez, the minister most responsible for *comercio libre*, clearly belonged to this school of political thought.

1 AGI, Mexico 1809, report by accountant-general Pedro Aparici to Soler, 23 September 1805.
2 AGI, Mexico 1775, consulado to Crown, 14 August 1787.
3 Campillo y Cosío, *Nuevo sistema*, p. 32.
4 BRP, MSS 2816, Miscelánea de Ayala 278, ff. 119–21.
5 Eli F. Heckscher, *Mercantilism* (2 vols.; London, 1934), II, 70–1.

The consequences of this famous decree, both for the merchant community and for the economy at large were all-important. It benefited both American consumer and Spanish producer. The industries and agricultural hinterlands of Bilbao, Santander, Malaga and Barcelona all increased their sales once direct access to the American market was established; the rising prosperity of the Catalan industry depended upon the freedom of Barcelona merchants to enter the New World.[1] In general, the well-known emergence of the geographic periphery as the leaders of the Peninsula's economy was intimately related to the new direct contact with colonial markets and the elimination of the Cadiz monopoly.

For New Spain the reform proved equally momentous. During the 1780s the colony received an unprecedented influx of European goods, and with its markets soon saturated both prices and profits tumbled. The very pattern of distribution changed: Mexico City's monopoly disappeared and Veracruz, previously a mere point of transit, soon housed a group of merchants who despatched their wares directly to the north. They bypassed the Mexico City almaceneros and dealt directly with provincial traders. Moreover, a new breed of travelling dealers, who bought at Veracruz and sold wherever they found a market, sprang into existence.[2] The lines of credit also changed. The Veracruz merchants obtained their imports from Spanish shippers who, financed in many cases by foreign trading houses, did not expect immediate cash payment. By 1807 Abad y Queipo estimated that Mexican merchants owed overseas traders up to twenty million pesos, a debt on which they were charged a 15 per cent discount.[3]

The Spanish Crown dealt a second blow to the old system of Mexican commerce when in 1786 it forbade the district magistrates to engage in trade. In the same key decade of the 1780s the price of cochineal—the most valuable commodity in this line of business—fell from over 30 ps. to a mere 11 ps. a pound.[4] Respectable merchants no longer cared to finance magistrates who wished to continue undercover trading; the profits were no longer sufficiently attractive to outweigh the possibility of prosecution.

The effect of these two reforms upon the great merchant houses of Mexico City was remarkable. They found that the age of relatively safe monopoly profits had ended. They were confronted with a more vigorous and numerous competition, since the expanded volume of

[1] Pierre Vilar, *La Catalogne dans l'Espagne Moderne* (3 vols.; Paris, 1962), III, 12, 559–66.

[2] Luis Chávez Orozco, ed., *El comercio exterior y su influjo en la economía de Nueva España en 1793* (Mexico, 1960), pp. 6–12, 99–102, 139–40.

[3] Mora, *Obras sueltas*, pp. 234, 235.

[4] Lerdo de Tejada, *Comercio esterior*, Appendix 55.

commerce soon attracted a new type of trader, men quite satisfied with small returns taken upon a quick turnover.[1] After a brief experience of the new system during the 1780s many merchant-capitalists, to cut what were already substantial losses, decided to abandon commerce. They then invested their capital in agriculture, mining and finance. Manuel Ramón de Goya, for example, changed from backing magistrates in the Indian south to financing a silver miner in Zacatecas. Pedro Alonso de Alles bought a sugar plantation. Gabriel de Yermo took over the management of his uncle's hacienda in Cuernavaca and at the cost of 200,000 ps. transformed it into a plantation capable of producing a million pounds of sugar a year.[2] The fiscal, Ramón de Posada, attributed this investment of mercantile capital in productive enterprise almost entirely to the decree of *comercio libre*. In 1792 he exclaimed: 'Many of the most wealthy [merchants] are in mining companies, no longer ashamed of these ventures which are so important to the state. Some are engaged in public supplies. Others are producing sugar with extraordinary diligence and expense sending unheard of amounts to Spain. What a happy revolution!'[3] In effect, the reduced commercial profits of the 1780s drove an entire generation of rich merchants to give up commerce in favour of mining and agriculture. But since, anyway, most mercantile capital was eventually destined to be invested in the land, its effect was more to accelerate and to concentrate within a quinquennium what otherwise would have been an individual and sporadic movement spread over several decades.

The mercantile oligarchy, however, did not greet this enforced retirement with Posada's enthusiasm. Their guild, the Mexican consulado, bitterly resisted the new policies and in general after 1778 became the centre of a wealthy, resentful opposition. After all, at an earlier period, in 1756, the consulado, acting through its agent in Madrid, Francisco Javier de Gamboa, had obtained the resumption of the convoy system after a 14-year intermission.[4] So now in 1786, after a brief experience of the greater influx of merchandise and the reduction in prices brought about by *comercio libre*, the guild presented a vehement memorial to the Crown demanding the restoration of the Cadiz monopoly and the convoy system.[5] The Crown, however, withstood this pressure, and instituted a detailed

1 Luis Chávez Orozco, ed., *El comercio exterior*, pp. 99–102.

2 See Martineña, *Verdadero origen*, *Documentos*, pp. 54–7. AGI, Mexico 2505, Revillagigedo to Gardoqui, 30 June 1792; other such merchants included Sebastián de Heras Soto, and Juan Fernando Meoquí.

3 AGI, Mexico 2505, report of Ramón de Posada, 27 January 1792.

4 Real Díaz, *Las ferias de Jalapa*, pp. 93–5.

5 AGI, Mexico 1554, consulado to Crown, 31 May 1788.

inquiry into the structure of colonial commerce. In 1788 the consulado of Santander, for example, praised *comercio libre* which had caused 'a prodigious increase' in their city and the surrounding valleys. The difficulties experienced in New Spain they attributed to the speculations of the Cadiz merchants who had oversupplied the market.[1] By 1792 Viceroy Revillagigedo was able to allay completely the Crown's apprehensions on this score. Far from declining, trade and the economy in general had undergone a remarkable expansion since 1778. In his report he singled out the Mexican consulado for attack. It wished to subordinate both Spanish and Mexican economic interests to the financial advantage of a few rich merchants resident in Mexico City. He suggested its total abolition or at least the establishment of similar bodies in all the principal cities of the colony.[2] At the same time the fiscal, Ramón de Posada, the most enlightened and honest of New Spain's public servants, roundly denounced the consulado and asked 'if the good of one city is preferable to that of two hundred; if the common good of this opulent empire should be sacrificed to the interest of a few rich merchants'.[3] Instead he pointed to the mercantile investments in agriculture and mining as the desirable results of *comercio libre*.

Subjected to official attacks and economic displacement the merchant-capitalists of Mexico City also experienced a challenge to their command of the consulado. At the general meeting held in January 1787 only 29 persons accepted the 30 listed electors selected by the four *calificadores* of the two parties of Montañeses and Basques. The remaining 56 voted for new lists of electors. In their protests to the audiencia at this reversal of a long-standing custom, the four *calificadores* stated that prominent merchants such as Antonio Bassoco, Juan Antonio de Yermo, Pedro de Vértiz, Miguel González Calderón and Miguel González de Cossío were rejected in favour of newcomers. Among the list of Basque electors proposed at the meeting were six men who had registered in the consulado but a month before and another five who had only entered recently. The audiencia backed the established group and ordered a return to past custom, despite the recommendation of both the viceroy and the fiscal, Ramón de Posada, that the general meeting should be granted the right of free election. The Council of Indies confirmed the audiencia's judgment.[4]

1 APS, Consulado 2/21, report of Santander consulado to Valdés, 24 April 1788.
2 Chávez Orozco, ed., *El comercio exterior*, pp. 31–4.
3 AGI, Mexico 1775, consulado to Crown, 14 August 1787.
4 AGI, Mexico 1775, consulado to Crown, 14 August 1787 (Council of the Indies, 14 April 1788).

Old Habsburg institutions thus combined to defend themselves against Bourbon innovations.

More challenging to the almaceneros' institutional dominance than internal revolt was the creation of independent merchant guilds in Veracruz and Guadalajara. These consulados, set up in 1795, were commissioned to foment trade, gather economic information and to build roads. They were granted 0·5 per cent duty on all merchandise entering their area.[1] The Veracruz guild, since it represented merchants who hoped to bypass Mexico City and deal directly with the provinces, assumed an especially active role. Prominent among its members was Tomás Morfi, a Malagueño of Irish descent, and a correspondent of the British firm of Murphy and Eliot; he maintained close relations with British dealers in Jamaica.[2] The new consulado soon showed its mettle. It initiated the publication of the invaluable *Balances of Trade*, which listed the imports and exports that passed through Veracruz. More importantly, it proposed to build a road to Mexico City via Jalapa. But in the first instance, its plans were obstructed by Viceroy Branciforte: he resented the consulado's independence, its direct correspondence with the Crown, and complained that it attempted 'to give the impression that this superior government was to be considered solely as an auxiliary to their operations'.[3] Later, he suggested the extinction of both new guilds, since they had done little but provoke dissension within the mercantile world; by contrast he upheld the authority and discretion of the Mexican consulado. They had proved their discretion by a gift of over 7,000 ps. given to Branciforte for his 'expenses' during a visit to the Desagüe of Huehuetoca.[4] But the Veracruz merchants enjoyed support in Madrid. In 1803 they received permission to begin their road, and its construction rapidly advanced until the revolt of 1810. The cost was estimated at three and a half million pesos. This sum was raised by advertisement in the Mexico City gazette: Bonds of a minimum four months' duration were issued, carrying the usual 5 per cent annual interest, raised from toll charges levied on all road users.[5]

1 AGI, Mexico 2512, *real orden*, 21 January 1795, establishing Veracruz consulado.

2 Murphy (Morfi) was the son of Juan Murphy y Eliot, a merchant of Malaga; see AGI, Mexico 1780. He became prior in 1807; see AGI, Mexico 2990, junta of Veracruz consulado, 2 April 1807. His wife was related by marriage to the Viceroy Miguel de Azanza; see AHN, Consejos 20728, *residencia* of Azanza, 25 November 1799.

3 AGI, Mexico 1572, Branciforte to Gardoqui, 27 August 1796. Between April 1795 and July 1797 Branciforte addressed nine letters to Madrid suggesting the extinction of the two new consulados. See AGI, Mexico 1783, Branciforte to Saavedra, 31 March 1798.

4 AGI, Mexico 1804, report by Pedro Aparici, 23 September 1805.

5 AGI, Mexico 1630, Iturrigaray to Soler, 18 November 1807.

The Mexican consulado disliked the Veracruz guild all the more because it too, after two centuries of neglect, had begun to build roads. During the early 1790s it backed the construction of a road to Toluca, from whence Mexico City obtained much of its wheat and maize. Then the consulado initiated a highway to Puebla which was later to extend to Veracruz via Orizaba. Thus in the colony's last peaceful decade two roads to connect the capital to the port were started almost simultaneously. Chief among the men responsible for this new activity in the Mexican consulado was Antonio Bassoco. In 1797 he was elected prior of the consulado for an unprecedented second term in order to superintend these road-building projects.[1] Naturally this concern was not entirely disinterested. As a retired merchant he sought new outlets for his capital, and the 5 per cent interest guaranteed by toll charges offered an attractive investment.

Reduced in prestige and importance by the creation of the new guilds, the Mexican consulado was further affronted by royal demands that it should present detailed accounts of income and expenses, and arrange its bookkeeping in accordance with the rules issued for the Guadalajara and Veracruz consulados.[2] But a more annoying attack occurred in 1806 when Viceroy Iturrigaray asked Bassoco to arrange the election of the young Count de la Cortina as prior of the Mexican consulado. Bassoco rejected the demand out of hand since Cortina was too young and, in any case, in that year the Basque party had the right to elect a prior and Cortina was a Montañés. In response Iturrigaray ordered the consulado to abandon its traditional system of election; instead, in conformity with the practice of the Guadalajara and Veracruz guilds, it should elect its officers by chance lot. Despite strong protests the viceroy refused to admit any appeal or discussion; he threatened a 6,000 ps. fine if the guild disobeyed his command. In 1807 the consulado reluctantly complied, but appealed to the Council of Indies where it obtained permission to return to the former custom. The Council sharply condemned Iturrigaray, stating that 'the viceroy proceeded with abuse and in excess of his powers when he suspended the consulado elections'.[3] This quarrel between the viceroy and the consulado was to have important repercussions in 1808. By then the almacenero class and the institution they controlled had good reason to oppose the new Bourbon regime. After all, they and the Church had been the prime victims of its reforming zeal.

[1] Humboldt, *Ensayo político*, pp. 464, 465. AGI, Mexico 1573, Branciforte to Gardoqui, 27 October 1796.

[2] AGI, Mexico 1809, report of Pedro Aparici, 23 September 1805.

[3] AGI, Mexico 1143, resolution of the Council of the Indies, 6 June 1807; also AGI, Mexico 1632, Iturrigaray to Soler, 24 May 1808.

IV

Two Merchants

The nature of colonial commerce and the changes it underwent during the eighteenth century can best be understood by an examination of two leading merchant houses of Mexico City. Their history has the advantage that it spans the century.

In the last decades of the seventeenth century Juan Bautista Arosqueta, a native of Lequeitio in Biscay, established an import house in Mexico City. His only heir, his daughter Josefa, married Francisco de Fagoaga, a wealthy silver banker, who then operated the trading firm in conjunction with his mining interests. In his turn, Fagoaga, a native of the valley of Oyarzu in Guipuzcoa, summoned his nephew, Manuel de Aldaco, both to manage his silver bank and to marry a daughter. Following Fagoaga's death in 1736 Aldaco appointed Ambrosio de Meave, from Durango in Biscay, to direct the trading house, granting him first 13·5 per cent of all profits, and then, after 1747, a full third. Meave remained in charge of the firm until his death in 1781.[1] During this period he drew up a series of inventories to present to Aldaco. From these statements we can gain some notion as to the process of capital formation and rate of return upon commercial capital in colonial Mexico. It is convenient to present summaries of selected inventories before discussing them[2] (see table 7).

It must first be emphasised that we are dealing with a series of inventories—periodic stock-takings—rather than with a record of total turnover and its profits. Profit here means the increase upon the former stock-taking. The trading capital represents the sum of the stock and credits advanced, after current debt has been subtracted. For the purpose of clarity the section 'credits advanced' has been broken down into current or good credits, uncollectable or lost, and those made to the *otra casa*, the silver bank managed by Aldaco, and the Fagoaga hacienda of Zambrano. It will be noticed that uncollectable debts were never written off: the original 37,911 ps. were still duly recorded in the 1781 inventory. To reach any notion of actual capital and its return, this item, therefore, must be first subtracted. The section 'current credits advanced' was composed of a multiplicity of small items—in 1754, 160 names can be counted—issued

[1] AGN, Vínculos 7, ff. 103–18. Arosqueta settled in New Spain in 1677. He died in 1730. See Rubio Mañé, *Gente de España*, pp. 31–2. For Meave and Aldaco see Obregón, *El real colegio*, pp. 48–50.

[2] AGN, Vínculos 10/3. The balances are included in the statement made by Manuel Ramón de Goya, 15 May 1782. The remaining information about Meave is taken from this source.

to correspondents resident both in Mexico City and in the provinces—in Chihuahua, Guadalajara, Durango, Zacatecas, Parras, Mazapil, Valladolid, Pátzcuaro and Guanajuato. Clearly this section covered all merchandise issued on credit. But, as the inventories demonstrate, the firm in large measure existed to supply the *otra casa*, the silver bank. In 1781, for example, over 57 per cent of all credits advanced (writing off the uncollectable items) were granted to the silver bank. Both institutions benefited from the arrangement. Meave found an outlet for his wares, and the bank presumably secured a moderately priced source of supply.

Other items in the assets column are self-explanatory. The large cash balances were assembled to await the next fleet, or in the case of 1781 were caused by a cessation of trade brought about by war with Great Britain. By October 1781, the 202,000 ps. which in March were held in cash had been invested in the purchase of stock. To turn to the debits column, current debts represented the sum of many small items most of which were owed to fellow merchants and correspondents. Meave himself was frequently listed as a major creditor—for 24,000 ps. in 1782. Deposits, clerical and private, were relatively large in early years, but later became barely noticeable. They comprised 41,000 ps. in 1750—about 16 per cent of all debts—but by 1757 they had fallen to 9,163 ps.

In general, the annual return upon capital was not as high as the monopoly conditions of colonial trade might have led one to suspect. Possibly the role of Meave's firm as supplier to the silver bank limited its profits. Whatever the explanation, if we write off the uncollectable credits to obtain a true notion of actual capital, then the annual return still appears low. In the 20 years 1738–57, on average, it amounted to 9·2 per cent, and once Meave's commission was subtracted, to no more than 5·6 per cent. During the 1760s and still more during the next decade, the return upon capital fell miserably. Since the profit of the years 1758–62 were paid into the silver bank, it is quite possible that the firm was being drained by its sister house. On the other hand, after Meave's death in 1781, the Fagoaga family found to its surprise that their manager had invested 100,000 ps. of his own capital in their business. Unfortunately, we can offer no explanation for the derisory 3·2 per cent return upon capital. Meave was old, he was interested in public affairs, he was looking after his own investments. Granted these personal considerations, it would be unwise to suggest that mercantile profits in general were falling during the 1770s; more evidence is needed.

The 1762 inventory does, however, record the history and profits of a particular transaction. In 1758 the first fleet since 1736 arrived at Veracruz,

Table 7 *Inventories and capital formation of the Fagoaga merchant house, 1736–81.* (In pesos)

January 1738			
Assets [a]		*Debits*[a]	
Stock in shop	105,737	Debts on current acct.	199,376
Current credits advanced	230,238	Trading capital at last inventory, Dec. 1736	162,205
Uncollectable credits advanced	37,911		
	373,886		361,581
less	361,581		
Year's profit	12,304	Return upon nominal capital	7·5%
Meave's commission	2,460		
Ploughed back	9,844	Actually reinvested	6%
		Return upon capital, with uncollectable credits written off	9·9%
New trading capital	172,049		

February 1762			
Assets [a]		*Debits* [a]	
Stock in shop	106,223	Current debts	280,428
Stock at Jalapa	52,252	Trading capital at last inventory	374,508
Cash	100,077		
Miscellaneous	13,430		654,936
Current credit adv.	90,591		
Credits to *otra casa* and hacienda of Zambrano	200,660		
Uncollectable credits	121,939		
	685.174		
less	654.936		
Three years' profit	30,237		
Management commission	10,079		
Profit	20,158		

1758 Fleet: Jalapa Purchase			
Costs [a]		*Sales* [a]	
Cost of 740 *tercios* *	290.817	Sale of 632 *tercios*, etc.	294,518
Taxes, transport	26,305	Remaining 103 *tercios*	52,252
	317,122		346.771
		less	317,122
		Profit over three years	29,649
		Profit on cost price	9·3%

* *tercios* = bundles

Table 7 (*cont.*)

March 1781 Inventory			
Assets [a]		*Debits* [a]	
Stock	164,148	Current debt	371,232
Cash	202,891	Trading capital at last inventory, Jan. 1770	465,183
Miscellaneous	20,984		836,415
Current credits adv.	175,875		
Credits to *otra casa*	241,737		
Uncollectable credits	138,221		
	943,956		
less	836,415		
Ten years' profit	107,541		
Management commission	35,847		
To firm	71,694		
		Annual return upon capital with uncollectable credits subtracted	3·2%
		Annual return less management costs	2·1%
December 1736–January 1757			
Nominal annual average increase	15,011	Return upon capital	9·2%
Increase less management costs	10,599	Return upon capital	6·5%
Actual increase with uncollectable credit adv. subtracted	11,538	Return upon capital	9·2%
Increase less management costs	7,117	Return upon capital	5·6%
February 1762–January 1770			
		Return upon capital	6·7%
		Return upon capital less management costs	4·4%
January 1770–March 1781			
		Return upon capital	3·2%
		Return upon capital less management costs	2·1%

[a] In this and in following tables the last digits often do not sum or subtract accurately. This is due to the omission of reales and granos from the accounts. Grand totals, therefore, often exceed by a few pesos the sum of their parts.

and by January of the following year Meave noted that he had purchased at Jalapa merchandise worth 225,802 ps. How did he manage to finance such a venture? In the first place he ran down his usual stock-holding, then he reduced his credits advanced by about 100,000 ps., and increased his debts, borrowing some 34,937 ps. from himself and 36,773 from the silver bank. As the 1762 inventory attests, the venture proved advantageous: in three years most of the stock had been sold, and a profit of nearly 30,000 ps. declared—a return of 9·3 per cent upon cost price and expenses spread over three years.

The fate of the Fagoaga merchant house subsequent to 1781 cannot be traced. But it should be emphasised that the very considerable capital that it came to employ was the accumulated product of at least 90 years of persistent trading. Meave built upon the foundations laid by Fagoaga and Arosqueta. By the 1780s, however, a new commercial climate had emerged which rendered doubtful the continued existence of the capital's old merchant houses.

Our second example permits us to examine the effect of *comercio libre* upon a leading almacenero. Sometime during the first half of the eighteenth century, Juan de Castañiza, a native of the valley of Gordejuela in Biscay, established an import house in Mexico City. His venture proved highly successful, and before his death in 1771, Castañiza had purchased two haciendas and a title of nobility; he became the first Marquis of Castañiza.[1] He did not, however, abandon his trading house. Instead he conferred its direction upon his nephew, Antonio Bassoco (1738–1814) whom he had summoned at an early age from Gordejuela to train him in the business. Bassoco received a salary of 3,000 ps. and a quarter of the profits, from which were deducted all costs of staff. In case of dispute both men agreed not to appeal to court but to submit to the arbitration of Castañiza's two Basque compadres, Ambrosio de Meave and Manuel de Aldaco. When, in 1763, Bassoco took over the firm its trading capital was valued at 250,000 ps., a sum which by 1771 he had almost tripled to just over 600,000 ps., a rate of increase of some 20 per cent a year—clear proof of Bassoco's exceptional talent. Table 8 lists the entire Castañiza estate.[2]

The inventory displays a pattern of business activity very similar to that of Meave's firm. The precise relation between the trading house and the two haciendas administered by Castañiza remains somewhat obscure, the

1 Ortega y Pérez Gallardo, *Historia genealógica*, I, *Marqués de Castañiza*, II, *Conde de Bassoco*.

2 AGI, Mexico 1427, inventory of estate taken by Juan Lucas de Lassaga, 17 May 1769. The above and following details about Bassoco are drawn from this source.

more so since among the firm's debts were counted 110,047 ps. owed to the Marquis and his wife. Possibly this sum, together with the 48,000 ps. owed to Meave, in part accounted for the remarkably high balance of cash and bills, accumulated, we may presume, for bulk purchase of

Table 8 *Inventory of Castañiza estate, May 1769.* (In pesos)

Assets			*Deposits and debts on current account*	
Almacén (trading house)				
Stock in Mexico City Jalapa, San Miguel el Grande		377,074		218,263
Cash and bills of exchange		279,078		—
Shop at Durango, stock & credits		62,150		—
Credits advanced:				
collectable		180,912		—
lost		5,219		—
		904,433		218,263
Haciendas of Xochiapán, Carmen, Ventorillo		82,308		59,258
Hacienda of Agrantla		57,016		—
Capital for management		118,995		—
Stock		25,174		—
Credits advanced:				
collectable		23,668		—
lost		17,198		—
		324,359		59,258
Personal effects		20,146		—
Miscellaneous		10,925		
Gross total		1,259,863		277,521
	less	277,521		
		982,342		
			Capital at marriage, dowry	62,939
			Profits of Bassoco	45,978
	less	108,917		108,917
Net increase		873,425		

stock from the next fleet. The inventory does not distinguish between current debts and deposits received, but it appears that clerical deposits did not form an appreciable sum when compared to the total trading capital. The importance of the Durango store as a northern outlet needs no emphasis; its low quantity of stock could be easily replenished from the warehouse; its manager received a third of the shop's profits.

Castañiza's death could have easily destroyed the merchant house. True, the haciendas were entailed, but by law the remainder of his estate had to be divided—one-half to his widow, and the rest in equal shares to his four children. And it was found, once certain legacies and charities were paid off, that each child was entitled to 90,000 ps. Bassoco, himself, having ploughed back his profits, had a right to 80,000 ps. But the firm was not dissolved. The dowager marchioness asked her nephew to continue to manage her half of the estate; the eldest son, who inherited the title, devoted himself to his entailed haciendas; the two younger sons had both joined the priesthood; and the daughter, María Teresa, married her cousin.[1] In this happy, almost inevitable, fashion Bassoco inherited his uncle's business.

In the years that followed Bassoco expanded his operations. The Durango store raised the price it paid for silver, and hence considerably increased its business. When Father Juan Agustín de Morfi visited the town he commented upon Bassoco's enlightened commercial policy.[2] In July 1781, entering an entirely different field, Bassoco obtained permission from the viceroy to establish pulque booths in Mexico City.[3] No doubt the family haciendas produced maguey.

But *comercio libre* brought an end to this diversified expansion. In the years 1783–5 Bassoco sent to Cadiz over half a million pesos in cash and colonial produce. The venture proved disastrous. He received merchandise worth 250,000 ps. only to find that the market was flooded: a good part of the consignment he could not sell at all, and for the remainder he could only obtain low prices. He arranged for 100,000 ps. to be remitted from Cadiz in bills of exchange, but the other 150,000 ps. he was obliged to leave in Spain. Like so many of his generation, Bassoco, in the light of this experience, decided to abandon transatlantic commerce. As he later commented: 'These continuous bad events have forced me to leave mercantile enterprises and to accept the expedient of lending capital at interest.'[4] He had always traded with his own capital, he added, but despite his resources and connexions he had suffered considerable losses.

No doubt prompted by his friendship with the Fagoagas (his brother-in-law married a Fagoaga daughter), Bassoco decided to enter silver

[1] AGN, Vínculos 25/4–6, undated.

[2] Fray Agustín de Morfi, *Viaje de Indias y diario del Nuevo México*, ed. Vito Alessio Robles (Mexico, 1935), pp. 75–6.

[3] AGI, Mexico 1394, Mayorga to Gálvez, 31 December 1782.

[4] AGN, Consulado 123, Bassoco to Revillagigedo, 22 July 1791.

mining. As early as 1784, in conjunction with two partners, he offered to buy the principal mines of Bolaños for the sum of 600,000 ps.[1] Later in 1786 he became a principal stockholder in a company formed by the Fagoagas to drain the Vetagrande mine in Zacatecas. In addition he invested in mines in Bolaños and Capula, always, we may note, in partnership with more experienced miners.[2] But despite this precaution none of these investments bore immediate fruit; he had to wait 20 years before his shares in the Vetagrande began to yield a profit, and by that time he had contributed 235,000 ps. to its restoration.[3] As early as 1791 Bassoco's rueful comment upon his various ventures was that 'there is nothing less certain that the calculations made concerning the costs of mining and the time required, and this uncertainty prevents people from entering the industry, which is generally regarded with horror among merchants'.[4]

By the turn of the century a more secure form of investment presented itself. The much traversed route between Veracruz and Mexico City was suddenly, in the last pacific decade of colonial government, blessed with two highways, both of which required a great deal of capital to be raised from the public. Bassoco took full advantage of this guaranteed return upon capital: he placed 347,000 ps. in the road built by the Mexico City consulado and another 93,000 in the rival Veracruz consulado road.[5] At much the same time the mining tribunal sponsored public loans to the Crown, upon which it paid 5 per cent interest, again guaranteed from its income, a duty levied on mining production. By 1813 Bassoco, the largest contributor, had moved 633,000 ps. into these funds.[6] Bassoco also sought a more final assurance. He invested 300,000 ps. in the construction of the church of Our Lady of Loreto in Mexico City, a handsome neo-classic structure.[7] Patriotism similarly exercised its claims: in 1809 he donated 200,000 ps. to the beleaguered Spanish government, a gift that brought him the title of Count of Bassoco, just one step inferior to the marquisate of his father-in-law.[8] In 1814 he died, leaving his widow an estate worth 2,646,000 ps. It numbered among the greatest fortunes of New Spain. In

[1] AGN, Minería 225, Pachuca treasury officials to viceroy, 10 June 1805.

[2] AGN, Minería 46/3, statement 31 January 1805.

[3] AGI, Mexico, Iturrigaray to Soler, 26 February 1805.

[4] AGN, Minería 87/6, Bassoco to Revillagigedo, 15 June 1791.

[5] *Discurso sobre el testamento de la señora María Teresa Castañiza de Bassoco* (Mexico, 1830), p. 17. AGI, Mexico 2990, report by Veracruz consulado agent, 30 January 1808.

[6] Howe, *The Mining Guild*, pp. 371–83. AGN, Minería 211/1, List of debtors recognised by mining court in 1826.

[7] Ortega y Pérez Gallardo, *Historia genealógica*, II, *Condado de Bassoco*.

[8] Chávez Orozco, ed., *Comercio exterior*, Introduction, pp. xiv-xv.

many ways, Bassoco presents us with the very paradigm of the successful colonial merchant. He differed from his uncle's generation in the wider range of his investments. For Castañiza only a hacienda offered security, whereas Bassoco benefited from the new institutional funds, which, until 1810 at least, provided a sure return upon capital.

Both Bassoco and his brother-in-law, the second marquis, died without issue; the two remaining brothers, as we have seen, entered the priesthood. Thus within one generation the Castañiza title and family became extinct. The destiny of this great fortune provides us with an interesting conclusion. In May 1816 the Society of Jesus was at last re-established in New Spain. Two canons of the Mexican Cathedral Chapter, Dr Juan José de Gamboa and Lic. Andrés Fernández de Madrid, had sponsored the return. Both men were sons of judges of the Mexican audiencia who had resisted the expulsion in 1767. Gamboa was the son of the famous mining jurist. But only two aged priests had survived the long years of Italian exile. The inaugural ceremony, arranged to fall on the very day—May 19th—when the new Provincial, José María de Castañiza, had entered the order some 56 years before, was presided over by the Bishop of Durango, Juan Francisco, third Marquis of Castañiza.[1] Present at this affecting scene was the widowed sister of the two brothers, María Teresa de Castañiza, Countess of Bassoco.

The family did not for long survive their reunion; in November the Provincial died; and only a year later his sister followed him to the grave. In her last will, the childless widow bequeathed her entire fortune, estimated at over three million pesos, to establish an *obra pía*, a charitable foundation designed to foster and diffuse the cult of the Virgin Mary's Expectancy. Direction of the foundation was conferred upon the Jesuits. Certain subsidiary aims—to educate the poor and to aid the sick—were included, but clearly the *obra pía* was a device whereby the Jesuits gained control of the vast Bassoco inheritance.[2] The patient capital accumulation of two generations of Basque merchants thus found a traditional clerical resting place. And the Castañiza family disappeared, survived only by Bassoco's peninsular nephew, who came from Spain to settle in Mexico.

[1] Juan Francisco de Castañiza González de Agüero, *Relación del reestablecimiento de la sagrada compañía de Jesús en el reyno de Nueva España* (Mexico, 1816). José María Ramírez, *Elegía de la muerte del padre José María Castañiza, provincial de la compañía de Jesús de México* (Guadalajara, 1817); Ignacio Lerdo de Tejada, *Discurso que en la profesa solemne del cuarto voto. . . .* (Mexico, 1816).

[2] *Discurso sobre el testamento de la señora María Teresa Castañiza de Bassoco*, and also *Observaciones sobre el acuerdo de la cámara de senadores . . . relativo a la testamentaría de la señora doña María Teresa Castañiza de Bassoco* (Mexico, 1830).

CHAPTER 2

THE STRUCTURE OF SILVER PRODUCTION

The structure and development of Mexican silver mining offers to the economic historian and to the student of Mexico alike a theme of absorbing interest. Both the domestic market and the external balance of exchange depended upon the production of silver. During the 1820s Lucas Alamán, Mexico's most perceptive historian, declared: 'Without mining neither agriculture, internal trade nor industrious occupation of any kind, prospers; population decreases, or at any rate is stationary, consumption fails and annihilation of foreign trade follows.'[1] He wrote, of course, in the shadow of the great silver boom of the eighteenth century during which production more than quadrupled.[2] The prosperity of the Peninsula was equally affected: Mr Vilar has written apropos the Catalan textile industry, 'Catalan products were exchanged in general for growing quantities of colonial produce, and in particular, for Mexican silver.'[3]

Despite its central role both in the colonial economy and the Spanish monarchy at large Mexican silver mining has not received the attention it deserves. In part this abstention can be explained by the overwhelming excellence of Alexander von Humboldt's *Essai Politique*, in which the Prussian traveller, assisted by official and private reports, by his own mining experience and knowledge, and by his visits to Guanajuato and other camps, compiled a first-hand description of the industry which has never been superseded. Since then all students of Mexico's eighteenth-century economy have to some degree paraphrased Humboldt. Only Sir Henry Ward, the first English minister to Mexico, by reason of his extensive travels, was able to add further significant information. But behind Humboldt's brilliant chapter lay an extensive Mexican literature upon which the baron drew copiously. Francisco Javier de Gamboa's *Comentarios a las ordenanzas de minas* gave a picture of the industry's problems and conditions in the years prior to the great reforms launched by José de Gálvez. At least four books were written on the amalgamation method of

1 United Mexican Mining Association, *Reports* (London, 1827–9), Report by Lucas Alamán and Lewis Agassis, 7 March 1827, Appendix I, p. xxiv; afterwards cited as UMMA, *Reports*.

2 Humboldt, *Ensayo político*, p. 386.

3 Vilar, *La Catalogne*, III, 12.

refining silver.[1] In many respects Humboldt was as good as his sources and the works of Gamboa, Joaquín Velásquez de León, José Garcés y Eguía and Fausto de Elhuyar were very good. Humboldt arrived in Mexico during the final scene of the industry's development, just seven years before the curtain fell forever upon the colonial society which had created the industry. Yet the expansion in silver production was a continuous trend throughout the entire century: each decade, with the single exception of the 1760s, registered an increase over its predecessor. Moreover, this expansion was internally engineered; unlike its nineteenth-century counterpart, it did not depend either upon foreign technique or foreign capital. Nor was it, as in the sixteenth century, a spontaneous boom consequent upon new discoveries. Many of the old minefields, such as Zacatecas, Real del Monte and Guanajuato, continued to number among the leading producers until the end of the colony[2] (see figure 1).

The eighteenth-century boom becomes all the more interesting if we pause to consider that, in general, old extractive industries have to deal with resource depletion which subjects them to the law of diminishing returns.[3] The best ore is usually mined first: thereafter as shafts are driven ever deeper, costs of production mount and the quality of ore declines until the point is reached when mining ceases to be profitable. At such a stage mines are then abandoned until new techniques reduce costs or the market price of the product increases. But the precious metals labour under the additional disadvantage that their price changes are to be measured by the century rather than by the year or month. Moreover, Mexico did not, strictly speaking, market silver: by law all silver had to be minted; the end product of its industry was coin, principally the famous pieces of eight known in every nursery. Its mines and refining mills, therefore, only produced the raw material from which the exchangeable commodity was manufactured. And since silver coin enjoyed a fixed ratio of value to gold, which did not undergo significant variation during the eighteenth century, then the Mexican miner could not expect any stimulus from the market he supplied.[4] Any analysis of the industry can ignore the role of demand: it was changes in the organisation of supply that determined the curve of production.

1 Juan Moreno y Castro, *Arte ó nuevo modo be beneficiar los metales de oro y plata* (Mexico, 1758). Francisco Javier de Sarria, *Ensayo de metalurgia* (Mexico, 1784). José Garcés y Eguía, *Nueva teórica y práctica del beneficio de los metales* (Mexico, 1802). Frederick Sonneschmid, *Tratado de amalgamación de Nueva España* (Paris, Mexico, 1825).

2 See Humboldt, *Ensayo político*, p. 333.

3 Harold Barger and Samuel H. Schurr, *The Mining Industries 1899–1939. A Study of Output, Employment and Productivity* (New York, 1944), pp. 250–3.

4 Humboldt, *Ensayo político*, pp. 426–7.

Structure of silver production

The Mexican silver industry was organised into three distinct stages: the extraction of the ore-bearing mineral from the earth; the refining or separation of silver from the base metal; and the final conversion of all silver into coin. The structure of production was determined both by the

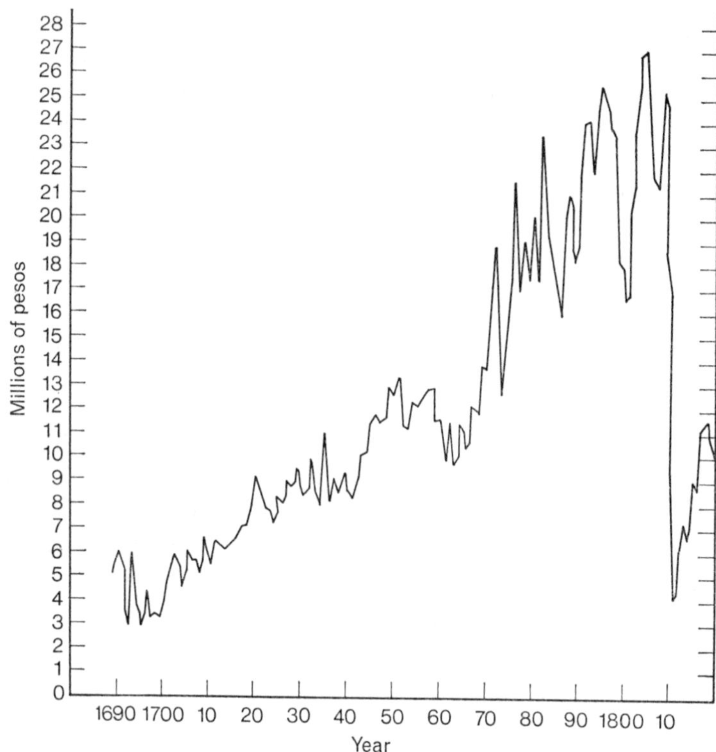

Fig. 1. *Mintage of Silver and Gold in Mexico 1690–1820.*

techniques employed and the regulations and fiscal demands of the Spanish Crown. We shall first analyse this structure and then describe in a succeeding chapter the progress of individual enterprises. It should be noted that the bulk of our material deals with the latter half of the eighteenth century.

I

By the legal definition of 1584 a mine comprised a rectangle staked above the surface, 120 yards long and 60 yards wide.[1] As was to be expected this ruling provoked innumerable disputes concerning interior demarcation,

[1] Gamboa, *Comentarios*, pp. 495–7.

so in the new code of 1783 all mines, by then extended to an area 200 yards long and 100 yards wide, were finally measured underground along the actual lode.[1] Although individuals were forbidden to own adjacent mines, companies could occupy four in a row, and the lode's discoverer three.[2] By the eighteenth century it was customary to divide a mine into 24 shares. But ownership depended upon effective exploitation since the Crown still regarded all precious minerals as its regalian property and hence only conceded working rights. All miners had to register their claim at the local treasury. Failure to maintain at least four workers within the site for a period of more than four consecutive months entailed a lapse of ownership; any newcomer was then free to open the mine afresh.[3]

But such textbook definitions tell us remarkably little about the three thousand odd mines found in New Spain by the last decades of the colonial period. Most were exploited by means of a perpendicular shaft cut directly from the surface to the lode. True, in the first years, and in some areas, especially in Chihuahua, these shafts amounted to little more than pits in the ground.[4] But for the most of the industry deep-shaft mining became the rule during the eighteenth century. At the beginning of the century depths of 130 yards were recorded at Parral.[5] Yet by 1797 the Vetagrande Company at Zacatecas had cut a general shaft 360 yards deep.[6] The extent of the change can be observed at the Veta Vizcaína in Real del Monte where depths increased from 143 yards in the 1720s to 375 yards by 1790.[7] Nor are these isolated cases. In Bolaños, a camp only discovered in 1736, the chief shaft had been driven 272 yards down by 1790 and the company which owned the property planned to drop it further to 345 yards.[8] None of these mines, however, could compare with the Valenciana, which by 1810 attained a depth of 635 yards, the deepest point then known in the entire world.[9] In Europe, for example, depths were less spectacular; in English coalmining no more than 331 yards; and in Saxon silver mines, 393 yards.[10] Moreover, the Valenciana's shaft was

1 Beleña, *Recopilación*, II, 242–5.
2 *Ibid.*, II, 258–62.
3 *Ibid.*, II, 249.
4 Gamboa, *Comentarios*, pp. 503–4.
5 West, *The Mining Community*, pp. 17–18.
6 AGI, Mexico 1587, statement by Vetagrande company's manager, March 1797.
7 Humboldt, *Ensayo político*, pp. 361–2; José Rodrigo de Castelazo, *Manifiesto de la riqueza de la negociación de minas conocidas por la Veta Vizcaína* (Mexico, 1820), p. 18.
8 AGN, Minería 94/5, agent of Bolaños company, 18 July 1791.
9 Ward, *Mexico in 1827*, II, 440.
10 T. S. Ashton and Joseph Sykes, *The Coal Industry of the Eighteenth Century* (Manchester, 1964), p. 10; Humboldt, *Ensayo político*, pp. 353, 356.

constructed on a scale that surprised foreign observers; its circumference extended 32 yards around.

Although many Mexican mines easily surpassed their European counterparts in depth and magnitude, their technology trailed far behind. No attempt was made to excavate by measured sections and since almost no cross galleries were cut, few mules or wagons could be used. Instead a series of small work tunnels led off from the foot of the shaft in all directions, to follow the lode wherever it took them.[1] A Mexican mine resembled a vast honeycomb, an underground city built of small streets twisting and turning at different levels.

To extract the ore from the lode the mine workers wielded a rather heavy, clumsy iron pick, an instrument much the same as that introduced by German miners in the sixteenth century.[2] Many mines set up under ground forges to sharpen these tools, which for the most part were locally fashioned from iron bar imported from Spain. But during the eighteenth century the Mexican miner came increasingly to rely upon gunpowder.[3] Just when the employment of blasting cartridges became widespread in New Spain is not known, but in Guanajuato local tradition asserts that José de Sardaneta, the proprietor of the Rayas, was the first Mexican to adopt the technique. Certainly in 1730 the *Mexico City Gazette* drew attention to a shaft 152 yards deep which Sardaneta had cut in two years using 'pick and gunpowder'.[4] Evidently, blasting was still not common, since in 1732 Zacatecas bought but 1,300 pounds of gunpowder, an insignificant quantity when compared to the 90,000 pounds annually consumed in Guanajuato during the years 1778–95.[5] Here then, we encounter a striking technical innovation. As a result mining became cheaper and more efficient. The rapid construction of the great shafts and adits of the eighteenth century clearly depended upon the introduction of underground blasting.

Once the ore was extracted and gathered into large leather bags, porters (called *tenateros*) carried the mineral on their shoulders, clambering through tunnels and climbing up narrow steps until they reached the foot

[1] Howe, *The Mining Guild*, Appendix C, pp. 472–89.

[2] Humboldt, *Ensayo político*, p. 366.

[3] West, *The Mining Community*, p. 21. We may note that underground blasting was first employed in Cornwall in 1689. In coal mining the technique spread slowly in the following century. See John Rowe, *Cornwall in the Age of the Industrial Revolution* (Liverpool, 1953), p. 9; Ashton and Sykes, *The Coal Industry*, p. 150.

[4] *Gacetas de México*, ed. Francisco González de Cossío (3 vols., 1944–50), I, 262.

[5] Joseph de Rivera Bernárdez, Conde de Santiago de la Laguna, *Descripción breve de la muy noble y leal ciudad de Zacatecas* (Mexico, 1732), p. 46. AGI, Mexico 1795, report of Guanajuato treasury officials, 27 October 1795.

of the vertically driven shaft. There, in the more shallow mines, not deeper than a hundred yards, or in the more remote regions like Durango, the men then had to mount a rough wooden ladder.[1] Since their loads could weigh anywhere between 150 and 330 pounds accidents were not infrequent.[2] Gemelli Carreri, who climbed one of those ladders unburdened, described the occasion as the most frightening experience of his life.[3]

But in the course of the eighteenth century, as mines were driven even deeper, Mexican miners came to reply upon whims—simple windlass hoists drawn by teams of four or more horses and mules—to haul the ore up the shaft. These machines belonged to the more advanced variety, with pulleys set over the pithead and the drum placed over 30 yards away. In 1738 in the Mellado mine at Guanajuato, the two whims which serviced its main shaft hoisted, every 24 hours, some 400 loads, each averaging up to 875 pounds of mineral.[4] This performance was later bettered at Real del Monte where in 1803 Humboldt found great double-sized whims drawn by eight horses with a load capacity of 1,250 pounds.[5] This report tallies with an estimate for the Veta Vizcaína mines which claimed a quadruple increase in haulage power during the century.[6] But many miners found it more efficient to install several medium-sized machines in one shaft. Here the Valenciana took the prize with no less than eight whims grouped around a main shaft constructed in octagonal form.[7] By this time four machines in one shaft were quite common in contrast to the one or two found at the beginning of the period.

These more powerful whims became all the more necessary as drainage problems increased. For most deep mines were engaged in an endless Canute's battle against rising water levels, to the point where they brought to the surface far more water than mineral. 'Water,' wrote the Mexican jurisconsult, Francisco Javier de Gamboa, 'is the greatest obstacle in mining. Strike the mine's lode, and water springs forth like blood from the veins of a body.'[8] There were only two methods to drain a mine. The first and simplest was to drive an existing or new shaft beyond the work area to the water's source, and then drain the level by daily employment of the whim. Provided no endless flooding occurred, this method was feasible and

1 Ward, *Mexico in 1827*, II, 565.

2 Luis Chávez Orozco, ed., *Conflicto de trabajo con los mineros de Real del Monte, año de 1766* (Mexico, 1960), pp. 36, 104, 228; Humboldt, *Ensayo político*, p. 368.

3 Gemelli Carreri, *Viaje*, I, 130.

4 *Gacetas de México*, III, 143.

5 Humboldt, *Ensayo político*, p. 369.

6 Castelazo, *Manifiesto*, p. 26.

7 Ward, *Mexico in 1827*, II, 444.

8 Gamboa, *Comentarios*, p. 354.

frequently successful. But if a continual heavy influx of water persisted, as distinct from the usual seepage, then the use of whims for drainage purposes alone could be prohibitively expensive. The Count of Regla reckoned that in 1801 he spent 250,000 ps. a year to maintain 28 machines in his Veta Vizcaína mines.[1] The chief cost, apart from initial capital expenditure, lay in the food and maintenance of the mules or horses. The 14–16 whims of the Quebradilla mine in Zacatecas required 800 horses to operate them, and these animals consumed 18,000 fanegas of maize a year.[2] The Veta Negra mine in Sombrerete required 29 whims operated by a thousand horses.[3] Any increase in the price of maize and hay could easily drive the miner close to bankruptcy. In addition, the leather and cord for the bags which had to be replaced every eight days were quite expensive. In 1732 Zacatecas miners spent 14,000 ps. on these articles, a sum roughly equal to what they paid for iron and steel (14,960 ps.) and much more than they paid for gunpowder (1,950 ps.).[4]

The second method of drainage was to cut a horizontal tunnel or adit at the foot of the mountain beneath the lode. By this device water drained off naturally leaving the lode relatively dry. Adits had been cut in the Americas since the sixteenth century; in 1617 an adit was completed at San Luis Potosí which was 250 yards long.[5] But for the Mexican miner such drainage tunnels required heavy initial expense; for him they represented a fixed capital investment—*obras muertas*, dead works—upon which no immediate return could be expected. Their construction demanded a certain mathematical expertise he did not always possess, and, more importantly, entailed financial backing upon a scale he could rarely command. The most successful adit in New Spain was cut to drain the Veta Vizcaína mine in Real del Monte. Although work began in 1739, errors in calculation wasted the first nine years' labour, and another 20 years passed before the owner, the Count of Regla, benefited from the project. By 1781 the adit reached a length of 2,881 yards. Admittedly the length of the Veta Vizcaína's adit was as exceptional as the depth of the Valenciana's main shaft.[6] At Tehuilotepec, for example, José Vicente de Anza took 12 years to cut a tunnel only 477 yards long.[7]

[1] Juan Burkart, 'Memoria de la explotación de las minas de Pachuca y Real del Monte', *Anales de la Minería* (Mexico, 1861), p. 44.

[2] Carlos de Berghes, *Descripción de la serranía de Zacatecas formada por I. A. Bustamante* (Mexico, 1834), pp. 22–3.

[3] AGI, Mexico 2214, Marquis of Apartado to viceroy, 31 August 1793.

[4] Rivera Bernárdez, *Descripción breve*, pp. 44–6.

[5] Borah, *Un gobierno provincial*, pp. 538–9.

[6] Castelazo, *Manifiesto*, pp. 10, 16; Gamboa, *Comentarios*, p. 477.

[7] AGI, Mexico 1571, Branciforte to Gardoqui, 28 September 1793.

Both methods were expensive, and since both shafts and adits represented heavy fixed investment many owners, accustomed to rapid easy profits, preferred to desert their mines rather than risk their fortunes. The productive life span of a Mexican mine was short; few enjoyed an uninterrupted cycle of production for more than 30 years; and most experienced short hectic booms which were soon broken by flooding and abandonment. In the course of the eighteenth century the Quebradilla at Zacatecas had three separate booms separated by long years of flooding. The Veta Vizcaína of Real del Monte was three times left deserted by its owners. Mining still remained a gamble; the trick was to know when to quit.

Within this cycle of discovery, abandonment and renovation, the tendency existed for the units of production to grow larger. In part this simply meant that shafts were driven deeper. But also it meant that by the close of the century many individual mines possessed several shafts. The Pabellón at Sombrerete comprised five shafts 'three of them with boxed compartments for eight whims in each one'.[1] The Quebradilla had five shafts and the Valenciana at Guanajuato four.[2] In certain camps the entire lode was dominated by one enterprise. By 1762 the Count of Regla, for example, had unified all the mines that lay along the Veta Vizcaína lode in virtue of which he dominated the Real del Monte camp.[3] In 1761 the five principal mines of Bolaños were abandoned following severe drainage problems. During the 1770s the entire lode was drained and its exploitation unified by Antonio de Bibanco.[4] In large measure this drive towards larger enterprises was imposed by the heavy costs of drainage. Its result was a startling increase in the number of persons employed. By 1766 Regla at the Veta Vizcaína hired over a thousand workers.[5] But in 1809 the Quebradilla required 2,550 men and women and the Valenciana, New Spain's largest enterprise, had over 3,000 workers.[6]

By the close of the century, therefore, the Mexican mining industry had attained a high degree of concentration. Its greatest firms represented fixed investments worth over a million pesos and employed over a thousand workers. Such mines were to be found in most of the great minefields and they accounted for a significant share of total silver production. Yet probably not more than ten such enterprises existed at any one time.

1 AGI, Mexico 2214, Marquis of Apartado to viceroy, 31 August 1793.
2 Berghes, *Descripción*, pp. 22–3; Humboldt, *Ensayo político*, pp. 553–4.
3 Chávez Orozco, ed., *Conflicto de trabajo*, p. 71.
4 See D. A. Brading, 'La minería de la plata en el siglo XVIII: El caso Bolaños', *Historia Mexicana*, 18 (1969), 3, pp. 317–33.
5 AGN, Minería 148/8, report of Pedro José de Leoz, 11 June 1770.
6 Berghes, *Descripción*, pp. 22–3; Humboldt, *Ensayo político*, pp. 553–4.

Moreover, a large amount of silver was also produced by small camps and solitary mines, often of ephemeral duration, which in the short term frequently yielded high profits to the speculative businessman. There was a continuum in the size of the industry's units of production—a scale which ranged from the barest pit in the ground to the Valenciana. A typical or average Mexican mine did not exist.

II

Since the chemical explanation of how silver was separated from the base metal in which it was found had yet to be defined, refining still remained a highly empirical art, a kind of cookery, governed by the practical tests of experienced workmen. Two methods could be used—a quick boil or a slow simmer. The metal could be smelted or subjected to a slow amalgamation with mercury. Which process was chosen depended upon the quality of the ore. All high-grade ore and mineral which contained admixtures of lead or lead compounds was smelted whereas average and low-grade ore was amalgamated.

Smelting, although a relatively simple affair, required elaborate equipment. The ore was first crushed by a stamp mill into a fine rice-like grain, after which it was burnt in small furnaces to eliminate all sulphur. Then it was mixed with litharge, lead and cinders and smelted in a large Castilian furnace, built in the shape of a pyramid. Depending upon local custom or the quality of the ore, other materials such as iron or copper pyrites were added to this central smelting process. Finally, the resulting compound was burnt again in small furnaces to separate the lead from the silver.[1] The actual smelting only took 24 hours so it offered miners the advantage of immediate access to their silver. Improvements were made during the 1780s by José Garcés y Eguía, who, by the addition of the salt known locally as *tequesquite*, was able to separate more silver.[2] For the general deficiency of this method lay in its inefficiency: it failed to refine all the silver. Besides it was expensive: the furnaces consumed great quantities of charcoal and wood, which in the older mining camps had to be brought from great distances since the surrounding countryside was long since deforested. Then again, the compounds, the lead, litharge and salts employed were required in bulk. Camps such as Guanajuato, Pachuca and Zacatecas were obliged to obtain their lead compounds from San Luis Potosí or Zimapán.[3]

[1] West, *The Mining Community*, pp. 27–30. Also Garcés, *Nueva teórica*, p. 105.
[2] Garcés, *Nueva teórica*, pp. 49–60.
[3] *Representaciones del real tribunal de minería a favor de su importante cuerpo* (Mexico, 1781), p. 6.

Tequesquite was found at Peñón Blanco, situated between Zacatecas and San Luis Potosí, so that Garcés' discovery was mainly applied in those camps which lay closest to its source. For these reasons smelting only yielded a clear profit when applied to high-grade ores, so that it was most commonly used in the first days of a mining bonanza. Similarly, in all camps occasional pieces of almost solid silver were encountered for which only smelting was suitable. In San Luis Potosí and Mazapil the mineral which had a high admixture of lead resisted amalgamation with mercury; in consequence at Zimapán all ore was smelted.[1]

The amalgamation, or patio method, was a lengthy, complicated process which could take up to two months to complete. The ore was first crushed by a stamp mill, operated by water power at Pachuca and other hill camps, or, as was more general in the north, by mules. The mineral was then transferred to an *arrastre* or *tahona*, a mule-drawn contrivance, in which it was ground into a fine powder by the constant movement of the arrastres' heavy stones.[2] At this stage mercury was sometimes added. The powder was then laid out in an open courtyard, and divided into piles containing between 15 and 32 cwt. For each hundredweight of ore about 2½ to 5 pounds of salt, 5–10 pounds of copper pyrites and 15-20 pounds of lime were added and thoroughly mixed together. Mercury was added in proportion, not to the ore, but to the expected yield of silver, some 3–4 pounds being needed for the separation of a mark of silver.[3]

The pile remained in the open patio, where it was periodically stirred. Experienced refiners inspected the mixture and added mercury, salt or copper pyrites according to their opinion of its progress. The process could last from two weeks to two months, varying in response to the season, the quality of the ore, and the skill of the workmen. The resulting blend was then washed by the river, along which refining mills were invariably situated. With the base metal washed away, the remaining amalgam was burnt to separate the mercury from the silver. About a quarter of the mercury used was lost in the process—about 12 ounces for every mark of silver produced.[4]

Few if any substantial modifications occurred in the patio method from its introduction during the sixteenth century until its final supersession in the 1890s by the cyanide process. In 1802 José Garcés y Eguía, a knowledgeable refiner, wrote: 'In general the patio process soon arrived at a certain point beyond which it has not passed in the space of two centuries.'[5]

[1] Ward, *Mexico in 1827*, II, 335–6.
[2] Bergher and Schurr, *The Mining Industries*, p. 151.
[3] Garcés, *Nueva teórica*, p. 91.
[4] Sonneschmid, *Tratado de amalgamación*, p. 53.
[5] Garcés, *Nueva teórica*, p. 105.

Significant change is hard to find. In 1777 José Cornejo sponsored the use of mules instead of men to stir the piles of metal in the patio. He conducted tests at Taxco, and proved that mules were cheaper and more efficient than men. His 'invention' was quickly adopted throughout the industry.[1]

At Catorce the *caso* method, first invented by the Peruvian Alonso Barba during the seventeenth century, was commonly used. This was a rapid amalgamation by fire. The ore was placed in a copper cauldron or pan, mixed with salt, copper pyrites and mercury, and then smelted. But only two-thirds or at most three-quarters of the silver was separated; moreover, the copper of the pan tended to mix with the silver.[2] For these reasons the method was not widely employed. But at Catorce, during the 1790s this process was substantially improved by a Basque miner, Francisco Miguel de Aguirre. He installed two circular discs of copper into the furnace, on which were deposited the usual amounts of mercury, salt, copper pyrites and ore. During the 24 hours' smelting the copper plates revolved, propelled by a lever, drawn by mules. Only between four and six ounces of mercury were lost for every mark of silver produced. But the initial expense was high, since some 80 cwt. of copper were required to construct the furnace. About half the silver was extracted from the ore; the residue was then subjected to the normal patio process.[3]

No dramatic technical innovation transformed the refining methods of Mexican silver mining. But during the eighteenth century existing techniques were better and more widely applied; and marginal improvements were more rapidly diffused throughout the industry. What T. S. Ashton wrote of British coal mining applies equally well to Mexican silver mining: 'No flash of genius of a Crompton or a Watt could transform coal-mining. Better methods had to be slowly forged from the painful experience of common men, and only gradually did a new idea or a new device spread from pit to pit, or from one coal field to another.'[4]

During the 1770s, however, one significant change in the pattern of refining did occur. In an earlier period up to a third of all silver was produced by smelting, whereas by 1803 Humboldt placed the ratio at one part smelted to three and a half parts amalgamated, and at the same time

[1] AGI, Mexico 1577, Branciforte to Gardoqui, 26 June 1796.

[2] Garcés, *Nueva teórica*, pp. 80–2; Sonneschmid, *Tratado de amalgamación*, pp. 88–9.

[3] AGI, Mexico 2247, report of Fermín de Reigadas, contained in letter of Pablo Macedo y Gama to Soler, 23 August 1803; Ward, *Mexico in 1827*, II, 512–15.

[4] Ashton and Sykes, *The Coal Industry*, p. 12.

Garcés y Eguía reckoned that no more than 13·5 per cent was smelted.[1] That the decisive decade for this changeover was the 1770s can be proved from the Zacatecas treasury records. In 1763, 34 per cent of the town's silver was separated by smelting; by 1770, 30 per cent; by 1779, 18 per cent; and by 1806, only 15 per cent.[2] The switch to the more efficient method of refining was largely caused by the royal decision to cut the price of mercury by half. The reduction in price of the most costly component of the amalgamation process permitted the application of the method to a far wider range of ores. We shall discuss the precise effects of this reduction somewhat later.

A refining mill, *hacienda de beneficio*, constituted a large industrial enterprise. It required a gallery to house the stamp mills and arrastres, a large open patio, furnaces, washing sheds, storage rooms for mercury and other raw materials, and stables for mules. Size was usually estimated by the number of arrastres it possessed since these measured capacity to treat ore. The units of production, as in mining itself, varied greatly from a mere collection of huts containing one or two arrastres or a small furnace to great fortified establishments. Once again, as in mining, enterprises tended to grow in size during the course of the century. To service the output of the Veta Vizcaína mines the Count of Regla constructed a huge refining mill at the cost of nearly half a million pesos.[3] It contained 24 arrastres moved by water wheels, furnaces, and two covered patios. At Zacatecas José de la Borda's Holy Family mill, in 1775 the largest in the north, housed 70 arrastres and 10 stamp mills, yet by 1800 at Sombrerete the Fagoaga family's mill had 84 arrastres and 14 furnaces.[4] Such establishments, the largest of their day, clearly represented capital investment upon a scale only made possible by the vast profits which resulted from the unification of entire lodes under a single ownership. But alongside these great mills there still persisted the petty refiners who bought small amounts of metal from the lesser miners or the mine workers. A typical refining mill no more existed than an average mine.

III

The Spanish Crown levied a 10 per cent tax on all silver extracted; it monopolised the sale of mercury and gunpowder; and it demanded that all silver be sent to Mexico City for coinage at the royal mint. At every

[1] Humboldt, *Ensayo político*, p. 372; Garcés, *Nueva teórica*, p. 126.

[2] AGI, Guadalajara, 477, 478; AGI, Mexico 2032, Zacatecas treasury officials' accounts.

[3] Humboldt, *Ensayo político*, p. 361; Ward, *Mexico in 1827*, II, 538.

[4] AGN, Minería 115/1, report by Borda's manager, 6 March 1780; Ward, *Mexico in 1827*. II, 540.

stage of production, therefore, the Mexican miner was loaded with a heavy burden of law and regulation.

After 1663 the Crown entrusted the distribution of mercury to the treasury officials, at much the same time setting up provincial cajas in all the chief mining camps.[1] These officials distributed the mercury in bulk on a six-months' credit to refiners, miners and their merchant backers. Before the year was out, each recipient had to pay into the treasury a quantity of silver exactly proportional to his allocation of mercury. The usual proportion was 100 marks of silver for a hundredweight of mercury, but rates varied from camp to camp, San Luis Potosí yielding but 80 marks whereas in Guanajuato 125 marks were demanded.[2] Overall supervision of the monopoly was exercised by a series of judges, recruited from the Mexican audiencia.[3] Following the retirement of Domingo Valcárcel in 1783, the monopoly's direction was first united to the superintendency of the mint, and then, in 1786, to the newly created *superintendente subdelegado de real hacienda.* But since, a year later, this office, as an independent entity was suppressed, the viceroy then assumed the responsibility. José de Iturrigaray, Viceroy of New Spain, 1803–8, converted this charge into a means of personal profit, taking bribes for extra awards of mercury to individual miners.[4]

Supply of this indispensable catalyst was always precarious. But here the Bourbon dynasty, aided by German mining experts, succeeded in thoroughly renovating Almadén. In consequence that great mercury mine, which at the beginning of the eighteenth century could rarely supply the 4,000–5,000 cwt. required by the Mexican industry, by 1775 despatched no less than 10,000 cwt. to New Spain.[5] At the same time production and transport costs evidently fell, since Gálvez, in two steps, reduced the price of mercury from 82 ps. 4 rls. 9 grs. (granos) per cwt. to 41 ps. 2 rls. 11 grs.[6] Even at this new rate the Crown still made a 10 ps. profit on each cwt. Transport costs from Mexico City to the treasuries were charged to the account of the recipients, a system which naturally added to the financial burdens of the northern miners. In 1796 it cost 10⅓ ps. to take a hundredweight of mercury to Chihuahua, compared to

1 Fonseca and Urrutia, *Historia general de Real Hacienda*, I, 311.
2 *Ibid.*, I, 383.
3 *Ibid.*, I, 325, 330, 357; see also AGI, Mexico 2207, Revillagigedo to Valdés, 21 April 1789.
4 AGI, Mexico 1633, Guanajuato deputation statement, 31 October 1808.
5 AGI, Mexico 2202, Tomás Ortiz de Landázuri to Gálvez, 27 February 1777.
6 Elhuyar, *Indagaciones*, pp. 125–7; Fonseca and Urrutia, *Historia general de Real Hacienda*, I, 343, 348. The old price was 82 ps. 5 rls. 9 grs.; on 24 November 1767, it was reduced to 62 ps. 4 grs.; and on 4 October 1776 it was reduced to 41 ps. 2 rls. 2 grs.

$4\frac{1}{2}$ ps. to Zacatecas, just under 3 ps. to Guanajuato, and less than 1 ps. to Pachuca.[1] The Crown itself paid the 3 ps. collected for carriage from Veracruz to Mexico City.

By the close of the 1780s the Mexican industry consumed over 16,000 cwt. of mercury a year, with Guanajuato the leading camp alone taking over 4,000 cwt.[2] Apprehensive that Almadén might prove unable to satisfy this rising demand, the Crown signed a contract with the Austrian court for an annual quota from Germany of not less than 8,000 cwt. of mercury for a six-year period.[3] Nevertheless, such heavy dependence upon an imported raw material made the industry highly vulnerable to the frequent British naval blockades brought about by Spain's alliance with France. Each time Spain declared war on Great Britain, Mexican silver production fell. In 1781 the Crown therefore abandoned its former prohibition against the exploitation of local mercury mines. Indeed, in 1778 Gálvez sent over Rafael Helling, a German mining expert, who since 1755 had worked at Almadén. Accompanied by the Mexican savant, José Antonio Alzate Ramírez, he inspected and tested all known mercury deposits, but found only a few surface veins, of poor quality. The expedition cost the Crown 151,000 ps. and achieved nothing.[4] Attempts were also made to stockpile. Between 13 November 1801 and 18 May 1803, 85,093 cwt. of mercury were despatched to New Spain; yet by January 1804 the viceroy reported that he had already distributed 64,011 cwt., leaving little more than a year's supply in stock.[5]

By law, all silver, once cast into bar, had to be presented at the nearest treasury. There a 10 per cent tax and 1 per cent charge for assay, and the cost of mercury supplied on credit were all deducted. During the seventeenth century a distinction was maintained between miners and refiners or merchant aviadores: the two latter classes paid 20 per cent. In actual fact, nearly all silver was registered under the name of miners; at Pachuca during the years 1671–3 only 45 marks were collected as fifths compared to the 8,381 marks paid as tithes.[6] In June 1723 this distinction was finally abolished and a flat 10 per cent levied on all silver, be it presented by merchant or miner.[7]

1 AGI, Mexico 1580, Branciforte to Varela, 28 March 1797.

2 AGI, Mexico 1545, Revillagigedo to Lerena, 29 November 1791.

3 AGI, Mexico 2208, Mangino to Crown, 26 September 1787.

4 AGI, Mexico 2203, Bucareli to Gálvez, 24 February 1779. Permission to mine mercury *real cédula*, 21 May 1781—in Mayorga to Gálvez, 1 October 1781.

5 AGI, Mexico 1620, Iturrigaray to Soler, 27 March 1804; AGI, Mexico 2213, Iturrigaray to Soler, 27 May 1803.

6 *Instrucciones que los virreyes dejaron*, p. 293.

7 Fonseca and Urrutia, *Historia general de Real Hacienda*, I, 20–2.

A significant change in the burden of taxation occurred in the decades that followed 1769. In that year Gálvez, to encourage José de la Borda to go to Zacatecas to drain the Quebradilla mine, granted the famous miner a complete exemption from the silver tithe until the initial cost of restoration was reimbursed, to be followed by a 50 per cent exemption for the subsequent 15 years. For the entire period Borda was also supplied mercury at the cost price of 30 ps. per cwt.[1] At much the same time two other miners, José de Moya at Pachuca and Cayetano Núñez de Ibarra at Temascaltepec, were conceded similar tax exemptions.[2] Thereafter such fiscal backing to miners who attempted to renovate old, waterlogged mines became quite common. By 1810 three of the major mines in Zacatecas—the Vetagrande, the Quebradilla and the San Francisco—all enjoyed these tax rebates. The Fagoagas at Sombrerete and Juan Sierra Uruñuela at Bolaños were also encouraged by such benefits.[3] On the other hand, in Guanajuato and Catorce, the industry's most successful camps, such exemptions were not to be found: it was only in the older, more marginal camps with waterlogged mines that the Crown granted these fiscal subsidies to production. Naturally it still retained the profits of mintage.

After taxation the treasury despatched all silver bar by mule-train to Mexico City. There, the royal mint cut 69 rls. from every mark of silver, of which 65 rls., the legal price, were returned to the owner.[4] At the beginning of the century mintage was a lengthy process, the more especially since the Crown had rented the office to private individuals who lacked funds to purchase the bar as it arrived in the capital. Most miners, therefore, preferred to sell their silver to merchants or silver banks resident in Mexico City at a discount of a real in every mark exchanged.[5] This unsatisfactory system was terminated in 1729 when the Crown appointed salaried officials, housed the mint in a magnificent new edifice, and set up a revolving fund of half a million pesos for immediate purchase of all silver. In 1732, the quality or grade of the silver in the coinage was reduced from 11 dineros 4 granos (268 grains) to a straight 11 dineros. In effect this meant that $69\frac{3}{10}$ rls. could be cut from a mark.[6] Yet at the same time the price paid by the mint to the public was reduced from 65 rls. to

[1] AGI, Mexico 2235, report by accountant-general, Tomás de Landázuri, 21 November 1767; *real orden* approving exemption, 12 April 1768.

[2] Fonseca and Urrutia, *Historia general de Real Hacienda*, I, 348, 355–6.

[3] See below, chapter on 'The Great Enterprises'.

[4] Fonseca and Urrutia, *Historia general de Real Hacienda*, I, iii–2.

[5] *Ibid.*, I, 145–6; Elhuyar, *Indagaciones*, pp. 8–9.

[6] Elhuyar, *Indagaciones*, pp. 14–39.

64 rls. 2 maravedis. The remainder went to the Crown. A further devaluation in the fineness of the coinage occurred in 1772 when the silver quality fell to 10 ds. 20 grs. (260 grains) and again in 1786 when the grade was stabilised at 10 ds. 18 grs.[1] Profits from this debasement, although great, were of course occasional and in no sense approached the annual yield. By 1804 the Mexican mint employed over four hundred workers and had the capacity to coin over 30 million pesos a year.[2] Its efficiency had improved considerably, since whereas in 1733 it cost 1¾ rls. to turn a mark into coin, by 1804 the cost had fallen to ¾rl.[3] By then the annual return to the Crown averaged at least one-and-a-half million pesos a year.

The Crown's monopoly of the third stage of Mexico's national industry weighed heavily upon the producers of the raw material. For the northern mines especially the cost in time was high: at Catorce or Durango miners might have to wait six months for the return of their silver in specie. The tardy development of the Sonoran minefields in part sprang from the Crown's insistence that silver could only be minted in Mexico City. It was only during the 1790s that this burden was lightened. In that decade each treasury established a revolving fund of specie with which to purchase silver directly when the miners presented it for taxation. Discounts on this exchange still varied according to proximity to Mexico City. In Guanajuato miners received 62 rls. 25 ms., whereas in Durango the treasury paid 62 rls. 17 ms.[4]

The Crown's new-found efficiency and flexibility further benefited the industry when during his Visitation Gálvez installed salaried officials to manage the production and sale of gunpowder, hitherto farmed out to private individuals. He reduced the price from 8 rls. to 6 rls. a pound. A large factory was constructed outside Mexico City, which employed 80 workers, and which in 1801 produced over 786,000 pounds of gunpowder.[5] It was in that same year that the price was further lowered to 4 rls. a pound.[6]

Finally, miners were exempted from paying the alcabalas, or sales tax, upon their raw materials and supplies. The new customs department, established in 1776, first tried to collect a 6 per cent duty on nearly all the

[1] Florescano, *Precios del maíz*, p. 80.
[2] Humboldt, *Ensayo político*, p. 458.
[3] Elhuyar, *Indagaciones*, p. 36.
[4] María Pilar Mariscal Romero, *Los bancos de rescate de plata* (Seville, 1964), p. 19, footnote.
[5] Fonseca and Urrutia, *Historia general de Real Hacienda*, II, 203, 210, First reduction, 3 February 1767. Humboldt, *Ensayo político*, pp. 454–5.
[6] AGI, Mexico 2247, Iturrigaray to Soler, 26 April 1804, *real orden*, 27 April 1801.

materials used by both miners and refiners. But in 1781 in response to the industry's vigorous protest, the viceroy, Mayorga decreed that all mining instruments should be relieved of the excise.[1] Four years later this exemption was extended to all raw materials needed for smelting and amalgamation. The excise officials protested against the concessions, and controversy between government departments as to the precise extension of these alcabala exemptions persisted until 1810. Dispute especially centered upon the maize brought into camps to feed the mules and workers employed by the industry. To encourage important discoveries, moreover, the Crown frequently granted temporary relief from all excise duties. Both Catorce in 1779 and Guarisamey in 1787 enjoyed total exemption from these imposts for periods of up to four years.[2]

Table 9 *Royal revenue raised from Mexican mining, 1789.* (In pesos)

	Gross	Net
Silver tithes	2,019,576	2,019,576
Mintage charges	1,766,202	1,417,140
Gunpowder	702,714	405,864
Spanish mercury	297,415	262,096
German mercury	495,388	465,297
Total	5,281,295	4,569,973

In general, therefore, in the decades that followed the Gálvez Visitation, royal policy towards the Mexican silver mining industry became more flexible and more intelligent. Old burdens were lightened or eliminated, and a series of extraordinary fiscal subsidies were extended to individual miners and particular camps. These concessions, general and particular alike, were justified in the official mind by the argument that all tax or monopoly price reductions had resulted in an increased production of such proportion that overall tax yield and monopoly profits, instead of declining, almost immediately augmented. Moreover, mintage profits rose steadily. In all the Spanish Crown gained the revenue shown in table 9 from the Mexican silver industry.[3]

It is estimated that taxation and mintage charges absorbed $16\frac{2}{3}$ per cent of all silver produced. But since part of the mint profits were gained by a

[1] AGI, Mexico 1133, *consulta* of Council of the Indies, 22 March 1786. See also the mining court's published *Representaciones* . . . (Mexico, 1781).

[2] For Catorce see AGI, Mexico 1730, audiencia gobernadora to Gálvez, 22 August 1779. For Guarisamey see AGI, Mexico 2242, Flores to Valdés, 26 September 1789.

[3] AGI, Mexico 2026, Revillagigedo to Lerena, 8 February 1791.

slight debasement of the coinage the actual total levy upon the miner was closer to 13 per cent.[1]

IV

Mexican mine-workers, far from being the oppressed peons of legend, constituted a free, well-paid, geographically mobile labour force which in many areas acted as the virtual partners of the owners. Sir Henry Ward noted: 'There are particular tribes of natives, who have been miners from generation to generation, and who lead a roving life, migrating with their wives and children, from one district to another, as they are attracted by fame of superior riches.'[2] His observations applied with especial force to the north: the rapidity with which new discoveries such as Bolaños and Catorce were able within a few years to attract and sustain populations of 12,000 and 20,000 persons indicates the mobility of the northern mine-worker. These men were largely mulattoes and mestizos. Lucas Alamán contrasted the labour force of camps near Mexico City with that of the the north.

> The inhabitants are not by any means, apt miners, being mostly Indians, who are much more ready at agriculture; whilst in the districts of the first group (Guanajuato, Zacatecas, Sombrerete) they are chiefly mulattoes and mestizos, both which castes are better adapted for occupations requiring energy of body or mind; the former are awkward and inefficient workmen, using a great deal more powder than is required.[3]

The vast majority of Mexican miners—they did not number more than 45,000 individuals—worked voluntarily.[4] Draft Indian labour was still recruited, however, especially in camps such as Real del Monte and Pachuca that lay near to Mexico City. The Count of Regla obtained a levy of 4 per cent of the male labour force from all villages that lay within a 30-mile radius of Real del Monte. But the alcaldes mayores, the hacendados, and the parish priests of the area all resisted his demands, arguing that their Indians were best suited for agriculture.[5] Elsewhere other miners appealed for these levies. But even where such Indians were recruited they served as little more than auxiliary workers. Within the Mexican mining industry at large the role of drafted Indian labour dwindled to insignificant proportions during the course of the eighteenth century.

On the other hand, in contrast to its concern for the Indian, the Crown explicitly permitted the forcible recruitment of any vagrant or unoccupied

1 Elhuyar, *Indagaciones*, p. 59; Humboldt, *Ensayo político*, p. 400.
2 Ward, *Mexico in 1827*, II, 145.
3 UMMA, *Reports*, Lucas Alamán and Lewis Agassiz, 2 October 1826.
4 Humboldt, *Ensayo político*, p. 48.
5 AGN, Minería 45/1, petition to viceroy, 18 June 1776.

mestizos and mulattoes.[1] Many Mexican mining camps, therefore, resembled British seaports of the same epoch. Mine-owners sent out collectors armed with whips who frequently seized anyone they met who was not respectably dressed. In 1792 the official in charge of the royal assay at Pachuca complained that local collectors had taken his peons: 'it has reached the point that they have been seized when they leave the furnace to go home for breakfast'.[2] In Guanajuato similar occurrences were reported. But in all likelihood the majority of such press-ganged workers were miners unoccupied for the moment.

The system of payment for free labour varied from camp to camp. The most common practice was to given all workers, be they pick and blast men, the barreteros and barrenadores, or porters and whim-minders, a standard 4 rls. a day. This rate may be compared to the earnings of hacienda peons who earned 1½ to 2 rls. a day together with food and land.[3] But what attracted men to mining was not their daily wage but a share in the ore. The size of these *partidos*, as the shares were called, also varied greatly. In Guanajuato and Real del Monte, once the worker finished a fixed daily quota of ore, he could split the remainder cut during that day on equal terms with the owner. It was the foreman's task to ensure that neither party was ill-done by the division.[4] In other camps workers took a percentage on all the mineral they produced. At Zacatecas and further north this amounted to a quarter of the total, but at Tlalpujahua José de la Borda only paid a twelfth.[5] In the early days at Catorce this proportion rose to as much as a third, and even a half.[6] But when partidos became so large the workers did not usually receive a wage; at Bolaños, for example, all they were paid was a third of the ore.[7] This latter arrangement resembled the practice common throughout the industry whereby impoverished owners took their workers into partnership, granting them half the mineral and paying little more than overhead costs such as drainage. But this could easily ruin a mine, since the pickmen, *buscones* as they were called, were soon tempted to destroy the ore-bearing pillars which alone prevented the collapse of the work tunnels.[8] Whatever the method of payment most Mexican mine-workers expected a share of the product, and at all times tried to hide the richest ore in their own bags.

[1] Beleña, *Recopilación*, II, 258–61.
[2] AGN, Minería 56/6, manager of Pachuca assay office, 2 May 1792.
[3] Gibson, *The Aztecs*, pp. 250–1, gives scheme of agricultural wages.
[4] Chávez Orozco, ed., *Conflicto de trabajo*, pp. 100–2.
[5] UMMA, *Reports*, 26 May 1826, p. 75.
[6] Ward, *Mexico in 1827*, II, 496.
[7] AGN, Subdelegados 2, treasury officials to Azanza, 17 August 1798.
[8] UMMA, *Reports*, 28 May 1826, p. 22.

Several efforts were made to reform the system but without success, since the miners were notoriously unruly and riot-prone. Many owners, therefore, suffered the mortification of seeing their mines' best mineral sold by their employees to independent refiners.

In the sphere of labour relations, as elsewhere, the Gálvez Visitation inaugurated a new stage. The ruthless suppression of the revolts in San Luis Potosí and Guanajuato, combined with the subsequent enrolment of the respectable classes into regiments of militia, strengthened the power of the mine-owners over their workers. In general, discipline became more stringent and in some camps earnings were reduced. At Real del Monte, for example, the Count of Regla attempted both to cut the daily wages of the peons from 4 to 3 rls. and to reduce the share of ore received by the pickmen. But in response, his men went on strike, closed down the Veta Vizcaína mines, and murdered the local magistrate. Francisco Javier de Gamboa, at that time a judge in the Mexican audiencia, was sent to arbitrate.[1] He restored much of the old order, since he stipulated that all employees, peons as well as pickmen, should be paid 4 rls. a day. As before, foremen were to assign variable quotas according to the type of mineral, especial care being taken to prevent workers reserving for themselves the richest ore. Both the porters and the labourers who repaired the tunnel and shaft supports were entitled to cut up to a bag of ore, subject, however, to division with their employer. Clearly a Mexican mine operated as much for the benefit of its workers as for the owner.

In Guanajuato, on the other hand, the Rayas mine successfully suppressed the payment of all partidos. But other mines only slowly followed this example. It was not until the early 1790s that the great Valenciana mine terminated the practice, being then obliged to more than double the wages of the pickmen. By 1803 they received 10 rls. a day instead of their former 4 rls. and partido.[2] In Zacatecas a similar movement to reduce labour costs occurred. When in 1767 José de la Borda went to that town he took advantage of the current unemployment to reduce the daily wage from the former 6 rls. to the more standard 4 rls. He also lowered the workers' share in all ore produced from a quarter to an eighth.[3] Later, during the first decade of the next century, the new owners of the Quebradilla finally succeeded in eliminating payment of all partidos. The

1 Chávez Orozco, ed., *Conflicto de trabajo*. The entire book is about this dispute.

2 AGN, Minería 58–5, Guanajuato treasury officials to viceroy, 30 March 1774; AGN, Minería 114/4, José Gómez Campos to viceroy, 5 May 1791. For wages see Silva Herzog, *Documentos*, pp. 75–81.

3 AMZ, leg. 23, letter of cura José Antonio Bugarín to intendant Felipe Cleere, undated, 1788/9.

workers in vain petitioned the viceroy to restore the old system.[1] It appears, therefore, that in the years following the Gálvez Visitation Mexican mine-owners launched a concerted attack upon what they considered to be the excessively high earnings of their labour force. Nevertheless in most camps, especially in the north, workers still received a large share of ore and acted as virtual partners if not active rivals of the mine owners.

V

Within the Mexican mining industry a great variety prevailed, both in the size of enterprises and in the degree of vertical integration. It was the great mines, however, such as the Veta Vizcaína and the Valenciana, which attracted travellers' attention. Yet not all these mines refined their own mineral. True, Regla at Real del Monte and the Fagoagas at Sombrerete operated vertically integrated concerns, but at Guanajuato and Catorce the great mines frequently sold a considerable part of their ore to independent refiners. In Zacatecas most mines also possessed refining mills, but even there the partners of the Quebradilla shared out the mine's ore among themselves for individual refining.[2]

In addition to these great enterprises the industry contained a host of small mines, in the same camps or on isolated lodes, whose owners were frequently obliged to sell their metal at once in order to obtain cash to meet their operating costs. Then again workers always sold their *partidos*. So a natural component of the industry was the independent refiner, or *rescatador*. These men bought at the pithead, after merely handling the ore. The prices they paid depended upon competition and their own informal valuation but were in general sufficiently low for them to make considerable profits. Clearly at times if his guess proved wrong, the refiner lost money, but his losses, unlike those of the miner were marginal and cumulative, never total. An English observer stated: 'The great mine-owners of Mexico generally speaking, formerly gained more by the haciendas [refining mills] than by their mines.'[3]

Simple miners, refiners and integrated enterprises all required financial backers or *aviadores*. In 1772 a knowledgeable report claimed that only twelve miners could finance their own operations.[4] Similarly, since independent refiners had to pay cash for all ore, then they too were obliged either to

[1] Miguel Othón de Mendizábal, *Obras completas* (6 vols.; Mexico, 1946–7), v, 207.

[2] UMMA, *Reports*, 28 May 1826, pp. 73–5.

[3] Edward James, *Remark on the Mines, Management, Ores etc. of the District of Guanaxuato, belonging to the Anglo-Mexican Mining Association* (London, 1827), p. 42.

[4] Lucas de Lassaga and Joaquín Velásquez de León, *Representación que a nombre de la minería de esta Nueva España, hacen al Rey* (Mexico, 1774), pp. 19–20.

sell their silver at once or to find an aviador. Miners especially suffered from lack of support; most merchants preferred to back refiners, and when they did support miners they demanded payment every eight to fifteen days, and were quick to cut off credit if a mine ceased to produce.[1] It was for this reason that many miners were forced to sell their ore as soon as it was produced.

The aviador, therefore, usually a local merchant, was an indispensable third agent in the industry. He supplied miners with iron, wood, leather and mules, and refiners with salt, copper pyrites, lime, maize and mercury. He charged these commodities upon account at current market price; upon European goods he added 25 per cent to invoice cost upon landing.[2] In addition the aviador paid the libranzas drawn upon him when the refiner or miner bought his own material. He also advanced the refiner the necessary cash with which to buy ore. In return for this financial backing all silver produced was sold to the aviador at a discount. Formal contracts were rare, balances were struck at infrequent intervals, and nothing was more common than for miners or refiners to overdraw their account. Many an aviador by progressive foreclosure found himself the owner of first a refining mill and then a mine. In mining, as distinct from refining, some aviadores took shares in mines from the outset. They then participated in overall profits rather than charging a discount on the silver. They still, however, received the normal commercial profit on the materials they supplied.[3]

Most provincial aviadores kept accounts with the almaceneros of Mexico City, to whom before 1729 they were accustomed to sell their silver. Even later, they still exchanged their silver for goods in the capital, so that relatively little coin actually returned to the mining camps. Many of the Mexico City almaceneros also maintained stores in the northern towns where their managers acted as aviadores or bought silver on the open market.[4] The six months' time-span between the actual payment of bar into the local treasury and its return in specie actually favoured the merchant.

Silver, therefore, possessed two prices: that which the mint paid and that for which bar could be exchanged in the mining camps. The latter price, unlike the former, was subject to considerable variation. In the first instance silver produced by smelting by reason of the frequent impurities

1 José Antonio Fabry, *Compendiosa demonstración*. . . (Mexico, 1743), p. 109. From unpaginated introduction by Manuel de Aldaco.
2 UMMA, *Reports*, 28 May 1826, Appendix, p. v.
3 Beleña, *Recopilación*, II, 271–2.
4 West, *The Mining Community*, pp. 83–4.

it contained always commanded less money than amalgamated silver. Then again, the value of both types increased with proximity to Mexico City. Finally, prices varied according to whether silver was sold to an aviador or on the open market. Ward stated that in the far north many miners were unable to obtain more than 4½ ps. or 36 rls. for a mark of silver worth 64 rls. 2 ms. at the mint.[1] But Gamboa, writing in 1762, declared that in Zacatecas miners received 54 rls. for a mark of amalgamated silver and 52 for smelted silver.[2] On the other hand, in Guanajuato as early as 1742, an aviador paid 56 and 52 rls. for the two varieties of metal.[3] Sometime after this, probably during the 1770s, prices began to rise. In Durango shortly before 1777 the two stores owned by Antonio Bassoco and Pedro Vértiz increased their prices from 52 to 54 rls. a mark for amalgamated silver.[4] By 1790 in Zacatecas aviadores paid 56 and 54 rls. respectively, and on the open market the current price was 57½ and 56 rls. for the two types.[5] Similarly, by 1786 in Guanajuato aviadores began to pay 58 rls. for amalgamated silver which by this time commanded 59 rls. on the open market.[6] Here then was a significant change. The local market price for silver rose and profits gained by aviadores declined: the balance shifted in favour of the producer as against his creditor.

These prices present one problem of interpretation. Who paid the 10 per cent and 1 per cent tax levied by the Crown—the refiner or his backer? This question relates to the discount charged by the aviadores and all purchasers of silver bar. In 1770 a report estimated that an aviador could expect to gain 3 or 4 rls. discount upon each mark.[7] If we accept Gamboa's testimony that they paid 54 rls. for amalgamated silver, then with discount the total rises to 57 or 58 rls. Now the 11 per cent tax amounted to just under 7 rls. in every mark, cutting the actual value to just over 57 rls. How then were aviadores in later years able to pay 59 rls. for a mark of silver? Here is a problem I have not been able to resolve. Whatever the case it remains clear that the discount rates declined by up to 50 per cent in the last third of the century.

In general Mexican mining suffered from a chronic lack of both credit for operating costs and capital for fixed investments. Whereas the industry

1 Ward, *Mexico in 1827*, II, 126.

2 Gamboa, *Comentarios*, p. 382.

3 AGN, Civil 256, contract between Juan Antonio Mendizábal and Andrés de Contreras, 1 December 1742.

4 Morfi, *Viaje*, pp. 75–6.

5 AGI, Mexico 2811, report of Zacatecas treasurer, Juan de Aranda, 18 November 1790.

6 AGN, Minería 120/1, Guanajuato mining deputation to mining court, 22 November 1786; AGN, Minería 76/18, Guanajuato deputation to mining court, 20 September 1791.

7 Lassaga and Velásquez de León, *Representación* . . ., p. 80.

had reached a stage where heavy fixed capital investment in the form of deep shafts, long adits and massive refining mills were all necessary, the merchant-aviadores upon whom the majority of miners depended preferred to supply only short-term credit to meet operating costs. Many merchants took no risk at all but simply purchased silver on the open market. Clearly the effects of the *comercio libre* decree of 1778 were all important: it drove mercantile capital into Mexican silver mining precisely at a time when the industry most needed it and when, moreover, it could justify such investments by the increased rate of profitability which the several tax and monopoly price reductions conceded by Gálvez had promoted. Mining profits rose and commercial profits fell. Former aviadores and silver merchants then directly entered the industry's productive stages which hitherto they had eschewed.

VI

At the close of the eighteenth century, José Garcés y Eguía estimated that to produce three million marks of silver—the annual output of the Mexican mint at this period—no less than ten million hundredweight of ore had to be cut, hauled to the surface and refined.[1] The expense of this vast operation can never be known with any exactitude. For a mine required the same number of workers to extract a given quantity of ore, be it rich or poor in quality. At the same time the problems and extent of drainage varied from shaft to shaft; a sudden influx of water could upset all calculations. Then again, what comparison could be made between a rich shallow deposit exhausted in a few months and an old mine, 300 yards deep, with but medium or low-grade ore. A lode could slowly peter out into base metal or, alternatively, suddenly yield an almost solid mass of silver. The costs of production, therefore, were infinitely variable and, as costs, related not to quality but to location and quantity. A mine produced ore, not silver.

Calculations become even more hypothetical if we consider that the mine-owners' basic item of expense was labour. At the Valenciana, wages and staff salaries absorbed some 75 per cent of all costs. Similarly, in a mine near Temascaltepec the pickmen and peons accounted for 73 per cent of the total bill.[2] Moreover, since the methods of remuneration varied from camp to camp, with workers taking different shares of the mineral, it is peculiarly difficult to deduce with any precision a generalised scheme of how much it cost to produce a hundredweight of ore. But clearly in

1 Garcés, *Nueva teórica*, p. 125. *Dictamen de la comisión especial nombrada para informar sobre el importante ramo de minería* (Mexico, 1821), p. 6.

2 Humboldt, *Ensayo político*, pp. 354–6; Ward, *Mexico in 1827*, II, 389–90.

comparison to labour, all other components—the gunpowder, iron, cord, wood, leather, and candles—dwindled in importance.

Once the mineral had been extracted from the shaft the picture changed. A refiner knew exactly how much it cost him to produce a mark of silver. In general terms, the cost of amalgamating a hundredweight of ore which contained the $2\frac{1}{2}$ ounces of silver—the average medium grade—amounted to 4 or 6 rls.[1] If we return to the figure put forward by Garcés y Eguía,

Table 10 *Average weekly cost of a refining mill with one stamp mill and twelve arrastres with a capacity of 193 loads (580 cwt. of ore) with an average quality of 9 ounces of silver per load (3 ozs. per cwt.).*

	pesos	*reales*
To maintain 12 mules for stamp mill at $1\frac{3}{4}$ rls. per day	18	3
Consumption of iron and depreciation of stamp mill each week	6	0
4 peons to work stamp mill at $4\frac{1}{2}$ rls. per day	10	0
Wages of 6 peons for arrastres for 5 days at 4 rls. per day; they grind 580 cwt. to form 29 mounds of 20 cwt. each	15	0
48 mules for arrastres at $1\frac{3}{4}$ rls.	73	4
Consumption of lead and litharge in arrastre at 1 rl. per day for 5 days	7	4
65 fanegas of crude salt for 29 mounts at 1 ps. each	65	0
9 cwt., 25 pounds of copper pyrites at $1\frac{2}{3}$ ps. per cwt.	15	3
Stirring of the 29 mounds at 1 ps.	21	6
To wash and load the mounds	5	0
To separate silver—cost of charcoal at 3 ps. 4 rls.	4	4
Wages: manager 16 ps., azoguero 12 ps., porter 4 ps., and others	44	0
Care of mules in stable and fields	12	0
Waterwheel to supply water to arrastres with 2 mules at $1\frac{3}{4}$ ps. per week	3	0
4 days of peon minding wheel at 3 rls.	1	4
Buckets and cord for waterwheel	1	0
Lime, candles and peons for cleaning	8	0
Loss of mercury, using 580 cwt. 173 pounds to produce 217 marks 4 ounces of silver	108	1
Total Cost for 193 loads (for each load 2 ps. 1 rl. 4 gr.)	419	5

then the total expense of refining ten million hundredweight of ore ranged from five to seven and a half million pesos, that is to say, from 20 to 30 per cent of the value of all silver minted. But in lieu of trusting such crude estimates it is preferable to examine a particular scheme which presents the breakdown in costs of the amalgamation of medium grade ore at Zacatecas[2] (see table 10).

If we group the items in table 10 somewhat differently we obtain the following results.

[1] Sonneschmid, *Tratado de amalgamación*, p. 92.

[2] AGN, Minería 82/3, mining deputation of Zacatecas, 16 May 1801.

	pesos	*reales*
Labour	70	4
Mules	106	7
Raw materials	103	7
Mercury	108	1
Miscellaneous	30	2
	419	5

Raw materials rather than labour absorbed the greater part of production costs. The mules—acquisition and depreciation costs apart—can be largely transmuted into the maize and straw which sustained them. The refiner, far more than the miner, was affected by changes in the prices of raw materials. Unfortunately, at present we possess little information as to the price trends of such commodities as salt, lead, firewood and copper pyrites. Similarly, the curve of maize prices has yet to be traced. But undoubtedly during the great drought of 1785–6 many refiners were obliged to cease production since they could no longer afford to feed their mules. Moreover, a knowledge of the market price of maize would not necessarily tell us what it cost the refiner since the more wealthy members of the industry frequently owned their own haciendas to supply them.

The scheme presented above lacked one vital component—the initial price paid for the ore. The following scheme drawn up in 1801 by the manager of the Regla refining mill at Real del Monte provides an indication of the magnitude of this item. He calculated the cost of refining poor and medium grade ore[1] (see table 11).

This we may assume to be a nominal scheme since the mill formed part of an integrated enterprise owned by the Count of Regla and existed to refine the Veta Vizcaína's mineral. The estimated price of the ore must therefore represent either its effective cost of production or the conventional market rate. The latter alternative appears more likely. Whatever the case, it was this acquisition price which largely determined the differences in the final cost of production. For the lower grade ore it amounted to 36·2 per cent of that cost and for the medium grade it rose to as much as 54·2 per cent. In the industry at large, refining profits depended upon what must remain, for the historian, an unknown factor—the price paid for mineral in the auctions held at the pithead.

The scheme also elucidates the peculiar role of mercury. The expense on

1 AGI, Mexico 1608, report of manager, 20 April 1801, in Marquina to Soler, 26 February 1802.

other items—labour, mules and raw materials—barely changed between the two classes of mineral. As costs they related to the quantity, not the quality, of ore refined. Mercury, on the other hand, varied in proportion to quality, that is to say, to the value of silver produced. Leaving to one side the acquisition price, we find that the cost of mercury needed to refine ore worth one ounce of silver per hundredweight amounted to only about 13 per cent of the total expense of production. But for the medium grade ore of 2½ silver ounces that proportion rose to 25 per cent. This latter percentage agrees with the previous scheme drawn up for Zacatecas

Table 11 *Cost of amalgamation at Real del Monte of two equal amounts of ore, each weighing 30 cwt. but containing different silver content, the first producing 1 oz. of silver per cwt. and the second 2½ ozs. per cwt.*

Costs	For 1 oz./cwt.		For 2½ oz./cwt.	
	pesos	*reales*	*pesos*	*reales*
Cost of ore	10	0	25	0
Transport to mill	3	1	3	1
Crushing by stamp mill	2	2	2	2
75 lbs. sea-salt	3	6	3	6
11 bbls. copper pyrites	3	7½	4	2½
			(12 barrels)	
Stirring of amalgam in patio	2	4	2	6½
Washing		1½		1½
Mercury lost	1	7	4	5½
	—	—	—	—
Total cost	27	5	46	1
Silver produced at 60 rls. per mark	28	0	70	2½
Costs	27	5	46	1
	—	—	—	—
Profits		3	24	1½

in which for ore worth 3 ounces of silver per hundredweight, mercury accounted for just over 25 per cent of production cost. Now more mercury was required to refine a greater sum of silver. So, if the quality of the Zacatecas ore was raised to 10⅔ ounces of silver per hundredweight, then total refining costs increased from 419 ps. to 734 ps., and the expense on mercury from 108 ps. to 386 ps., that is to say, from 25 per cent to over 52 per cent of the total bill. A point was then soon reached where it became more profitable to smelt than to amalgamate.

The significance of the reduction by half in the price of mercury effected by Gálvez becomes clear. If we double the mercury price to return to the pre-1767 situation, then its proportion of total refining costs rises to 41 per cent for ore containing 3 ounces of silver per hundredweight and to nearly 69 per cent for ore containing $10\frac{1}{2}$ ounces of silver. At Real del Monte it would have been impossible to refine the one-ounce quality ore. With the cut in the mercury price a wider range of mineral could be refined. During the 1720s treasury officials in Zacatecas, Guadalajara and Guanajuato all agreed that a consistent ratio of 2 ounces of silver per hundredweight gave a good profit to the miner; in many cases miners refined ore worth one or one-and-a-half ounces to keep their mills in operation. Only at Pachuca, it appears, were such ratios unprofitable: there a 2-ounce minimum was necessary.[1]

Writing in 1814, Fausto de Elhuyar, director-general of the mining court, declared: 'the lowering of the price of mercury, which amounted to 3 reales 11 maravedis in every pound, has been considered as the chief cause of the annual increase in mintage'. In effect, since it took a pound of mercury to refine a mark of silver the miner received a fall in costs of about 5 per cent.[2] The reduction in the price of mercury hence augmented profits upon all medium grade ores. But equally important, the range of mineral which could be profitably subjected to the patio process was extended at both ends of the scale. A greater amount of higher as well as lower grade ore could then be amalgamated. Moreover, since amalgamation was a more efficient method of separation than smelting, any conversion to the former process entailed a greater reduction of silver from the same, given quantity of ore previously smelted.

VII

Any explanation for the great Mexican boom must be tentative. Let us record two contemporary opinions. In 1793 Viceroy Revillagigedo wrote: 'The causes of this increase are not that there have been greater bonanzas, nor that the ore is of higher quality: it is caused chiefly by the greater number of persons who have devoted themselves to mining, to the small advance made in the manner of working them, to the conveniences in the price of mercury, the reduction in gunpowder and the exemptions from salestax.' He also pointed to the formation of mercantile companies to exploit some older mines.[3]

In 1803 Humboldt largely agreed with Revillagigedo.

> The enormous expansion in the produce of the mines observable in latter years is to be attributed to a great number of causes all acting at the same time, and among which

[1] Joseph Antonio de Villaseñor y Sánchez, *Respuesta que ... a la apología* (Mexico, 1742) unpaginated introduction by Bustamante, pp. 24, 51–2, 68.

[2] Elhuyar, *Indagaciones*, pp. 126–7.

[3] Revillagigedo, *Instrucción*, p. 118.

the first place assigned must be to the growth in population on the tableland of Mexico, the progress of knowledge and national industry, the freedom of trade conceded to America in 1778, the facility of procuring at a cheaper rate the iron and steel necessary for the mines, the fall in the price of mercury, the discovery of the mines of Catorce and Valenciana, and the establishment of the *tribunal de minería.*[1]

Clearly, in this hunt for causes, the Mexican viceroy scored over the Prussian traveller. Several of Humboldt's agents were simply concurrent phenomena. At best, the growth in population formed but a prerequisite; and as for *comercio libre* its success may well have been the effect of the rise in silver output. Revillagigedo pointed more precisely to the question of costs and the entrance of capital and entrepreneurs into the industry. Now it is necessary to be quite clear about what one is trying to explain.

There are, in this context, three facts which demand explanation. The first is the century-long upward curve in silver production: in each succeeding decade, with the single exception of the 1760s, more silver was minted. Secondly, the great spurt forward of the 1770s, in which production leapt from 12 million to 18 million pesos a year. Thirdly, the maintenance of this new level, followed by another slow rise. We here ignore the yearly fluctuations, in large part caused by British naval blockades, and drought. It is the continuous upward curve which offers the greatest difficulty and which in part works to refute several possible lines of argument. It especially illumines the danger of the *post hoc propter hoc* fallacy. The efficacy of any particular measure, be it *comercio libre* or the Jesuit expulsion, could always be proved by the subsequent increase in silver production. This, needless to say, was a favourite manner of argument among both statesmen and miners of the period, wishing to laud a favoured measure or to secure further concessions. Clearly it is absurd to invoke one cause to explain a century-long process. At different times different agents worked to produce the same effect.

Granted these difficulties, it seems best to concentrate upon the boom of the 1770s which followed the recession of the 1760s. Here we can perceive several factors at work which combined to create a significant lowering of production costs sufficient to increase profits quite considerably. In mining itself, owners gained a greater control over their workers, and in some cases were able to reduce their partidos and wages. Then the more extensive use of gunpowder was encouraged by a cut in price and a more efficient supply. Finally, several risky enterprises were encouraged by tax exemptions. The refining industry benefited equally. The cheaper and more abundant supply of mercury led to a greater reliance upon amalgamation

[1] Humboldt, *Ensayo político*, p. 385.

as against smelting. At the same time the local price of silver bar rose appreciably. Here again, individual exemptions included a further reduction in mercury to 30 ps. By contrast the industry's merchant-aviadores experienced a setback. Trading profits in general and premiums on silver in particular both fell during the 1780s. Here, then, is a possible causal sequence. The great boom of the 1770s sprang both from general cost reductions affecting all the industry and from a remarkable series of concurrent bonanzas in particular mines. Then, in the 1780s this boom was sustained and pushed still further by the widespread entrance of mercantile capital into the industry and matched by a greater willingness to plough back mining profits. Moreover, an increasing number of miners and companies in the older camps obtained tax exemptions. Now all these cost reductions may well have acted as so much bait; quite possibly it was the entrance of investment capital which made the difference. Proofs, however, are lacking. In the last resort until long-term account books are discovered and studied, any explanation must remain, at best, hypothetical.

CHAPTER 3

THE MINING COURT

The Bourbon dynasty assisted Mexican silver mining most effectively when it lightened the heavy burden of taxation and monopoly profit levied by the Habsburgs. But in addition to this fiscal relief, the Crown also attempted to raise the public status of the industry to a level equal to that enjoyed by the colonial merchants. It therefore organised the miners into a guild with a central court and deputations in each camp; it furthermore established both a bank to finance the industry and a technical college to train its young men. In striking contrast to the mercantile campaign against *comercio libre* several of these reforms sprang from the proposals and petitions of the miners themselves. Indeed measures similar to those actually applied had been the object of public and official debate in Mexico for nearly half a century.

As early as 1716 the viceroy, the Duke of Linares, pronounced Mexican silver mining to be deficient in technique, pointing to the widespread use of smelting as proof for this assertion. Moreover, the industry lacked capital; many leading miners ended their careers bankrupt and in consequence merchants despised the profession and refused to give it financial backing. The viceroy's chief remedy for this deplorable situation was to abolish the old distinction in the rates of taxation paid by miners and by refiners and their aviadores when they presented silver bar in the treasury. If this difference was eliminated, he claimed, merchants would more readily buy silver and pay miners a higher price.[1] By 1723 his suggestion was accepted by the Crown and passed into law.

The next viceregal proposal to assist the industry did not gain royal approbation so rapidly. In 1727 the viceroy, the Marquis of Casafuerte, summoned a general meeting of leading officials to discover whether it would be desirable to lower the price of mercury. Great quantities of low-grade ore, it had been alleged, were simply cast aside because the high cost of mercury made amalgamation unprofitable. Convinced by this line of argument, the junta urged a cut in price from 82½ ps. to 55 ps. a cwt., a recommendation which did not, however, command royal

[1] BN (Madrid) MSS 2929, f. 41.

assent.[1] Debate on this subject became public during the 1740s when the erudite José Antonio Villaseñor y Sánchez, the accountant for the mercury monopoly, published a short work in which he argued, with the support of José Alejandro Bustamante, owner of the Veta Vizcaína, that mercury formed an insignificant part of amalgamation costs; other materials were equally or more important. A reduction in its price would not provoke an overall increase in silver production sufficiently great to cover the loss in revenue that the reduction entailed.[2] His arguments were rebutted in detail by Manuel Fabry, a mint official, who, with the backing of Manuel de Aldaco, the silver banker, asserted that many miners barely cleared their costs; they worked in hope of future bonanzas; therefore any lowering of costs would stimulate production. Aldaco pointed out that to cut the mercury price by half would give the miner an additional $3\frac{1}{2}$ rls. in each mark, no small encouragement for the larger enterprise.[3]

A second significant proposal emerged in these years of discussion. In 1743, a Genoese, Domingo Reborato y Soler, suggested the formation of a general investment company with a capital of two million pesos: its purpose was to finance the mining industry. The viceroy, the Count of Fuenclara, favourably impressed, asked two silver bankers, Francisco Manuel Sánchez de Tagle and Manuel de Aldaco for their opinion. But although Aldaco had earlier fixed upon the shortage of capital as a cause of the industry's current difficulties, he and his fellow banker attacked the scheme. The new company would lose money, or if successful, would replace existing institutions, i.e. would drive them out of business. Their lobbying impressed the viceroy who dropped the idea.[4] Nevertheless, in 1748 José Alejandro Bustamante put forward a similar scheme to the effect that a company should be set up with a five million pesos capital; it would collect a real on every mark of silver produced and administer the distribution of mercury and other supplies.[5]

The proposals of the 1740s were reiterated and transformed by Francisco Javier de Gamboa in his influential *Comentarios a las ordenanzas de minas*, published in Madrid in 1761. Far from being a mere legal commentary, his book included a description of the industry's current condition, proposals of reform for its improvement, and much valuable technical information. The book soon acquired a high reputation and was

[1] Gamboa, *Comentarios*, pp. 28–30.
[2] Villaseñor y Sánchez, *Respuesta*, *passim*.
[3] Fabry, *Compendiosa demonstración*, unpaginated introduction by Aldaco, *passim*.
[4] Gamboa, *Comentarios*, pp. 144–8.
[5] *Ibid.*, pp. 151–5.

later to be translated into English.[1] Gamboa's fellow American, the jurist Pedro Cañete y Domínguez, in his compendium on Potosí, roundly declared: 'I venerate all of the opinions of our wise author, as much for the ingenious depth and fertility of his doctrine as for his mastery in mining matters.'[2] The work was also useful to the practical miner since Gamboa inserted lengthy descriptions and diagrams of the best instruments and methods to employ in the interior measurement and excavation of mines; the appropriate mathematical tables were also appended. He drew upon Mexican manuscript sources to assist him, especially the works of the creole fiscal, José Saénz de Escobar, whom he claimed was 'as expert a geometrician as he was a weighty jurisconsult'.[3] He also provided a valuable guide to contemporary mining literature, including works recently published in French and German. Fr Christian Rieger, SJ, a former professor of experimental physics at the Teresian College at Vienna, translated for him the gist of the latest works in German.[4] Gamboa's purpose in all this was to combat what he deemed to be the deplorable technical ignorance of the colonial miners.

The central argument of the book, however, was essentially political. In his preface Gamboa declared that the Mexican mines barely produced a tenth of the silver possible under better management. He dismissed the substantial increase in mintage during the previous decade—that was simply due to fortuitous discoveries, especially of Bolaños. Instead, he fixed upon the ruin of Zacatecas, Sombrerete, San Luis Potosí and Parral, and the decline of Guanajuato and Taxco. Among the older camps only Pachuca and Real del Monte appeared to be thriving. To remedy this disastrous state of affairs, Gamboa advocated that the price of mercury should be reduced and that permission should be granted for it to be freely mined in New Spain. He attacked the restriction of mintage to Mexico City as injurious to the northern camps and supported the erection of a second mint at Guadalajara, his native city. Furthermore, he urged the implementation of a never-invoked law which conceded tax exemptions to enterprises of great difficulty or risk.[5]

More importantly, and here we approach the book's political *raison d'être*, Gamboa, adopting the ideas of the 1740s, proposed the formation of

[1] *Commentaries on the mining ordinances of Spain: dedicated to his Catholic Majesty, Charles III. By Don Francisco Xavier de Gamboa* . . ., trans. from the original Spanish by Richard Heathfield (2 vols.; London, 1830).

[2] Pedro Vicente Cañete y Domínguez, *Guía histórica, geográfica, física, política, civil y legal del gobierno e intendencias de la Provincia de Potosí* (Potosí, 1952), p. 718.

[3] Gamboa, *Comentarios*, prologue, unpaginated, and p. 229.

[4] *Ibid.*, p. 247.

[5] *Ibid.*, p. 61.

a general company or bank to solve the industry's financial crisis. The company would have a capital of 4 million pesos, divided into shares worth 500 ps. each. It would purchase mercury from the Crown at Veracruz for 40 ps. a cwt. and then distribute it directly to miners, bypassing the treasuries. More generally, the company would act as the industry's chief aviador, supplying both cash and raw materials in return for silver. The originality of Gamboa's scheme, however, lay in his suggestion to place this company under the direction of the Mexican consulado. Its guarantee, he claimed, would be sufficient to attract ecclesiastical capital into the bank. Moreover, mining litigation could be then summarily despatched in the consulado court rather than suffering the current prolonged delays in the audiencia.[1] To provide the guild with an income to meet the costs of management, he advised that the farm of Mexico City excise duties (restored to the Crown in 1754) should be returned to the consulado. Now, at the time of the book's composition, during the years 1755–65, Gamboa acted as the Madrid agent of the Mexican consulado. He was also a personal friend of Manuel de Aldaco, director of the Fagoaga silver bank and the leader of the Basque community of Mexico City.[2] The inference is obvious. Despite the legal and technical brilliance of his commentaries, Gamboa emerged as the political advocate of the great import houses and silver banks of Mexico City. Precisely at the time when the statesmen of the Bourbon dynasty were moving to undercut the position of the colonial merchant-monopolists, Gamboa wished to subject the entire Mexican silver mining industry to the control of the consulado and the mercantile oligarchy.

The 1760s proved to be the one decade of the eighteenth century in which mintage fell below its predecessor, indeed production dropped to a level not known for fifteen years. In 1764 Tomás Ortiz de Landázuri, the accountant-general, painted a depressing picture of the chief camps. Even the mines of Bolaños, the phoenix of the 1750s, lay under water. Only Sonora and Sinaloa seemed to hold out hope for the future.[3] Warned by this memorandum the visitor-general, José de Gálvez, immediately consulted with the leading miners of the colony—with Manuel de Aldaco, whom he termed 'the father of his country', and with the Count of Regla, 'the restorer of his profession'.[4] He accepted a long petition

[1] Gamboa, *Comentarios*, prologue and pp. 160–72.

[2] See Real Díaz, *Las ferias de Jalapa*, p. 93; Obregón, *El real colegio*, p. 72; also AGN, Vínculos 6–3, where Aldaco, writing to José Joaquín de Fagoaga, refers to 'Amigo Gamboa' and letter from Gamboa to Aldaco.

[3] BRP MSS 2824, Miscelánea de Ayala X, Report of Tomás de Landázuri, ff. 132–59.

[4] Gálvez, *Informe general*, pp. 42–3.

presented by José de la Borda and Juan Lucas de Lassaga, which proposed a 50 per cent reduction both in the silver tithe and in the price of mercury.[1] Presumably he also talked to Gamboa, who by then was serving as a criminal court judge in the Mexican audiencia. The upshot of these discussions was an ambitious programme of reform which dramatically altered both the costs of production and the public status of the mining industry.

The economic effects of this programme we have already described—the cut in the price of mercury and gunpowder, the individual tax exemptions given to Borda and other miners, the greater control over labour brought about by the establishment of militia forces, and the entrance of mercantile capital following the abolition of the convoy system. But Gálvez also introduced other, more institutional reforms, designed to give the industry a public voice and social prestige. Here he accepted the ideas of a memorandum drawn up by the Mexican savant Joaquín Velásquez de León and Juan Lucas de Lassaga, a Basque miner. Indeed his almost total acceptance of this plan would seem to indicate that Gálvez himself instigated the report.

Like both Gamboa and Landázuri, Velásquez de León and Lassaga assumed that Mexican silver mining was decaying. They rejected Landázuri's hope for Sonora, since although that region was rich in mineral, it lacked sufficient population apart from hostile Indians. They stressed the technical ignorance of the Mexican miner and the lack of esteem in which the industry was held; only those driven by blind avarice or economic despair became miners. They singled out the industry's lack of capital, however, as the chief cause of its current decline. After Aldaco's death not a single silver bank remained in business.[2] Their remedy greatly differed from Gamboa's scheme. For they wished to form a mining guild, to be governed by local deputations and a central court in Mexico City. The court was to manage both a finance bank and a technical college; it would receive a real in every mark of silver produced, a charge already collected by the Crown since 1732 as an extra seigniorage duty. With this secure income it could easily raise capital to finance the industry.[3]

After his appointment as Minister of the Indies in 1776, Gálvez moved rapidly to implement these proposals. In the same year the viceroy, Bucareli, summoned six delegates from the chief mining camps to establish the court and its guild. Velásquez de León, delegate for Sultepec, became

[1] BM Add. MSS 20999, ff. 559–605.

[2] Lassaga and Velásquez de León, *Representación*, pp. 4–7, 19.

[3] *Ibid.*, pp. 41–74.

the first director-general, an office especially charged with technical education and experiment. Lassaga, the representative of Bolaños, was elected administrator-general. Three deputies-general, Tomás de Liceaga of Guanajuato, Marcelo de Anza, an associate of Borda in Zacatecas, and Julián del Hierro from Temascaltepec, completed the court. Aniceto del Barrio, delegate for Taxco, a merchant, was appointed factor or business manager.[1] None of the great miners of that epoch deigned to attend the meeting or accept office on the court. Of the six men only Anza was a full-time miner; Lassaga and Liceaga had abandoned their mines.

The court's first achievement was the publication in 1783 of a new mining code to replace the existing ordinances which had been issued by Phillip II in the sixteenth century.[2] Velásquez de León, a lawyer as well as mathematician, was its chief author; he drew heavily upon Gamboa's *Commentaries* and corresponded in detail with Gálvez. The aim of the new code was the encouragement of silver production. Patent rights for discoveries, limited liability for miners, careful definitions of aviador contracts, labour payments and mine measurements were all lucidly stated in language easily comprehensible to the deputation courts charged with its administration. Its impact is hard to measure but our impression is that after its promulgation fewer mines were closed or ruined by litigation.

The court's second achievement, the establishment of a finance bank, proved disastrous. It began operation in 1784 but in less than two years the viceroy intervened to suspend further investments. During this short time the bank raised and advanced 1,204,903 ps. to over 20 separate enterprises, received back in silver 509,397 ps., and hence lost 702,000 ps. In addition to a reckless lending policy, corruption entered the picture; the tribunal's business manager misappropriated 126,938 ps.; Velásquez de León himself had been awarded 20,000 ps. for his labour in the creation of the court. A badly run group of mines in Pachuca, owned by a mercantile company, had wasted a large portion of the bank's loans.[3]

After the bank's suspension—the *raison d'être* of its creation—the court suffered a further blow when in 1786 both Velásquez de León and Lassaga died, each bankrupt. The Crown ordered an inquiry into the court's future, and the viceroy installed two merchants, Antonio Bassoco, our old friend, and Antonio Barroso as interim deputies-general. During the 1790s the Crown obtained from the court three loans worth a total value

[1] Howe, *The Mining Guild*, pp. 46–59. A later critic described the deputies as 'obscure men . . . who were never miners. . . .'; see AGI, Mexico 2241, Miguel Pacheco Solís to Gálvez, 26 March 1787.

[2] They are printed in Beleña, *Recopilación*, II, 212–92.

[3] Howe, *The Mining Guild*, pp. 136–55.

of two-and-a-half million pesos; most of the bank's income was absorbed by the payment of the interest upon these loans.[1] Possibly, therefore, the court's net effect was to divert capital from mining and instead to lay the foundation of the Mexican national debt.

The residual task left to the court was the diffusion of technical knowledge. In 1786 the Crown appointed the distinguished Spanish mineralogist Fausto de Elhuyar as director-general. His initial task was to lead a German technical mission to New Spain, and there introduce the method of amalgamation discovered in Austria by the Baron de Born. The mission was welcomed by Mexican miners. At Sombrerete the Fagoagas permitted a German professor to conduct experiments in their refining mills and mines; at Guanajuato, Elhuyar was able to use the mill owned by the Count of Valenciana. But the results of their tests were dismal.[2] The Born method proved to be little more than a variant upon the old *caso* process or hot amalgamation invented by Alonso Barba in the seventeenth century. It cost more and produced less silver than the standard patio method. In all the Crown spent 145,371 ps. upon a mission which Viceroy Revillagigedo dismissed as a complete failure.[3]

Nevertheless, Elhuyar, encouraged by the viceroy, pushed forward with the establishment of a technical college modelled on the Basque institute at Vergara where he had once taught. In 1792 Mexico's first secular school began to teach a handful of pupils the elements of mineralogy, metallurgy, and other less specialised subjects such as French and mathematics. Given prestige by a distinguished staff, among which was included Andrés del Río, a brilliant mineralogist who had studied with Humboldt at Freiburg, the college soon became fashionable.[4] In August 1809 the court stated: 'Many sons of the first nobility who wish in general to devote themselves to the sciences which although suitable for their rank and military career are not taught in other schools, find in our college an education which is appropriate to their status and convenience.'[5] Critics of the college, however, charged that it had acquired the reputation of being 'a lodging house

[1] Howe, *The Mining Guild*, pp. 95, 371–83.

[2] Arthur Whitaker, 'The Elhuyar Mining Mission and the Enlightenment', *Hispanic American Historical Review*, 31 (1951), pp. 558–83. See Introduction to Sonneschmid, *Tratado de amalgamación*, written by D.J.M.F. (Don José María de Fagoaga?) who concluded: 'In spite of their scientific knowledge, the German miners who went to teach America could not advance a single thing, neither in the method of working mines, nor in the refining of the metal.' Howe, *The Mining Guild*, pp. 302–19.

[3] Revillagigedo, *Instrucción reservada*, pp. 122–8. Clement G. Motten, *Mexican Silver and the Enlightenment* (Philadelphia, 1950), pp. 46–63.

[4] Howe, *The Mining Guild*, pp. 320–45.

[5] AGI, Mexico 2248, Report of Mining Court, 5 August 1809.

for gentlemen'. Students came and went at will; many abused their freedom; several had to be expelled for misconduct.[1] An anonymous pamphlet, written somewhat later, asserted that its students proved rarely able to apply their theoretical knowledge to actual mining problems. The professors undertook little research. The author concluded that the institution should be transferred to a mining town where its pupils could acquire practical experience.[2] Nevertheless, despite persistent criticism, the college undoubtedly trained several men who proved acceptable to the mining industry. The most outstanding alumnus, Casimiro Chovel, became general manager of the Valenciana mine. In general, the college did not fulfil the high hopes of its founders; it contributed more to the advance of Mexican education than to Mexican mining.

Fausto de Elhuyar and Andrés del Río did attempt, however, to provide the industry with more efficient drainage machinery. They experimented with hydraulic pumps of the Hungarian variety in the Morán mine at Pachuca. They favoured hydraulic power rather than steam engines since the latter were expensive not only to acquire but, by reason of fuel costs, to operate. Four years' work and 40,000 ps. of the court's funds were invested in this attempt. But the first shaft in which the pump was installed collapsed under the weight of the apparatus, and in the second shaft, after limited success, a sudden influx of water nullified its entire work.[3] Once again, foreign methods had failed.

If neither its technical nor its financial ventures proved successful, wherein lay the court's value to Mexican mining? In the first place, it acted as the industry's public voice in all its dealings with the fiscal bureaucracy. It was the court which in 1778 expressed the miners' protests against the exactions of the new excise officials, and which secured from Viceroy Mayorga a declaration that essential mining supplies were to be exempted from alcabalas.[4] In addition, the court almost invariably backed the claims of individual miners for tax exemptions for dangerous undertakings. Its most valuable service was rendered in 1801. In that year the British naval blockade, provoked by Spain's alliance with Napoleon, interrupted mercury shipments to the point where many refining mills suspended operation, and other miners smelted metal to obtain cash for drainage costs. The court, therefore, after much bureaucratic shuffling and

1 AGI, Mexico 2254, Defence of Elhuyar from court attacks, 11 April 1811.

2 *Discurso sobre la minería de este imperio* (Mexico, 1822). For its attack on Elhuyar see pp. 34–5.

3 See AGI, Mexico 1617, Iturrigaray to Soler, 26 June 1803, where can be found a description of the machine; also AGI, Mexico 2254, Elhuyar to Lizana, 24 August 1809.

4 *Representaciones del real tribunal de minería a favor de su importante cuerpo y declaración del excmo. señor virrey de estos reinos* (Mexico, 1781).

snuffling, obtained from the colony's chief finance committee a temporary 50 per cent overall tax reduction on all silver produced. Granted for a seven-month period, January to August 1802, this exemption amounted to a 515,798 ps. fiscal subsidy. The court had used vigorous language to extract the concession: it protested, 'the mining industry [is] always the victim and never protected from circumstances'. It even accused the Crown of being 'so slow to help, so quick to harm'.[1] Naturally Madrid did not approve: the viceroy was ordered to reprimand both the finance committee and the court for their invasion of royal prerogative. The lost taxes, however, were not repaid.

The court could better represent the industry since after 1793 it attracted the service of several leading miners. Between 1787 and 1793 its future had remained in doubt. A viceregal inquiry into the previous financial fiasco provided old opponents with an opportunity for attack. In 1790, for example, Francisco Javier de Gamboa, by this time regent of the Mexican audiencia, proposed the court's abolition on the grounds that it had totally failed to fulfil the objects of its creation. He criticised the new code which he claimed was inferior to the old one; he regretted the elimination of the audiencia from mining litigation; he still favoured the consulado to manage the finance bank.[2] But Gamboa's criticism was rejected. Instead the court emerged stronger than before. It was erected into a court of appeal for all mining litigation. The private jurisdiction over all mining cases, granted to the locally elected deputations set up in each mining camp, had provoked numerous controversies. The court was now given powers to reverse local judgments; in consequence it became the true head of the industry. Two of the three administrators-general elected between 1793 and 1810 represented Guanajuato, the leading mining camp. Two of them, the Marquis of San Juan de Rayas, owner of the Rayas mine in Guanajuato, and José Mariano de Fagoaga, manager of his family's mines in Sombrerete, came from families engaged in mining for nearly a century. When in 1801 the court so confidently attacked the financial committee for its lentitude in assisting the industry it possessed Fausto de Elhuyar as director-general, José Mariano de Fagoaga as administrator-general, the Marquis of San Juan de Rayas and Marcelo José de Anza of Zacatecas as deputies-general. Two years later Colonel Ignacio de Obregón, the chief miner of Catorce, joined the court as deputy-general. It was these men who in 1803 declared to the Crown: 'The interests of the mining community, intimately bound

[1] AGI, Mexico 1608, mining court to viceroy, 29 December 1801, found in Marquina to Soler, 20 February 1802. AGI, Mexico 1786, Council of the Indies, *Consulta*, 2 July 1803.

[2] Howe, *The Mining Guild*, pp. 182–91.

to those of the State, are of transcendental importance to commerce, to the arts, to industry, to royal revenue, and to all Europe.'[1]

The mining court succeeded in changing the climate of opinion. In 1716 the viceroy, Linares, wrote: 'Miners are commonly despised by merchants.'[2] This contempt for all but the greatest miners continued until the Gálvez Visitation. But then, slowly, as mining became more profitable and less risky, it acquired respectability. The magnificent, neo-classic palace which housed the court visibly demonstrated to the world the industry's new status. As the court itself attested: 'If heed be taken of moral and political influence, then it cannot be denied that the court is principally responsible for that change in public opinion which destroyed the former general prejudice against this profession, and which to some degree opened the door to the freedom with which persons of other occupations have devoted themselves to mining or have invested in it a part of their wealth.'[3] Naturally such a claim cannot be proved; possibly the increased rate of profits provides a sufficient explanation for the greater flow of capital into the industry. But above all else, the existence of the court expressed the royal preference for mining over trade.

Gálvez brilliantly succeeded in his plans to increase Mexican silver production. That success, we have argued, can best be attributed to his strictly economic reforms. The effects of his institutional programme cannot be easily measured. But it appears that neither the financial nor the technical undertakings of the court promoted additional production. Yet certainly the industry became more respectable. Gálvez, as a good mercantilist, conferred public prestige by organising industry into a guild to which he gave private jurisdiction and a central court with an income greater than the consulados. He liberated mining from the jurisdiction of the audiencia and rejected Gamboa's plan to subject the industry to the economic management of the consulado. Yet neither fiscal inducements nor institutional independence would have raised silver production if there had not been present in Mexico both enterpreneurs and investors able to profit from the changes introduced by Gálvez. It is to these men and their enterprises that we now turn.

1 AGI, Mexico 2246, mining court's agent, 18 June 1803.
2 BN (Madrid) MSS 2929, f. 28.
3 AGN, Minería 193/1, mining court, 22 April 1815.

CHAPTER 4

THE GREAT ENTERPRISES

The sociology of Mexican silver mining presents an almost insurmountable problem to the historian. The difficulty lies in the absence of information about the failures, the bankruptcies, about the depressing social tragedy underlying the industry's progress. Velásquez de León once asserted that for every ten persons who entered mining eight lost their money. Men only became miners because they were 'either gripped by a blind avarice or by a depressing necessity'.[1] But those who fled to the mining camps in search of economic redemption all too often sank still further down the social scale, lost amidst the prevailing rough camaraderie and debauchery. As Gamboa noted: 'The first enemy of the miner is the miner himself. They are generally prodigal, without bounds nor end to their expenses, luxuries, superfluities and vices.'[2]

At the same time, many of the greatest colonial fortunes were made in silver mining. During the eighteenth century at least sixteen titles of nobility were acquired by Mexican miners, a considerably higher number than those gained by their cautious rivals, the merchants. Information about these men and their enterprises is in some cases abundant; if not, however, entirely reliable, since it mainly comes from lawsuits and petitions for tax exemptions. Nevertheless, a series of entrepreneurial studies can be compiled from this evidence. The discussion, granted the absence of long-term account books, must concentrate upon capital recruitment and the entrepreneurs. A list of the titled nobility is shown in table 12.[3]

The shift from Zacatecas in the first half of the century to Guanajuato in the years after 1770 is striking: the two camps between them account for half of all the titles, with the one mine of Valenciana supporting no less than three counts. Equally noteworthy is the fact that whereas the chief miners of Zacatecas appear to have been peninsular, in Guanajuato they were, as we shall see later, nearly all creoles. At all levels of the industry an active competition existed between the two halves of the Spanish nation. Although several leading peninsular miners began as merchant-aviadores and silver bankers—the Count of San Pedro del Alamo, the

[1] Lassaga and Velásquez de León, *Representación*, p. 42.

[2] Gamboa, *Comentarios*, pp. 378–9.

[3] Taken from Ortega y Pérez Gallardo, *Historia genealógica*.

Count of Regla and Manuel de Aldaco—other peninsulars, such as the Count of Bibanco and José de la Borda, plunged, like the creoles, directly into mining.

Table 12 *Mexican mining nobility of the eighteenth century (creations).*

Title	Year of creation	Camp	Origin
Count of Santiago de la Laguna	1727	Zacatecas	Peninsular
Count of San Mateo Valparaíso	1727	Zacatecas	Peninsular
Marquis of San Clemente	1730	Guanajuato	Creole
Count of San Pedro del Alamo	1734	Silver Bank Zacatecas, Mazapil	Peninsular
Marquis of Valle Ameno	1740	Real del Monte	Peninsular
Count of Nuestra Señora de Guadalupe del Peñasco	1768	Guadalcázar, Catorce	Creole
Count of Regla	1768	Real del Monte	Peninsular
Marquis of Panuco	1772	Rosario	Creole
Marquis of Apartado	1772	Silver Bank, Sombrerete	Creole
Marquis of San Juan de Rayas	1774	Guanajuato	Creole
Count of the Valle de Suchil	1776	Durango Sombrerete	Peninsular
Count of Valenciana	1780	Guanajuato	Creole
Count of la Cortina	1783	(?)	Peninsular
Marquis of Bibanco	1791	Bolaños	Peninsular
Count of Pérez Gálvez	1805	Guanajuato	Peninsular
Count of Casa Rul	1804	Guanajuato	Peninsular

These titles, moreover, can serve as a rough guide to the relative importance of the various mining camps. Guanajuato consistently produced from between a fifth and a quarter of all Mexican silver. Bolaños and Catorce were the century's great discoveries. But elsewhere camps such as Taxco, Real del Monte, Pachuca, and in particular Zacatecas, all experienced an irregular cycle of flooding and bonanza. The great boom in production that started during the 1770s and which kept up until 1810 sprang from both the renovation of old mines and the more efficient exploitation of new ones. To illustrate this complex trend we have chosen for detailed discussion Bolaños and Zacatecas. But to fully understand the situation before 1770 it is necessary to examine a hitherto relatively unknown institution.

I

In 1716 the viceroy, the Duke of Linares stated that although the Mexican mining industry required the service of four to five silver banks, in fact only two, owned by Isidoro Rodríguez and Luis Sánchez de Tagle, transacted business.[1] A third banker, Nicolás de Landa, had recently been declared bankrupt; he was later to be joined by Rodríguez.[2] By 1730 we find mention of two banks belonging respectively to Francisco de Valdivielso and Francisco de Fagoaga.[3] But apparently in no year of the eighteenth century were there more than three of these institutions operating together, and by 1770 all three had withdrawn from circulation.[4]

The origin of these banks was to be found in the six months delay caused by the Crown's decision to farm out the mint to private individuals. A group of merchants arose to exchange silver for coin as soon as it arrived in Mexico City, charging a discount of one real a mark. These men then arranged for the silver's final assay and smelting into bar and frequently rented the machinery and plant of the mint itself.[5] The silver bankers, therefore, were simply merchants who up to 1730 controlled the third stage of Mexico's silver industry. The Fagoagas, for example, rented from the Crown the Apartado office, where the gold found in silver bar was finally separated. But in addition to this exchange and mintage business, the silver bankers acted as the chief aviadores of Mexico, opening accounts for important miners, honouring libranzas drawn upon them, and sending them cash, mercury and other raw materials. Gamboa stated that they only charged a discount of $1\frac{3}{4}$ rls. on the silver produced by their contracted miners.[6] What distinguished the silver banks from the normal aviadores was their greater capital resources, their more generous rates of discount and their participation in the mint. These firms often accepted loans from private institutions and individuals, upon which they paid the normal 5 per cent interest. But in no sense did they serve as banks of deposit or issue; as regards the type of their transactions they formed little more than enlarged versions of the traditional silver merchants.

The scale of operation, however, was at times extraordinarily large. In 1738 Francisco de Valdivielso, by then Count of San Pedro del Alamo, agreed to back Manuel Ginoesio, the owner of mines and refining mills at Sombrerete, a camp situated in the modern state of Zacatecas.[7] Valdivielso gave 20,000 ps. in cash at once; despatched to Sombrerete such indispensable materials as mercury, cord, iron, and gunpowder; and honoured all

[1] BN (Madrid) MSS 2929, f. 137.

[2] Gamboa, *Comentarios*, pp. 149, 355.

[3] Fonseca y Urrutia, *Historia general de Real Hacienda*, I, 152.

[4] Lassaga and Velásquez de León, *Representación*, p. 19.

[5] Elhuyar, *Indagaciones*, pp. 8, 39.

[6] Gamboa, *Comentarios*, p. 149.

[7] AGN, Vínculos 174, contains a full account of the lawsuit.

libranzas drawn upon his bank by Ginoesio in payment for supplies of maize, straw, mules, salt and copper pyrites. In return for these extensive services, the contract stipulated that Ginoesio had to pay a discount of 2½ rls. on every mark of silver he sent to Mexico City. As so often happened in these arrangements, the miner overdrew his account. In retaliation Valdivielso first increased his discount rate to 4 rls., then, in 1742, installed a manager to improve production, and finally, in 1749, initiated a lawsuit to embargo and auction Ginoesio's estate. He reckoned that during the entire period 1738–49 he had advanced 703,645 ps. in cash, supplies and bills for which he had only received 472,183 ps. in actual silver. Ginoesio contested the case, asserting that he had paid into the bank bar worth 1,106,474 ps., so that in fact the Count owed him over 350,000 ps. Since more precise information is not at present available we have no reason to accept either party's testimony.

But from whence did Valdivielso, a Montañés immigrant, procure sufficient capital to establish himself as a silver banker? As was so often the case in Mexico, the answer appears to lie in his marriages. His first wife, Luisa Sánchez de Tagle, daughter of the second Marquis of Altamira, brought him a dowry of 200,000 ps.[1] Possibly, she also inherited the silver bank founded by her grand-father, the first Marquis of Altamira, Luis Sánchez de Tagle, once prior of the consulado. Both he and her father, like her husband, were natives of Santillana del Mar.[2] Her sister also married a Montañés. Following his wife's death, Valdivielso, not content with one such matrimonial prize, succeeded in winning the hand of the Marchioness of San Miguel de Aguayo, the heir to vast territories in the modern state of Coahuila. By some genetic quirk the inheritance of this great entail, set up in the sixteenth century by the well-known Francisco de Urdiñola, had passed through four generations to daughters. Each in her turn had chosen a peninsular Spaniard husband.[3] Valdivielso, in both of his matrimonial alliances, benefited from these ingrained social preferences.

Little evidence has come to light as to the outcome of the wide circle of mining investments into which Valdivielso poured his wives' fortunes. He figured prominently in Guanajuato and Pachuca as an aviadoa; he himself owned mines in Zacatecas and Mazapil.[4] But when he died in 1749

[1] Francisco González Cancino y Aguirre, 'Santillana del Mar en el año de 1753', *Altamira*, 2 (1934), pp. 73–178. Also *Aportación al estudio de la historia económica de la montaña*, pp. 707–11.

[2] Rubio Mañé, *Gente de España*, pp. 258–9.

[3] AGI, Mexico 1370, Bucareli to Arriaga, 24 June 1772, contains printed memorial of the services of the Marquis de Aguayo. Leopoldo Martínez Cosío, *Los caballeros de las órdenes militares en México* (Mexico, 1946), pp. 88–9, 193–4, 290.

[4] BRP, MSS 2824, Miscelánea de Ayala, I, ff. 132, 136, 137.

apparently his two sons found their vast patrimony to be heavily burdened with debts. One source mentions the figure of half a million pesos 'in deposits'.[1] Certainly, when the Mexican ecclesiastical funds were amortised during the years 1805–8, the Marquis of San Miguel of Aguayo of that epoch was called upon to repay no less than 450,000 ps.[2] It is not clear, however, whether this huge mortgage originated in Valdivielso's prodigality as a silver banker.

II

If any one family could lay claim to the leadership of the Mexican silver-mining industry it was the Fagoagas. For three generations, throughout the entire span of the eighteenth century they participated in many of the industry's greatest enterprises. Until the 1770s they operated the colony's largest silver bank; then, during the 1780s they emerged as the chief miners in the province of Zacatecas. In addition the family always stayed close to the seat of power. Both Francisco de Fagoaga and his son-in-law Manuel de Aldaco became priors of the Mexico consulado. On the other hand, José Mariano de Fagoaga, who was mainly responsible for the great bonanza at Sombrerete, accepted election as administrator-general of the mining court.[3] After Independence the Fagoagas, along with their Villaurrutia cousins, numbered among the leaders of the aristocratic Bourbon party.[4] Frances Calderón de la Barca, the wife of the Spanish minister during the 1840s, knew the family well and visited their estates.[5] She clearly had them in mind when she wrote: 'There are in Mexico a few families of the old school, people of high rank, but who mingle very little in society. ... Being nearly all allied by birth, or connected by marriage, they form a sort of clan ... and whatever elements of good society exist in Mexico, are to be found amongst them.'[6]

It was in 1706 that Francisco de Fagoaga, a Basque from the valley of Oyarzu in Guipuzcoa, laid the foundation of his descendants' future prosperity when he rented the Apartado office from its nominal manager.[7] For the Apartado office, a royal institution leased to private individuals,

[1] AGI, Mexico 1511, Cossío to Gálvez, 26 November 1780.

[2] Romeo Flores Caballero, 'La consolidación de vales reales en la economía, la sociedad y la política novohispanas', *Historia Mexicana*, 18 (1969), 3, pp. 334–78.

[3] *Gacetas de México*, II, 79, Fagoaga was elected prior in 1733. His grandson José Mariano was Administrator-general in 1800–6. See AGI, Mexico 2246, Azanza to Soler, 30 January 1800.

[4] Mora, *Obras sueltas*, p. 27.

[5] Frances Calderón de la Barca, *Life in Mexico* (London, Everyman ed., 1960), p. 420.

[6] *Ibid.*, pp. 223–4.

[7] AGN, Vínculos 8/6, account by Lic. Oláez, 1808.

was charged with the task of separating gold from silver in the bar sent to Mexico City. Naturally, if operated efficiently, it could yield a handsome profit to the owner. Moreover, since it was desirable to exchange the bar for cash upon presentation, the office provided an ideal basis for a silver bank. So it is not surprising to find that by 1730 Fagoaga was described, along with Valdivielso, as a leading silver banker. By then he had purchased the lease from its former owner for 60,000 ps., the Crown charging 36,000 ps. on the transaction. Marriage completed the circle of Fagoaga's undertakings when his wife Josefa inherited a trading house worth 118,464 ps. set up in the previous century by her father, Juan Bautista de Arosqueta, a Basque merchant.[1] Our knowledge of both the structure and progress of Fagoaga's group of enterprises is mainly limited to what can be gleaned from the inventory of his estate, drawn up in December 1736, just after his death[2] (see table 13).

Caution is required to interpret the inventory: this was a balance of stock, cash, credits and debts struck at a particular moment in time, not an account of a year's trading. In effect, Fagoaga ran three separate businesses—the merchant house, the Apartado office, and the silver bank. Unfortunately, although all credits advanced by the almacén and bank were listed separately, the debts they owed on current account—*cuenta corriente*—were presented together. But from another balance drawn up by Ambrosio de Meave, the trading house's manager, we can estimate that the current debts of his firm did not amount to more than 200,000 ps. If this be the case then the remaining 750,000 ps. represented sums owed by the silver bank and the Apartado office. In fact two merchants, Domingo Mateos and Francisco de Vértiz respectively held credits of 418,274 ps. and 236,722 ps. These debts accounted either for Fagoaga's surprisingly large stock of specie or, alternatively, for the great store of merchandise which was far in excess of the firm's usual stock. According to a later estimate the Apartado office required a revolving fund of 400,000 ps. for the purchase of silver bar. The rest of the specie probably belonged to miners or silver merchants.

The deposits section was divided into two parts: that for which a 5 per cent interest was paid and that which did not carry any interest. The first part comprised a series of small sums lent by ecclesiastical institutions and a few private individuals. A large proportion of the second class were deposited by the judge of testaments and wills; the customs house held

1 For Arosqueta, see Rubio Mañé, *Gente de España*, pp. 31–2. He died in 1730.

2 AGN, Vínculos 7. The inventory was drawn up at the end of 1736, and approved 8 April 1737.

another 30,000 ps. Presumably Fagoaga offered safe storage. But whatever their origin these deposits represented an additional source of capital rather than the mainstay of the business.

Table 13 *Inventory of estate of Francisco de Fagoaga, December 1736.* (In pesos)

Assets		*Debits*	
Apartado office instruments, premises	167,775	Deposits paying 5% int.	68,500
		Deposits without int.	95,920
Cash	757,259	Debts on current acct.:	
Silver and gold bar	131,293	Domingo de Mateos	418,274
		Francisco de Vértiz	236,772
Silver Bank:		Marquis of San Clemente	96,896
collectable credits	262,582	Juan Domingo Guraja	78,638
doubtful credits	107,507	Many smaller items	203,969
lost credits	67,358		
Trading House:		Legacies, etc. owed to Fagoaga family	121,612
Current stock	125,013	Small misc. items	20,066
Merchandise last fleet	216,843		
Merchandise present fleet	308,011		
Collectable credits	97,632		
Doubtful credits	6,951		
Lost credits	37,582		
Stock, cash, credits of shop in Oaxaca	45,422		
Personal effects	34,421		
Misc. items	14 072		
Gross assets	2,379,721		
Debits	1,331,647		1,331,647
Net total	1,048,074		
		Principal of Josefa de Arosqueta	159,070
		Principal of Francisco de Fagoaga at marriage	176,909
		Lesser charge	12,742
	348,721		348,721
Net increase	699,353		

The silver bank's range of activity can best be gauged from its credits advanced. It supplied clients in Guanajuato, Zacatecas, Mexico City, Tlalpujahua, Taxco, Pachuca, Temascaltepec and Chihuahua. Sums varied from the 234 ps. advanced to Francisco and José de la Borda to the 57,493 ps. granted to Simón Francisco de Arroyo, a partner in the Rayas mine of Guanajuato. Over 40 per cent of all 'good' credits went to Guanajuato. That town's importance for the bank is confirmed by the debit side of the accounts: Fagoaga owed the Marquis of San Clemente, the principal shareholder of the Mellado and Cata mines, some 96,896 ps. Zacatecas was less well covered: the bank had lent 27,895 ps. to one miner and owed 20,150 to another. Silver banking also offered considerable risks: the doubtful or lost credits amounted to over 150,000 ps.

After Fagoaga's death, his widow conferred full management of the entire estate upon Manuel de Aldaco, her husband's nephew from Spain, who had married her eldest daughter. From 1736 until he died in 1770 he received half the profits of the enterprise. But, apparently this arrangement contained some hidden clause since after his death Aldaco's only son was granted but one-third of the estate, the remainder going back to the still surviving widow. Whatever the precise agreement, in effect Fagoaga's great firm was not subjected to any testamentary division. On the strength of his marriage and his cousinhood, Aldaco became the leading silver banker of his day, prior of the consulado and co-founder of the Vizcaína college. He backed many of the industry's chief enterprises. He acted as aviador to José de la Borda, the most skilled miner of the time and greatly profited from the latter's bonanza at Tlalpujahua during the 1740s. But most of his ventures did not prove so successful.[1] At Real del Monte, where the Count of Regla was later to make a vast fortune, Aldaco, in company with Juan de Barandiarán, attempted to drain the Santa Brígida mine by the construction of an adit. He installed Pedro de Anza, a close associate of Borda, as his manager. Nevertheless, despite this combination of capital resources and technical skill, Aldaco lost about half a million pesos on the project.[2]

The risks of silver banking were further demonstrated when in 1749 the leading miner of Guanajuato, the Marquis of San Clemente, died owing Aldaco 160,000 ps. His heirs proved unable either to redeem the principal or to pay the yearly interest on the huge sum. In consequence Aldaco took the case to court, and in 1753 the audiencia ordered the heirs to cede to Aldaco their main asset, the Villachuato hacienda.[3] Other investments proved equally unfruitful. In 1757 Aldaco foreclosed upon certain miners

[1] See José Antonio Ximénes y Frías, *El fénix de los mineros ricos* (*Mexico*, 1779), p. 55; also Manuel Toussaint, *Tasco* (Mexico, 1931), p. 90.

[2] AGI, Mexico 2240, Domingo Valcárcel to Crown, 29 August 1777.

[3] AGI, Mexico 2214, Marquis of Apartado to viceroy, 31 August 1793. See also Chávez Orozco, *Conflicto de trabajo*, pp. 96–9.

at Fresnillo; he appointed his own administrator but lost 80,000 ps.[1] Similarly, at the same time, José de la Borda, despite his earlier success at Tlalpujahua and Taxco, failed to drain the Canal mine at Zacualpán. By 1766 he owed Aldaco 102,000 ps.[2]

Clearly, only the richest of firms could have withstood such a range of losses. Presumably—our records are by no means complete—other investments must have yielded a good return. Then again, during the years 1758–62, all the profits made by the trading house, managed by Ambrosio de Meave, were paid directly into the silver bank.[3] Moreover, according to an independent estimate, the Apartado office averaged an annual income of 25,435 ps. during the period 1742–62, at least enough to cover the loss in the Santa Brígida.[4] A family lawsuit, however, offered a different scale of profit, taken after the deduction of 5 per cent upon the capital value of the plant.[5]

Profits of apartado office, 1751–78

August 1751–November 1756	10,604 ps. loss (42,388 ps. interest paid)
November 1756–January 1767	98,124 ps. profit
January 1767–October 1772	194,495 ps. profit
12 years 1766–78	392,045 ps. profit

An obvious explanation of the losses suffered during the 1750s would be that Aldaco financed the bank from the income of the Apartado office. The matter was somewhat delicate, since by this time the office had been inherited by José Joaquín de Fagoaga, his brother-in-law, a colonel resident at the Court of Naples. In 1764 Aldaco wrote a paternal letter to Fagoaga advising him of the family's current financial difficulties. He asked him to be more economical, 'avoiding all superfluous expense, which only tends to discredit business houses no matter how opulent they are, since they become objects of censure and gossip among all persons of good sense. . . .'[6] Fine talk from a man who had just lost 500,000 ps. down a mine!

1 AGN, Vínculos 150, the audiencia adjudged the hacienda to Aldaco, 7 June 1753.
2 BRP, MSS 2824, Miscelánea de Ayala X, report of Tomás de Landázuri, ff. 133–4, 157; AGN, Minería 202, Manuel de Aldaco to viceroy, 13 February 1768.
3 AGN, Vínculos 106/4, José de la Borda to viceroy, March 1775.
4 See balances in AGN, Vínculos 10/3, statement by Manuel Ramón de Goya, 15 May 1782.
5 AGI, Mexico 1382, Bucareli to Gálvez, 27 July 1777. AGN, Vínculos 6/3, statement by J. A. Rangel, 7 July 1794.
6 AGN, Vínculos 6/3, Aldaco to José Joaquín de Fagoaga, 22 October 1764.

The final results of Aldaco's management can be ascertained from the inventory of the Fagoaga estate, drawn up after his death[1] (table 14).

Table 14 *Partial inventory of Fagoaga's estate, August 1772.*[a] (In pesos)

Assets		*Debits*	
Apartado office, instruments, premises	138,000	Deposits	280,186
Bullion and cash	1,442,718	Debts on current acct.: to consulado	400,000
		to Echeveste trading house	310,845
Credits, current and good	318,280	Smaller items (various)	417,318
Credits at Fresnillo	271,665		
Credits at Sombrerete	170,881	Debts on Villachuato hacienda	17,601
		To Marquis of Apartado	73,296
Almacén (trading house): Stock, cash, credits	525,000	Libranzas to Sombrerete and Fresnillo	18,000
Haciendas: Villachuato	253,544	To Manuel Aldaco, personal costs	19,084
Zambrano	111,303		
Temepantla	44,769		
Smaller properties	54,682	Misc. items	55,577
Personal Effects	43,000		
Misc. items	8,004		
Gross total	3,381,846		
less	1,591,727		1,591,927
Net total	1,789,919		
		Principal of Josefa de Arosqueta (*c.* 1736)	546,508
		Principal of Aldaco (*c.* 1736)	80,000
less	626,508		626,508
Net increase	1,163,411	(Divided equally between Aldaco and Arosqueta)	

[a] It should be noted that the 1772 inventory only gives a round total for debts and deposits on current account. The partial breakdown in this section is taken from an earlier inventory drawn up in January 1771.

The main difference from the previous inventory lay in the acquisition of haciendas and the actual direction of mines at Fresnillo and Sombrerete. Largely through foreclosure the Fagoagas had entered productive enterprise. The geographical concentration of their interests in the area which

[1] AGN, Vínculos 6/3, inventory approved 31 December 1770, and AGN, Vínculos 8/8.

now forms the state of Zacatecas was to become even more pronounced in the years to come. The silver bank still continued in business, but since individual items were not listed, we have no indication of its range. Once again, the great fund of silver bar and specie reflects both the Apartado and silver bank's mode of operation rather than directly realisable assets. On the debit side, the firm had somewhat increased its deposits, which as before represented an agglomeration of small sums supplied by confraternities, convents and private individuals. Domingo Valcárcel, senior judge of the Mexican audiencia, had placed 22,529 ps. with Aldaco. We are not informed whether all deposits, or only some, received the 5 per cent interest. As before, the current accounts comprised an extensive range of petty debts; in addition the firm owed 400,000 ps. to the consulado and 310,849 ps. to the 'house of Echeveste'—the associate of Meave and Aldaco in the construction of the Vizcaína college. Over a period of 30 years the total value of the combined businesses had risen by 741,845 ps.—an annual average of 21,819 ps. The figure, of course, excluded the income which supported the Fagoaga family. But it does indicate that Aldaco's decision to plunge heavily into mining had not met with much success.

When Fagoaga's widow finally died in 1772 she was survived by only two sons, Francisco Cayetano, Marquis of Apartado, and Juan Bautista, whom she had recently summoned home from Spain. At her instance the two heirs had already agreed not to divide the vast estate; instead they appointed a peninsular cousin, José Luis de Fagoaga, to act as their general manager. However, by the 1780s, the two brothers, after a few years of prosperity, began to experience considerable financial difficulties. For in 1778 the Crown, inspired by Gálvez, terminated their lease of the Apartado office, paying in compensation for the machinery, houses and plant just under 100,000 ps.[1] Only a few years later, in 1781, Ambrosio de Meave died, leaving the trading house exposed to all the commercial vicissitudes of the 1780s. In a word, two of the three pillars which upheld the great Fagoaga enterprise were suddenly removed. At the same time their mines at Sombrerete began to lose money. In 1779, under threat of total abandonment, they obtained from the Crown a full tax exemption for the initial renovation of the Veta Negra mine, to be followed by a 50 per cent reduction for a period of 16 years, during which span mercury was to be supplied at cost price. These concessions, granted in view of Sombrerete's complete dependence upon the Fagoagas, kept the firm afloat.[2] Nevertheless, by 1790 the mine's shafts, cut to a depth of 290 yards, required ten

[1] Bernard Bobb, *The Viceregency of Antonia María Bucareli, 1771–79* (Austin, 1962), p. 239.
[2] AGI, Mexico 1533, Revillagigedo to Lerena, 29 July 1790.

whims to stem the persistent flooding. Silver output did not cover the costs of production.[1] By the end of that decade, traumatic for so many established commercial and financial houses, the Fagoagas had accumulated debts at Sombrerete and elsewhere that approached 716,000 ps. It then appeared that, with the prop of the Apartado office removed, the family was doomed to follow many a lesser miner into the bankruptcy courts.

But at this point José Mariano de Fagoaga, Juan Bautista's Peninsula-born son who managed the Sombrerete mines, decided to cut a cross-tunnel from the Veta Negra to the Pabellón mine which lay 400 yards away. The estimated cost was 200,000 ps. and the chances of failure high. The Fagoagas therefore petitioned for a complete exemption from the silver tithe for 15 years and a 50 per cent reduction for another 15 years; during the entire 30 years mercury was to be supplied at cost price. These concessions, applicable only to the Pabellón mine, were approved by the Council of the Indies in view of the project's cost and risk.[2] But almost as soon as work began on the tunnel an extraordinarily rich mass of ore was encountered. Between October 1791 and June 1793 the mine produced 185,882 marks of silver. A disgruntled viceroy protested against the tax exemptions; but not until 1801 did the Crown finally decide to cancel the concessions and demand the retroactive payment of a third of the taxes hitherto ceded. The Fagoagas resisted this demand, proclaimed their impressive record of service to the silver-mining industry, and presented an account of their most recent investments. The list in table 15, suspect like all tax declarations, indicates both their profits and the use to which they were put.[3] Table 16 gives an overall picture of the Fagoaga family's mining investments at this time.

The Crown lost 939,110 ps. in taxes on the Pabellón mine. But as the Fagoagas pointed out, their workers took an eighth of all silver produced, upon which the full tithe was charged. Moreover, all silver continued to pay mintage charges. They claimed that the Crown had obtained 943,451 ps. in taxes directly attributable to the Pabellón mine. In addition, other branches of revenue, such as tobacco and alcabalas, had benefited from the purchasing power generated by their employees. Between 1791 and 1803 the Sombrerete treasury received 1,042,167 ps. from the local tobacco monopoly officials. Convinced by these impressive claims, the

[1] AGI, Mexico 2214, Marquis of Apartado to viceroy, 31 August 1793.

[2] AGI, Mexico 1554, Revillagigedo to Crown, 31 August 1793; *real orden* granting exemptions, 11 September 1792.

[3] AGI, Mexico 1815, Iturrigaray to Soler, 27 January 1806, statement of José Mariano Fagoaga, 15 February 1805.

Table 15 *Production of Pabellón mine 1790–November 1804.*

Year	Production (in marks)	Taxes exempted (in pesos)
1792–3	336,608	320,243
1794	162,778	154,987
1795	101,074	96,237
1796	97,881	93,190
1797	96,211	91,607
1798	60,908	57,993
1799	57,368	54,622
1800	26,248	24,992
1801 (Jan.–Oct. 28)	22,696	21,616
1801 (Oct. 28–Dec.)	3,828	1,822
1802	16,628	7,916
1803	17,970	8,555
1804 (Jan.–Oct. 31)	11,195	5,330
	1,011,393	939,110

Costs and profits, 1791–1804

	Costs	*Production*
Costs of production	4,758,013 ps.	8,834,820 ps.
Transport costs, assay, Mining court charges	550,703 ps.	
	5,308,716 ps.	5,308,716 ps.
Profits		3,526,104 ps.

Table 16 *Mining investments of the Fagoaga family, c. 1804.* (In pesos)

	Losses incurred	Taxes paid [a]
At Fresnillo until 1801	43,321	103,964
At Sultepec until 1803	156,365	45,118
At Zacualpán	25,108	696
At Vetagrande in Zacatecas	549,500	exempt
At Animas in Guanajuato 1800–4	105,259	taxes paid by Guanajuato refiners
In Sombrerete:		
Quebradilla 1796–1804	379,338	150,594
Santa Catalina (both abandoned)	123,428	13,426
San Nicolás, since 1802	49,129	518
Lost in Veta Negra and Pabellón on capital construction	412,566	156,892
Total	1,844,014	471,208
	Mintage charge	227,266
	Total	698,474

[a] Including 1 rl. to Mining Court, assay, etc.

viceregal finance committee accepted the Fagoagas' offer to pay back 38,188 ps. of past taxes and to give outright the 50,000 ps. loan already subscribed to the Crown by the Marquis of Apartado.

José Mariano de Fagoaga, who presented the family's case, stressed that the Pabellón's true bonanza only lasted from 1792 until 1795. Since then costs had eaten into profits as the mine soon required five separate shafts serviced by some 29 whims. At the same time the Veta Negra had to be kept drained to prevent its water flooding into the Pabellón. Presumably the 412,566 ps. listed in the scheme of investments as 'lost' in these two mines referred to the construction cost of these shafts. At Sombrerete the Fagoagas operated a vast integrated enterprise, which comprised mines, a refining mill with 84 arrastres and 14 furnaces, and haciendas to supply maize, straw and mules.[1] They also ran company stores to the point where one merchant called the town 'a closed door' for other traders.[2] For nearly 40 years Sombrerete formed the special domain of one, almost never resident family.

The Fagoagas differed from other Mexican miners in at least two different respects. They maintained a united management for a century and throughout that period they ploughed back their profits into mining. Their losses were phenomenal and their profits the reward for years of persistent heavy investment. The transition from silver banker to simple miner was a perilous one. Moreover, the withdrawal from trade and the termination of the Apartado lease dealt mortal blows to the basis of their enterprise. Only the extraordinary success of Sombrerete, after 20 years of mediocre returns, permitted them to continue as leaders of the industry. Their ability to invest over half a million pesos in the Vetagrande at Zacatecas clearly sprang from this bonanza.

During the 1790s as death drew close, the two brothers, the Marquis of Apartado and Juan Bautista, decided finally to split their jointly managed estate, since they both had numerous heirs. By then the brothers had acquired several distinguished relatives. The Marquis himself had married a daughter of the creole judge Antonio de Villaurrutia; he therefore possessed two influential brothers-in-law, Jacobo, an alcalde del crimen in the Mexican audiencia, and Antonio, regent of the Guadalajara audiencia. Similarly, a daughter of Juan Bautista married the second Marquis of Castañiza, son of the former compadre of Manuel de Aldaco. In these circumstances it was perhaps to be expected that when the two brothers quarrelled over the division of their estate they should have called their

[1] See Ward, *Mexico in 1827*, II, 534–43.

[2] FV 3, Manuel García Herreros to Diego Rul, 22 January 1793.

business partner and relative by marriage, Antonio Bassoco (in that year prior of the consulado), to adjudicate. They did not accept, however, his verdict and took the case to the audiencia. In the end the estate was divided among eight children and 26 grand-children.[1] The heirs proved less devoted to mining than their ancestors and invested their capital in haciendas and in the new interest-paying funds of the mining court and the consulados. In 1813 the court listed debts of 242,000 ps. owed to the Count of Alcaraz, husband of a Fagoaga daughter, and 240,000 ps. held by the dowager Marchioness of Apartado.[2] By then, of course, the Fagoagas had lost that unity of direction which had maintained their enterprise at the head of Mexican mining for nearly a century. As always, the laws of inheritance and the absence of joint stock companies worked to destroy the capital accumulations of colonial Mexico.

III

The tendency for entire camps to fall under the domination of a single company or family can be clearly demonstrated from the history of Real del Monte and Pachuca, two camps situated just northeast of Mexico City. Both had been discovered in the sixteenth century and both enjoyed bonanzas in the first years of the eighteenth century.[3] But then the mounting level of water cut short their prosperity. Extraordinary measures were called for and in one case supplied. By the 1760s the chief mines in each camp were operated by a single owner, in Real del Monte by the Count of Regla and at Pachuca by a mercantile company. Their contrasting fortunes indicated what constituted the necessary prerequisites for the successful renovation of old mines.

Pedro Romero de Terreros, a native of Cortegana in Andalusia, first went to New Spain to inherit the considerable fortune left by a deceased brother. He then moved to Querétaro, there to assist his uncle Juan Vásquez de Terreros, a prominent merchant. When the latter died he bequeathed his nephew all his worldly goods. This pattern of inheritance, common among the immigrant community, laid the basis of Regla's fortune.[4] He consolidated it by his friendship with José Alejandro Bustamante, a miner whom he backed with the full weight of his resources.

In 1739 Bustamante decided to renovate the Veta Vizcaína mine at Real

[1] For this dispute see AGN, Vínculos 6/3.

[2] AGN, Minería 211/1, statement 1826. After June 1813 the court did not pay any interest on its funds.

[3] Gemelli Carreri, *Viaje*, I, 130–2. Lassaga and Velásquez de León, *Representación*, p. 87.

[4] Ortega y Pérez Gallardo, *Historia genealógica*, II, *Conde de Regla*.

del Monte by means of an extensive drainage tunnel or adit. The lodes of that camp were already famous for their wealth: in the single year, 1726, the Veta Vizcaína and Jacal mines had produced 292,774 marks of amalgamated silver. But its mines were equally renowned for their deep flooding. The silver banker Isidoro Rodríguez de la Madrid had bankrupted himself at Real del Monte when he imported English machinery at a cost of 100,000 ps. in a vain attempt to clear his property of water. To share the costs of construction, Bustamante formed a company with other mine-owners of the camp—with the Marquis of Valle Ameno and Juan de Barandiarán. He himself was backed by Romero de Terreros, and Barandiarán by Manuel de Aldaco. But after nine years' labour the drainage tunnel had to be abandoned: it had been cut for 1,200 yards but it did not drain the lode.[1] Work on a new tunnel began, but soon after, in 1750, Bustamante died leaving Romero de Terreros both his property and his commitments. The adit was not completed until 1762: only then did the true Veta Vizcaína bonanza begin. By this time the other mines in Real del Monte had flooded. Nor had the Veta Vizcaína as yet yielded much profit since between 1741 and 1758 the mine only produced 216,093 marks of silver. Romero de Terreros claimed that he had invested 1,428,906 ps. in the construction of shafts, drainage tunnels, and the famous Regla refining mill which alone cost 425,708 ps.[2]

In the years that followed, despite the serious labour troubles which have already described, the Veta Vizcaína made its owner the richest man in New Spain. In all, between 1738 and 1781, the mine's output amounted to about 20 million pesos of silver, of which possibly two million were taken by workers as partidos.[3] Profits matched production and Romero de Terreros expended his fortune in prodigal fashion. He purchased first a title for himself, and then two other titles for his younger sons. He became the Count of Regla, and his sons, the Marquises of San Cristóbal and San Francisco. He obtained royal favour by the gift of a warship, built at Havana for a million pesos. A pious man as well as a patriot, Regla helped the northern missionary activity of the Franciscan College at Querétaro; his own cousin was killed by Apaches when engaged on this work. He also donated 300,000 ps. to erect the national Monte de Piedad or pawnshop, which today continues to do business in the same massive building situated in the main square of Mexico City.[4] Unlike the Fagoagas, Regla

[1] Gamboa, *Comentarios*, pp. 477–8.
[2] AGI, Mexico 2251, statement by Regla, undated *c.* 1758.
[3] Castelazo, *Manifiesto*, pp. 8–10.
[4] Ortega y Pérez Gallardo, *Historia genealógica*, II, *Conde de Regla*.

did not re-invest his profits in mining. It appears that apart from a lead mine at Zimapán he restricted his activity to Real del Monte, a camp which he dominated as much as the Fagoagas in Sombrerete.[1] Instead, intent upon the establishment of a noble family, he purchased chains of haciendas. In 1777 he acquired all the estates belonging to the former Jesuit colleges of Tepotzotlán and St Peter and St Paul of Mexico City. Although they were then valued at 1,979,595 ps., he bought them outright, cash down, for 1,020,000 ps.[2] These estates were then divided among his three sons to form separate entails each worth about 300,000 ps.

While Regla busied himself with these new possessions the source of his wealth, the Veta Vizcaína, experienced difficulty as its shafts penetrated beyond the levels drained by its great adit. In consequence, soon after Regla's death in 1781, the mines were effectively abandoned. The second count, however, renovated the mine once more, so that between 1794 and 1801 it produced another six million pesos. But by then the cost of its 28 whims had risen to a quarter of a million pesos a year, so that when the British blockade interrupted mercury shipments he proved unable to meet these enormous overhead costs and terminated work.[3] His son, the third count, started a fresh restoration of the mine, but his efforts were cut short by the 1810 insurrection. The financial success of the Count of Regla, consummated by 1762, offered an obvious lesson to all potential miners. But most investors, we may suspect, were more impressed by the size of his fortune rather than by the patient years of investment in drainage shafts and adits. As economists put it, his success operated as a demonstration effect: it made mining more attractive to investors. It was a royal official who in 1764 perceived the effort behind the achievement: 'Don Pedro Romero de Terreros has begun and concluded a magnificent work at the cost of his spiritual tenacity, constancy and great expense.'[4]

Not all miners possessed Regla's perseverance or capital resources. In 1767 Manuel José de Moya registered ownership of a group of flooded mines at Pachuca known collectively as the Four Peaks; he proposed to cut an adit at an estimated cost of 700,000 ps. To assist Moya in his ambitious scheme to restore this ancient but decadent camp Viceroy Croix granted him full tax exemption and the supply of mercury at cost price.[5] But unlike Borda or Regla, the two great exemplars of the industry, Moya lacked both skill and capital. Between February 1770 and September 1773

[1] Ward, *Mexico in 1827*, II, 335.
[2] AGI, Mexico 1772, statement of accountant-general of *Temporalidades*, 16 December 1777.
[3] Castelazo, *Manifiesto*, pp. 10–11. Burkart, *Memoria*, pp. 22–3, 44.
[4] AGI, Mexico 2251, fiscal report, 30 May 1764.
[5] AGI, Mexico 2200, Ortiz de Landázuri to Arriaga, 30 April 1769.

the mines produced 255,426 ps. but the cost of renovation and the construction of a refining mill amounted to 462,406 ps.[1] By then Moya had died, leaving debts of over 200,000 ps. His principal debtor, his aviador, the Count of San Bartolomé de Jala, a wealthy merchant and landowner of Mexico City to whom he owed over 96,000 ps., refused to invest more money in the venture. Another merchant of Mexico City, José de la Torre Calderón, to whom Moya owed 52,000 ps., then formed a company composed of the principal creditors to keep the mine in production and hence redeem their debts.[2] But this company did not care to invest further capital in the Four Peaks mine. Instead they gave their workers half the ore, in lieu of wages, only insisting that the partidos had to be sold to the company's own refining mill and not to independent refiners. They spent very little on deepening the main shaft. Moya had driven it to a depth of no more than 73 yards out of the 233 yards deemed necessary. But between 1773 and 1779 it was extended only another 34 yards.[3] Yet throughout this period, indeed until 1801, the company enjoyed full exemption from the silver tithe and was supplied mercury at cost price. An indignant royal official who later inspected the neglected mine, exclaimed: 'the owners have not contributed a penny to develop it'.[4] Yet it was to this ruinous enterprise that in 1784–6 the mining court supplied 472,272 ps. in avíos. The mine's production accelerated somewhat, but not enough to cover the money advanced. By June 1787 the company owed the court 170,855 ps.[5] Presumably these funds had been invested in the main shaft, since by 1789 it had reached a depth of 140 yards.

During the next decade the company was subjected to official scrutiny since it did not appear to merit its tax exemptions. Nevertheless work continued, in part by the company, in part by individuals who had rented several of its mines. Finally, in 1801, the Crown terminated the tax rebates; the treasury officials then estimated that between 1770 and February 1801 the company had produced 511,695 marks of silver (4,469,814 ps.). The value of the royal concessions for this period amounted to 553,376 ps. In spite of this, however, the company's managers claimed that total costs had exceeded the value of the output by 213,258 ps.[6] In all, the company was in debt for about half a million pesos. Naturally these figures were highly suspect, as the treasury officials declared, since the company

1 AGI, Mexico 1765, statement by accountant-general, 6 April 1775.
2 AGI, Mexico 1768, meeting of creditors, 29 August 1772.
3 AGI, Mexico 1728, Pachuca treasury officials, 1 May 1778.
4 AGN, Minería 26/1, Francisco Saavedra to viceroy, 21 September 1790.
5 AGN, Minería 30/9, contract, December 1784.
6 AGN, Minería 75/3, Pachuca treasury officials, 25 September 1804.

had spent so little on the mine's development. It is difficult to know whether simple inefficiency or false accounts explained these losses. Whatever the case, neither tax exemptions nor mining court loans nor mercantile intervention had worked to redeem the enterprise. But then its mode of paying labour invited ruin, and the absence of investment in shafts or adits prevented effective exploitation.

IV

Since in many respects the history of Bolaños in the eighteenth century epitomises the general course of Mexican silver mining this little-studied camp deserves extended attention. Situated in the Sierra of northern Jalisco at roughly equal distances from Zacatecas and Guadalajara, Bolaños was a frontier town, for the province of Nayarit had been but recently subdued by the Spaniards. The nearest source of labour was the ancient Tlaxcalan settlement of Colotlán. First discovered by an Indian in 1736, Bolaños soon attracted more experienced miners, but it was not until 1747 that a true mining bonanza began. Then, in the years that followed until 1761, Bolaños produced nearly two million pesos a year, a total that amounted to 15 per cent of all Mexican silver production during that period.[1] This is a minimum estimate: Francisco Javier de Gamboa reckoned that Bolaños in this initial epoch produced between three and four million pesos, or nearly a third of all silver minted.[2] The camp's importance was signalised in 1752 when the viceroy, the Count of Revillagigedo (the Elder), established a royal treasury at Bolaños. Two years later he also gave the town an independent corregidor in order to provide some measure of public order.[3] By this time Bolaños possessed a population of 12,000 persons, a number which later rose to 16,000—clear proof of the mobility of northern mining labour.[4]

But by the 1760s the town's industry faced a crisis. Its principal mines, the Conquista, Castellana, Perla, Montañesa, and Zapopa, were situated along the same lode; for drainage they required common action; but each mine was owned by different groups of partners, many of whom lived in Mexico City or Guadalajara, and the shares of one leading miner, Juan de Echazaureta, had been divided among his children, and were managed by a guardian. In 1757 quarrels over the demarcation of individual mines began. Yet at this moment, after fourteen years of continuous production,

1 Ward, *Mexico in 1827*, II, 139.

2 Gamboa, *Comentarios*, p. 502.

3 *Instrucciones que dejaron los virreyes* (2 vols.; Mexico, 1873), I, 379–92. See also AGI, Guadalajara 203, Viceroy Marquis of Amarillas to Crown, 18 July 1757.

4 AGN, Civil 142/19, corregidor to viceroy, 21 July 1760.

the mines of Bolaños suffered from extensive flooding and required heavy capital investment in the form of a new central shaft cut sufficiently deep to provide effective drainage.[1] Already the four principal mines were losing 500 ps. a week, having doubled the number of whims in operation. Confronted with this situation the mine owners of Bolaños collectively agreed to abandon their property; they had made a certain fortune; they preferred not to lose it in a possibly vain attempt at drainage.

Within two years, by 1762, production halved, and in the next decade, up to 1775, languished at a level that barely reached a quarter of the silver produced during the 1750s.[2] The town's population, so rapidly assembled, fled with equal rapidity, and soon numbered barely a quarter of the former total.[3] Any future revival would have to deal with a serious labour shortage. Equally alarming for the future was the decline in the quality of Bolaños ore: it proved increasingly refractory to the amalgamation process, using more than the normal amount of mercury. In 1772 the superintendent of the mercury monopoly officially recognised this deterioration: whereas in most camps the treasury demanded 100 marks of silver for every hundredweight of mercury distributed, in Bolaños only 75 marks were required.[4]

Bolaños was restored to prosperity by Antonio de Bibanco, a native of Villalasara, in the district of Montija in Castile; his family was probably of Basque extraction.[5] Why Bibanco entered mining, when he came to Bolaños, or what was his previous occupation remains unknown; but by 1771 he was already registered as the owner of two small mines, the Cocina and the Espíritu Santo. Evidently a skilful miner he soon attracted attention when he began to extend his general shaft to a level deep enough to drain the entire lode. It was then, in 1773, that he obtained the financial backing of Juan de Sierra Uruñuela, a merchant of Mexico City who owned shops in Bolaños. Bibanco borrowed 25,000 ps. from Sierra and then took possession of the Conquista, Perla, Castellana, and Montañesa mines which lay waterlogged and unworked.[6] In addition he received the strong support of the local treasury officials who had previously urged the viceroy to find a rich merchant of Mexico City to revive the local mines

1 BRP, MSS 2824, Miscelánea de Ayala X, f. 136.

2 Ward, *Mexico in 1827*, II, 139.

3 AGN, Minería 151/3, treasurer Sebastián de la Torre y León to viceroy, 16 October 1772.

4 AGI, Mexico 2235, superintendent to Crown, 26 May 1772; see also Fonseca and Urrutia, *Historia general de Real Hacienda*, I, 383.

5 For his birthplace see AGI, Mexico 1745, Bibanco to Crown, 23 June 1789. Note his nephew, Pedro Manuel de Bibanco was a native of Biscay; see AGN, Historia 130–3.

6 AGS, Guerra Moderna 7015, treasury officials to viceroy, 5 March 1784.

upon whose continued production depended the prosperity of the surrounding province. Bibanco was granted mercury at a price a third less than the standard rate of 1775.[1] Furthermore, the Bolaños corregidor was forbidden to interfere in mining affairs, so that he was subject only to the local treasury, acting as the viceroy's delegate.

Assisted by this combination of mercantile backing and official benevolence, Bibanco deepened his general shaft to the depth of 250 yards necessary for effective drainage. He later claimed that the shaft cost him 300,000 ps. to cut, a sum largely raised by ploughing back profits, since from 1775 onwards his mines began to produce silver in great quantity. Even so, in his will he stated that as late as February 1780, when his wife died, he only possessed a capital of 40,000 ps., and owed his partner Sierra and the treasury some 160,000 ps.[2] Moreover, in July 1781 he suffered a major setback when the river overflowed into his central shaft, filling it to a depth of 150 yards. True, Bibanco appealed for, and obtained, full exemption from the silver tithe to repair the damages; but this concession was cancelled by Gálvez, and he had to repay some 25,000 ps. to the treasury.[3]

To solve the problem caused by the flood Bibanco constructed a new shaft, 257 yards deep, on which he expended over 400,000 ps. No doubt, however, this second shaft was an essential part of the general restoration of the mines.[4] Certainly the 1781 flood did not seriously lower production which was maintained at a high level from 1776 until 1783 when it abruptly fell. Presumably the great famine of 1785–6, which affected all mining camps, had cut off the supply of labour. Whatever the case, Bibanco, who was engaged in a series of disputes with the local deputation and the audiencia of Guadalajara, decided to abandon his mines. He ceded ownership to his aviador or backer Sierra Uruñuela for the paltry sum of 73,000 ps. Clearly he reckoned that continued investment would no longer yield a profitable return.[5]

Bibanco, although lesser known than José de la Borda or the Count of Regla, must be numbered among that select band of entrepreneurs who directly engineered the mining boom of the 1770s. He too had learnt the lesson that success in mining, initial discovery apart, lay in persistent heavy capital investment. The foundation of his enterprise rested upon the

[1] AGI, Mexico 2235, 18 May 1775.

[2] AGN, Vínculos 214, Will of Antonio de Bibanco, 20 August 1799.

[3] AGI, Mexico 1396, viceroy Mayorga to Gálvez, 28 February 1782; AGI, Mexico 1046, Posada to Gálvez, 2 February 1782.

[4] AGI, Mexico 2242, viceroy Flores to Valdés, 26 February 1789.

[5] AGN, Minería 25/1, Bibanco statement, 3 October 1787.

construction of two deep drainage shafts. His ability was recognised by the local treasury officials, who as early as 1772 wrote to the viceroy that 'Antonio de Bibanco, we can say, without offence to the rest, is the chief and only miner who today maintains the camp due to his indefatigable activity and skill in the art of mining'.[1] Bibanco himself wrote that the cost of draining the flooded mines had frightened off previous competitors. 'It was then [in 1773], moved by the impulse of my spirit and confidence in my skill, that I took possession of these mines, without obtaining the slightest help, although it was necessary to construct great works at the cost of an immense fortune, a consideration which might have made a coward of the most courageous.'[2]

The revival of Bolaños provoked a certain labour scarcity since the resident population could not supply a sufficient work force. Bibanco had recourse to the Tlaxcalan settlement of Colotlán; he raised the wages of his Indian workers from four to five and even six reales a day. He appealed to the magistrate to ensure the despatch of contingents of workers. But apparently this source of labour proved troublesome; the Indians were undisciplined and prone to riot.[3] To deal with the problem Bibanco suggested the recruitment of an extensive militia, over which, of course, he was to preside as colonel, an office which would give him virtual control of Colotlán. In 1781 the viceroy issued his approval, and Bibanco proceeded to raise some fourteen companies of dragoons and ten companies of infantry, recruited from a wide area that comprised Bolaños, Colotlán and the alcaldías mayores of Fresnillo, Aguascalientes and Jerez.[4] Trouble immediately began, since all the local authorities—alcaldes mayores, ayuntamientos and the audiencia of Guadalajara—were opposed to the establishment of the milita. Bibanco himself provoked further reaction when he vigorously quelled a riot in Colotlán, seized the five leaders of the disturbance, and sent them for trial to Mexico City. In the subsequent hearing Bibanco's advocate was at pains to refute the common accusation: 'It is said that my client solicited and obtained the colonelcy by means of cash, in order to have the power to force the Indians of Colotlán to work in his mines.'[5] He also pointed out that after 1783 Bibanco paid up to six reales a day for unskilled labour as compared to the standard four reales paid elsewhere. Furthermore he had financed the construction of both a school and a church, paying for the upkeep of

1 AGN, Minería 151/3, treasury officials to viceroy, 16 October 1772.
2 AGN, Minería 25/1, Bibanco to viceroy, 30 October 1787.
3 AGN, Minería 138/3, Bibanco, 4 April 1774.
4 AGI, Mexico 1396, Mayorga to Gálvez, 26 March 1782.
5 AGS, Guerra Moderna 7015, statement by Pedro Manuel de Bibanco, 14 February 1784.

two priests and a teacher. Whatever the truth of these accusations and refutations their interest was terminated by the withdrawal of Bibanco from the area.

Bibanco did not leave Bolaños empty-handed. In 1789 he successfully petitioned the Crown for the title of Marquis of Bibanco, Viscount Bolaños. To justify his plea he presented an estimate of his fortune, the fruits of his years as a miner.[1] He owned two haciendas: Chapingo, a former Jesuit estate, which he bought for 136,000 ps.; and Ojo de Agua, a pulque estate valued at 162,000 ps. and purchased from the Count of San Bartolomé de Jala. In Mexico City he had a house and a pulquería, the latter worth 13,000 ps. In addition to these properties, which he proposed to entail upon the marquisate, he possessed 440,000 ps. invested in trade, loans and personal silver. In all, therefore, his fortune amounted to three-quarters of a million pesos.

However, in the years that followed until his death in July 1799, the Marquis of Bibanco maintained rather than increased his fortune. In company with Antonio Bassoco, the Mexico City merchant, he invested some 80,000 ps. in mines at Capula, but without profit.[2] Similarly he took out shares in the Vetagrande company in Zacatecas, but he did not live to see the final success of that venture. Finally, he subscribed to the company that planned to revive once more the mines of Bolaños. But none of these enterprises yielded immediate return, and Bibanco died leaving a fortune of 590,000 ps. to his heir, the second Marquis.[3]

For Juan de Sierra Uruñuela, who owned a warehouse and store in Mexico City and three shops in Bolaños, the camp's continued prosperity was all-important. It was the chief market for his merchandise. Hitherto, from 1752 onwards, he had acted as aviador of several of the town's chief miners.[4] Now, confronted with Bibanco's termination of their partnership and virtual abandonment of the town's principal mines, he was obliged to choose between a similar retirement and further expenditure. If the mines went out of production, then his shops in Bolaños would lose their business, and if his northern market was closed, his Mexico City store would, no doubt, dwindle in value. Moreover, since the 1780s were a decade of crisis for old-established merchants such as Sierra Uruñuela, he was forced to rely all the more upon the Bolaños market. Bibanco had

[1] AGI, Mexico 1745, Bibanco's petition, 23 June 1784. The title was conceded on 17 October 1791; see Ortega y Pérez Gallardo, *Historia genealógica*, II, *Marqués de Bibanco*.

[2] AGN, Minería 225, Pachuca treasury officials to viceroy, 10 June 1805.

[3] AGN, Vínculos 213/2, Lic. Oláez, July 1809.

[4] AGI, Mexico 2243, fiscal of Council of the Indies, 23 April 1789.

deserted his mines at a moment when production was falling and extensive investment was required. Sierra Uruñuela formed a new partnership with Isidoro Sarachaga, a Basque miner resident in Bolaños, and in the period from April 1786 to March 1787 they cut a new central shaft to a depth of over 250 yards at an estimated cost of 390,000 ps. At that level they encountered good quality ore. But in March 1787 a fire swept through the mine destroying their work.[1] Sierra Uruñuela was faced with complete ruin. He had poured into the mine his entire fortune, and had borrowed another 261,000 ps. All that remained was the stock of his shops and the surviving equipment of the mine and its refining mill.

Sierra Uruñuela met his thirteen creditors and, with the approval of the consulado obtained a five-year postponement on the payment of his debts.[2] Furthermore, he petitioned the Crown for a 15-year total exemption from the silver tithe. In view of his long services to the industry and the complete dependence of Bolaños upon his efforts, in May 1789 this plea was granted.[3] Equally important, he secured a 160,000 ps. loan from *temporalidades*, the Crown department that managed the former Jesuit properties. This loan, it should be noted, was guaranteed by sixteen of the leading merchants of Mexico City, including Antonio de Bibanco.[4] But Sierra Uruñuela, by this time no doubt an old man, did not for long survive his financial collapse. Sometime in the year 1790 he died: certainly by May 1791 in a lawsuit presented by his creditors he was mentioned as deceased. The contents of his shops had been auctioned for 88,000 ps. to meet his debts.[5]

Before his death Sierra Uruñuela had begun his fourth and final renovation of the Bolaños mines. This time he formed a company composed of the sixteen Mexico City almaceneros who had guaranteed his loan from temporalidades. It was this company which took over the management of mines; inherited Sierra Uruñuela's tax exemption; and succeeded in restoring the production of Bolaños to the level of the early 1780s. Among its shareholders were to be found several leading Mexican merchants. The Marquis of Rivascacho, Antonio Bassoco, Sebastián de Heras Soto, Francisco Baso Ibáñez, Manuel Ramón de Goya, Juan Fernando de Meoquí, and Juan Fernández Peredo all possessed large fortunes. Many had made

1 AGI, Mexico 1533, Viceroy Revillagigedo to Lerena, 29 July 1790.

2 AHN, Consejos 20688, contains a list of these creditors and a description of Sierra's problems; see fiscal of Council of Indies, 6 October 1794.

3 AGI, Mexico 1533, Revillagigedo to Lerena, 29 July 1790.

4 BN (Mexico) MSS 1388, ff. 244–9, loan approved, 19 January 1789.

5 AHN, Consejos 20688, statement by Antonio de Bibanco in 1792.

several investments in mining. Fernández Peredo joined the Vetagrande company in Zacatecas, along with Bibanco and Bassoco.[1] Francisco Martínez Cabezón, who acted as the company's general agent, owned two small refining mills in Bolaños and had small properties in Fresnillo and Matehuala.[2]

But these merchants, desirous of new outlets for their capital, soon found that silver mines, especially old silver mines, could as easily ruin as enrich. By July 1791 the company's agent estimated that a new shaft had been cut to the depth of 275 yards out of the 345 yards now deemed necessary. So far 825,000 ps. had been invested in the mines, including in this figure, no doubt, ploughed-back profits.[3] This investment bore its fruit: in 1792 the company produced 115,474 marks of silver, about 4·5 per cent of total Mexican mintage for that year.[4] This initial success by no means solved the company's problems. The supply of labour was costly and inadequate, and the ore extracted was of poor quality. In 1792 the company's agent complained that the Indians of Colotlán were unwilling to work in their mines, and petitioned that the president of the Guadalajara audiencia should compel all Indian villages within a 40-league radius to send labour contingents to Bolaños. But the Crown reiterated the established ordinance which decreed that such Indian labour could be only ordered from a distance of ten leagues and should comprise no more than 4 per cent of the male tributaries of any village.[5]

Another threat to the company's labour recruitment was posed by the declining quality of metal. For in Bolaños the skilled pick and blast men relied entirely upon their partidos, which amounted to a full third of all the ore they cut. By 1796 these workers experienced considerable difficulty in selling their ore to the independent refiners, owing to its poor quality. They were obliged, therefore, to sell it to their company, which bought the mineral more to provide its employees with means of subsistence rather than to make a profit. The company then unsuccessfully petitioned the Crown that this workers' share should also enjoy tax exemption.[6]

If the workers' ore was of such low quality we may presume that the company's metal was equally bad. Further information is largely lacking,

[1] The list of shareholders can be found in BN (Mexico) MSS 1388, f. 247. For Goya see AGI, Mexico 2212, Viceroy Azanza to Crown, 27 July 1799.

[2] AGI, Mexico 2206, Viceroy Matías Gálvez to Gálvez, 30 April 1785.

[3] AGN, Minería 94/5, statement by Francisco Martínez Cabezón, 18 July 1791.

[4] See Bolaños treasury accounts, AGI, Mexico 2119, for year 1792.

[5] AGI, Mexico 2243, company petition, 23 April, *real orden*, 11 May 1792. See also AGN, Minería 97/3, Governor of Colotlán to Revillagigedo, 11 June 1791.

[6] AGN, Minería 137/3, company petition, 28 June 1796.

but already by 1797 production had more than halved. And in August 1798 the river once more flooded, overflowing into the mines and wrecking the town.[1] At this point the company closed its accounts and left Bolaños to its fate. Some measure of the subsequent decline can be obtained from the treasury records. In the three years 1794–6, 70,796 ps. were collected in excise duties (alcabalas) whereas in 1798–1800 this branch of revenue yielded only 9,106 ps.[2] The history of Bolaños as an important mining centre had ended. In effect, it appears that the company had suffered from that chronic ailment of old mines—persistent diminishing returns. Production was abundant: in the years 1792–6 it averaged 103,327 marks, some 3·7 per cent of all Mexican mintage during those years.[3] But the initial investment was heavy, and the ore of such poor quality that much of it was barely worth refining. Despite the tax exemptions, therefore, production barely covered its costs. Antonio Bassoco, a principal shareholder, later declared: 'in spite of the tithe exemptions that they enjoyed, the shareholders of that company abandoned their mines in order not to ruin themselves, without having gained a penny from the use of their capital. Those shareholders who did not remain in the company throughout the restoration, lost their initial investment'.[4] In other words, the company had virtually subsidised the town for eight years without return upon its capital.

V

The process by which Bolaños was restored revealed patterns prevalent throughout the industry. The surprising extension of fiscal exemptions, the greater influx of mercantile capital, the ploughing back of mining profits, and the increased reliance upon heavy capital investment in drainage shafts and adits—these elements were to be found at work not merely in Bolaños but also in Pachuca, Zacatecas, Sombrerete and Taxco. They did not, however, play such an important role in Guanajuato or Catorce, the two camps which between them by the 1790s produced at least two-fifths of all Mexican silver. Not a single miner of these two camps obtained tax exemptions. Similarly, although their merchants entered mining they did not dominate the local industry. We have described, therefore, the process whereby special cost reductions and heavy capital investment succeeded in restoring the older, more marginal sector of Mexican mining to effective production. These camps accounted for between a quarter

1 AGN, Subdelegados 2, treasury officials to Azanza, 17 August 1798.

2 AGI, Mexico 2120, treasury accounts for years 1794–1800.

3 Calculated from treasury accounts, AGI, Mexico 2119, 2120.

4 AGN, Minería 108, statement by Bassoco, 27 July 1804.

and a third of all silver minted. But the contrast must not be pushed too far. Mercantile capital developed new mines as well as restoring old mines. Two examples will illustrate this trend.

In 1780 José Gómez Campos, a merchant of Mexico City, registered a group of mines in Jilotlán, a remote district of Colima, He had to hire workers from Real del Monte, Valladolid, and Zapotlán. Furthermore, he had to rent and farm land in order to feed his workers and mules with meat and maize. Gómez Campos later stated that he was prepared to place up to 200,000 ps. in the venture; by 1788 he had yet to receive any profit.[1] In the district of Villa alta, a wealthy Basque merchant resident in Oaxaca, Juan Francisco Echarri, invested 200,000 ps. to establish six silver mines at Talea, a copper mine at Ixtepeji, and a refining mill. The copper mine was to supply his mill with copper pyrites for the amalgamation process. He brought in workers from Pachuca, Taxco and Real del Monte. Echarri stated that in the first five years his mine only produced 6,831 marks, but then in the eighteen months between 1785 and August 1786 production increased to 8,112 marks. At this stage he secured full tax exemptions from the Crown, especially since he estimated that his enterprise required another 450,000 ps. investment spread over fourteen years.[2] Both of these merchants, in effect, opened mines in areas where hitherto little silver had been found. It was for this reason that they were obliged to obtain labour from old but decadent mining camps. The amount of capital they invested, and the decade—the 1780s—when they entered the industry, equally indicate general trends.

But what of Guanajuato: surely as a camp first founded in the sixteenth century it should have been numbered with Zacatecas and Real del Monte? In part it was.[3] By the 1760s several of its great mines, the Mellado, the Cata and the Sirena, lay waterlogged with only their upper reaches still scavenged by workers. On the other hand, the Rayas, despite a heavy burden of debt, continued to prosper, and with deeper shafts struck rich ore. But it was a new discovery, the Valenciana, located on a section of the lode between the Mellado and the Rayas previously deemed barren, which transformed Guanajuato. For the Valenciana yielded consistent profits from 1770 until 1810. Moreover, its owners never attempted to integrate their enterprise: a large share of its ore was always sold to independent refiners. The Guanajuato industry, therefore, possessed a complex

1 AGI, Mexico 1540, Revillagigedo to Lerena, 15 January 1791.
2 AGI, Mexico 1533, Revillagigedo to Lerena, 29 July 1790; AGI, Mexico 2242, Flores to Valdés, 24 December 1788.
3 See below, Part Three, 'Guanajuato'.

structure of production (described in a later chapter) not to be found in Zacatecas or Real del Monte. But the Valenciana's success sprang from its heavy reinvestment of profits in the construction of new, extraordinarily deep shafts. It only differed from other mines in that skilful management rescued it from the usual cycle of abandonment and renovation. Elsewhere in Guanajuato, several older mines were restored by merchant houses or by the partners of the Valenciana. Fiscal inducements apart, Guanajuato experienced the play of the same factors which had revived Mexican mining in other camps. But the engine of its prosperity, the Valenciana, gave those factors a different perspective.

Information about Catorce is sparse. Discovered in 1778, its growth was remarkably rapid, as the following list demonstrates.[1]

Early production of Catorce, 1779–84

	marks		*marks*
1779	169,007	1782	295,522
1780	181,767	1783	368,187
1781	273,144	1784	372,000

Profits were high: Father Flores received three-and-a-half million pesos in the years 1781–3. Ores were so rich that refiners from Guanajuato, Sierra de Pinos and León came to buy it. By the late 1780s, however, these halcyon days had ended: the rich mass of ore that lay close to the surface had been exhausted. But instead of entering a decline, Catorce's position was consolidated by more efficient methods of production. A new mine, the Purísima, was developed by two partners. Miguel Francisco de Aguirre, a talented Basque miner, and Ignacio de Obregón, son of the first Count of Valenciana. Later estimates claim that their mine averaged 200,000 ps. a year profit from 1788 to 1806; by that time its chief shaft had been driven 550 yards deep, the second deepest in all Mexico.[2] During these years Catorce produced about four million pesos a year; unfortunately little more information is available about this camp, which like Bolaños suddenly leapt to second place among Mexican camps, but which unlike Bolaños progressed from first bonanza to deep-shaft mining, without passing through the usual intermission of flooding and abandonment. Moreover, it appears that the Catorce miners followed the practice of the Valenciana and sold their ore to independent refiners.

[1] AGN, Minería 110/6, treasury officials of San Luis Potosí, 24 January 1785.

[2] Ward, *Mexico in 1827*, II, 489–502; Santiago Ramírez, *Noticia histórica de la riqueza minera de México* (Mexico, 1884), pp. 566–7.

Finally, to conclude our catalogue of omission, we have not attempted to examine the mining industry of the far north—Durango and beyond—where camps such as Guarisamey, Santa Eulalia, Batopilas, Cosalá and Alamos produced up to a quarter of all Mexican silver. Several of these camps enjoyed booms during the 1780s and after. They await their historian.

VI

For nearly two hundred years Zacatecas maintained its place at the head of the Mexican mining industry, producing silver on the average worth two million pesos a year, a figure roughly equal to a quarter of all mintage during the first decades of the eighteenth century. In 1732 the town possessed 25 mills that used the amalgamation process and 20 furnaces for smelting.[1] But then, in the ensuing years, one by one the mines of Zacatecas flooded and were deserted by their owners. By 1760 Francisco Javier de Gamboa commented, 'its mines have been very rich, but are no longer worked owing to their depth and water'.[2] Clear evidence of the town's decay was provided by the closure of its refining industry: by 1767 only five mills and two furnaces remained at work.[3]

The causes of this decline are still unresolved. Writing in 1732, the Count of Santiago de la Laguna, a leading miner of the town, cited several cases of bankruptcy among fellow mine owners, and claimed that in the past two years he himself had lost 50,000 ps. He ascribed his losses to the low quality of ore by then found in Zacatecas and the high price of mercury which did not permit the profitable refining of large ranges of low and medium grade ore. The margin between costs and returns was very small, and hence bankruptcy became only too easy. Furthermore, it appears that quarrels over drainage duties led to the abandonment of some mines, and in others, notably the Quebradilla mine, drainage techniques were not adequate to conquer the rising level of water.[4] Zacatecas suffered from the typical problems of an ageing mining centre: its mines were deep, so that drainage costs were high, yet its ores were by then of medium or low grade, hence production costs tended to swallow up profits. Moreover, local drainage techniques were defective and local mine owners peculiarly litigious. Whatever the precise cause, when José de Gálvez

[1] Rivera Bernárdez, *Descripción breve*, pp. 44–50.

[2] Gamboa, *Comentarios*, p. 510.

[3] BM Add. MSS 20999, 'Representación sobre el estado de los reales de minas por Juan Lucas de Lassaga y José de la Borda', f. 565.

[4] BRP, MSS 2824. Miscelánea de Ayala, 10, f. 132.

reached Mexico, Zacatecas retained but a shadow of its past glory. Yet by 1803, when Humboldt visited New Spain, he found the town to occupy third place among Mexican producers, inferior only to Guanajuato, another long-established centre, and Catorce, a relatively new discovery.[1]

The decisive step in the restoration of Zacatecas was taken by José de la Borda, the most notable miner of his day, who in a career that stretched from 1716 had already made and spent several fortunes gained at Taxco and Tlalpujahua, two camps that lay near to Mexico City.[2] But by 1767 Borda, although famous, was virtually bankrupt; he had invested nearly half a million pesos in the construction of the famous Santa Prisca in Taxco, a church which still numbers among the architectural glories of Mexico. In addition Borda owed 400,000 ps. to various persons, including 112,000 to Manuel de Aldaco.[3] Moreover, although his mine of Chontalpa near Taxco had produced over two million pesos, his most recent venture had proved unsuccessful. In order to pay off his debts and recoup his fortune, Borda decided to abandon the mining camps of the centre and go north—to Zacatecas. Already, in an influential report to José de Gálvez, he had argued that the Crown should grant special assistance to miners engaged in risky and costly renovations, pointing to an old, never-invoked law that permitted tax reductions for the operation of old, deep mines.[4] He soon followed this general argument with the proposal that he himself should attempt the renovation of the Quebradilla, a Zacatecas mine rich both in ore and water.

Gálvez and the viceroy, the Marquis of Croix, who had already discussed with Borda ways to develop the industry, immediately approved his project and gave him extraordinary fiscal assistance. He was conceded full exemption from the silver tithe during the period of initial renovation; then, once his initial costs were recouped, he was granted a 50 per cent tax reduction for 20 years. In addition, during the entire period he was to receive mercury at the cost price of 30 ps. a cwt.[5] These exemptions, the first of their kind to be awarded, became the model for many similar individual concessions. Naturally, Borda's reputation helped him in all this. As early as 1761, Gamboa wrote: 'By reason of his vast understanding and management of this occupation, José de la Borda can be pointed to as

1 Humboldt, *Ensayo político*, p. 333; by this time its share in total production amounted to about 12 per cent.

2 Ximénez y Frías, *El fénix de los mineros ricos*, pp. 90–2.

3 AGN, Minería 106/4, José de la Borda to Bucareli, March 1775.

4 BM Add. MSS 20999, ff. 562, 598, 604.

5 AGI, Mexico 2235, *real orden*, 12 March 1768; see also Fonseca and Urrutia, *Historia general de Real Hacienda*, I, 38, 343.

the first miner in the world.'[1] And indeed Viceroy Croix expressly emphasised his technical superiority to justify the tax concessions: 'José de la Borda is without doubt the person in this kingdom who knows most about mines and the machinery for their excavation and drainage. . . . By means of his renovation [of the Quebradilla] the miners of Zacatecas and of the far north will learn how to manage his machines, and hence the means to drain and restore many rich mines.'[2] Thus the Crown employed fiscal weapons to promote the diffusion of technical knowledge.

At first, however, Borda delayed his attack upon the Quebradilla, a notoriously difficult mine, since, despite his fame and royal backing, he was unable to find a financial backer. Instead, he addressed his efforts to a separate lode in the Zacatecas camp, the Vetagrande, where he opened seven mines. Even so, he was obliged to borrow 30,000 ps. from friends, and this spent, another 18,000 ps. from the Crown, before the venture proved successful. But in the succeeding eight years these mines produced over one-and-three-quarters of a million pesos. With his profits Borda constructed a huge refining mill, the Sauceda, which, he claimed, could handle 3,000 cwt. of ore a week, being at that time the largest in the entire north. He also acquired the nearby hacienda of Malpaso for 102,000 ps. to supply the mill's 1,400 mules with maize and straw as well as maize for his workers.[3] Since the Vetagrande mines were not included in his tax exemptions, Borda took advantage of local unemployment to reduce his labour bill. Hitherto, mine workers in Zacatecas—the pick and blast men —earned 6 rls. a day and took a quarter of the ore they produced. Borda cut their daily wage to 4 rls. a day and reduced their share of the ore to an eighth.[4]

By 1775 Borda found that the San Acasio, his best mine, had reached a depth of 240 yards, and its ore only yielded a mediocre two ounces of silver per hundredweight, so that its operation was barely profitable. At last he decided to drain the Quebradilla, in which a local company of merchants had earlier lost 300,000 ps. But Borda's superior technique soon conquered the mine. As he later wrote in triumph: 'when the water taken out by my whims is compared to theirs [the previous company] then everyone must agree that water which was insuperable for them is like a

[1] Gamboa, *Comentarios*, p. 380.

[2] AGI, Mexico 2235, Croix to Crown, 26 May 1767. We may note that Borda's assistant, Juan Pablo Echegoyen, a Basque, had studied mining techniques in England; in 1761 he was denounced to the Inquisition as an Englishman. See Manuel Toussaint, *Don José de la Borda restituída a España* (Mexico, 1933), p. 9.

[3] AGN, Minería 106/4, Borda to Bucareli, March 1775.

[4] AMZ, 23, Dr Antonio Bugarín to intendant Felipe Cleere, undated, 1788/9.

toy for me'.[1] Moreover, from April 1775 to November 1779, when the mine produced 93,774 marks of silver, he enjoyed full tax exemptions, which together with cheap mercury amounted to a grant of 98,053 ps., otherwise due to the Crown. From this sum and his profits he built another huge refining mill, 'The Holy Family'.[2] Some measure of the Quebradilla's production and the tax concessions it enjoyed can be gauged from the scheme, shown in table 17, drawn up by the Zacatecas treasury.[3]

Table 17 *Production and tax exemption of the Quebradilla mine.*

Year	Total production (in marks)	Nominal tithes at unexempted rate (in pesos)	Value of tithe exemptions (in pesos)	Amount of mercury supplied at 30 ps./cwt. (in cwt.)	Value of reduction in mercury price (in pesos)
1777	2,103	2,002	2,002	—	—
1778	36,768	35,005	35,005	321	3,648
1779	62,179	59,203	55,690	539	6,125
1780	32,841	31,270	15,635	—	—
1781	52,356	49,851	24,925	400	4,545
1782	30,282	28,832	14,416	250	2,842
1783	35,010	33,335	16,667	—	—
1784	3,001	2,858	1,429	—	—
1790	1,820	1,733	866	—	—
	256,360	244,089	166,635	1,510	17,160

The absence of more detailed accounts makes it difficult to rank the relative importance of the several financial advantages enjoyed by Borda. Compared to his predecessors he was able to cut costs in both the mining and refining stages of his enterprise; in addition he obtained considerable tax exemptions. His superior technique, the indispensable prerequisite of his success, did not, we may presume, of itself reduce expenses. All calculations, however, are partially vitiated by our ignorance of one vital ratio: the distribution of total production cost between mining and refining; hence we cannot assess the eventual weight of any percentage reductions at either stage. Nevertheless, we can point to considerable economies. If we roughly calculate (using information from other mine-fields) that the wage bill comprised about 75 per cent of the total cost of mining, then Borda, by cutting wages from 6 rls. a day to 4 rls. a day, reduced total mining costs by 25 per cent. Furthermore, he obtained a

1 AGN, Minería 106/4, Borda to Bucareli, March 1775.
2 AGN, Minería 115/1, report by Borda's manager, Ventura de Arteaga, 6 March 1780.
3 AGN, Minería 115/1, report by Zacatecas treasury, 23 March 1791.

greater proportion of the ore produced. At the refining stage we have already pointed out that for the amalgamation of a medium grade ore of three ounces of silver to a hundredweight of ore, mercury, at the new price of 41 ps. 2 rls. 11 grs. a cwt., absorbed about 25 per cent of total refining costs. Borda's supply of mercury at 30 ps. per cwt. reduced the proportional cost of mercury to about 18 per cent. But in addition to the greater return on medium range ores that this cheap mercury provided, Borda was also able to refine profitably a wider range of low quality ore. Finally, his tax rebates in the years 1778–90 totalled 166,639 ps., a sum which taken as a percentage of overall production amounted to 7·3 per cent, in itself a reasonable return upon capital. Clearly Borda did not depend upon his tax exemptions: they acted as a stimulus, especially since he had worked the Vetagrande mines without such support. Nevertheless, without their incentive he might never have dared transfer to Zacatecas. As it was, at the time of his death in 1779, Borda had paid off his debts and in 1790 his only son, a priest, Manuel de la Borda, estimated his property at a million pesos, of which 300,000 ps. was invested in houses in Mexico City. But by then the Quebradilla lay once again flooded and Borda's heir vainly petitioned the Crown for a 100,000 ps. loan to renovate his property.[1] In Mexico a mining success or bonanza rarely lasted for more than a decade without the need arising for major capital investment in the form of new shafts or adits.

Owing to Borda's intervention the Zacatecas mining industry underwent a major renewal of personnel. A repoıt, written in 1784, stated that the city's chief miners were Ventura Arteaga, Borda's former manager; Marcelo de Anza, the nephew of his principal associate; and his two French 'nephews', Francisco Javier and Julián Penmartin.[2] A new wave of Basque immigrants began to enter the industry, acting as merchant-backers and refiners. For it must be remembered that the workers always sold their share of the ore they produced to independent refiners, so that all the great integrated enterprises which mined and refined their own ore were surrounded by a group of petty refiners and merchants.

[1] AGN, Vínculos 123/3, Manuel de la Borda to audiencia, 22 August 1790.

[2] AGI, Mexico 2205, Mint superintendent to Gálvez, 26 September 1790. The Penmartins were natives of Oloron, France, and were in danger of arrest during the 1790s. Their Zacatecas guarantor, Fausto de Arce, then, on 25 February 1795, wrote to the viceroy of Francisco Penmartin: 'he is a man as addicted to Spanish rule as his uncle D. José de la Borda'. Contrary to Manuel Toussaint's claim that Borda was Spanish, he continued: 'D. José de la Borda conducted himself without remembering his French origin.' See AGN, Historia 503/47.

If Borda had succeeded by superior technique, the next generation relied upon heavy capital investment. Zacatecas had reached the stage where companies, by reason of their better staying power, stood more chance of success than individual entrepreneurs. In 1783 two competing companies formed to drain and operate the Vetagrande group of mines. The first, initiated by Marcelo de Anza and Ventura de Arteaga, and backed by Antonio de Bibanco, the chief miner of Bolaños, and Manuel Ramón de Goya, the Mexico City merchant, petitioned the Crown for tax exemptions since they estimated initial drainage costs at half a million pesos. The second company, however, organised by the local parish priest, Dr Antonio Bugarín, and supported by a mixed group of lawyers, priests and widows, put the cost of renovation at only 50,000 ps.[1] Eventually, in July 1786, a united company was set up. Anza and his backer, Goya, withdrew; Arteaga became the general manager; and a miscellaneous group of local Zacatecas residents and Mexico City merchants and financiers subscribed to some 40 shares.

Anza then decided to continue to work the Canteras and San Francisco mines which he had inherited from his uncle. Production held up quite well, but his costs soared. During the 20 years from 1772 through 1792 the mines' output amounted to 720,329 marks of silver—but the price for this continued production was paid by Anza's backer, the merchant Manuel Ramón de Goya who lost half a million pesos in the venture. In the subsequent meeting of creditors it was discovered that Goya, abusing his position as the Mexico City receiving agent for the silver of the Count of Valenciana, had misappropriated 300,000 ps. from his account. Goya's own fortune was valued at about 200,000 ps.[2] As an act of mercy, more to the creditors than to the two men, the finance committee reduced Anza's taxes from a tithe to a twentieth and ordered mercury to be supplied at cost price, both concessions to run for ten years.[3] Clearly, the mines of Zacatecas operated very close to the margin: most required, and obtained, fiscal relief. The unfortunate fate of Goya, a former cajero of Meave in the Fagoaga trading house, amply demonstrates why so many merchants feared to enter the industry.

During the 1780s Zacatecas attracted another major entrepreneur. Manuel de Rétegui, a Basque immigrant, had made his fortune during the period 1772–87 at the neighbouring camp of Fresnillo. He then transferred to Zacatecas where he soon succeeded in restoring the old Malanoche

[1] AGN, Minería 107/1, united company established 19 July 1786.

[2] BN (Mexico) MSS 1374, in petition of José Antonio Ansac, 19 June 1786; for his misappropriation see AHGP, Cabildo, 25 October 1791 and 1 December 1792.

[3] AGI, Mexico 2212, Azanza to Crown, 27 July 1799.

mine, a feat that numbered him among the town's richest miners. Despite certain failures—he lost 150,000 ps. in the San Bernabé and a similar sum when he attempted to invade the Vetagrande company's territory—by 1804 Rétegui estimated his estate at half a million pesos, invested in mines, refining mills and commerce. His production figures compare favourably to those of Anza or the Vetagrande: between 1787 and 1805, he presented 756,785 marks of silver at the local treasury.[1] Moreover, he was about the only major Zacatecas miner who was not eventually granted tax exemptions, although he petitioned for them during his unsuccessful attempt to renovate the San Bernabé mine.

By the end of the 1780s at least three groups of mines were in production—the San Francisco of Anza, the Vetagrande and the Malanoche of Rétegui; and in all these mines the workers received shares of the ore they produced. Rétegui, for example, permitted his workers to take a sixth as compared to the eighth that Borda had introduced. But whatever the proportion enough ore was sold for a group of independent refiners, mainly Basque in origin, to become sufficiently wealthy to consider the renovation of local mines. Two such men, Fermín de Azpezechea and Bernardo de Iriarte, both Basques, first seized virtual control of the local guild court, or deputation, and then, in 1792, acting in conjunction with Manuel de Rétegui, registered mines that lay within the territory of the Vetagrande company. They used the deputation's authority to confirm the legality of this invasion. However, the company protested to the viceroy and demanded that the case be tried by the mining court of appeal in Mexico City.[2] The upshot was a truce: Azpezechea and his partners abandoned their claims to the company's mines; in return, it appears, he was conceded a free hand to take over the property of the Borda family. And by 1794, the Quebradilla and Cabras mines were acquired by a company formed by Azpezechea, the local deputation rejecting the protests of Borda's grandchildren. Admittedly the family lacked capital to renovate the flooded mine, but the seizure was an undoubted piece of legal chicanery.[3]

The new company, divided into the usual 24 shares, was entirely recruited from Zacatecas: Azpezechea took eight shares, Bernardo de Iriarte six, and Francisco Javier Penmartin, Borda's unfaithful 'nephew', three. Work on this second renovation of the Quebradilla began in April 1804, and proceeded until January 1808 without any profit to the partners. They spent 150,000 ps. before producing a single mark of silver and by

[1] AGI, Mexico 2248, Iturrigaray to Crown, 26 September 1806.
[2] AGN, Minería 107, company's agent to viceroy, undated 1792.
[3] AGI, Mexico 2245, Branciforte to Crown, 26 June 1797.

1808 their investment, they claimed, amounted to 862,606 ps. In this sum, however, the partners without doubt included ploughed-back profits. But in view of their difficulties, in January 1809 the company was granted a 50 per cent tax reduction and a supply of mercury at cost price.[1] To facilitate this concession the company had subscribed 50,000 ps. to the patriot War Fund, clear evidence of the value of such exemptions.

The enterprise was surprisingly large. Some five shafts, serviced by 14–16 whims were required to drain the mine. The central shaft, although not very deep—it had only reached 168 yards in 1804—needed eight whims alone. These whims were operated by some 800 horses that consumed 18,000 fanegas of maize a year. The labour force was correspondingly high—2,500 persons, of whom 1,415 worked underground. With such a labour force weekly expenses were high: in 1809 a possible 18,000–20,000 ps. per week.[2]

Confronted with such heavy costs the company, dominating as it did the local deputation, took the decisive step of suppressing the system whereby the workers received a certain share of the ore they produced: instead they were reduced to a simple daily wage, and, moreover, part of this was paid in goods and not in cash, despite laws to the contrary. In 1810 the workers protested without avail to the viceroy that 'in addition to the fact that in the mine of Quebradilla they do not pay us in the customary fashion [i.e. with shares] they are destroying us by giving us our salary in goods'.[3]

Yet by 1810 the company had struck rich, and in addition to normal profits, the partners enjoyed tax reductions and the share of ore that the workers would normally have taken. How much the mine produced, or how great were these profits we do not know, but a later account reckoned that in less that nine years the Quebradilla company paid the Crown 528,413 ps. in taxes, which at 5 per cent would roughly amount to a production of over a million pesos a year.[4]

The most important enterprise in Zacatecas belonged to the company which owned the Vetagrande group of mines. Its road to financial success, however, proved to be a peculiarly long and difficult one. For the renovation of its mines required far more capital than anyone had anticipated. By December 1788 the company had called up and spent without return some 3,000 ps. per share. Most of the local residents—the original partners of Dr Bugarín—then cancelled their subscriptions so that only 22 out of

[1] AGI, Mexico 1634, Garibay to Crown, 16 July 1809.
[2] Berghes, *Descripción*, pp. 22–3.
[3] Cited in Mendizábal, *Obras completas*, v, 207.
[4] AGN, Minería 180/6, Zacatecas mining deputation to Crown, 20 May 1818.

the initial 40 shares remained operative.[1] And, despite a short spurt in production in 1791–2 when some profits were distributed, costs continued to exceed returns, so that shareholders had to pay in well beyond the original stipulated 10,000 ps. a share. In consequence most of the other partners were obliged to withdraw, several after making quite heavy investments. For example, Gaspar Martín Vicario, a Mexico City merchant, lost 88,550 ps. in the venture; Juan Fernández Peredo, 55,000; Dr Luis Beltrán, 38,500; and so on. In the upshot only five shareholders stayed the course.[2]

The size of the mine is hard to estimate. By 1797 the main shaft had reached a depth of 360 yards, out of the 450 yards deemed necessary. To drain this and other shafts some 17 whims were required, serviced by 660 mules at a cost of 2,400 ps. a week. In all, the mine cost 6,000 ps. a week to run. Naturally most operating costs were financed from production: the shareholders' capital was mainly invested in the plant. For by 1803 the company had purchased or constructed three refining mills (including Borda's Sauceda). The total value of these mills together with the plant of the mine was reckoned at 931,768 ps., amounting to most of the current subscribed capital.[3] The Vetagrande company thus formed a vast integrated enterprise which ranked among the greatest in Mexico. Certainly it was the largest in Zacatecas. In 1803 the intendant stated that out of a total 460 arrastres then in use the company possessed 138, whereas the next most important refiners, Marcelo de Anza, the Borda family and Manuel de Rétegui respectively held but 64, 50 and 24 arrastres.[4]

In an attempt to balance their accounts, the surviving shareholders had already, in 1797, petitioned the Crown for tax relief. Evidently impressed by their tale of woe, the finance committee granted the company a full tax exemption for six years, and a supply of mercury and gunpowder at cost price. These concessions were to become effective once the British naval blockade occasioned by Spain's alliance with Napoleon was lifted. That the company had a good case could not be doubted: by 1804 the total deficit, i.e. capital invested without return, stood at 1,198,930 ps.[5] Thus after some 17 years of production the mine had yielded almost no profit to its owners. Its scale of operation can be gauged from table 18.[6]

[1] AGI, Mexico 1587, Azanza to Crown, 27 August 1798.

[2] AGN, Minería 46/3, inquiry into company's shareholding, 31 January 1805.

[3] AGI, Mexico 1587, statement by company's agent, March 1797.

[4] AGN, Historia 49/26, Rendón to viceroy, 3 May 1803.

[5] AGN, Minería 108, statement of company's agent, undated 1805.

[6] For 1786–93, AGN, Minería 46/3, Zacatecas treasury report, 5 March 1793. For 1795–1801, see Ward, *Mexico in 1827*, II, 45.

As the table shows it was only in 1805, after some 17 years of almost continuous investment, that the mine finally struck rich, By then the five remaining partners had subscribed 922,205 ps. on their 11¾ shares. Their reward was sudden and commensurate. In the three years 1805–7, for which we have figures, the Vetagrande paid a dividend of 3,021,647 ps.[1] But who were the five men capable of sustaining such heavy demands upon their resources? What was the origin of their capital?

Table 18 *Production of the Vetagrande Company, Zacatecas, 1786–1810.*

Year	Marks	Ozs.	Year	Marks	Ozs.
1786	167	2	1795	41,900	3
1787	6,296	1	1796	35,570	4
1788	2,947	3	1797	10,533	3
1789	7,262	5	1798	15,702	6
1790	18,419	3	1799	8,178	5
1791	27,057	4	1800	17,348	3½
1792	77,060	4	1801	14,326	7
1793 (to March)	14,359	4	1802	20,996	1
			1803	64,291	3
	153,570	2	1804	136,836	3½
			1805	299,944	7½
			1806	193,533	2
			1807	102,999	6
			1808	184,230	2
			1809	65,293	6
			1810	101,550	4
				1,313,237	2½

The two leading partners with four and three shares respectively were the Fagoaga brothers, the Marquis of Apartado and Juan Bautista. The 549,000 ps. they subscribed came, of course, from the Sombrerete bonanza of 1792–4. Thus the very same family, which in a previous generation had lost nearly half a million pesos at Real del Monte, barely escaped the same experience in Zacatecas. As it was, both men had died before their investment yielded any return. Bolaños as well as Sombrerete helped to sustain Zacatecas. The Marquis of Bibanco paid 117,500 ps. on his share and a half. The other partner of note was Antonio Bassoco, the Mexico City merchant, who put up 235,000 pesos on his three shares. The final shareholder, Vicente Olloquí, only subscribed 19,625 on his quarter of a

[1] AGN, Vínculos 213/3, statement by Bibanco's estate lawyer, July 1809. Bibanco's daughter received 377, 164 ps. on 1½ shares. There is no reason to suppose she was paid proportionally more than the other partners.

share.[1] The Vetagrande owed its success, therefore, to that small group of Mexico City merchant-capitalists and finance houses which had dominated entire sections of the mining industry throughout the eighteenth century. They formed a tight circle of magnates. Bassoco's brother-in-law, the second Marquis of Castañiza, had married a daughter of Juan Bautista de Fagoaga. The daughter of Gaspar Martín Vicario, another albeit less resilient shareholder, married the second Marquis of Bibanco. Bassoco's widow was later to comment: 'The Marquis of Bibanco and Don Gaspar Vicario enjoyed the closest friendship with my husband.'[2]

For both the Fagoagas and Bassoco the crisis of the 1780s had marked an epoch in their lives. The many reforms which Gálvez had introduced in the very structure of trade and mining manifestly threatened their interests. They were forced to change their methods of business. The prolonged gestation of their Vetagrande bonanza demonstrated the risks involved in this transition. But where lesser men, like Manuel Ramón de Goya, went to the wall, their vast resources permitted them to weather the storm. They became even richer than before. The very ease with which they obtained tax concessions on their investments at Sombrerete, Bolaños and Zacatecas showed that they still stood close to the seat of power. Their mining profits in part depended upon these extensive fiscal subsidies. If any group of families and enterprises could be said to constitute a colonial establishment, it was the Fagoaga brothers and Bassoco with their Castañiza and Villaurrutia brothers-in-law in both the Church and the judiciary.[3] All these men, by reason of their connexions and wealth, contrived to ride the wave of Bourbon reforms and to emerge as entrenched and as influential as ever. It was left to the more powerful tide of Jacobin revolution after Independence to dislodge them. When the state of Zacatecas moved to attack the dominance of Mexico City over the provinces, may not its politicians have had the Fagoagas somewhat in mind? After all, Francisco García, its radical, federalist governor, had once worked for them at the Vetagrande.[4]

[1] AGN, Minería 46/3, inquiry into company's shareholding, 31 January 1805.

[3] AGN, Guerra 5 (B), Countess of Bassoco to Calleja, 28 October 1815.

[2] During the 20 years 1796–1816, among the members of this group were to be found a prior of the consulado, an administrator-general of the mining court, a bishop of Durango, the first Jesuit provincial of the revived company, the regent of the audiencia of Guadalajara, a canon of Mexico City cathedral chapter, an *alcalde del crimen* of the Mexican audiencia, and three titles of nobility.

[4] Salvador Vidal, *Señor Francisco García Salinas, 'Tata Pachito'* (Zacatecas, 1962), p. 10.

CHAPTER 5

THE CREOLE INHERITANCE

During the eighteenth century the Crown granted some 50 new titles of nobility to persons resident in New Spain. In most cases the only observable criterion of selection was the possession of great riches. The Mexican aristocracy was recruited from the financial élite, and in general can be accepted as a representative sample of the colony's wealthy classes. An analysis of its composition, therefore, will yield revealing evidence as to the formation of great fortunes in New Spain.[1] The scheme shown in table 19 will best illustrate this pattern.

Table 19 *Mexican nobility of the eighteenth century (creations).*

	Peninsulars	Americans	Unknown	Total
Miners	9	6	1	16
Merchants	10	—	—	10
Landowners	2	10	—	12
Officials	7	1	—	8
Unknown	1	2	—	3
	—	—	—	—
Total	29	19	1	49

Two significant facts emerge from this scheme. In the first place the importance of mining and commerce as compared to landowning and office-holding. The significance of mining is increased if we note that the two younger ennobled sons of the Count of Regla are placed in the category of landowners although their estates were purchased from their father's mining profits and that one official gained his wealth and title through marriage to a daughter of the Count. The second striking phenomenon is the great quantity of peninsular Spaniards, not merely in trade and office-holding, but also in mining. They obtained 60 per cent of all new creations of nobility.

Clearly the scheme—and the arguments of previous chapters which it largely confirms—provokes the query: Why were the creoles unable to compete with the immigrant Spaniards? For here we have a society

[1] Calculated from Ortega y Pérez Gallardo, *Historia genealógica*. See also Fonseca y Urrutia, *Historia general de Real Hacienda*, IV, 234, 243, 350–1.

established for over two hundred years which still required—or permitted—immigrants of relatively humble extraction to seize control of commerce and a good part of mining, to assemble great fortunes, and to crown their achievements with the purchase of titles of nobility. The gachupín success rested upon the failure of the creole. Why was the creole unable to compete with his immigrant cousin, and what were the consequences of this failure?

Most contemporary observers of colonial society gave a forthright and harsh response to our query. The American Spaniard of the respectable classes, they asserted, was idle. True, the more sympathetic hastened to qualify this judgment, declaring that the creole best exercised his talents in the professions, in literature and the arts. But most agreed that he lacked all sense of business. In consequence there existed a universal tendency for the American Spaniards to consume their inherited estates. Now admittedly, evidence for these generalisations is almost entirely literary but the unanimity of both passing travellers, permanent residents, and even accounts written by creoles themselves is sufficiently striking as to demand discussion. For if we accept this testimony as reliable then we are confronted with an unexpected and indeed controversial conclusion to our study of Mexican miners and merchants.

In 1763 Father Ajofrín, an itinerant Capuchin friar, stated: 'Notwithstanding that the natives or creoles are so capable and fit for letters and the professions, it has been found that they do not have the required economy for trade, the management of haciendas and the administration of their households; it happens all the time that gachupín fathers leave their sons great fortunes in commerce and haciendas, and within a short time these are consumed or diminished.'[1]

In 1809 Pedro de Fonte, later Archbishop of Mexico, made a similar but more hostile observation:

> Since their education is in opulence and comfort, they view with distaste serious occupation and fall quickly into a languid inertia which at the same time buries them in vice and misery. Most can glory in the wealth of their fathers and ancestors, but there are few who have not wasted their fortune and property, or if they retain a part, then the profit barely exceeds the interest of the mortgages with which their estates are charged. Favoured or exalted by their noble origin, they despise the Indians and mixed breeds, and ashamed of their own vices and dissipations, entertain a secret aversion to, and envy of, the Europeans, who by their toil, sobriety and energy enjoy consideration and comfort. This class, rival to all the rest, wishes to enjoy alone the advantages of this soil.[2]

[1] Ajofrín, *Diario*, I, 85.

[2] AGI, Mexico 1895, Pedro de Fonte to Benito Hermida, 24 April 1809.

Both priests were, of course, peninsular Spaniards; they expressed the opinions and prejudices of the gachupín community resident in Mexico. But corroboration for their views can be gleaned from various declarations made by the Mexican creoles themselves. At the beginning of the eighteenth century, for example, Juan Antonio de Ahumada in an open letter to the new king, Philip V, asseverated that the American Spaniards were little better than pilgrims in their own country. They were rarely if ever appointed to high office in the Church or the royal administration. Without such reward they lacked all incentive to study or to undertake arduous achievements and in consequence they relapsed into a vicious sloth, the source of all their evils and failure.[1]

The ayuntamiento of Mexico City, a creole stronghold, largely concurred with Ahumada's argument. In 1771 in a petition presented to the Spanish Crown they demanded that public office in New Spain should be reserved to natives of the country. They were at pains to emphasise the noble ancestry of the American Spaniards; many of the best families in the Peninsula, they asserted, had despatched their younger sons to the New World. The common gachupín insinuation that most creoles possessed Indian blood was vehemently denied. Furthermore, they affirmed that their children 'are bred and educated in the same splendour [as their forefathers], enjoy delicate foods, ornate clothing, the pomp and attention of servants, sumptuous buildings and exquisite furniture ... they are ignorant of manual work and for the most part dedicate themselves to their studies.... Mechanic jobs neither agree with the lustre of their birth nor offer a decent subsistence.'[2] Given this upbringing the American Spaniard depended upon public office in order to subsist. Without it, so the ayuntamiento argued, the creoles were forced to enter the priesthood or to remain bachelors. If they did risk marriage, economic necessity would drive their children into the ranks of the populace.

In effect, both Ahumada and the author of the 1771 petition agreed with the observations of Ajofrín and Fonte; they differed only in their explanation: the peninsular clerics ascribed creole failings to their character and the nature of their talents, whereas the two Mexicans explained the disastrous situation of their class by its virtual exclusion from public office. That the creole was idle and that he tended to waste his fortune no one denied.

[1] BN (Madrid) MSS 1187, 'Representación política y legal de Juan Antonio de Ahumada a Felipe V', ff. 33–8.

[2] Juan Hernández y Dávalos, *Colección de documentos para la historia de la guerra de Independencia de México de 1808 a 1821* (6 vols.; Mexico, 1877–82), I, 427–55.

Clearly, what we have here is a description of a colonial élite denied its birthright—the governance of the country. The American Spaniard, by reason of his family and race, was born, bred and educated within a socially privileged and materially comfortable class, demonstrably superior to the surrounding coloured population. 'All creoles are born to be hidalgos', wrote Juan López de Cancelada, an acute observer.[1] Now hidalgos, generally speaking, rarely sought to enter business; instead they expected public employment. And in the New World the American Spaniards from the sixteenth century until Independence besieged the Crown with petitions for office and complaints at their exclusion. The creole wanted to be a viceroy, a governor, a bishop, a general, a high court judge. It was from the exercise of political power that he aspired to obtain both prestige and profit. Denied access to such positions he did not, unless driven by extreme necessity, engage in economic enterprise; instead, he lived off his estates, took up a profession, and consumed his inheritance.

Juan López de Cancelada wrote an amusing dialogue about the consequences of the creole's dislike of business as seen by gachupín cousin and creole son.[2]

Gachupín—I came from Spain without a penny: I received 20,000 pesos from my uncle's business in the ten years during which I worked for a third of the profits, leaving my uncle 350,000 pesos; and my cousin, who then inherited the money, has wasted it, and now wants to support himself, his wife and children, without knowing more than Latin.

Creole—He came to my father's house from Spain without shoes, a brute of a fellow, and now that he is rich he wishes to be consul. These gachupines come here to be somebody and to take possession of all that our land produces: we are to be blamed for permitting it.

It was Lucas Alamán who summarised the final effect of the American Spaniard's character and ambitions:

The result of these unhappy propensities [of creole character] was the short duration of fortunes, so that the Europeans' efforts in working to gather and leave an estate to their children can be compared to the bottomless tunnel of the Danaides which was never filled no matter how much was thrown into it. Hence in order to endure in prosperity and opulence the Spanish race in America required to be remade continuously by European families as those formed by their predecessors fell into obscurity and poverty.[3]

Himself the son of an immigrant merchant, Alamán cited the Andaluz proverb, 'Father a merchant, son a gentleman, grandson a beggar.' The

[1] Juan López de Cancelada, *El Telégrafo Americano*, No. 20, 19 February 1812, p. 254.
[2] *Ibid.*, p. 251.
[3] Alamán, *Historia*, I, 16, 17.

cycle of three generations is, of course, echoed in the proverbs of many nations. The rise and fall of wealthy families is a constant within most societies. Equally frequent is the recruitment of successful merchants into the ranks of the landed classes and the preference of their sons to enter the professions.[1] But in one important respect New Spain differed from other such traditional societies. In Mexico it was generally immigrants who made fortunes, it was the native-born who lost them. The usual circular process of rise and fall was therefore broken. For the most part it was European Spaniards who ascended the social scale, it was American Spaniards who descended. There was small chance of upward social mobility for any creole. New Spain, therefore, possessed a peculiarly colonial society—colonial in the sense that both prestige and wealth went to immigrants rather than to the native-born. Our argument of course depends upon the assumption that the populace, by reason of its racial composition and lack of education, was unable to climb to the level of the respectable classes, so that a creole family, once submerged among the masses, could rarely hope to regain its lost status. Naturally this process of social decline did not affect all families with equal rapidity: in general it was the grandsons of the successful immigrant who most felt the pinch of economic necessity. By then, the original estate had been subjected to two testamentary divisions. It was in this generation that the battle of existence began in earnest.

Our presentation of Alamán's theory has been both extreme and schematic; many exceptions to the rule can be advanced and in any case it foreshortens what was often a century-long struggle for social survival. Moreover, as so far argued, it must leave us more puzzled than convinced. For Alamán, like Ajofrín and Fonte, explained the process of social decline by appeal to the creole's education and character. Yet surely economic reasons must be adduced if we are to explain why inherited capital was consumed or dissipated. Was it just indolence and unsatisfied political ambitions that prevented the creole from accumulating wealth or maintaining his estate? Or did his financial ruin spring from his choice of occupation? What in fact could the creole do; what jobs were open to him?

1 Compare: 'A general feature of the social and economic history of English towns . . . was the remarkable constancy with which successful urban families came and went in a matter of three generations at the most. No merchant patrician class ever formed in the English towns. Recruited largely from the younger sons of the free peasantry and the minor gentry of the adjacent countryside, the successful merchants returned to the land within a hundred years—usually much less; and their business dissolved into farms and fields, crops and stock.' W. G. Hoskins, *Provincial England* (London, 1963), p. 74.

Once posed in this form, the problem becomes more manageable. For the most cursory examination immediately reveals the fact that the professions—the creole's chosen field of activity—provided sustenance for remarkably few people. In 1803 an official inquiry found that New Spain possessed 386 lawyers, of whom only 210 actually practised. The great majority (over 171) lived in Mexico City.[1] Yet even this small number found it difficult to gain a livelihood. In 1807 Carlos María de Bustamante complained that after eight years of practice, 'I hardly have sufficient bread for my family'. He averred that a mere handful of men monopolised litigation in the audiencia, making great fortunes while 'the remainder of the lawyers groan in poverty'.[2]

Other careers were hard to seek. There were fewer doctors than lawyers; in 1793 they did not number more than 140. Notaries were similarly sparse—no more than 180.[3] The regular army, recruited since the 1760s, formed a new but limited source of employment. By 1800 it did not have more than 200 creole officers.[4] We can now better appreciate the importance of the royal bureaucracy. But its numbers are not easy to calculate. Whereas nearly all lawyers, doctors and notaries were creole, the bureaucracy was precisely the profession most dominated by peninsular Spaniards. Possibly there were up to a thousand posts on which were assigned salaries sufficient to maintain in comfort a family of the respectable classes.[5] But we do not know the proportion held by creoles.

All these occupations dwindle, however, in comparison to the Church. By 1809 New Spain possessed 7,431 priests and religious, the overwhelming majority of whom were native-born Spaniards.[6] True, many clergymen, particularly the encumbents of country parishes, were recruited from the lower levels of society—not all seven thousand men were born into families of the 'gente decente'. Moreover, in the higher offices and the religious orders some peninsular Spaniards were to be found. But in general it was the creole who staffed the multitude of clerical institutions—the cathedral chapters, the university, the colleges, the hospitals, the monasteries and the parishes. For the Church offered both social prestige

[1] AGI, Mexico 1811, audiencia to Council of the Indies, 21 October 1806.

[2] AGI, Mexico 1817, Petition of Carlos María de Bustamante, 1 September 1807.

[3] In 1790 Mexico City possessed 51 physicians, 237 surgeons and 'barbers'. The intendancy of Guanajuato, which comprised about a tenth of the population, had 9 physicians, 9 surgeons and 97 'barbers'. See AGN, Historia 523, ff. 76, 90.

[4] See AGS, Guerra Moderna 7276–7, the listed service sheets of all officers give birthplaces.

[5] See López de Cancelada, *El Telégrafo Americano*, 13, 1 January 1812, pp. 139–41. Also *Guía de Forasteros* (Mexico, 1809), *passim*.

[6] Navarro y Noriega, *Memoria*, foldpaper, p. 30.

and generous stipends; the clergy were the natural leaders of Mexican society.

But of course the entrance of numerous young creoles of the upper class into a celibate priesthood abruptly terminated the course of many wealthy families. No doubt the Church offered an asylum for the impecunious—a refuge for the progeny of families descending the social scale. But many cases could be cited where the unexpected death of an elder brother brought a considerable inheritance to the surviving son who had become a priest. Nor could such estates be legally passed on to illegitimate children. The Church, therefore, was a key institution which by its insistence upon celibacy contributed to undermine the stability of the colonial élite.

Apart from the professions the impecunious creole could always enter some form of economic enterprise. But here, especially in commerce, he was confronted by the clannish confraternity of gachupín merchants who distrusted his capacity and honesty and who frequently refused to concede him necessary credit. Many American Spaniards did become traders but few attained more than a mediocre success. The conventional stereotypes about creole character—his lack of business sense and his unreliability—became self-fulfilling predictions. Moreover, as Dr Mora pointed out, whereas the gachupín was supported by an extended network of paisanos, the creole had to struggle as an individual.[1]

If in general the slow, penny-pinching routine of shopkeeping did not attract the American Spaniard, by contrast the speculative, lucky-strike quality of silver mining exercised a perennial fascination. But silver mining tended to attract men who were either foolishly avaricious or hopelessly impoverished.[2] It was all too easy for a creole of moderate means to lose his entire fortune in an unsuccessful mine; it was even more common for a creole of good family and no means to sink without trace amidst the rough camaraderie of the mining camp. Then again, in an industry so heavily dependent upon mercantile capital, the creole miner and refiner suffered the effects of gachupín prejudice and competition. Nevertheless, despite the industry's hazardous nature, it undoubtedly offered the American Spaniard far better opportunities for social redemption than was possible in commerce. But as a prescription it was a remedy that more often killed than cured. It certainly injected a feverish quality into colonial society.

In the last resort, neither the limited number of professional jobs, the

1 José María Luis de Mora, *Méjico y sus revoluciones* (3 vols.; Mexico, 1950), I, 76–8.

2 Lassaga and Velásquez de León, *Representación*, p. 42.

celibacy of the clergy, the gachupín control of trade, nor the risk-laden nature of silver mining will suffice to explain the social and economic debility of New Spain's native-born élite. For the stronghold, the basis, of the creole class was the land. The immigrant merchants, the wealthy miners, creole and gachupín alike—these men all invested their fortunes in the purchase of haciendas. In a country without joint stock companies or banks only the land offered rich entrepreneurs the prospect of a well-endowed and secure future for their descendants. Lucas Alamán's theory, therefore, stands or falls upon the economic viability of the Mexican hacienda. If these large estates were profitable then it is difficult to explain why the families which owned them should have been subject to a continuous process of social replacement. No description of the Mexican élite can be complete without a discussion of the hacienda and its problems.

Whereas the 6,680 ranchos and the 4,680 Indian villages listed in 1809 of necessity mainly lived off their own crops, New Spain's 4,945 haciendas and estancias produced for a market.[1] A hacienda existed to provide its owner with an income. True, many were left deserted as mere parks for semi-wild herds of cattle and sheep, but in such case they served no observable purpose. For in general most landowners preferred to live in a town; they visited their estates for a few months in a year, if at all, and for the rest entrusted their property to the care of a manager.[2] The Mexican hacendados formed an absentee landlord class who relied upon their estates to yield an income sufficient to maintain an upper-class town-dwelling family in style and comfort. Almost no one bought a hacienda to live on it, still less to feed himself. Many large estates frequently had to support two élite families—the owner's and that of his manager.

But as a unit of production the hacienda was notoriously defective. For there was a peculiar disproportion between the number and average size of the Mexican hacienda—some covered over a hundred square miles—and the minuscule market it supplied. Travellers of the period, such as Father Morfi, lamented over the vast tracts of land left derelict by their owners.[3] But to what point cultivation, if the crops could not be sold? Only the sparsely distributed chain of towns and mining camps offered an adequate market. True, certain regions such as the Bajío and the Valley of

[1] Navarro y Noriega, *Memoria*, foldpaper, p. 30.

[2] Francisco Pimentel, *La economía política aplicada a la propiedad territorial en México* (Mexico, 1866), p. 116. For a general characterisation of the haciendas see Eric R. Wolf and Sidney W. Mintz, 'Haciendas and Plantation in Middle America and the Antilles', *Social and Economic Studies*, 6 (1957), pp. 380–412.

[3] Morfi, *Viaje*, pp. 46–75. See also Andrés Molina Enríquez, *Los grandes problemas nacionales* (Mexico, 1909), pp. 80–93.

Mexico presented urban markets situated at an economic distance. But elsewhere most haciendas made use of but a small portion of their land, and rented out the remainder to their peons, vagrant squatters and neighbouring Indian villages. Moreover, the depressed price level of most agricultural produce did not permit landowners, even on favourably situated estates, to make much profit. For example, the one district of Chalco, with some help from Toluca, satisfied Mexico City's demand for maize; yet in 1773 it was estimated that average production per hacienda amounted to no more than 3,000 fanegas a year, which, with maize prices varying from one to two pesos a fanega, provided a return of at most 6,000 ps., from which the production costs had still to be subtracted.[1]

In general, the Mexican hacienda yielded a poor return upon the large quantity of capital usually invested in its purchase. The Marchioness of Bibanco owned two haciendas, Chapingo situated in Texcoco, and Ojo de Agua located in Sepuala. The latter estate produced pulque. Her income and average yield upon capital is shown in table 20.[2]

Table 20 *Income and return upon capital of two haciendas, 1800–5.* (In pesos)

Year	Chapingo	Ojo de Agua
1800	19,825	10,368
1801	4,695	8,844
1802	10,365	9,047
1803	8,217	10,914
1804	6,414	10,250
1805	16,325	10,034
	65,843	59,459
Average annual income	10,940	9,909
Capital value of estates	193,082	140,442
Annual return upon capital	5·6%	7%

The Jesuits enjoyed fame as the most efficient managers of haciendas. Yet M. Berthe, in his study of the order's sugar plantation at Xochimancas, found its profits, especially in the early eighteenth century, to be remarkably low.[3] It can be proved that the vast estates belonging to the Mexico City College of St Peter and St Paul and the seminary at Tepotzotlán yielded but a low return upon their capital value. These estates, which

[1] Florescano, *Los precios del maíz*, p. 92; and Gibson, *The Aztecs*, pp. 328–9.

[2] AGN, Vínculos 213/3, Statement of Lic. Oláez, July 1809.

[3] Berthe, 'Xochimancas,' pp. 104–5.

comprised 'a substantial fraction of all the land in the northern part of the valley' in 1767 passed into royal administration after the expulsion of the Jesuits, and in 1775 were sold to the Count of Regla.[1] At the time of the sale a scheme of income for the years immediately before and after confiscation was drawn up, which we present in summary in table 21.[2]

Table 21 *Value and income of former Jesuit haciendas purchased by the Count of Regla, c. 1775.* (In pesos)

	Haciendas					
	Jalpa and subsidiaries	Santa Lucía, San Javier	Gavía	Portales	Molino	Total
Value	575,830	1,151,694	184,440	52,186	2,500	1,966,650
Sale price	—	—	—	—	—	1,020,000
Annual income before occupation	35,000	23,065	5,979	3,594	436	68,074
After occupation: avg. of 8½ yrs. (1767–75)	28,793	16,486	2,733	336	314	48,662
Tithes & excise: annual avg. (only charged after occupation)	—	—	—	—	—	8,317
Avg. return on capital by Jesuits	—	—	—	—	—	3·5%
Return on capital after occupation, including tithes and excise	—	—	—	—	—	2·9%
Return on sale price to Regla	—	—	—	—	—	4·7%

Our eighteenth-century evidence, therefore, supports the estimates of Francisco Pimentel, who, writing in the 1860s, reckoned that in Mexican agriculture the average return upon capital was no higher than 6 per cent.[3]

A contributory cause for the colonial hacienda's low income was to be found in the taxes to which its produce was subject. The Crown levied an excise duty of 6 per cent, and sometimes 8 per cent, on the value of all its sales. In addition the Church collected a tithe of all its produce. The Jesuit estates mentioned above, once confiscated, paid, in both excise and tithe, over 14 per cent of their total income. The Church bore heavily upon Mexican agriculture: in the period 1779–89 its tithes in New Spain (excluding Yucatán) averaged 1,835,000 ps. a year.[4]

[1] Gibson, *The Aztecs*, p. 290.

[2] AGI, Mexico 1772, a statement of the accountant-general of temporalidades, 16 December 1777.

[3] Pimentel, *La economía política*, pp. 208, 236–7.

[4] Humboldt, *Ensayo político*, p. 85.

Moreover, the Church also acted as the colony's land bank. By 1805 it possessed a capital of about 44 million pesos, which was mainly invested in mortgages and loans secured upon urban and, more especially, rural property.[1] This huge sum represented the accumulated product of three centuries of pious donations, testamentary bequests and invested interest. It comprised the annuities that supported the secular clergy and the endowments that sustained hospitals, asylums, orphanages and colleges. Thus the Mexican hacienda, upon which largely fell the burden of paying the 5 per cent interest accruing from these clerical mortgages and annuities, maintained not merely the fabric and liturgy of the Church, but also the entire charitable, medical and educational establishment of the colony.

The explanation for this peculiarly heavy burden can be found in the reciprocal needs of the Church and the land-owning class. Most haciendas required credit, and hence tended to accumulate debts. A bad harvest, a drought, a mining or commercial venture, a charitable donation, a daughter's dowry, an annuity for a younger son, mere conspicuous consumption: all these expenses were met by mortgages charged upon haciendas, and although in the first instance such loans were usually only granted for five-year periods, an almost perpetual extension was common.[2] It was not infrequent to encounter haciendas which bore inherited mortgages worth up to 50 per cent of their market value. For its part the Church—almost the only source of long-term credit open to the hacendado—clearly deemed haciendas to be far safer prospects than silver mines or an *obraje*; only urban property offered comparable advantages. Moreover, such mortgages yielded an income—at 5 per cent—without the labour that outright ownership of an estate entailed. Thus most clerical capital was charged upon the hacienda, invested in land, the colony's only tangible security which provided an income. Naturally this reciprocity of interest between Church and landowner soon led to situations where the impecunious hacendado became little more than a manager for his clerical creditors. The intendant of Puebla reported that the 38 haciendas and 17 ranchos of Cholula were worth 788,442 ps., of which value 550,504 ps. were held by the Church.[3] Although Cholula was probably atypical, the tendency it represented was universal. By the end of the eighteenth century most haciendas bore a heavy burden of debt.

The Mexican hacienda thus constituted a weak foundation for a stable class of landed families. The cycle which Gómez de Cervantes observed at

[1] Mora, *Obras sueltas*, 'Escritos de Abad y Queipo', p. 231.

[2] *Ibid.*, p. 221; see also Chevalier, *Los grandes latifundios*, pp. 201–5.

[3] AGN, Intendencias 48, Intendant Flon to viceroy, 12 May 1790.

work in the seventeenth century proved to be a continuous process, equally applicable to the eighteenth century. Apart from a handful of magnates, the owners of entire provinces such as the Rincón Gallardo or the Marquises of San Miguel de Aguayo, the average hacendado family found it difficult to weather the passage of the generations. In general a contemporary student of clerical mortgages declared that few families held their estates for more than three generations.[1] Francisco Pimentel stated that barely a hacienda existed which had not been purchased with capital acquired in mining, industry or trade.[2] If such be the case then the Mexican hacienda was a sink through which drained without stop the surplus capital accumulated in the export economy. The fortunes created in mining and commerce were invested in land, there to be slowly dissipated or to be gradually transferred into the coffers of the Church. In consequence, a continuous replacement in the hacendado class occurred. New Spain's élite was unstable in composition precisely because its chosen economic basis, the hacienda, absorbed and wasted the greater part of the colony's accumulated capital. This instability was not to end until the Mexican Revolution.

[1] José María de Jaúregui, *Discurso en que se manifiesta que deben bajarse los réditos a proporción del quebranto que hayan sufrido en la insurreción los bienes y giros de los deudores* (Mexico, 1820), p. 76.

[2] Pimentel, *La economía política*, p. 59. See also Otero, *Obras*, I, 26–32.

PART THREE

GUANAJUATO

Real Apprehension is . . . in the first instance an experience or information about the concrete.

CARDINAL NEWMAN

CHAPTER 6

THE BAJIO

Four days horse-ride north of Mexico City the traveller reaches a fertile, low-lying plain already known in the eighteenth century as the Bajío. This plain stretches from Celaya to León; it is bounded to the south by Lake Yuririapúndaro and to the north by a ridge of mountains which sharply interrupts the flat surrounding landscape. It is within these mountains that the silver town of Guanajuato is located, connected to the plains by a narrow descending river valley. Prior to the Spanish Conquest the area lay outside both the Aztec and the Tarascan empires; it was inhabited by wild, Chichimeca Indians belonging to the Cuachichile, Guamare and Pame tribes.[1] But by the close of the colonial period the Bajío was renowned both for the fertility of its fields and the wealth and number of its towns; it was second in density of population only to the Valley of Mexico itself.[2]

The precise stages of the region's colonisation remain obscure but the available evidence indicates that it was not until the eighteenth century that it emerged as the pacemaker of New Spain's economy. For the early settlement was tentative and designed mainly to occupy and guard the largely vacant territories that stretched between the Valley of Mexico and the rich mining north. San Felipe (1562), San Miguel el Grande (1555) and León (1585) were established to act as garrison towns against the still unpacified Chichimeca Indians and to serve as way stations along the great road north that led to Zacatecas and Durango.[3] At much the same time, a chieftain of the Otomí tribe, Don Fernando de Tapia, founded the town of Querétaro.[4] Some Tarascan Indians from the Michoacán also came to settle. The Bajío's ultimate prosperity, however, was assured during the 1550s when a small mining camp, called Santa Fé de Guanajuato, was staked out in the mountains.[5] The circle of settlement was closed by the foundation of Celaya in 1571 as a centre of agricultural production.

[1] Wigberto Jiménez Moreno, *Estudios de historia colonial* (Mexico, 1958), p. 57.

[2] Eric R. Wolf, 'The Mexican Bajío in the 18th Century: An Analysis of Cultural Integration', *Synoptic Studies of Mexican Culture*, ed. Munro S. Edmundson (New Orleans, 1957), *passim*.

[3] Jiménez Moreno, *Estudios*, pp. 57, 81–2, 89.

[4] José María Zelaa e Hidalgo, *Glorias de Querétaro* (Mexico, 1803), p. 147.

[5] Lucio Marmolejo, *Efemérides guanajuatenses* (4 vols.; Guanajuato, 1884), I, 145, 166.

During the following century the region was more noted for its agriculture than for mines. Whereas Celaya received its charter as a city in 1655, Guanajuato was not dignified with even the title of town until 1679.[1] The camp's population was correspondingly small: an estimated 4,000 in 1600 rising slowly to 16,000 in 1700.[2] Similarly, its silver production did not become important until the last decades of the century. In the mercury distribution of 1636 Guanajuato was given 7·2 per cent of the total issue, compared to the third allotted to Zacatecas. Furthermore, a comparison of the town's massive but simple parish church, built in the years 1671–96, with its splendid baroque equivalent in Zacatecas constructed at much the same period, reveals how provincial Guanajuato still remained.[3]

By the eighteenth century, however, the Bajío had come to form a prosperous intermediary zone quite distinct from either the vacant ranges and scattered mine camps of the north or the central valleys with their blend of Indian communities and latifundia. In the first place, its population was both heavily urbanised and mainly mestizo. Moreover its towns were industrial: Querétaro and San Miguel el Grande were New Spain's leading centres for the manufacture of woollen textiles; Celaya and Salamanca wove cotton; León made leather goods; and Guanajuato had become the chief silver producer in all Mexico. Then again, with such an extensive town market to supply, the region's agriculture greatly prospered. It was precisely this combination of urbanisation, textiles, mining and agriculture which made the Bajío an area exceptional not merely in Mexico but in all Spanish America.

II

Without a plentiful and mobile work force, the economic progress of the region would have been impossible. At the same time, the wide range of employment possibilities either attracted immigration from Michoacán and the centre, or, alternatively, offered a peculiarly propitious environment for natural increase. Whatever the cause, the population of the five districts which later composed the intendancy of Guanajuato grew at a much faster rate than in the central valleys or the south. Whereas for New Spain as a whole the demographic growth between 1742 and 1793 amounted to about 33 per cent, for the Guanajuato intendancy it reached 155 per cent. In 1742 the intendancy's area contained 4·6 per cent of the

1 Silva Herzog, Documentos, p. 75; José Guadalupe Romero, *Noticias para formar la historia y la estadística del obispado de Michoacán* (Mexico, 1862), p. 157; Marmolejo, *Efemérides*, I, 102.

2 Matilla Tascón, *Minas de Almadén*, p. 223.

3 Marmolejo, *Efemérides*, I, 212, 226.

total population of New Spain, a percentage which by 1793 rose to 9·4.[1] Reasons for this phenomenal increase are hard to find. The parochial records suggest that much of it can be accounted for by the clear excess of births over deaths. Apparently even the heavy toll of deaths exacted by the great famines and epidemics of 1759–60, 1779–80, and 1784–6 did not destroy this favourable balance. The scheme of table 22 and figure 2 will best indicate these trends.[2]

Table 22 *Population of Guanajuato intendancy with various records of births and deaths, 1742–1812.*

Guanajuato intendancy	Population 1742	1793	1810
Alcaldías mayores:			
Guanajuato	48,750	114,344	—
León	16,970	54,952	—
Celaya	55,200	141,918	—
San Miguel	23,800	55,965	—
La Paz (San Luis de)	11,420	30,745	—
	156,140	397,924	576,600
Parochial records 1797–1802	*Births*	*Deaths*	*Increase*
City of Guanajuato	12,666	6,294	6,372
Marfil	3,702	1,904	1,798
Santa Ana	3,629	1,857	1,772
Jurisdiction of Querétaro			
14 January 1784 to 13 April 1795 (6 years, 3 months)	44,179	13,759	20,420
1 January 1796 to 13 December 1801 (6 months)	40,024	24,308	15,716
Dolores Hidalgo			
1756–1801	61,258	24,123	37,135
Marfil			
1743–1812	53,594	21,680	31,914

Clearly not too much can be made of these scattered figures. A person was always more likely to receive a Christian baptism than a church burial; moreover during the years of famine many Indians and peons roamed the countryside in search of food only to die unattended in the

[1] For 1742 see Gerhard, *México en 1742*, pp. 21–8; for 1793 see AGN, Historia 523, f. 88; for 1810 see Navarro y Noriega, *Memoria*, foldpaper, p. 30.

[2] For districts see references in note 9. The parochial figures are taken from Humboldt, *Ensayo político*, p. 40; Querétaro figures from BN (Madrid) MSS 18636, report made by parish priests of Querétaro, 10 July 1802. For the graph of Marfil baptisms and burials see AHG, Insurgencia 1812–14, report of Marfil parish priest, Lic. José Ignacio Franco, 10 May 1813.

fields. Such mobility distorts, where it does not destroy, the value of lists for individual parishes. Nevertheless as straws in the wind, they serve as useful indicators.

The degree of urbanisation, although difficult to calculate, was remarkably high. In 1790 the town of Querétaro possessed nearly 30,000

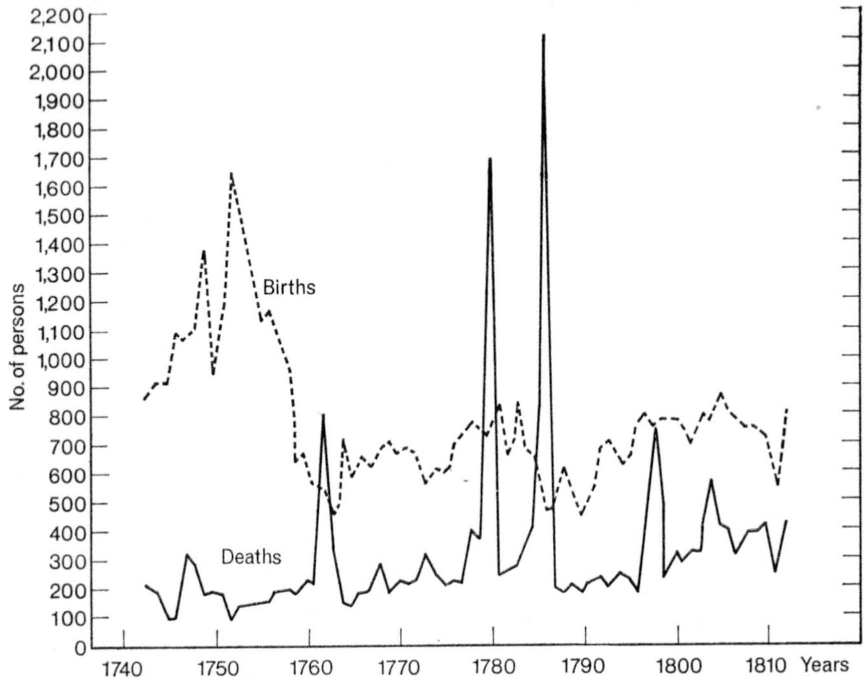

Fig. 2. *Registered births and burials in parish of Marfil, Guanajuato, 1743–1811.*

inhabitants and San Juan del Río, 6,173.[1] Guanajuato comprised 32,000 persons within its centre; but if we add the population of the mining and refining villages, no more than three miles away, which formed so many suburbs of the city, then the total reaches 55,000.[2] Precise figures for the towns, as distinct from the jurisdictions, of Celaya, San Miguel and León are lacking. But Celaya probably had over 20,000 inhabitants and San Miguel at least 12,000; León was much smaller—under 6,000 in 1781.[3]

[1] José Antonio del Raso, *Notas estadísticas del departamento de Querétaro, año de 1845* (Mexico, 1846), p. 97.

[2] AGN, Historia 523, f. 88.

[3] Romero, *Noticias*, p. 190. But it is claimed that by 1810 the population of Léon had risen to 18,000.

In addition to these major urban centres the Bajío had a considerable number of smaller towns such as Irapuato, Silao, Salamanca, Salvatierra, Acámbaro, San Felipe and Dolores Hidalgo. It appears reasonable to suppose that by 1793 about a third of the population in the intendancy of Guanajuato lived in towns of over 5,000 persons. A similar percentage prevailed in the area of the corregimiento of Querétaro.

Granted this situation, it is not surprising to learn that in the Bajío's population persons of mixed blood predominated. A scheme extracted from the published summaries of the 1792 census will illustrate its proportions.[1]

Population of the Intendancy of Guanajuato, 1793

Spaniards	103,584	(26·1%)
Mulattoes	72,281	(18·2%)
Castes	46,982	(11·5%)
Indians	175,182	(44·2%)
	398,029	(100·0%)

Since the majority of persons listed as Spaniards undoubtedly possessed some admixture of Indian or African blood, then we can assume that by the end of the eighteenth century the Bajío had achieved what other provinces were to reach much later—the formation of a predominantly mestizo population. The Indians were already in a minority. Furthermore, the available evidence suggests that the Indian community was considerably hispanised and well on the road to losing its identity as a separate cultural group.

Historically, the Otomíes and Tarascans of the Bajío were a settler group which had set up relatively few constituted villages. In 1810 only 62 such *pueblos* were listed, and the 1793 census enumerated but 37.[2] Moreover, as an inquiry made in 1797 revealed, these villages retained little communal land. In San Felipe and Dolores no pueblo had either community funds or communal maize plots (*siembras de milpas comunes*). In San Luis de la Paz four villages still retained some land but all four were engaged in lawsuits against local landowners over possession. To the south in Salamanca the two villages which owned land rented it out, and in Salvatierra the few fields which belonged to two villages there did not yield any profit. Neither in Celaya nor in the smaller towns of its jurisdiction, such as Apaseo, Jerécuaro or Chamacuero, did the Indians have

[1] AGN, Historia 523, f. 88.

[2] AGN, Historia 523, f. 75.

any land. In León the 702 tributaries of San Francisco de Rincón lacked communal fields. Of San Miguel el Grande it was reported: 'There is no distribution of land among the Indian labourers since they live on the haciendas and ranchos of the district, and those who dwell in the town support themselves as artisans.'[1]

The weakness of the villages was further demonstrated by the distinctive method of tribute collection employed in the Bajío. In 1776 the alcalde mayor of San Miguel el Grande complained that 'this jurisdiction [is] the only one in all the kingdom where the tributaries are migrants (*vagos*); nor does there exist any means of a return to payment by village as is the custom in the rest of the kingdom'.[2] At much the same time, the alcalde mayor of Guanajuato remarked upon the increasing number of such vagos—both migrant labourers and tenant farmers—'whose tribute is paid neither by their village nor by their hacienda'. He suggested that the local hacendados should be made responsible for tribute collection.[3] It was in view of these complaints that Viceroy Bucareli granted the alcaldes mayores of Guanajuato, León, San Miguel and Celaya a 9 per cent commission on all tributes they collected directly from individuals as distinct from those forwarded by villages and haciendas.[4] By the close of the century most Indians in the Guanajuato intendency were classified as vagos—some 168,879 as contrasted to the 76,852 whose tribute was gathered by their villages.[5] If this proportion is compared to that found in the adjacent Mexican intendancy where out of a total 982,621 Indians only 13,554 were designated as vagos, then the distinctive nature of the Bajío's Indian community stands clearly revealed.

Other, more literary evidence points in the same direction. In 1811 Juan López de Cancelada, a shrewd observer, who had lived in Silao, stated: 'The Indians from Querétaro to the far north barely differ from the other castes either in presence or in civilization.'[6] Yet it seems that this process of acculturation was a fairly recent phenomenon, and that it moved faster in the towns than in the countryside. In 1746 José Villaseñor y Sánchez, in his *Theatro Americano*, estimated that a thousand families of Tarascan Indians lived in Marfil; he also noted large Otomí and Tarascan settlements in Silao and Irapuato.[7] But by 1779 Guanajuato's hospital for

[1] AGI, Mexico 1454, Riaño to viceroy, 25 September 1797.
[2] AGI. Mexico 1378. Bucareli to Gálvez, 24 February 1777.
[3] AGI, Mexico 1370, Baltazar de Bersabal to viceroy, 9 March 1771.
[4] AGI, Mexico 1370, Bucareli to Gálvez, 20 June 1772.
[5] Wolf, *The Mexican Bajío*, p. 191.
[6] López de Cancelada, *Ruina de la Nueva España*, p. 70.
[7] José Antonio Villaseñor y Sánchez, *Theatro americano* (2 vols.; Mexico, 1746–8), II, 41.

these tribes had fallen into disuse since the Indians had 'merged with the *lobos* (a mixture of Indian and negro) and the mulattoes'.[1] The extent of acculturation is demonstrated by a municipal edict issued in 1781 by the Count of Valenciana, at that time acting magistrate of Guanajuato. He forbade Indians to wear European dress since otherwise it was difficult to find them for taxation, and encouraged them to think themselves equal to the mestizos and mulattoes.[2] Admittedly the edict was annulled by the viceroy, since royal policy wished to promote the wearing of European cloth in order to benefit Spanish industry, but the incident throws clear light upon the blend of races in the mining town. An interesting implication of the edict is that an 'Indian' could only be distinguished from a 'mestizo' if he wore distinctive costume.

Table 23 *Distribution of occupations in Guanajuato Intendancy.* (c. *1793*)

Occupation	No. of persons employed	per cent
Farmers	53,867	48·7
Miners	9,369	8·5
Merchants	1,031	0·9
Industrial workers (*fabricantes*)	10,753	9·8
Artisans (*artesanos*)	16,605	14·9
Day wage-earners (*jornaleros*)	17,680	15·9
State and military employees	250	0·2
Professional	272	0·2
Religious	299	0·2
Nobility and hidalgos	807	0·7
Total working population	110,933	100·0
Total population	388,029	
Total working population as a % of total population		28·6

If Indian communities lacked stability and property there is no reason to suppose that the mestizos or most Spaniards were any better off. But in what occupations was this mass of workers engaged? The intendant drew up a chart for 1793 that threw some light on this question[3] (see table 23).

This scheme is unsatisfactory since we have no means of knowing what the men described as *jornaleros*, day wage-labourers, actually did; they could be agricultural peons, odd-jobs men in the towns, or occasional

[1] BN (Madrid) MSS 17618, Sale of Guanajuato Jesuit lands, Vicente Herrera to Gálvez, 26 April 1785.

[2] AGI, Mexico 1396, Mayorga to Gálvez, 14 February 1782.

[3] AGN, Historia 523, ff. 76, 90.

miners. Then again, the *muleteers* who formed a not insignificant group are omitted or included in an unspecified category. For the rest, the distinction between *fabricantes* and *artesanos* presumably denotes the difference between a weaver and a tailor, a leather-curer and a cobbler. What the scheme does prove, however, is the relatively complex nature of the Bajío economy. Contrary to some notion about 'traditional' societies, agriculture employed at most 60 per cent of the work force and probably as little as 50 per cent. On the other hand industry, including mining under this head, occupied some 18 per cent of all workers. Equally notable is the small number of persons who could be defined as belonging to the élite: in all they could not have amounted to more than 3 per cent of the total population.

There is no reason to suppose that this distribution of labour did not change. Labourers could easily obtain casual employment in a variety of jobs. A brief consideration of the Bajío economy will serve to show both the mobility of labour and the interdependence of its diverse sectors. Agriculture, which absorbed at least half the work force, was especially organised in a loose structure. In 1793 the intendant listed the following divisions.[1]

Pueblos	37
Estancias	29
Haciendas	448
Dependent ranchos	1046
Independent ranchos	360

Since the Indian pueblos owned very little communal land their inhabitants obviously worked on the haciendas and the ranchos in company with mestizo and mulatto labourers. The units of production, therefore, reduce themselves to the two main categories, haciendas and ranchos. But since most ranchos were classified as dependent, then clearly many hacendados preferred to divide and rent a good part of their estates. Evidence is at present lacking to state how common was this practice. But in 1772 we know that the Mariscal de Castilla, José Pedro de Luna, the owner of three large haciendas—La Rosita in the jurisdiction of San Miguel, Las Arandas in Guanajuato, and Nuestra Señora de la Concepción in Piedra Gorda—did not directly farm any of his property.[2] Instead, he leased out these haciendas to some 594 tenants, whose rents varied from 8 ps. to 550 ps. a year, and from whom he collected a total of 21,820 ps. Many tenants sub-rented their land in smaller plots, and nearly all

[1] See above and AGN, Historia 523, f. 76.

[2] AGI, Mexico 1370, manager's report, 4 February 1772.

employed peons and seasonal labour. The Mariscal's business manager complained that quite frequently he did not know how many persons actually lived on these estates.

This example should not be accepted as necessarily typical. For although leasing was clearly a common practice many hacendados farmed their land directly. This was particularly true of the owners of mines, refining mills and textile workshops. In these cases the hacendados effected a sort of vertical integration. They used their estates to provide them with raw materials—with maize for their mules and workers, and with wool for their looms. The haciendas existed, therefore, both to feed the people of towns and to serve their industries.

If the markets were extensive, supply was even more abundant. The fertile plains of the Bajío produced the usual Mexican staple crops in great profusion. In the jurisdiction of Celaya the average yield of maize ranged between 100 and 150 grains for every one sown. Wheat gave less: some 40 or 50 to one on irrigated land.[1] Chili, beans, fruits and pasture for livestock completed the picture. For tropical crops Guanajuato relied upon the *tierra caliente* of Michoacán. There, in 1793, the intendant calculated that his province grew three million pounds of sugar a year, of which a half was sold in Guanajuato.[2] This gave the intendancy an annual consumption of four pounds of sugar a head.

Precise figures as to both the value and bulk of the Bajío's agricultural output are lacking. We do not possess any consistent series of prices. Granted both the fertility of its land and the close proximity to markets it appears reasonable to presume that prices were somewhat lower than in Mexico City. In 1808 one source stated that some 26,160 fanegas of maize were sown within the Guanajuato intendancy.[3] At a yield of a hundred to one this amount would result in a harvest of about three million fanegas, with a value of three to six million pesos. Since by this time the annual consumption of the town of Guanajuato—including its 14,000 mules—amounted to 400,000 fanegas, this estimate does not appear improbable.[4] A somewhat later calculation for the adjoining state of Querétaro gave 624,880 fanegas of maize as the product of that rather arid province.[5]

Despite its fertility, however, the region occasionally experienced bad harvests caused by drought or frosts. During such years maize prices could rise to excessive heights. Once the level of 20 rls. a fanega was

1 Humboldt, *Ensayo político*, pp. 251, 257; see also Raso, *Notas estadísticas*, p. 37.
2 AGI, Mexico 1887, report by intendant of Michoacán to Revillagigedo, 4 October 1794.
3 Romero, *Noticias*, p. 29.
4 AGI, Mexico 2213, Marquina to Soler, 27 July 1801.
5 Raso, *Notas estadísticas*, p. 38.

reached then the refining mills which depended upon mules began to stop work.[1] If prices rose still higher then thousands of the poorer classes of society could die. The years 1785–6 were especially disastrous. In Guanajuato prices soared to over 5 ps. a fanega of maize. The town council borrowed 165,000 ps. to encourage new harvests in the *tierra caliente* and on irrigated land and to purchase any remaining stocks of grain.[2] Yet despite these extraordinary measures the town's priests estimated that about 19,000 persons died during 1786 alone, no less than 35 per cent of the population. Other towns were equally affected. San Miguel lost 3,356 persons, Celaya 4,049, León 3,794 and so on. In all the intendancy suffered 64,000 deaths in 1786. But the parish priests who supplied these figures all emphasised that many more hundreds had expired in the fields and elsewhere. For example, the vicar of Salvatierra registered 2,460 burials but reckoned that some 6,000 persons had probably perished in his parish.[3] In any case, the proportion of deaths to the total population amounted to at least a fifth.

Such crises proved all the more devastating because a considerable proportion of the urban population was employed in the region's flourishing textile industry. In 1804 the corregidor of Querétaro counted 18 factories (*obrajes*) and 327 workshops (*trapiches*) in his town, the former group operating 280 looms and the latter up to 1,000. The larger firms wove woollen ponchos, blankets, serges, and sarapes while the smaller produced coarse cottons. In addition, there were another 35 workshops making hats and ten treating leather and suede goods. Estimates as to how many people were engaged in this industry varied.[4] In 1803 the factory owners admitted that they kept over 2,000 men shut up within the walls of their prison-like establishments.[5] In the same year the corregidor stated that some 9,000 persons of both sexes were occupied in the spinning, weaving and finishing of cloth. The industry's consumption of wool averaged about a million pounds and the value of its product was later reckoned to reach over a million pesos a year.[6] These figures, moreover, excluded the 3,000 workers employed by the tobacco monopoly. Information concerning the other textile towns of the Bajío is peculiarly sparse. Yet San Miguel el Grande, for example, was renowned for its carpets, rugs, sarapes and fine woollens.

[1] AGI, Mexico 1418, Guanajuato city council to viceroy, 10 October 1785.

[2] AGN, Minería 18–8, report by Manuel García de Zeballos, 28 March 1786.

[3] ACM, 598, contains reports of all parishes within Guanajuato intendency; all give precise figures with the exception of Guanajuato itself where a mere estimate was given.

[4] Zelaa e Hidalgo, *Glorias de Querétaro*, p. 5; BM, Add. MSS 17557, ff. 147–9. Report by corregidor, Lic. Miguel Domínguez, 1804.

[5] AGI, Mexico 1809, Iturrigaray to Crown, 27 July 1806.

[6] These estimates vary considerably. See Raso, *Notas estadísticas*, pp. 57–61.

Its scale of production, however, was much smaller than its neighbour since at no time did the town possess more than four obrajes; in 1802 total capacity only amounted to 318 looms.[1] Finally, although Celaya and Salamanca spun a great deal of cotton, almost nothing is known about the organisation of their industry.

For raw materials the manufacturers turned to New León and Coahuila and to Michoacán. In a good year the latter province sold up to half a million pounds of cotton to the intendancy of Guanajuato—about a quarter of its crop.[2] The north provided both wool and cotton. Many obraje-owners, in an attempt at vertical integration, purchased haciendas not merely in the jurisdictions of San Miguel and Querétaro, where large flocks of sheep were to be found, but also in the north in the provinces of New León and San Luis Potosí. But this tendency added fuel to the resentment entertained by the natives of these areas.[3] They complained that the merchants and manufacturers of the Bajío treated them like colonies, buying or producing raw materials at a cheap price, ordering it down to Querétaro and San Miguel for manufacture, and then returning the finished article to be sold for high profit at the trade fairs of Saltillo and San Juan de los Lagos.[4] Whatever the truth of these accusations, we must remember that a wealthy market was available at the very doorstep, so to speak, in the city and mining villages of Guanajuato with their 50,000 inhabitants in need of clothing and with money enough to buy it. In the last analysis, therefore, although the Bajío benefited from its geographical position straddling the lines of communication and transport between the north and the central valleys, its own domestic economy was remarkably self-contained.

III

For the people of the Bajío the events of the 1760s marked an epoch in their political education, a time in which they became aware as rarely before of their colonial status. In Guanajuato the populace strongly resented the new régime introduced by José de Gálvez. As early as July 1766 some 6,000 persons tried to storm the treasury, shouting 'Long live the King! Death to bad government!' They were protesting against the imposition of excise duties on maize, flour, meat and wood; against the badly made cigars that the new tobacco monopoly demanded they buy;

[1] Silva Herzog, *Documentos*, pp. 83–4.
[2] AGI, Mexico 1887, intendant of Michoacán to viceroy, 4 October 1794.
[3] AGN, *Boletín*, 2nd series, II (1961) 3, pp. 371–2.
[4] Ramos Arispe, *Memoria*, pp. 85, 89–92.

and against the formation of a militia into which they could be enrolled. The town council and the parish priest succeeded in pacifying the mob only by abandoning the plan to establish a militia regiment.[1] Nor were the rioters imprisoned or punished.

A far more serious disturbance occurred the next year following the announcement of the expulsion of the Jesuits from Mexico. In July 1767 'a great number of workers from the mines and refining mills together with many vagabonds from the town and its district rioted, throwing stones at the treasury, the tobacco and gunpowder monopoly and at many other houses'. For over three days the mob remained in control of the streets forcing respectable citizens to barricade themselves within their houses.[2] Both rich and poor, however, united to deplore the expulsion. The Jesuits had only arrived in Guanajuato a generation before. The wealthy classes had made generous donations to construct a college and a church. Mine workers had laboured free of charge to finish the building. The magnificent new Jesuit Church was only completed and publicly dedicated in November 1765, barely eighteen months before the fruits of the town's generosity were destroyed by the exile of the order from America.[3]

To José de Gálvez the uprisings that occurred simultaneously in Guanajuato, San Luis de la Paz and San Luis Potosí gave notice of what he took to be a widespread Jesuit plot. He later wrote to the viceroy, Croix: 'If the expulsion of these black enemies had been delayed for a few months more, America would have been lost.'[4] Backed by the Spanish regiments recently despatched to Mexico, Gálvez suppressed the revolt with unprecedented severity. In Guanajuato alone he imprisoned 600 men for examination, and out of these he hung nine, sent 31 for life imprisonment in the frontier garrisons, and sentenced another 148 for terms of confinement ranging from six to ten years.[5] To prevent any further outbreaks he forbade any miner to carry firearms; prohibited Indians from wearing Spanish costumes, and made the mine-owners responsible for the maintenance of order among the workers—who 'are made immediately subject to the managers and foremen who have the power to restrain and punish them privately . . . when the faults are not sufficiently grave to require a magistrate and trial'.[6] Gálvez also abolished

1 AHG, Insurgencia 1767, report of municipal notary, 17 July 1766.

2 AHG, Insurgencia 1767, report of alcalde mayor, 16 July 1767.

3 *Rasgo breve de la grandeza guanajuatense* (Puebla, 1767), p. 12; see also Marmolejo, *Efemérides*, II, 108, 161, 170, 217.

4 AGI, Mexico 1365, Gálvez to Croix, 24 September 1767.

5 Priestley, *José de Gálvez*, pp. 223–5.

6 AGI, Mexico 1365, Croix to Crown, 26 November 1767.

the exemption from the payment of tributes hitherto enjoyed by the town's Indian and mulatto mine workers.

By these measures Gálvez wished not merely to punish a single revolt but rather to terminate 'the perpetual disturbances and scandalous unruliness which the populace had maintained for so many years'. He wrote: 'It is indispensable to establish and perpetuate in this great community the respect and obedience for the commands of the superior Government, which until now it has not known.'[1] The chosen instrument to consolidate this new régime was the militia. Gálvez seized the opportunity to enrol the law abiding citizenry of Guanajuato, San Miguel, León and San Felipe into a newly raised regiment, the Príncipe, composed of 1,700 men. With satisfaction he noted that 'in this city, where before on erroneous grounds the formation of a militia was opposed, they now clamour to have them, owing to the repeated experience that without such a force the respectable citizens live at the mercy of the lower classes and the mining rabble'.[2] Clearly, with the Jesuits gone, new methods of social control had to be employed.

Equally decisive was the creation of a permanent platoon of 46 soldiers to patrol the streets. This para-military police force was later expanded to 75 men led by four sergeants. The town council which paid the men two-and-a-half to three reales a day relied upon them 'to control the insults of a populace as numerous as it is vicious and insolent'.[3] Apparently these measures proved successful: no record survives of any further public disturbances in Guanajuato until 1810, when the masses took their final revenge.

To equip the regiment and to maintain the permanent picquet Guanajuato required additional revenue. Gálvez therefore levied a new municipal excise duty upon all maize and flour entering the city. The result was a considerable increase in the costs of foodstuffs. Each load of maize then paid a duty of $2\frac{1}{2}$ rls. and each load of flour 4 rls. By 1770 these charges, when combined with certain other funds, yielded the city an income of over 41,000 ps. a year, more than sufficient to finance the new military establishment.[4] The surplus was to be employed, so Gálvez decreed, on public works, and in particular for the construction of a paved road to the refining village of Marfil.

A later scheme, drawn up by the intendant in 1800, indicated the precise

1 AGI, Mexico 1365, Gálvez to Croix, 24 September 1767.
2 AGI, Mexico 1857, Gálvez to Arriaga, 25 October 1767.
3 AGI, Mexico 1528, Azanza to Saavedra, 27 November 1798.
4 Gálvez, *Informe general*, pp. 339–40.

destination of this much augmented municipal revenue. By then the city's income amounted to 51,418 ps. of which no less than 45,813 ps. derived from duties on maize and flour; auctions of stalls in the market, and of the plaza for the annual bullfights completed the sum.[1] Expenditure is listed in table 24.

Most of this chart is self-explanatory. Expenditure on the militia amounted to some 9,519 ps., the largest individual item listed. Basically the city did two things: it maintained public order by paying a police force and by operating a prison; and secondly, it regulated the sale and supply of grain by the upkeep of a municipal granary.

Table 24 *Estimated expenditure of Ayuntamiento.* (c. *1800*)

Salaries:	*pesos*
Teniente Letrado	1,000
Cabildo notary	500
Copyist	50
2 porters of Cabildo	500
Lawyer, legal advisor for the Cabildo	200
Legal agent for prisoners	200
Lawyer for the poor	300
Doctor of prisons	150
Surgeon of prisons	150
Parish clockman	150
Manager of granary	700
Copyist for granary	208
Managers for lesser granaries	1,000
2 sentry guards for Marfil road	1,248
2 guards for Excise	900
2 guards for dams	400
2 guards of wood deposit and slaughter-house	737
Hangman and crier	100
Various misc. items	710
	9,203
Charges:	
To Franciscans	100
To Belemites for school of First Letters	300
Hospital of San Hipólito in Mexico, for Guanajuato sick	200
Ditto to Hospital of San Lázaro in Mexico	600
Academy of San Carlos	200
	1,400

[1] AGI, Mexico 1463, Marquina to Caballero, 26 September 1802.

Festivals:	*pesos*	*reales*
Mass of Holy Spirit said before elections	12	5
Good Friday procession	97	5
Corpus Christi procession	250	5
Santiago celebration	100	
San Ignacio Loyola celebration	141	6
Thanksgiving mass for king	63	2
Holy Sacrament celebration	61	—
Guadalupe celebration	100	—
Holy Thursdays in Guadalupe Chapel	50	—
	876	7

Extraordinary Expenses:	*pesos*	*reale*
Sentry-box rent in Marfil	162	
Main granary rent	240	
Lesser granary rents	144	
Dam cleaning costs	1,085	
River cleaning costs	1,690	4
Food for prisoners	1,701	1
Medicine for prisoners	688	6
Curfew	50	
Wages and upkeep of militia	7,779	
Uniforms of militia	1,500	
Porter's uniform	28	
Cabildo seats	89	6
Mayordomo of revenues at 1½% commission of all charges	793	6
4% of revenues to Contaduría General de Propios y Arbitrios	2,116	5
Copyist of accounts	129	4
Rogation mass	358	2
Repairs of militia barracks	300	3
Wages of bullion shipment guards	51	
Reception of Intendant	431	1
Residencia Judge's costs	120	
Fund for royal celebrations	88	4
Half Annates of city	23	4
Postal charges for Cabildo, correspondence	71	8
Costs of city's lawsuits	1,413	1
Public works repairs	2,414	3
	23,470	2

	pesos	*reales*
Salaries	9,203	
Charges	1,400	
Festivals	876	7
Extraordinary expenses	23,470	2
Total Exp.	34,950	1
Income	52,918	
Surplus	17,967	7

If Gálvez began the militarisation of colonial society it was left to the Sicilian viceroy, Branciforte, to complete the work. Under Revillagigedo several militia regiments, including the Príncipe, were dissolved on the convincing grounds of their inefficiency. But Branciforte, seeing here a great opportunity for peculation, revived New Spain's volunteer forces upon an even more extensive scale. The colonels of those new regiments paid a high fee for their ranks: they were usually expected to provide about 40,000 ps.—the cost of equipping 300 men. By 1810, as a result of local ambition and viceregal avarice, the Bajío possessed no less than four regiments of cavalry and one battalion of infantry. Querétaro, Celaya and San Miguel each raised a cavalry regiment numbering between 350 and 400 men. The city of Guanajuato maintained an infantry battalion, with 407 men including sergeants, and contributed to a new Príncipe cavalry regiment, which also levied men from León, Silao and Irapuato.[1] The officers of this small brigade were recruited from among the local wealthy; they comprised gachupines and creoles, and merchants, miners and landowners. The Bourbon state trusted somewhat blindly that its lavish distribution of military honours would bind the colonial élite, especially the younger men, to its service.

Reliance upon military loyalty among the upper classes became all the more necessary since greater pressure was being exerted upon the population at large. By the close of the century each town in the Bajío housed directors and accountants of both the excise service and the tobacco monopoly, these officials, of course, being assisted by a numerous group of guards and clerks. In addition, the registration of Indians and mulattoes for tribute purposes was more rigorous than before. Here the decisive decade was the 1770s. In León, for example, Rafael de Monterde y Antillón, commissioned by Gálvez to compile new lists of tributaries, by 1771 collected 19,000 ps. compared to the former 7,000 ps.[2] The gain for Guanajuato, after the creation of the intendancy in 1786, was, however, considerable. Prior to that year, the tributes, the alcabalas and the tobacco revenue of the other districts were despatched directly to Mexico City. But then, following the promulgation of the ordinances, all these monies went to the Guanajuato treasury. Since many tax collectors preferred to settle their account by issue of libranzas made out upon merchants or miners in Guanajuato, then this traffic in bills helped to convert the city into the financial as well as the administrative centre of the province. A comparison of the treasury accounts in 1742 and 1793 will best demon-

[1] AGI, Estado 23, Branciforte to Alcudia, 30 August 1795.

[2] AGI, Mexico 1370, Bucareli to Arriaga, 26 June 1772.

strate the change in the tax system. It should be noted, however, that the payments from the tobacco monopoly varied greatly year by year[1] (see table 25).

Table 25 *Guanajuato Treasury receipts 1742 and 1793.* (In pesos)

1742 Receipts		1793 Receipts	
Amalgamated silver [a]	167,068	Amalgamated silver [b]	515,811
Smelted silver [a]	87,317	Smelted silver [b]	89,226
Amalgamated gold	42,092	Amalgamated gold	1,295
Smelted gold	10,891	Smelted gold	648
Mercury sales	179,617	Castilian mercury	68,481
Mercury transport	3,747	German mercury	208,600
		Mercury transport	15,727
Media Anata	1,336		
Sealed paper	2,016	Tributes	70,786
		Excise duties	190,869
Home brandy	147		
		Tobacco monopoly	94,702
Misc. small items	10	Misc. small items	62,406
	494,241		1,318,551

[a] Tithe, 1% and Seigniorage.
[b] Tithe and 1%.

By 1792 the town of Guanajuato alone possessed about 50 revenue officers. Of these the treasury employed 17, with an accountant, a treasurer, 3 assistant clerks, 2 copyists, a porter and another 8 men subject to the chief assayer. Apart from the 2 senior officials only 3 were peninsulars. An identical pattern was manifest in the excise service, where the director, the accountant, 4 guards and a copyist were European Spaniards against 9 creole guards. Then again in the tobacco monopoly, the director, the receiver, a guard and 2 tercianistas were peninsulars whereas all 4 salesmen in the surrounding mining villages and 1 guard were American-born. Finally we may note that the 3 tribute collectors were creoles.[2]

The establishment of the intendancy made Guanajuato the political capital of a province which comprised the five former alcaldías mayores of San Miguel, Celaya and Salvatierra, San Luis de la Paz, Guanajuato and

[1] AGI, Mexico 2122, Guanajuato treasury accounts, 1742. AGI, Mexico 2125, the Guanajuato treasury accounts, 1793.
[2] Calculated from AGN, Padrones, 30–3.

León. Querétaro was included in the intendancy of Mexico, but by 1793 the viceroy appointed a *corregidor de letras* to govern the city, the only post of this sort in New Spain. Hitherto Guanajuato had been ruled by military men, captains on half-pay who came expecting to make their fortunes only to find that the town offered its magistrates few chances of profit. With such an active merchant body the alcalde mayor could not engage in *repartimientos de comercio*. The fruits of justice were largely absorbed by the municipal magistrates, and after 1768 the mining deputation collected tributes. So derisory indeed had the normal channels of revenue become that in 1770 the town council allocated a thousand pesos a year from municipal funds to maintain its president. When in 1782 Captain Manuel de Sello y Somoza, the scion of a distinguished Malagueño family, was named alcalde mayor, he found that the charges of office amounted to 200 ps. and that he only received 600 ps. from the town council, since a former magistrate's widow had been assigned the remaining 400 ps.[1]

Table 26 *Subdelegates' incomes in 1792 for Guanajuato Intendancy.* (In pesos)

	5% of Tributes	Fruits of Justice and Commissions of Office
Celaya with Salvatierra, Salamanca, Valle de Santiago	2,267	500
San Miguel and San Felipe	478	100
Dolores	205	700
León	688	45
Piedragorda	508	—
Pénjamo	420	—
San Luis de la Paz	452	250

The subdelegates who replaced the alcaldes mayores in all but Guanajuato itself did not differ greatly from their predecessors. For the most part they continued to form a mixture of peninsular military men on reserve and a few wealthy creoles. On the other hand, the creation of three new subdelegations reduced the value of the León and San Miguel districts so that only Celaya offered much chance of profit. In 1792 the intendant submitted a list of subdelegates' earnings[2] (see table 26).

Little information can be gleaned about the subdelegates apart from the encumbents in Celaya. There, between 1791–6 and 1802–7, the town was governed by Captain José Belloquín, a native of La Rioja, who first came

[1] AGI, Mexico 1859, ayuntamiento to viceroy, 17 November 1770; AGI, Mexico 1871, Sello y Somoza to Gálvez, 22 September 1782.

[2] AGI, Mexico 1579, Riaño to viceroy, 6 August 1792.

to New Spain to train the cavalry militia of Querétaro.[1] After his second term at Celaya he obtained the subdelegation of San Miguel el Grande where he remained until 1810. In the period 1796–1802 Celaya was ruled by Antonio Pedro de Septién Montero y Austri, *alférez real* of Querétaro, a wealthy creole who belonged to a distinguished local family.[2] His son, Manuel de Septién y Primo, after acting as his father's general lieutenant, was nominated to be subdelegate of San Luis de la Paz.[3]

For Guanajuato itself the 1786 reform made a great difference. The town as a provincial capital housed an intendant, a semi-permanent governor with wide powers, prestige, and an income of 6,000 ps. He was assisted by a legal lieutenant, a trained lawyer, the greater part of whose 1,500 ps. salary was paid out of municipal funds. Both intendants, Andrés Amat y Tortosa (1786–90) and Juan Antonio de Riaño (1792–1810) were peninsular Spaniards recruited from the armed forces. Amat, a lieutenant-colonel in the artillery, had served in the Canary Islands, where he had attempted to publish 'a miscellaneous weekly, an elementary encyclopedia'. In Guanajuato he accomplished little, and in 1790 went mad and tried to shoot himself.[4] His legal lieutenant, José Soriano, a peninsular lawyer already sixty-three years old when he took office, was lazy and soon acquired a reputation for venality. Riaño, decidedly unimpressed with the man, completed his record sheet as follows: 'Aptitude-scarce; talent-doubtful; conduct-average; application-none.'[5]

Soriano, however, was not typical of the other senior officials whom Riaño encountered upon his arrival in Guanajuato. The accountant at the treasury, for example, Ramón Gutiérrez del Mazo, had been commissioned in 1787 to introduce the double-entry system of bookkeeping into New Spain. He had acted as interim accountant in Mexico City where he was highly praised by Viceroy Revillagigedo.[6] Evidently a man of ability, he was later chosen by Viceroy Iturrigaray to direct the capital's cigar factory. His reward finally came in 1810 when he was appointed intendant of Mexico. Gutiérrez del Mazo later managed other revenue departments and clung to office until at least 1824, well after Independence.[7]

[1] AGI, Mexico 1975, Belloquín to Crown, 21 April 1809.

[2] AGI, Mexico 1790, Marquina to Caballero, 26 June 1802.

[3] AHGP, Cabildo, 25 February 1803.

[4] AGI, Mexico 1883, Amat's widow to Crown, 8 April 1791; *Jovellanos en la real academia de la historia* (Madrid, 1911), pp. 206–8; AGI, Mexico 1973, Revillagigedo to Valdés, 3 July 1790.

[5] AGI, Mexico 1793, Revillagigedo to Lerena, 27 May 1791; AGI, Mexico 1555, Revillagigedo to Gardoqui, 30 October 1793.

[6] AGI, Mexico 1532, Revillagigedo to Lerena, 29 October 1790.

[7] AGI, Mexico 1975, installed as intendant, 26 May 1810.

His colleague, the treasurer Norberto de Corres, was less distinguished. Before coming to Guanajuato he had served in the postal service in Havana and in the treasuries at Veracruz and Alamos. Corres, a native of Burgos, probably obtained promotion through the efforts of his influential brother, Francisco Javier de Corres, who was the accountant of the Gálvez Visitation.[1] He remained in Guanajuato from 1780 until his death in 1797.

The other senior officials had similar careers. José Pérez Becerra, the excise director, worked in the Acapulco treasury, the viceregal secretariat, and as excise director in Querétaro before coming to Guanajuato in 1782 where he stayed until his death in 1802. Apparently a man of both culture and enterprise, he possessed a library of 450 titles worth 3,700 ps. and a refining mill.[2] His long tenure in office was only surpassed by Francisco de Bustamante, the director of the tobacco monopoly, who arrived in Guanajuato in 1766 and remained there until 1805 when he was finally suspended after certain errors were discovered in his accounts. The subsequent inquiry revealed that although his fixed stipend only amounted to 1,600 ps., less than the 2,500 paid to Pérez Becerra, various commissions augmented his receipts to over 6,000 ps.[3]

The careers of these men, if considered together, disclose the salient features of the Bourbon fiscal bureaucracy. Strict departmental lines were not observed; men transferred quite easily from the customs and excise to the treasuries, from the viceregal secretariat to the tobacco monopoly. Once appointed to Guanajuato, however, most officials did not move on. Their terms of office in the town were remarkably long, ranging from Bustamante's 38 years to the 17 years of Corres. If we accept these periods of tenure as representative of the colonial bureaucracy at large, then clearly the new Bourbon state inaugurated since the Gálvez Visitation was peculiarly stable in its personnel: it barely spanned two official lives.

Whereas all of Guanajuato's senior officials were peninsulars, men with wide experience, who had influential friends and relatives in Madrid or Mexico City, the majority of their assistants were American Spaniards, for the most part recruited in Guanajuato itself. The treasury best illustrates this contrast. Between 1787 and 1810 the senior official was Francisco Marino, a native of the town, who had first entered the treasury in 1771. For three years he worked as an unpaid supernumerary before he was

1 AGI, Mexico 1554, Revillagigedo to Gardoqui, 1 March 1793; AGI, Mexico 1377, Bucareli to Gálvez, 27 May 1777.

2 AGI, Mexico 1396, Mayorga to Gálvez, 6 March 1782; for his library see Henry Bernstein, 'A Provincial Library in Colonial Mexico', *Hispanic American Historical Review*, 26 (1946), pp. 162–83.

3 AGI, Mexico 1140, Council of the Indies, *consulta*, 6 February 1807.

named as second official, at which level he lingered for 13 years. His salary as senior official amounted to 800 ps. a year as compared to the 3,300 ps. earned by Gutiérrez del Mazo.[1] The contrast of background was even more striking in the case of José María Robles, who in 1787 succeeded Marino as second official. For his grandfather, a native of Peru, had been alcalde del crimen in the Mexican audiencia, and his father had served as senior official in the Guanajuato treasury. Robles worked for six years as an unpaid supernumerary before obtaining a post which carried an annual salary of 500 ps.[2] Neither of these men secured further promotions before 1810. Creoles could attain to high positions in the Bourbon bureaucracy, but much depended upon the right backing in Madrid or Mexico City.

The most talented and the best connected official in Guanajuato was undoubtedly the intendant Juan Antonio de Riaño. Later historians of all shades of opinion united to praise his administration. Carlos María de Bustamante and José María Luis Mora both eulogised him as belonging to the school of Floridablanca, Jovellanos and Gálvez, as a very model of enlightened government.[3] Lucas Alamán, who knew him well, painted an attractive picture of a cultured man, anxious to promote the public good. His home and family acted as the centre of French language and ideas in Guanajuato.[4] At his table could be found such visitors as Manuel Abad y Quiepo, the bishop-elect of Michoacán, and the energetic parish priest of Dolores, Miguel Hidalgo y Costilla.

As a mere naval lieutenant serving in Louisiana, Riaño assured his future when he won the hand of Victoria de Saint-Maxent, the daughter of a wealthy French creole. Her sister Felícitas married Bernardo de Gálvez, the nephew of the Minister of the Indies and later himself Viceroy of Mexico. When Riaño became intendant of Valladolid, relations by marriage included the intendants of Puebla and Oaxaca, the superintendent of the mint and the *fiscal de real hacienda.* Not that Riaño relied entirely upon his family connexions. He obtained his transfer from Valladolid to Guanajuato through the recommendation of Viceroy Revillagigedo who described him as 'very well informed as to his obligations which he discharges with knowledge, discretion and execution'.[5] Viceroy Azanza—

[1] AGI, Mexico 1544, Revillagigedo to Lerena, 26 September 1791.

[2] AGI, Mexico 1554, Revillagigedo to Gardoqui, 1 March 1793; AHGP, Presos, 4 March 1787.

[3] Carlos María de Bustamante, *Cuadro histórico de la revolución mexicana* (3 vols.; Mexico, 1961), I, 41. Mora, *Méjico y sus revoluciones*, III, 45–6.

[4] Alamán, *Historia*, I, 55–6, 274.

[5] AGI, Mexico 1973, Revillagigedo to Valdés, 3 July 1790.

another *afrancesado*—wished to appoint him intendant of Mexico.[1] Clearly Riaño belonged to that central group of enlightened public servants who at this time did so much to transform New Spain.

Soon after his arrival in Guanajuato in 1792, Riaño gave proof of his quality as an administrator when he abolished all the restrictions and regulations imposed upon workers by the artisan guilds. He declared that henceforth anyone could enter whatever occupation he wanted and could buy and sell his wares in the public market without hindrance.[2] At the same time, however, he insisted upon a higher degree of social discipline. Each street was named, each house numbered, and the town divided into eleven wards presided over by *alcaldes de barrio*, ward magistrates, responsible for the maintenance of public order. By November 1792, Riaño assessed the effects of these measures:

> The numerous masses which until the present were restive and insubordinate are now docile and obedient. If my predecessor did not believe himself safe without armed guards, I walk through the most obscure places without other defence than my cane of office and hat. It especially pleases me to see the liking with which they greet me, and the docility with which they suffer my corrections: corrections more repeated than before and more severe, since, subject to a supervision which they never knew, it is difficult for them to escape punishment.[3]

In contrast to this policy of more government for the masses, Riaño chose not to interfere with the power of the local oligarchy. He once declared: 'Experience, preferable to all theory, has proved to me the effective advantages enjoyed by communities which in the first instance are governed by local citizens of adequate means and good standing.'[4] He discouraged all appeals from the decisions of the municipal magistrates and supported the mine-owners' right to punish their workers for minor offences. Riaño deferred to the town council's advice in the choice of lieutenants of justice for the mining villages. His attitude to the annual elections of municipal magistrates was described in the following terms: 'In these matters the intendant does not count; he blows neither hot nor cold; nor does he know who is elected until the pie is baked.'[5] Riaño, however, possessed an important advantage when dealing with the local élite. He was a Montañés, a native of Liergnes in the Vallecarriedo, precisely the same province in Spain from which many of Guanajuato's

[1] AGI, Mexico 1581, Azanza to Soler, 2 June 1799.
[2] AGI, Mexico 1660, Riaño to Crown, 24 December 1792.
[3] AGN, Minería 23/2, Riaño to Revillagigedo, 3 May 1792.
[4] AGN, Intendencias 8, Riaño to viceroy, 4 April 1800.
[5] FV, 5, José Joaquín Peláez to Diego Rul, 13 December 1805.

most influential gachupines had emigrated.[1] His daughter married a son of the rich Montañés merchant and miner, Francisco de Septién y Arce.[2] Moreover, the intendant entrusted some 30,000 ps. to another compatriot from Vallecarriedo to invest in a refining mill.[3] Riaño's power and prestige, therefore, in part rested upon his informal leadership of the town's immigrant community.

At the same time the intendant enjoyed the favour of the wealthy creoles. Carlos María de Bustamante later wrote that Riaño 'loved the Americans'. Certainly he did not hesitate to choose Lic. Fernando Pérez Marañón, the *alférez real* and a native of Guanajuato, to act as his legal lieutenant and advisor following the death of the incompetent Soriano.[4] This interim appointment, which Riaño recommended should be made permanent, was not however accepted in Madrid, and the inevitable Peninsula-born lawyer arrived to take office. Nevertheless, the intendant's choice illustrates his close relations with the local élite.

Power to the wealthy, discipline for the masses: such an assessment, true enough in outline, would fail to do justice to Riaño's humanity. Appointed as intendant during a year when thousands died of hunger, he took firm steps to avert future catastrophes. Soon after his arrival in Guanajuato he borrowed 20,000 ps. to establish in the municipal granary a public deposit of maize which, when needed, could be sold in sufficient quantity as 'to subject to a just price the remainder which is brought in by private individuals'.[5] Not content with the existing facilities, Riaño, in conjunction with the town council, obtained the viceroy's permission to build a new granary. Work began in 1797 at an eventual cost of 218,306 ps., the money being raised from the annual surplus of municipal revenue. The *alhóndiga de Granaditas* was constructed in a simple neo-classic style, but its ample proportions and austere exterior gave it the appearance of a fortress, while the colonnaded courtyard resembled a mansion rather than a granary.[6] By the 1790s neo-classicism had become the favoured architectural style of the Mexican élite. The churriguerresque splendours of the past decades were by then the object of derisory comment. Both the style and the purpose of the granary, therefore, symbolised the new spirit of enlightened despotism which Riaño and his generation of peninsular officials and immigrants introduced into New Spain. The *alhóndiga de*

[1] Fermín de Sojo y Lomba, *Lierganes* (Madrid, 1936).
[2] AHGP, Cabildo, 10 June 1809.
[3] AHGP, Cabildo, 13 October 1810; Bustamante, *Cuadro histórico*, I, 41.
[4] AGI, Mexico 1893, Iturrigaray to Caballero, 26 November 1804.
[5] AGI, Mexico 1660, Riaño to Crown, 24 December 1792.
[6] AHG, Alhóndiga, initial proposal to Branciforte, 6 August 1796.

Granaditas was the architectural equivalent and expression of the new Bourbon state. Ironically it was also to serve as the mausoleum for Riaño and the régime he represented.

In the last resort, however, the intendant's public measures, beneficial and sensible as they were, did not much affect or greatly alter the society and the economy over which he presided. His influence was largely confined to the town of Guanajuato. And there, in a sense, he simply gilded the cake. He mediated between quarrelling members of the local oligarchy; he influenced its younger members; he contrived the construction of a handful of public buildings; he propagated the neo-classic style in architecture; he kept the peace and ran an honest government. And yet, if Riaño had been corrupt, quarrelsome, idle and uncultured, would Guanajuato have been so very different? Clearly not. The structure of its society and the prosperity of its silver mines rested not upon the efforts of an intendant but upon the enterprise and the parsimony of the town's miners and merchants. These were the men who made Guanajuato what it was—the creole miners and the immigrant merchants. These are the men who will occupy most of the following pages. But first it is useful to ascertain from the 1792 census some elementary notions about the racial and occupational structure of the town's working population.

CHAPTER 7

A CENSUS

Information about the structure of society in colonial Guanajuato is remarkably hard to come by. True, a handful of travellers sketched their impressions of the miners of the town—their debauchery, their high earnings, the hard conditions under which they laboured. Then again, a series of genealogical and prosopographic exercises yield a fairly convincing picture of the upper élite. A few scattered statistics can also be adjoined. But none of this material, by its nature descriptive, particular and occasional, tells us much about the division of this society into classes and races, the distribution of occupations and the significance, if any, of these predications for the individual. The only source which can help us here is the 1792 military census of the town and district of Guanajuato.[1] This document—which comprises four stout manuscript volumes—lists the name, age, birthplace, residence, occupation and race of all adult males—priests and Indian commoners excepted—together with similar, although not so complete, data for their wives and children.

At the outset, however, it must be emphasised that since there is no means of checking the accuracy of the census, then all our tables and conclusions derive from the exegesis of one, possibly mendacious, source; they do not necessarily depict a historical reality. Nevertheless, we may well ask, why should the residents and officials of Guanajuato conspire to record erroneous information? What purpose would be served by lies about age, birthplace and occupation? Almost none at all: errors in these categories of inquiry, therefore, spring from ignorance, carelessness, or lack of precision. For example, many persons probably could not remember their age; others may have been recorded as merchants rather than as dealers, as miners rather than mine-workers. But it is plausible to assume that most people knew their age by decade if not by year, and that tailors were rarely described as shoemakers or notaries as lawyers. There were limits to the possibilities of error. On the other hand, concerning one class of information there was a good chance of conscious distortion. Individuals in colonial Mexico were highly sensitive about their racial designation. Indians and mulattoes suffered from a stigma of social inferiority and, moreover, had to pay a price for this burden in the form of a special

[1] See AGN, Padrones 30–3. All the tables in this chapter are based on these four volumes.

capitation tax. Clearly then, members of these groups (we refer to town dwellers) strove, where opportunity arose, to promote themselves into the ranks of the mestizos or Spaniards. But this step was difficult to make if one stayed at home, since the parish priests kept three separate baptismal registers for Indians, for mulattoes and for the hispanic community. In certain measure, therefore, social advancement depended upon geographic mobility. Now since in Guanajuato four-fifths of all adults were born within the town and its adjacent villages, then the probability of a successful lie to the census-taker, himself no doubt a native of the district, was quite restricted.

Although ignorance and even distortion can be hence discounted, not much can be done about the omissions. And here all our calculations are in part vitiated by the one glaring deficiency of the census—it does not enumerate any Indians apart from non-tribute-paying chiefs and those women who married out of their racial group. True, some notion about Indian numbers can be gained from the summary of the census, printed in 1793 where they amount to some 11,800 persons or a fifth of the population.[1] But, then, the printed summary in no sense tallies with the manuscript totals. The magnitude of this divergence is best presented as in table 27.

Small hope exists of a reconciliation between the two versions. Differences in the grand totals could be explained by the exclusion of outlying territorial units; and in the case of the town itself by different definitions of its area. But the discrepancies in the figures as to the racial breakdown are inexplicable and irreconcilable. The printed summary claims 24,160 Spaniards whereas the manuscript only enumerates, 15,374; the former lists 922 European Spaniards, the latter 314. Obviously, persons counted as Spaniards in the summary were described as mulattoes or mestizos in the manuscript. In the absence of any mediating evidence, it seems best to rely upon the more ample source and dismiss the summary as tendentious.

II

Let us now move forward to the analysis. After a certain amount of laborious computation, we were able to devise tables 28 and 29 dealing with the distribution of occupations and races and their geographical origin.

Contrary to our usual impressions about mining towns, Guanajuato's population by its own account was geographically immobile. A full 77·7 per cent of adult males were born in the town and the immediate circle of

[1] See AGN, Historia 523, ff. 88, 90.

mining villages and ranchos. Only among the élite, especially among the merchant class, was any marked degree of immigration to be found. The mine-workers, for example, were largely recruited from the town itself;

Table 27 *Population of town and district of Guanajuato, 1792–3.*

Printed summaries [a]	Town	Town and district (incl. town figures)
Spaniards	18,068	24,160
Indians	4,385	11,814
Castes	9,645	19,038
	32,098	55,012
European Spaniards	922	
American Spaniards	17,146	
Castes	2,428	
Mulattoes	7,217	
Indians	4,385	
	32,098	
Manuscript Census Totals [b]		
Spaniards	7,446	15,374
Castizos	1,194	2,308
Mestizos	5,260	11,281
Mulattoes	3,481	10,733
	17,381	39,696
Add Indians (above)	4,385	11,814
	21,766	51,510

[a] Source: AGN, Historia 533, ff. 88, 90.
[b] Source: AGN, Padrones, 30–3.

Table 28 *Geographical provenance of adult male work force, Guanajuato, 1792.*

	Guanajuato	Province	Outside	Total: Number	Total: Percentage
Spaniards	3,176	461	461	4,098	38·4
Mestizos	2,389	282	111	2,782	26·0
Mulattoes	2,469	481	182	3,132	29·3
Caciques	166	39	26	231	2·2
Castizos	98	18	6	122	1·1
Europeans	—	—	314	314	3·0
	8,298	1,281	1,100	10,679	100·0

a mere 21 per cent came from outside. In part, we may attribute this relative immobility to the prolonged cycle of prosperity that preceded the 1792 census; possibly a count taken during the 1770s might have revealed a higher proportion of migrant workers.

The distribution of occupations offers little surprise. The entire mining industry employed 55 per cent of the listed male work force. The remainder ran the gamut of jobs beginning with water carriers, charcoal makers, and muleteers and finishing with the equally familiar crafts of tailors, cobblers, and blacksmiths. A few items call for comment. The number of domestic servants would be much augmented by the inclusion

Table 29 *Distribution of occupations of adult males, Guanajuato, 1792.*

Occupation	Number	Percentage
Mining	5,057	47·3
Refining	792	7·6
Commerce	681	6·4
Clothing	590	5·5
Food and drink	364	3·4
Servants	511	4·8
Transport	283	2·6
Agriculture	686	6·4
Metal and wood workers, construction, pottery	596	5·6
Fuel, candles, soap, lime, etc.	271	2·5
Professions, copyists	117	1·0
State and Municipality	118	1·1
Fine Arts, entertainment	96	0·9
Miscellaneous	517	4·9
	10,679	100·0

of females. The agriculturists, some market gardeners apart, were farmers and labourers who lived on farms and estates included within the municipal jurisdiction; their number has no particular meaning. The section *clothing* is largely composed of tailors, hatters and cobblers; Guanajuato possessed but a handful of weavers and spinners. In broad perspective the population can be divided into three groups: the workers engaged in the mining industry, the élite those workers supported, and the artisans and labourers who served the needs of the two preceding groups.

The chief point of interest and indeed problem of interpretation presented by the census surely lies in the significance we are to attach to the racial categories into which it divides the population and the relation of these designations to the town's occupational and social hierarchy. Did race dictate choice of jobs or jibe with class? Here the picture is blurred both by the absence of the Indians and by the extraordinary propinquity and number of American Spaniards, who spanned the entire scale of jobs from lawyer and priest to mine-workers and muleteers. Granted these difficulties it is convenient to tread the firmest ground first and to begin at the top of society, and then work downwards.

III

A detailed examination of Guanajuato's 314 resident peninsular Spaniards, as given in table 30, offers a twofold advantage. First we can use these men

Table 30 *Provincial origin and occupations of Guanajuato's peninsular Spaniards, 1792.*

Provinces of origin		Occupations		
		Trade		
Santander	92	Merchants	77	
Basque Provinces and		Apprentices	72	
Navarre	43	Agents	1	
Andalusia	30	Dealers	14	
Castile	26	Taverners	7	
Galicia	20		—	
Asturias	11		171	(54·4%)
Canaries	6	*Mining*		
Extremadura	4	Miners	37	
La Rioja	2	Managers	6	
Murcia	1	Foremen, workers	11	
Granada	1		—	
Catalonia	1		54	(17·5%)
Orán	1	*Refining*		
European Spaniards	36	Refiners	16	
Kingdoms of Castile	27	Managers	8	
Foreigners	13	Petty refiners	4	
	—	Azogueros	8	
	314		—	
			36	(11·5%)
		Crown municipal service		
		Officials, assistants,	11	
		guards	17	
			—	
			28	(8·9%)
		Miscellaneous		
		Craftsmen	8	
		Farmers	3	
		Priests	3	
		Misc.	11	
			—	
			25	(8·0%)
			—	
		Total	314	(100%)

as a yardstick by which to measure élite status. Secondly, we can test certain more general hypotheses already adduced about the nature of the immigrant community. The most striking feature of this group's provincial recruitment was the predominance of Montañeses. Men from the coast and mountains of Santander comprised at least a third of all immigrants resident in Guanajuato. Unfortunately, our percentages cannot be fully accurate because the 62 persons who described themselves as European Spaniards or who gave their birthplace as the kingdoms of

Table 31 *Occupations, ages, and marital status of Guanajuato peninsular Spaniards, 1792.*

	Age groups														
	11–20		21–30		31–40		41–50		51–60		61–70		Totals		
Occupations	B	M	B	M	B	M	B	M	B	M	B	M	B	M	Total
Merchants	4		15	4	20	10	5	8	3	4	1	3	48	29	77
Apprentices	19		42		5	1	4	1					70	2	72
Dealers			1		3	3	1	2	1	1	1	1	7	8	15
Taverners			3	1	1		1	1		1			5	2	7
Miners [a]			6	4	10	7	11	6	4	4	1	1	32	22	54
Refiners	1		6	1	6	4	1	5		3		1	14	14	28
Azogueros	2		5					1					7	1	8
Government	1		3	3	2	5	3	6	2	2		1	11	17	28
Misc.					4	3	2	3	4	5		1	10	12	22
Priests															3
Totals	27		81	13	51	33	28	33	14	20	3	8	204	107	314

KEY: B = Bachelors; M = Married.

[a] Miners include workers and foremen; refiners include managers; the one agent has been added to dealers. The 19 widowers are listed with the married.

Castile cannot be placed. All Spain, apart from the kingdoms of Aragon (including Cataluña and Valencia) and Navarre, technically belonged to the kingdoms of Castile. If we omit these men and the foreigners, then of the remainder whose provincial birthplace is known, Montañeses amounted to 38 per cent and men of the northern seaboard to 69 per cent.

The immigrants' choice of employment followed traditional lines (see table 31). By far the great majority engaged in trade. But as was to be expected in a town like Guanajuato a large percentage entered the mining industry. By contrast, the bureaucracy, including both guards and clerks in that term, supported less than 10 per cent of all peninsular Spaniards. This, then, was a working community. But not everyone by any means secured desirable jobs. The group of dealers (*tratantes*) can best be defined as commercial odd-jobs men; they had to compete with large numbers of creoles, mestizos and mulattoes, also busy in petty trading transactions. Similarly, the five mine-workers registered with the foremen had clearly failed to attain financial success. The craftsmen—two tailors, a baker and a hairdresser—were mostly foreign. Among those persons listed as miscellaneous we may note the presence of an 'author of comedies', as well as a blind man, a cripple and a retired soldier. No significant correlations existed between provincial origin and choice of occupation. For example, about a third of the peninsular merchants were Montañeses. And these proportions were observed throughout. A partial exception to this rule was constituted by the presence of only one Basque in royal service compared to ten Montañeses. Then again, the group described as European Spaniards was largely composed of young *cajeros* (apprentice merchants). But for the remainder noticeable deviations from the normal distribution of employment cannot be found.

At different ages men entered different jobs. About half of Guanajuato's peninsular Spaniards under thirty described themselves as cajeros—apprentice or journeymen merchants. The managers of the refining mills and the *azogueros* who directed the amalgamation process were equally young. Most men, however, terminated their period of apprenticeship by the time they were thirty. They then became merchants or acted as dealers. After this age more owners than managers of refining mills were listed. Now whereas in their twenties and, to a lesser extent, in their thirties, most immigrants engaged in trade, after forty as many miners as merchants were to be found among them. It is difficult to assess the significance of this progression. Possibly it indicates a career pattern in which young men began as cajeros, graduated as merchants, and then, if successful, diversified their investments and entered mining. Alternatively, the predominance of the younger age group as registered in absolute numbers may reflect a relatively recent influx of young immigrants, most of whom entered trade. After all, this was 1792, only fourteen years after the declaration of *comercio libre* had expanded commercial opportunity. Such hypotheses, however, must remain speculative. For a census is a sort of an inventory taken at a particular moment in time, not a balance sheet of loss and gain. Some immigrants returned to Spain; others arrived quite late in life; we do not know the average age of entry into New Spain, still less the usual period of residence.

With youth went celibacy. By definition a cajero was a bachelor, but then, more importantly, most merchants also preferred not to marry until they were forty and many never married at all. The same rule held for men in other occupations. Very few immigrants married under thirty and most waited until they were at least forty. Clearly the peninsular Spaniards gave few hostages to fortune. By choice or necessity, their business careers were built upon celibacy as much as parsimony. In terms of numerical predominance the typical gachupín of Guanajuato was a young bachelor from the north of Spain who sat behind a shop counter.

IV

How different were the peninsular Spaniards from their American cousins? Only a comparison between the two groups can indicate what was peculiar to the immigrants' behaviour and what was common to both sections of the Spanish nation. But here the terrain becomes decidedly treacherous. To compare 314 persons of approximate élite status with the 38 per cent of the town's population described as Spaniards would be manifestly inappropriate. But how are we to separate creoles from the mestizo masses? In this context the only plausible way to define an upper-class Spaniard is by his choice of profession. But how can we determine

Table 32 *Occupational structure of commerce and mining, Guanajuato, 1792.*

Occupation	Peninsular Spaniards	American Spaniards	Castizos	Mestizos	Caciques	Mulattoes	Total
Commerce							
Merchants	77	75	—	6	—	4	162
Apprentices	72	71	—	4	2	—	149
Dealers	14	215	5	58	10	39	341
Agents	1	15	—	—	—	—	16
Taverners	7	5	—	1	—	—	13
	171	381	5	69	12	43	681
Refining							
Refiners	16	24	—	2	—	—	42
Managers	8	18	—	—	—	—	26
Azogueros	8	58	1	5	—	2	74
Petty refiners	4	85	1	86	4	79	259
Workers	—	143	8	138	6	101	396
	36	328	10	231	10	182	797
Mining							
Miners	37	201	—	66	2	23	329
Managers (Foremen)	12	57	—	—	—	—	69
Workers	5	1,323	46	1,332	72	1,881	4,659
Total	54	1,581	46	1,398	74	1,904	5,057

the social prestige of Guanajuato's manifold occupations? Now admittedly here the argument appears to be moving in a circle, since the best measure of status was racial. Nevertheless, the middle element in the spectrum, the American Spaniards, can be differentiated by its association with the two mutually exclusive poles, the European Spaniards and the mulattoes. Those creoles who entered the same occupation as the peninsulars probably belonged to a social stratum superior to those who worked alongside

Table 33 *Occupations of creole élite, Guanajuato, 1792.*

Occupation	Number	Percentage of total
Merchants	75	
Apprentices	71	
Agents	15	
Taverners	5	
	166	21·2
Miners	201	
Managers	24	
Foremen	33	
	258	33·0
Refiners	24	
Managers	18	
Azogueros	58	
	100	12·7
Crown officials	4	
Crown guards, assistants	33	
Municipal officials, guards, assistants	21	
	58	7·4
Notaries	6	
Lawyers	11	
Doctors	12	
Priests	52	
	81	10·4
Silversmiths	86	10·9
Copyists	35	4·4
Total	784	100·0

mulattoes. Conversely, those jobs that offered employment to a considerable number of mulattoes must be regarded as socially inferior to those from which they were excluded. If such assertions sound presumptuous let us quickly adduce some proofs (see table 32).

Here at once it can be observed that the census was fairly reliable in its definitions. The term *comerciante* for merchant and *cajero* for apprentice or journeyman merchant was used sparingly and with a certain degree of precision. The ambiguous position of the *tratantes*, with a clear predominance of American Spaniards, qualified by a heavy inclusion of mestizos and mulattoes, is also disclosed. In the refining industry the same pattern emerges; an *hacendado de plata*, a refiner, was easily distinguished from a *rescatador*, a petty refiner. The *azogueros* were obviously a cut above the *rescatadores*. Unfortunately, in the mining industry the picture is blurred by a certain imprecision in the use of the word *minero*, miner, contrasted to *operario de minas*, mine-worker. It could refer to an owner, a skilled technician or to some independent impoverished prospector.

With the efficacy of our divining rod thus proven, let us now compare European Spaniards and American Spaniards. Table 33 lists the chief creole occupations. Dealers and petty refiners have been excluded for reasons mentioned above, the silversmiths (with a membership 87·7 per cent Spanish) and the more obvious professions such as lawyers and doctors have been added.

The total number is somewhat bloated by the inclusion of so many *mineros*. Nevertheless, some broad conclusions immediately emerge. At most, Guanajuato's upper social stratum comprised a thousand male adults, that is to say, about a tenth of the population, of which number a good quarter were immigrants. Also striking is the lack of professional employment. The town had one priest for every thousand persons, and a lawyer and a physician for every four thousand. The Crown and the municipality offered opportunities equal in extent to all the professions combined. One surprising feature is the large number of creole merchants and their assistants, a phenomenon which other types of evidence do not usually indicate. However, if we inspect more closely what appear to be two very similar groups, the salient differences come to light, as table 34 reveals.

To take the commercial category first, we may note that creole cajeros pursued the same celibate career as their peninsular co-evals, but preferred either to start or to finish their period of apprenticeship at a somewhat younger age. On the other hand, oddly enough, creole merchants tended to be older than their peninsular rivals. Thus whereas in the age group

31–40 there were 16 creole merchants as compared to 30 peninsulars, in the succeeding decade the equivalent ratio was 24 to 13. Equally significant is the fact that the creoles married much earlier. Already in their twenties two-thirds of the American-born merchants had found wives, whereas only a third of the European Spaniards aged 31–40 were married. Here

Table 34 *Occupations, ages, and marital status of Guanajuato creoles, 1792.*[a]

	Age groups												Totals		
	11–20		21–30		31–40		41–50		51–60		61–70				
Occupations	B	M	B	M	B	M	B	M	B	M	B	M	B	M	Total
Merchants	6	—	4	9	3	13	7	17	—	8	—	8	20	55	75
Apprentices	38	—	21	1	6	2	1	1	1	—	—	—	67	4	71
Agents	—	—	—	2	2	1	1	5	—	4	—	—	3	12	15
Taverners	—	—	—	2	—	1	—	—	—	2	—	—	—	5	5
Miners	28	3	26	43	11	55	7	45	2	24	—	14	74	184	258
Refiners	1	1	6	4	1	13	2	8	1	2	1	2	12	30	42
Azogueros	12	—	12	12	2	7	1	8	—	3	1	—	28	30	58
Government	2	1	7	11	3	12	2	13	—	6	—	1	14	44	58
Professional	1	—	1	4	2	5	2	10	1	3	—	—	7	22	29
Silversmiths	19	1	14	14	5	17	3	8	—	4	—	1	41	44	85
Copyists	3	1	5	6	3	10	1	3	—	3	—	—	12	23	35
Priests															52
	110	7	96	108	38	136	27	118	5	59	2	26	278	453	783

KEY: B = Bachelors; M = Married.

[a] Petty refiners (rescatadores) excluded; widowers (54) included with the married.

then we encounter two very different patterns of behaviour for men of the same profession and nation. In effect, in any competition for commercial success, the gachupín enjoyed the marked advantage of being, on average, younger and a bachelor. Nor was this pattern restricted to the trading community since in refining about half the creoles married during their twenties as compared to one out of twenty peninsulars. All eleven of the American-born mill owners had found wives whereas five out of the eight peninsular mill-owners remained single. And so on. Enough has been said first to show immigrant idiosyncracy, since after all the creoles followed fairly normal lines of behaviour.

V

The remaining nine-tenths of the population can be divided into two great sections—the industrial workers engaged in mining and refining and the variegated host of artisans, servants, dealers and muleteers. Following our previous method let us now examine the correlations, if any, between race and occupation. In the scheme of table 35 are listed all designated professions in which more than a hundred persons were employed. For the sake of clarity the handful of castizos (the mixture of Spaniard and mestizo) are included with the mestizos.

Table 35 *Racial membership of adult male workers in selected occupations, Guanajuato, 1792.*

Occupation	Spaniards		Mestizos		Caciques		Mulattoes		Total
	No.	%	No.	%	No.	%	No.	%	No.
Carpenters	85	62·5	40	29·4	—	—	11	8·1	136
Bacon-curers	69	58·9	35	29·9	—	—	13	11·2	117
Dealers	229	67·2	63	18·5	10	2·9	39	11·4	341
Tailors	138	48·2	104	36·2	9	3·4	35	12·2	286
Blacksmiths	81	48·1	60	36·8	1	0·6	24	14·5	166
Farmers	320	54·1	125	21·3	7	1·1	139	23·5	591
Masons	23	20·2	47	41·3	12	10·6	32	27·9	114
Servants	185	36·3	177	34·7	5	0·9	143	28·1	510
Millworkers	143	36·2	146	36·8	6	1·5	101	25·5	396
Petty refiners	89	34·4	87	33·5	4	1·6	79	30·5	259
Bakers	34	33·0	25	24·3	12	11·6	32	31·1	103
Charcoal-makers	39	36·9	29	27·2	—	—	38	35·9	106
Cobblers	24	11·8	90	44·5	15	7·5	73	36·2	202
Mine-workers	1,328	28·5	1,378	29·6	72	1·6	1,881	40·3	4,659
Muleteers	71	30·8	47	20·5	5	2·3	108	46·4	231
Total male work force (less upper stratum)	3,324	34·7	2,904	30·3	231	2·4	3,132	32·6	9,589

To rank these occupations we have used the percentage inclusion of mulattoes as the defining mark of status. On the whole, it tallies with the corresponding proportional absence or presence of Spaniards, with the mestizos, as always, forming an ambiguous middle layer with no particular characteristics of their own. In effect, a handful of crafts—tailors, blacksmiths, carpenters, along with the dealers—can be separated from the masses to constitute a social stratum best defined as upper-working-class. Do we have here a poor white element, the victims of a downwardly mobile society? For the rest (cobblers apart), the deviations from the usual proportions, although at times pronounced, do not emerge with any great clarity. Nor, with such small numbers, as was the case of the bakers and masons, should too much be made of the precise percentage. An addition of ten more men in any one group would largely change the picture. Granted this difficulty, it seems best to concentrate upon the mine-workers. Here, alas, despite the great variation in wages, no distinction was observed between the pick and blast men and the whim-minders or peons. As it is, a noticeable divergence becomes manifest if we calculate the percentage of all members of each racial group (still subtracting the Spanish upper stratum) engaged in mining. It yields the following result:

Percentage of racial groups engaged in mining

Mulattoes	60
Mestizos	47·4
Caciques	31·6
Spaniards (less upper stratum)	39·6
Population (less upper stratum)	48·6

At first sight, therefore, it appears that within the ranks of the populace race, to some degree, did dictate choice of occupation. The mulattoes followed distinct lines of behaviour from the rest. However, if we subtract from the Spanish total those professions in which the proportion of mulattoes was very low, i.e. carpenters, bacon-curers, tailors, dealers and blacksmiths, and assume that they form an intermediary layer in society, then the divergences become less marked. Of the remaining, truly proletarian, Spaniards some 48·9 per cent were mine-workers. Mulatto 'difference' is thus reduced to about 10 per cent deviation from the normal pattern of employment.

Our inquiry is now honed down to one simple question: What significance, if any, did race possess for men who worked side by side in the mines and who lived in much the same streets? Can we conclude that among that 85 per cent of Guanajuato's population which did not enter the skilled crafts, commerce and management, ethnic designations were little more than arbitrary labels, meaningless survivals from the past, perpetuated only by fiscal obligations and parochial registration? One last test of group homogeneity remains: marriage. Did these mine-workers choose their mates haphazardly from different races? Table 36 contains the answer.

A rapid glance might suggest that the overall intermarriage rate of 29·5 per cent was sufficiently high to prevent the formation of stable ethnic groups. If the rate was continuous for a century, then in four generations there would be no significant difference between the several racial categories, two of whom, anyway, the mestizos and mulattoes, were defined in terms of their genetic mixture. Such a conclusion, however, would not be warranted. A closer inspection of the chart reveals that intermarriage, when it occurred, followed the lines of social esteem. In general, Spaniards married mestizos, mulattoes married Indians, and mestizos married Spaniards and Indians. Spaniards rarely chose mulatto women, whereas mulatto men more frequently secured Spanish and mestizo women. For both Spaniards and mestizos marriage with an Indian was preferable to an alliance with a mulatto woman. Moreover, if we assume that proletarian Spaniards and mestizos in effect formed a single community, then their intermarriage rate with Indians and mulattoes drops to just over 10

Table 36 *Mine-workers: intermarriage rate.*

Male	Female: Spaniard	Castizo	Mestizo	Cacique	Indian	Mulatto	Un-married	Total	Inter-marriage
Spaniard:									
number	566	6	150	7	33	13	548	1,323	199
percentage	73·0	0·8	19·4	0·9	4·3	1·6			27·0
Castizo: a									
number	5	2	14	1	1	1	22	46	8
percentage	20·8	8·3	58·3	4·2	4·2	4·2			33·4
Mestizo:									
number	127	4	491	7	76	26	601	1,332	236
percentage	17·4	0·5	67·2	0·9	10·4	3·6			32·9
Cacique: b									
number	12		20	13	9		18	72	32
percentage	22·2		37·0	24·1	16·7				59·4
Mulatto:									
number	71	6	79	3	198	875	649	1,881	357
percentage	5·8	0·5	6·4	0·3	16·0	71·0			28·9
Total							1,838	4,654	832 29·5

a Marriage with mestizos is not counted as intermarriage.
b Marriage with Indians is not counted as intermarriage.

per cent. After two centuries of inter-breeding the mulattoes and the Indians formed separate, inferior groups, with whom the hispanic-mestizo group chose not to marry despite their social proximity. The only exception to the rule lies in the Indian *caciques*, but these men, to judge from their intermarriage rate, were simply mestizos who for some reason clung to an Indian, noble status.

Our evidence for Guanajuato, therefore, suggests that racial distinctions, although not by themselves indicative of class, in part did define the individual's status in the esteem of his fellows and, more importantly, in the eyes of his womenfolk. Seven-tenths of all men married women drawn from their own ethnic group. Racial consciousness still remained strong, and hence within any occupation persons of different race enjoyed a somewhat different status. The hierarchy of race bisected and disordered the pyramid of class.

CHAPTER 8

THE MINES

At the close of the eighteenth century Guanajuato was the leading producer of silver in the world. Its annual output of over five million pesos amounted to one-sixth of all American bullion, gold and silver combined, and equalled the entire production of either viceroyalty of Buenos Aires or Peru. Yet despite the prominence conceded to the town by Humboldt in his *Essai Politique*, Guanajuato has never obtained the historical attention that its importance warrants. Moreover, unlike Potosí, the town did not even find a contemporary chronicler. Humboldt's invaluable study apart, very few printed sources deal with Guanajuato in its colonial heyday. In consequence, the modern historian must rely almost exclusively upon archival material to reconstruct the outlines of its economic history. Unfortunately, a good part of the intendancy and treasury records were destroyed in 1810 when Hidalgo's forces captured the city. Other documents were lost during the last century and within living memory the account books of the great mines—until then religiously preserved—were sold for pulping to a local cardboard factory. Our knowledge, therefore, is restricted to what can be pieced together from lawsuits, petitions to the Crown and notary records. On many points we still lack information; for others the evidence we do possess is sparse and at times confusing. Nevertheless, even the most cursory reading of the available material soon reveals that silver mining in Guanajuato differed considerably from the remainder of the industry. Its production was much more consistent than elsewhere, so that although individual mines experienced great fluctuations, the town as a whole regularly produced between a fifth and a quarter of all Mexican silver throughout the eighteenth century. This record was all the more remarkable for a camp in which several principal mines had been worked since the 1550s. Then again, no other camp had a mine like the Valenciana. This one great enterprise, which from 1769 until 1810 consistently yielded a high level of profits, virtually freed Guanajuato from its former reliance upon the merchant houses and silver banks of Mexico City. Moreover, its success both generated and depended upon a complex structure of production and credit within Guanajuato itself. By the end of the eighteenth century, in striking contrast to Zacatecas, the local industry had achieved complete financial autonomy. Our object then, in the pages to follow, is to describe the way in which this autonomy was secured. Of necessity, granted the absence of detailed account books, we must concentrate upon the supply of capital and changes in the organisation of production.

I

A brief note about the physical basis of the industry is necessary to understand the subsequent discussion. All the chief mines of colonial Guanajuato—the Rayas, Mellado, Cata, Sirena, Tepeyac, and Valenciana—were situated, within a distance of 2,170 yards, along one central lode, the Veta Madre, which ran in a fairly straight line southeast to northwest of the town. The lode itself inclined 45 degrees southwest and measured about 66·8 yards across, dividing within this area into three parallel seams. Both horizontally and vertically these seams varied in quality, in some places converging to form a solid mass of silver ore, and in others petering out into base metal. According to Humboldt the richest ores were to be found at depths between 83 and 290 yards.[1] Apparently the lode was relatively dry so that central shafts serviced by horse-whims sufficed to keep the mines free of water; adits were not required.[2] Drainage, therefore, did not constitute much of a technical problem for the Guanajuato miner.

In any one year the multitude of shallow ephemeral shafts cut both along the Veta Madre and on the lesser lodes of the area produced a considerable amount of mineral. But, in the long run, it was the handful of great mines occupying substantial portions of the Veta Madre which dominated production. Even when they lay waterlogged their upper reaches were still scavenged to good effect by independent pickmen. Moreover, nearly all these mines—the Valenciana, Rayas, Mellado and Sirena—continued to yield great quantities of ore in the nineteenth century. If some mines, therefore, lay waterlogged for years, their condition sprang from an insufficient capital investment in shafts deep enough to drain the work area, or from a superabundance of low-grade ore which did not cover contemporary production costs.

II

That it was undercapitalisation and inadequate and costly credit facilities which hindered Guanajuato's mines can be proved from their history during the first half of the eighteenth century. For at this time the industry was characterised by its dependence upon capital largely recruited in

[1] Humboldt, *Ensayo político*, pp. 350–1, UMMA, *Reports*, report by Lucas Alamán, 28 May 1826, viii-xiii, pp. 8–9. Rafael Orozco, *La industria minera de México, distrito de Guanajuato* (Mexico, 1921).

[2] Humboldt, *Ensayo político*, p. 352.

Mexico City; by its indebtedness to the local treasury over the payments for mercury; by the excessive division of mine ownership; and, as a consequence of the previous features, by frequent bankruptcy among leading miners resulting quite often in the abandonment of their mines. Particular case studies will best illustrate the prevalence of these factors.

Between 1694 and 1699, Dr Juan Diez de Bracamonte produced 1,200,000 ps. from the Rayas. Calculating that the enterprise required 200,000 ps. in avíos to finance its operating costs, he contracted with the Sánchez de Tagle silver bank in Mexico City to receive his silver, honour his libranzas, and send him cash and supplies. With this backing he purchased four small haciendas in the immediate vicinity of Guanajuato to supply the mine with maize and he constructed a refining mill and furnace on the hacienda of Burras situated just outside Marfil to handle all his ore.[1] But despite this outlay neither Bracamonte nor the succeeding owner appear to have met with much success.

In 1712 the superintendent of the mercury monopoly intervened to embargo and auction the Rayas to satisfy debts on mercury supplies that amounted to over 60,000 ps.[2] Such embargoes of property were then quite common since at much the same time three leading miners in Guanajuato all suffered the same fate.[3] Indeed, so stringent were the local treasury's debt-collecting measures that at least twice, in 1725 and 1740, the Guanajuato mining deputation protested to the monopoly's superintendent to point out that the town's prosperity depended upon the care with which the payments for mercury were arranged.[4]

In the case of the Rayas, since no purchaser appeared, the superintendent agreed to rent the mine to Pedro de Sardaneta for 10,000 ps. a year. But although he paid off the mercury debt, Sardaneta fell into arrears with his Mexico City aviadores. The Rayas was then acquired by his brother, José, a more knowledgeable and enterprising miner, who in 1727 bought the property outright.[5] In three years he cut a new shaft to a depth of 150 yards, serviced by two whims.[6] Tradition has it that he was the first miner in Guanajuato to employ gunpowder for underground blasting. In addition

[1] Juan Diez de Bracamonte, *Por la justicia . . .* (Mexico, 1699), pp. 3–5, 23–31. AGI, Mexico 1045, audiencia to Bracamonte, 22 September 1704.

[2] AGN, Minería 50, statement of José de Sardaneta, 27 October 1724.

[3] AGN, Minería 111/2, 3, 6, contains those embargo cases that occurred between 1714–25.

[4] AGN, Minería 111/4, Guanajuato mining deputation to mercury monopoly superintendent, 14 August 1725; AGN, Minería 40/1, Guanajuato mining deputation to mercury monopoly superintendent, 11 October 1740.

[5] AGN, Minería 50/1, José de Sardaneta statement, 13 October 1740.

[6] *Gacetas de México*, I, 262–3.

it was Sardaneta who invented the arrastre, a crushing device which was far more efficient than the old stamp mill.[1] Yet despite his skill as a miner and the abundant production of the Rayas in these years, when Sardaneta died in 1741 he left an estate charged with debts amounting to 508,000 ps. In consequence, the creditors installed Juan Jiménez, a local merchant-aviador, to manage the mine. It was not until 1757 that Sardaneta's son, Vicente Manuel, regained control of the family property. He then had to rebuild the enterprise, since Jiménez, in an effort to reduce costs, had simply sold the crude ore at the pithead, abandoning all attempt to refine on the Burras hacienda.[2] Thus although the Rayas produced a substantial quantity of silver—a possible seventeen million pesos between 1715 and 1777—its owners received an extraordinarily poor return. Part of their problem lay with the mine itself: its ores were at best medium grade. But, more importantly, the Sardanetas took over the Rayas without much capital at a time when the mine clearly required heavy fixed investment in the form of new and deeper shafts. A low level of profit together with undercapitalisation drove them even deeper into debt. Yet in the 1720s a treasury official declared that 'with its wealth the Rayas is the best jewel that decorates the Crown'.[3]

The other two great mines in Guanajuato at this period, the Mellado and the Cata, were both largely ruined by much the same factors combined with the effects of the laws of inheritance and the inability of their shareholders to devise an efficient and unified system of management. First discovered in the 1550s, the Mellado was renovated towards the end of the seventeenth century by Francisco de Busto y Jerez. But the mine's 32 shares were then divided among his four children, so that his eldest son, the first Marquis of San Clemente, only received eight shares. In fact, the marquis gained most of his wealth from the Cata, a mine which enjoyed a striking bonanza in the years 1724–35 and in which he owned half of its 24 shares.[4] The other chief shareholder in both these mines was Manuel de Aranda y Saavedra, a merchant-aviador of Guanajuato who married the marquis' sister Josefa.

Each man acquired a fortune of about 300,000–400,000 ps. from his mine—sufficient, one might suppose, to establish their enterprises upon a secure footing. But both the marquis and Aranda begot ten children, and

[1] AGI, Mexico 1130, Council of the Indies, *consulta*, 22 December 1777.

[2] AHGP, Cabildo, Will of Vicente Manuel de Sardaneta, 19 December 1786.

[3] AGN, Minería 51, treasury officials to viceroy, 19 November 1727. They also testified to Sardaneta's use of gunpowder.

[4] Marmolejo, *Efemérides*, I, 145, 165–6; II, 29. See also AGN, Minería 5/1, testimonies of descent.

since neither purchased an entail, the estates were divided equally among their heirs. Aranda died about 1730 when the Cata was still experiencing a full bonanza, so the distribution of his fortune between his widow and children had little immediate effect apart from obliging the marquis to seek credit from the Fagoaga silver bank. But by the late 1730s, both the Cata and the Mellado required new shafts. Yet Aranda's widow had donated 60,000 ps. to found a Jesuit college in Guanajuato and the marquis had bought two haciendas.[1] The result was that when the marquis died in 1747 he left an estate heavily encumbered with debt and two ailing mines both in need of renovation[2] (see table 37).

Table 37 *Estate of first Marquis of San Clemente*, c. *1747*. (In pesos)

Assets			Debts	
Hacienda of Villachuato		325,000	Manuel Aldaco	160,000
Hacienda of San José de la Cañada		54,834	Church	80,000
Refining mill		28,943		
House		45,162		
8 shares in Mellado	no value assigned			
12 shares in Cata				
		453,939		240,000

Distribution of the estate was delayed until the huge debt owed to Aldaco could be paid off. But the mines yielded little profit and no buyer appeared to pay the 200,000 ps. finally demanded for the Villachuato hacienda. Aldaco then added 20,000 ps. to his bill as interest upon principal. In 1753, to meet his claims, the audiencia decreed that the Villachuato should be ceded outright to Aldaco.[3] With the burden of debt eliminated, the San Clemente estate was eventually apportioned in 1756. The widow (his second wife) was given 115,800 ps., $3\frac{2}{3}$ shares of the Cata and $2\frac{2}{5}$ of the Mellado. The ten children received sums ranging between 24,000 and 30,000 ps., and each obtained $1\frac{1}{5}$ shares of the Cata and $\frac{4}{5}$ of a share in the Mellado. But much of this partition was nominal, comprising dowries already paid and bad debts that were quite irredeemable. Whatever the case, it provoked intense quarrels among the heirs and effectively destroyed the capital accumulation of two generations. A further, almost immediate consequence of this testamentary division was the virtual abandonment of the Mellado and Cata mines.

1 AGN, Historia 109/5, 23 May 1732.
2 AGN, Vínculos 158/1, contains an inventory of the estate.
3 For the subsequent lawsuits and disputes arising out of the division of the San Clemente estates see AGN, Vínculos 150.

San Clemente's employment of the Fagoaga silver bank and his mounting balance of debt exemplified a general problem confronting many Guanajuato miners at this period who relied upon these Mexico City institutions to supply them with credit. In 1736, the Fagoagas maintained accounts with the local miners[1] shown in table 38.

Table 38 *Fagoaga silver bank accounts with Guanajuato miners, c. 1736.*

Credits advanced		*pesos*
Good	Simón Francisco de Arroyo	57,493
	José Antonio Mendizábal	44,464
	Tomás de Zertuche	13,331
Doubtful	Bernardo Fernández de Riaño	24,800
	Alonso Fernández	19,787
		159,875
Debts owed by bank		
Marquis of San Clemente		96,896
Baltazar Pardo de Figueroa		19,995
Manuel González de Zedillo		7,417
Francisco Alipasolo		513
		124,821

The silver bank owned by the Count of San Pedro del Alamo also did business with Guanajuato miners. In the years 1737–40 Bernardo Fernández de Riaño, listed above by the Fagoagas as a doubtful payor, drew over 31,000 ps. from the Count in the form of libranzas.[2] Similarly, Antonio Jacinto Diez Madroñero relied heavily upon the bank to finance his mining enterprises.[3] But this use of the silver banks to obtain credit and cash for operating costs turned sour as several leading miners followed the Marquis of San Clemente into debt. It is noteworthy that three of the marquis' six sons-in-law all bequeathed estates encumbered with more debts than assets. Two of the three sons-in-law of Manuel de Aranda died bankrupt.[4]

During the 1750s, as the situation of the Guanajuato industry grew worse, two major attempts to renovate mines were initiated with the assistance of the silver banks. In 1749 Juan de Quintana, a son-in-law of

[1] AGN, Vínculos 7, inventory of Fagoaga estate, verified 10 December 1736.

[2] AGN, Vínculos 176/2, Count of San Pedro del Alamo suit, 12 May 1741.

[3] AHG, Bienes Difuntos 1761–79, Madroñero's will, 16 November 1779.

[4] These were Lorenzo de Olazábal, Antonio Jacinto de Diez Madroñero, and Gonzalo de Aranda Saavedra: AGN, Minería 158/3, Olazábal's will, 18 September 1733. For Diez Madroñero, see note 3 above; and for Aranda see AHGP, Cabildo, 11 October 1770 and 26 June 1777. The Aranda sons-in-law were José Antonio Mendizábal and Juan Antonio de Quintana; see respectively, AGN, Vínculos 144/1, embargo of goods, 11 October 1751, and below, p. 267, note 1.

Manuel de Aranda, borrowed 51,000 ps. from Manuel de Aldaco to restore the Mellado. In the upshot, he failed and after his death in 1756 his estate was embargoed to pay off 64,000 ps. to Aldaco, 15,715 ps. to the treasury for mercury and 11,040 to the Church.[1] During the same decade the Valdivielso silver bank backed another leading miner, Lorenzo de Incháuregui, in a major renovation of the Sirena mine. Some 400,000 ps. were invested but apparently with little success.[2] Thus both the two chief ventures of the 1750s were financed by silver banks and both experienced an equally disastrous outcome. After this decade of setbacks it is not surprising to find that the silver banks abandoned their operations in Guanajuato.

III

As the silver banks retired from the scene with fingers burnt, their place was taken by a group of merchant-aviadores resident in Guanajuato. Acting with considerable caution and skill several dealers had contrived to make their fortunes precisely at the time when many local miners became bankrupt. By 1760 these men imported European commodities directly from the Jalapa fair without any intervention of the Mexico City almaceneros.[3] They then distributed these wares on credit to the lesser traders of the town and the mining villages. They dealt heavily in the industrial supplies required by the mining industry. They also acted as aviadores to independent refiners and, in some cases, to miners. Competition was vigorous: in 1743 the town was reckoned to contain 80 *tiendas de gruesa*, shops which stocked foreign goods, and another 73 shops located in the mining villages. In 1793 the intendant counted 335 merchants in the town alone, one for every 96 persons.[4] Such a concentration inevitably drove many businessmen to act as aviadores in order to obtain an outlet for their goods. For it must be remembered that the aviador enjoyed the right of providing his partner with all industrial materials required either in mining or refining.

Such necessary components of refining as lead, salt and copper, all attracted mercantile enterprise. Naturally at times traders attempted to

[1] AHG, Bienes Difuntos, 1742–61, settlement of estate, 27 July 1756. Also AHGP, Cabildo, 29 February 1804.

[2] BRP, MSS 2824, Miscelánea de Ayala 10, f. 154.

[3] BN (Mexico) 1396, f. 415, protest of Veracruz merchants against termination of the Jalapa Fairs, 8 January 1785: 'neither the powerful merchants of Mexico nor the rich men of Guanajuato, nor of other opulent cities in the kingdom have come here as they used to Jalapa to employ their wealth in the purchase of our goods'.

[4] Villaseñor y Sánchez, *Theatro americano*, p. 41. AGN, Historia 523, ff. 76, 88.

drive up prices by cornering the market. For example, in 1790, a wealthy merchant of Guanajuato, José Pérez Marañón, signed a contract with the owner of the Targea lead mine, situated in the jurisdiction of San Luis de la Paz, the chief source of supply for the Guanajuato smelters. He bought a thousand loads at 10 ps. each on condition that the owner did not sell to anyone else for another six months. He then forced up prices. His manoeuvre, however, backfired, since the mining deputation intervened to fix the price at 13 ps. a load and fined Pérez Marañón 500 ps.[1] The deputation also defended the industry from outside commercial speculations. In 1804 a group of merchants in Guadalajara bought up all the existing stock of salt in Colima, the usual supplier to Guanajuato. So the deputation, which estimated the town's weekly needs at 500–600 loads, entered the market, and bought 4,000 loads in the northern camp of Guarisamey and found another 2,000 loads in Tonatlán and Colima itself.[2] No doubt similar manoeuvres at times occurred over the purchase of *magistral* (copper pyrites) from Tepezala situated near Zacatecas.[3]

Table 39 *Entrance of goods into Guanajuato, January–August inclusive, 1778.*

Salt	10,802 loads
Copper pyrites	1,903 loads
Litharge (lead oxide)	549 loads
Lead	108 loads
Pinewood (Ocote)	832½ loads
Cordage (Jarcia)	131 loads
Wooden rollers	747½ doz.
Arrastre wooden parts	577 pieces
Planks of wood	517,060
Nails	480,512
Iron	1,926 cwt.
Steel	300 cwt.
Mules	162
Horses for whims	58

Some idea of Guanajuato's annual consumption of such commodities can be gathered from the list shown in table 39, compiled by the town's excise officials.[4] Unfortunately they only gave quantities and not values.

Whatever the returns upon wholesale and retail transactions, they could not compare to the profits available in the mining industry. All the

[1] AGN, Minería, 52/16, Guanajuato deputation to viceroy, 28 February 1790.

[2] AGN, Minería 80/4, Guanajuato deputation statement, 9 July 1804.

[3] Henri St Clair Duport, *De la Production des Métaux Précieux au Mexique* (Paris, 1843), pp. 94–5.

[4] AGI, Mexico 1391, report of excise director, 7 October 1778.

wealthiest merchants of Guanajuato styled themselves: *comerciantes y mercaderes de plata* (merchants and dealers in silver). These men often began by buying silver on the open market from small independent refiners; soon, however, they became contractual aviadores to refiners, and, more rarely, to miners. Where did they obtain their capital to finance these operations? Generally they began business with a small loan from fellow traders, usually relatives or paisanos, or from the Church or a rich widow. In Guanajuato several leading merchants started on the road to success by marrying an heiress. With a few thousand pesos in hand, it was then always possible to build up a fortune by acting as an aviador. Possible, but difficult: it required considerable business acumen to profit from refiners and miners without becoming too heavily involved in their enterprise. Maintenance of liquidity was the key to success. To give substance to this generalisation let us examine the business operations of a successful *mercader de plata.*

By 1761, that is to say, after a decade of misfortune for the Guanajuato mine owners, Martín de Septién y Montero, a Montañés merchant, had established a business worth over 300,000 ps. He had accumulated this fortune 'on my own account and at the expense of my industry, care and personal work'. Not that his success was fortuitous: he had two uncles engaged in local commerce, one of whom, Agustín de Septién y Montero, was himself worth over 200,000 ps. Such connexions provided invaluable backing. For instance, in 1744, Martín's brother, Juan Fernando, borrowed 20,000 ps. from a widow resident in Mexico City, offering as security the guarantee of his uncle and his brothers.[1] Nevertheless, the use made of such backing depended upon the commercial talent of the individual merchant. Neither of Martín de Septién's two brothers, Francisco and Juan Fernando, became particularly rich. How then did Martín make his money? An examination of the inventory of his estate, given in table 40, will give us some indication.[2]

Not all these debtors can be identified; López, Miera, Uribarren, and Díaz de Cossío were recipients of mercury from the treasury, and hence were at least refiners and possibly miners. On the other hand the two Pérez Marañón, and Otero were fellow merchants; Otero was a small tradesman with a business in the mining villages, and no doubt Septién supplied him with goods on credit.

The curious distribution of resources found in the inventory is hard to explain, unless we presume that Septién was at that time deliberately

[1] AHGP, Cabildo, 13 February 1744.
[2] AHG, Bienes Difuntos, 1742–61, inventories, 6 May 1761.

accumulating a stock of cash. This presumption is strengthened by the fact that May 1761 fell between the arrival of the two convoys of 1760 and 1762; no doubt, Septién himself went or sent an agent to Jalapa.[1] This then

Table 40 *Estate of Martín de Septién y Montero, May 1761.* (In pesos)

	Assets	*Debits*
Shop and merchandise	19,186	
Property in houses	18,700	
Silver, gold in bar	135,028	
Credits advanced	144,926	
Smaller items	1,625	16,314
	319,465	
Less debits	16,314	
Balance	303,151	
(A list of debtors was provided, among whom the most important were the following):		
Pedro Gerardo López	20,589	
Fernando de Miera	27,090	
José Antonio de Uribarren	9,883	
Francisco Díaz de Cossío	10,000	
Juan José de Angulo	11,002	
Francisco Javier de Rodríguez	13,134	
José Pérez Marañón	5,549	
Joaquín Pérez Marañón	6,000	
Pedro Luciano Otero	1,719	
Smaller items	39,960	
	144.926	

would explain why he kept a third of his capital in hard cash, and why his stock of merchandise had run so low. The large quantity of silver and gold bars he either gathered from casual purchase on the open market or derived from contracts with his refiners to whom he had advanced cash and supplies. Unfortunately the statement of debtors does not indicate whether these were simple loans at 5 per cent covered by mortgages, or contractual aviador credits.

The salient feature of Septién's estate lay in its extreme liquidity; he owned a few houses and some mercantile stock, yet these items together amounted to little more than a tenth of his capital; the remainder was invested in cash, bullion and loans. And in contrast to Bassoco or the Fagoagas he did not employ deposits or loans to finance his

[1] Lerdo de Tejada, *Comercio esterior*, Appendix 1, 2, unpaginated.

operations, so that his capital was entirely his own. He was far more an aviador and a finance banker than a merchant.

His business continued to prosper in the years following 1761, so that when a second inventory was taken in December 1779 after his death, the estate had nearly doubled in value. It was then divided into the branches shown in table 41.[1]

Table 41 *Estate of Martín de Septién y Montero, December 1779.* (In pesos)

Shop managed by Francisco de Septién y Arce	36,325
Shop managed by Manuel García de Quintana	274,975
Property in houses	94,044
Private silver, jewellery, etc.	10,881
Loans advanced on interest covered by mortgages	110,073
Legacies already paid	47,928
Smaller items	19,600
	593,926

Table 42 *Shop managed by Francisco de Septién y Arce, December 1779.*

	Assets (in pesos)		*Debits* (in pesos)
Merchandise	17,558	Capital in November 1776	33,344
Cash	1,705		
Credits advanced	24,160		
Total	43,423		
Capital	33,344		
Profits	10,078		
Profits to be subtracted	7,097		
Remainder to estate	36,325		

Septién had persisted in his refusal to acquire refining mills, mines or haciendas; the only fixed investment he cared to make was in urban property, situated within Guanajuato. However, with the termination of the convoy system, there was no longer any need to accumulate large cash balances, so that more capital was placed in merchandise and loans. The inventories of the two shops, shown in tables 42 and 43, permit us to understand their range of business.

[1] AHG, Bienes Difuntos, 1761–79. Septién's will, 19 December 1778; inventory approved 10 December 1779.

Of the credits advanced by the shop managed by Septién, the largest item was 16,793 ps. advanced in avíos to the refiner Felipe de Soria. Francisco de Septién y Arce, the manager, received 547 ps. as his share of the profits for the period 1776–9.

The inventory of the larger shop, directed by Quintana, was much larger and more confusing.

Table 43 *Shop managed by Manuel García de Quintana.*

	Assets (in pesos)		*Debits* (in pesos)
Merchandise	82,679		
Cash	15,679		
Silver bar	20,757		
Avíos to refiners	122,978		
Credits advanced to merchants	45,537		
Invested in public supply of meat to municipal slaughterhouse	42,153		
Invested in Arce's shop	32,965	Invested in Arce's shop	32,965
Costs of Quintana	9,613	Quintana's capital plus $\frac{1}{3}$ or profits since 1776	36,803
Bad debts	602	Debts owed	21,146
Smaller items	2,542	Other items	9,616
Gross Balance 1779	375,505		100,530
Previous balance (1776)	308,942		
Profits in 3 years	66,563		
Net Balance in 1779, less debits	274,975		

Quintana as manager took a percentage of the profits which he then left in the business to fructify, so that already in 1776 he owned 24,224 ps. of the firm's capital. The range of the shop's activity is quite clear; it still distributed goods on credit to smaller merchants, and avíos to refiners; it had also branched out and secured the contract for the municipal supply of meat. The list of refiners indicates the concentration of the firm's financing.

	pesos
Pedro de Palencia	31,611
Alejandro de Araujo	21,996
Pedro de la Riva	22,576
Pedro de Quijano	5,073
José Campero Montero	10,115
Manuel Güemes de la Concha	31,604
	122,978

The importance for the mining industry of this backing is hard to quantify; but in 1782 the Septién firm was granted just over 9 per cent of that year's mercury allocation for its refiners.

In addition, Septién also lent out money at the standard interest of 5 per cent; his chief debtors were:

	pesos
Bernardo Fernández de Riaño	38,000
Manuel Rodero de Garnica	10,000
Antonio de Briones	12,000
Antonio de Septién y Castillo with his wife María Gertrudis Jordán y Primo	16,000
Smaller items	—
	110,073

Fernández de Riaño, a prominent miner, in 1763 had borrowed 18,000 ps. for ten years, offering his haciendas in Silao as security; in 1776 he renewed the loan and borrowed another 20,000 ps.[1] Antonio de Septién was a distant relative who had settled in Querétaro.

If we now organise the inventory, we obtain the following balance for the main items:

	pesos
Merchandise	100,237
Cash and bullion	38 141
Total credits advanced and loans	302,748
Invested in purchase of meat	42,153
Property in houses	94,044

Septién, above all else, lived off his ability to supply credit; in an industry chronically undercapitalised he avoided any fixed investment but instead was careful to keep his capital highly liquid, placing it mainly in short-term loans; and where he did extend long-term credit he demanded firm security and a 5 per cent rate of interest. Septién thus represented the typical merchant-capitalist who financed the refining industry. We may note that the return on capital was not extravagant; Septién doubled his capital in a period of 18 years; the 5 per cent that he received on his long-term loans was not much inferior to what he could expect from his mercantile or aviador business; Quintana's shop made an average of 5·9 per cent return on capital in the three years 1776–9, and Septién y Arce's averaged 9 per cent. Such figures did not differ greatly from Meave's estimates for the first 20 years of his management of the Fagoaga trading house.

Septién bequeathed his entire estate to his young wife and their only

[1] AHGP, Cabildo, 26 February 1776.

daughter. The widow married his nephew Francisco de Septién y Arce.[1] The close connexion between business success and family ties is further illustrated by the fact that the other manager, Manuel García de Quintana, married a niece of his employer. The third cajero, Martín de la Riva, later emerged as a leading merchant. His brother Pedro ran a refining mill which was backed by the Septién house. All these men, like most of the refiners listed above, were Montañeses.

Another extended mercantile family were the Pérez Marañón. Their case illustrates the fact that commercial fortunes, as much as those made in mining, could be easily dissipated by the laws of inheritance. As in the case of the Septiéns, three brothers arrived in Guanajuato; two died in modest economic circumstances, the third, José Pérez Marañón, became a leading merchant-aviador. At his death in 1793 he left an estate valued at 327,572 ps. It included three shops, a petty refining mill, a small ranch and two houses. The stock of merchandise was worth 158,106 ps, and the shops had advanced credits to the order of 130,466 ps.[2] The fixed property, therefore, only comprised about 12 per cent of the value of the entire estate. Pérez Marañón acted as an aviador to no less than 19 refiners but he carefully avoided any entanglement in mining.[3] Presumably the one small refining mill that he owned came to him through foreclosure for debt. The pattern of investment is hence very similar to that of Martín de Septién.

This evidently flourishing business was almost entirely destroyed by a classic testamentary apportionment among Pérez Marañón's widow and seven children. After certain charitable legacies were paid and the small prenuptial capital subtracted from the widow's share, each child received 15,085 ps. in property and merchandise and 12,598 ps. of the credits advanced—a mere 27,687 ps. in all. For example, María Manuela, the daughter who married Lic. José María de Septién y Montero, obtained a small house worth 7,313 ps. and the rest of her inheritance in merchandise and credits advanced. Oddly enough, the stock and loans of the three shops were shared equitably among all the children. Thus within one generation a leading merchant fortune was dissolved and the greater part of the enterprise terminated.

IV

By the early 1760s the situation of the Guanajuato mining industry appeared to be decidedly precarious. Several of its greatest mines lay waterlogged and those which continued to produce yielded but small

[1] The daughter died soon after. AHGP, Cabildo, 10 November 1789.

[2] AHGP, Cabildo, 20 December 1790, 17 August 1793.

[3] AGI, Mexico 2209, Valcárcel to Mangino, 15 July 1782.

profits to their owners. A representative of the city complained to the Crown that 'the population was obviously declining and was very poor, that most of the known mines were not worked, and that their owners were losing money and abandoning business'. And in support of this declaration the Rector of the Jesuit College, Father Ignacio Coromina, stated that 'of those who really operate the mines, there is not a single person who is well off and who is not burdened with debts and charges'.[1] It is significant that Coromina restricted his comments to the owners. For clearly the town had several wealthy merchants. Moreover, at this time Guanajuato's mine-workers were notorious for their high earnings. Many shafts relied entirely upon *buscones*, men who took half the ore they found. Up to 1757 the Rayas too sold its mineral. In consequence the town possessed numerous independent refiners who bought ore from workers and miners alike.

A curious situation existed in which owners of highly productive mines found themselves in debt and unable to obtain credit while what should have been *their* profits went to the workers, to the independent refiners and to the merchants. Moreover, the withdrawal of the silver banks drove these mine-owners into the arms of the local aviadores, who, however, as we have seen, were highly reluctant to back them. For example, Vicente Manuel de Sardaneta, the owner of the Rayas, found it extraordinarily difficult to get credit to finance his operations. And within seven years of regaining control of his mine, by 1764, he was again obliged to cede the management to his backers, Juan José de Compains and Gabriel de Arechederreta, two Basque merchants who had married into the Busto family connexion.[2] Not until 1769 did he pay off his debts.

This new reliance upon local merchant-aviadores can be further proved from the testimony of Bernardo Fernández de Riaño, the principal shareholder in the San Lorenzo mine. In his will he left a list of all his aviadores from the 1720s until 1784.[3] In the early years he had relied upon the alcaldes mayores of Guanajuato and the two silver banks of Mexico City operated by the Fagoagas and the Count of San Pedro del Alamo. But these were replaced by merchants resident in Guanajuato itself—by 'Juan Compains and his partner Gabriel de Arechederreta' and then by Martín de Septién. But he was only able to borrow 38,000 ps. from Septién because he owned several small haciendas in the neighbouring district of Silao. Septién did not act as his aviador he merely loaned him capital for

[1] AGI, Mexico 2251, Guanajuato mining deputation to viceroy, 30 October 1760.
[2] AHGP, Cabildo, will, 19 December 1786.
[3] AHGP, Cabildo, 26 February 1776.

ten years at an annual 5 per cent interest. In addition Fernández de Riaño, once more offering his estates as security, borrowed 23,000 ps. from the Church.[1] All this indicates clearly enough that the withdrawal of the silver banks had left a credit vacuum which the local trading houses were unwilling to fill save in the most cautious fashion.

During the 1770s, however, the trends that appeared to dominate the previous decade were reversed. A new structure of production emerged in which the balance of profit moved in favour of the mining section of the industry. Hitherto, Guanajuato's mine-workers had been notorious for both their indiscipline and for the large amount of ore they took as their partidos. As early as 1663 the ayuntamiento promoted the establishment of a Franciscan convent in the town, since the friars enjoyed a greater influence among the populace than the secular clergy, and hence could better control their disturbances. They declared that 'the mining populace, uncontrollable and wild in their temper, frequently and for the simplest causes start terrible riots and tumults'.[2] The Franciscans, it was hoped, could contain the disorders.

It is doubtful whether any diminution in these riots occurred, since in 1732, for example, an attempt by the Crown to collect tribute from the mine-workers immediately provoked an armed uprising that required the presence of an oidor to pacify them by a continued exemption from tribute.[3] Further corroboration can be obtained from the description of Guanajuato left by the Spanish Capuchin, Father Ajofrín, who visited the town in 1763. He found the miners' style of life to be wild and lavish. The friar asserted that it was not uncommon for workers to finish a week with 300 ps. in their pocket.[4] These gains they invariably spent at once. 'They buy taffeta, fine cambric, delicate lace and other rich fabrics so that they dress like princes. By Monday they find themselves without a penny ... and descend the mine nearly naked.' He thought the men very strange: 'It makes one laugh to see these people of all shades of colour, with faces like devils and huge hands, black and ugly in the extreme, festively dressed in velvet breeches, gold tissue dresscoats, Dutch ruffled shirts etc.' He gave an account of a mulatto who had discovered a small mine. During the brief five-week bonanza some two thousand people arrived to join in the great debauch on which the mulatto spent all his profits—some 40,000 ps. in all.

The money for these debauches came not so much from wages—for the

[1] AMM 150, 13 September 1806.
[2] Marmolejo, *Efemérides*, I, 207–9.
[3] AGN, Minería 76/2, report of mining deputation, 6 April 1735.
[4] See Ajofrín, *Diario*, I, 213–15.

standard rate was but 4 rls. a day—but from partidos. Pedro de Anza, the close associate of José de la Borda, declared: 'In the custom of partidos there is much diversity. . . . I have seen shares of a quarter, an eighth, a twelfth and even a twentieth if the ore is rich, but in Guanajuato, the practice is so outrageous that after a small fixed quota all the remaining ore is shared equally [between owner and workers] and in my opinion it is from this and other abuses in favour of the workers that the backwardness of that camp results.'[1]

Both the indiscipline and the excessively high earnings were terminated in the years following the harsh suppression of the 1767 revolt. The new militia regiment, and, even more, the permanent patrol picquet, gave the mine-owners more effective control of their employees. They were not slow to exercise their new power. In 1774 the treasury officials noted that Manuel Jiménez, the manager of the Rayas, had abolished all payments of partidos in his mine. Moreover, he refused to pay more than 4 rls. a day and established a company store in which the greater part of this exiguous wage was spent. The treasury officials complained: 'Never has the town's commerce been so destroyed and reduced as at present. The cause is that the mine-workers no longer receive the partido, which according to ancient custom, they used to be given until a few years ago—a custom which still prevails in the north.'[2] It appears, then, that the Rayas mine was trying to secure the profit which hitherto had been made both by the workers and the merchants. Further corroboration that a marked change had occurred in popular spending habits was indicated in 1793 by a mercantile petition to close the town's shops on Sundays. In earlier times episcopal permission had been granted for stores to cater for workers coming on Sundays to the town centre to enjoy their week's earnings. But by 1793 the miners made their purchases in the villages.[3] Clearly the weekends of riots and dissipation described by Ajofrín were long since past.

With partidos eliminated the next obvious step for the intelligent mine-owner to take was to establish a vertically integrated enterprise. Such was certainly the pattern prevalent in camps like Real del Monte and Sombrerete. In Guanajuato the best attempt at such integration was made by the Rayas. By 1773 the mine produced about 600–700 loads of ore a week. All this was refined on the Burras hacienda, a property outside Marfil, which was both a refining mill and an agricultural estate. At both Rayas

[1] Chávez Orozco, ed., *Conflicto de trabajo*, p. 99.

[2] AGN, Minería 11/1, Guanajuato treasury to Bucareli, 3 February 1774.

[3] ACM, 688, petition of Guanajuato merchants, 2 January 1793.

and Burras, company stores were set up. Taken with the termination of the workers' partidos, this meant that the owners, the Sardanetas, at last received profits commensurate with their scale of operations. Vicente Manuel de Sardaneta, the principal shareholder, estimated that in the period 1757–74 the mine made a total profit of 480,768 ps., little more than an average 28,280 ps. a year. But it was not until 1772 that he finally paid off all the debts charged upon the mine since 1729. During the 1770s as the income from the integrated enterprise at last increased, Sardaneta purchased a string of haciendas and ranchos in Irapuato and Silao.[1] He also became the Marquis of San Juan de Rayas. However, this spurt of prosperity did not survive the decade, since in 1780 the mine suddenly flooded and was not restored again until 1799.

The Rayas pattern of vertical integration did not, however, prove to be the rule of the future. The owners of the newly discovered Valenciana mine followed a different policy. In 1760 Antonio de Obregón y Alcocer opened the mine on a section of the lode hitherto deemed to be composed of base metal. And so it was—down to a depth of about 60 yards. It took Obregón eight years to cut a shaft to the rich middle region of the lode. During this period he was backed by a petty tradesman, Pedro Luciano de Otero, who in turn took goods on credit from Martín de Septién's store. Each man owned ten shares in the mine with the remaining four held by an inactive partner, one Juan Antonio Santa Ana.[2]

After 1769 the Valenciana's output mounted at a phenomenal pace so that by 1774 it was producing between 800 and 1,000 loads of ore a week, more than the Rayas.[3] Such a rapid development naturally entailed extensive operating costs and a heavy investment in the constructions of shafts, whims and refining mills. Where did Obregón and Otero, neither of whom possessed financial resources, obtain their capital for such investments?

In the first place, they cut labour costs: they granted their workers a moderate partido, but insisted that out of this share of mineral the pick and blast men should provide their own gunpowder, candles and picks.[4] Then, secondly, Obregón and Otero sold their own ore to independent refiners. These weekly sales yielded sufficient cash to pay for all operating costs and to finance further development of the mine. Whether this policy was voluntary or forced upon them by circumstances, its effect was the same: they escaped any contractual dependence upon a merchant-aviador. Yet of

1 See Sardaneta's will, AHGP, Cabildo, 19 December 1786.
2 AHGP, Minas, 15 and 24 September 1760; Humboldt, *Ensayo político*, p. 353.
3 AGN, Minería 11/1, report of Guanajuato treasury, 3 February 1774.
4 AGN, Minería 114/4, report of Francisco Pallares, 5 May 1791.

course it was precisely these merchant-aviadores who provided the refiners with the cash to buy ore from the Valenciana partners and their workers.

Now there was nothing very exceptional in this triple structure; many mines started off in such a fashion. But the situation of the Valenciana differed from others in that the mine proved to be extraordinarily rich and that its owners pushed forward its production so rapidly, reinvesting their first profits in the construction of new shafts. Moreover, although both Obregón and Otero bought refining mills, at no time did they ever attempt to refine all the ore produced by their mine. No evidence exists to suggest that they ever tried to establish a vertically integrated enterprise.

At first sight their policy appears to be self-defeating. Surely most of the profits of their mine went to the refiners and their aviadores? Were they not working for the benefit of others? At the outset this was clearly the case. But as sales of ore brought a steady return the two partners, rather than investing all the capital in the purchase or construction of further refining mills, themselves became aviadores. That is to say they gave independent refiners cash to buy ore from both the Valenciana and other mines. In part this was a device by which they could participate in the profits made from the sale of their partidos, since workers never sold ore to their employer. But its effects were much broader. In essence, Obregón and Otero were able to establish a circulating stock of relatively liquid capital. They escaped the heavy burden of fixed investment in refining plant. In this way they made a twofold gain upon the ore they produced. This policy, of course, depended upon the existence of a large number of independent refiners, backed in the first instance by merchant-aviadores. Small wonder, then, that in 1781 the mining tribunal wrote of the Valenciana: 'Almost alone this famous mine has maintained the town's growing number of workers, refiners and merchants.'[1] In the same year the treasury drew up a scheme of mercury allocations which demonstrated the mine's overwhelming importance.[2]

Table 44 gives a clear picture of the complex structure of production which then prevailed in Guanajuato. The obvious importance of the Valenciana partners needs no emphasis. They refined about a fifth of all silver separated by amalgamation. But they also figured as the largest aviadores, so that in all they received a total of 1,506 cwt., or 38·9 per cent, of all mercury issued. This figure can be compared to the 9·3 per cent taken by the Septién, and the 7·1 per cent of the Marquis of San Juan de Rayas.

[1] AHH, 204/15, mining court to viceroy, 19 July 1781.
[2] AGI, Mexico 2209, Valcárcel to viceroy, 15 July 1782.

Table 44 *Structure of Guanajuato's mining industry, 1780–1, as demonstrated by the distribution of mercury.*

Mercury issued to:	*cwt.*
miners	1,799
aviadores	1,648
refiners (independent)	420
Total	3,867

Mercury issued to miners	
Valenciana partners:	*cwt.*
Antonio de Obregón	512
Pedro de Otero	218
Manuel Santa Ana	100
Other miners:	
Marquis of Rayas	275
Bernardo Fernández de Riaño	184
Ramón de Aranda	150
Francisco Azpilcueta	61
José María de Irizar	140
Ventura Carrasco	36
Manuel de Otero and partner	30
Manuel García de Zeballos	30
Ramón Liceaga	15
Lucas de Arriaga	18
José de Obregón	30
Total	1,799

Mercury issued to aviadores

	cwt.	*haciendas*	*zangarreros*
Antonio de Obregón	476	16	—
Pedro de Otero	200	6	7
Martín de Septién	360	8	—
Juan de Revuelta and Manuel Cobo García	115	1	24
José Pérez Marañón	100	2	17
Bernabé Bustamante	69	?	?
José María de Irizar	50	2	—
Juan Compains	70	—	—
Juan Vicente Alamán	69	2	5
Pedro Aguirre	42	1	6
Miguel Mendizábal	9	—	6
Agustín Pérez Marañón	18	—	—
Francisco Zamora	35	—	—
Francisco Sierra	9	—	6
Cayetano Cobo	8	—	—
Francisco de Septién	6	—	—
Lesser items	12		
Total	1,648	38	71

Table 44 (*cont.*)

Mercury issued to independent refiners

35 individuals—average assignment: 18½ cwt.

The largest were:

	cwt.
Domingo Aribe	39
Hipólito de Busto	32
Juan Villamor	30
Gregoria de Busto	25
Salvador de Ocio	29
Francisco Múrquiz	24
Carlos Villaseñor	20
Félix Aguirre	20
Smaller items	201
Total	420

Valenciana partners took: 1,506 cwt. (38·9%)
Martín de Septién took: 360 cwt. (9·3%)
Marquis of Rayas took: 275 cwt. (7·1%)

The number of effective miners was surprisingly small: some 15 men, and even if the suspended assignments are added, we still only reach a total of 23. Granted the lack of information, it is difficult to ascertain how important were the listed mines. Their owners, however, were all attached to recognisable connexions. Fernández de Riaño, Ramón de Aranda, Francisco Azpilcueta and Ramón Liceaga were all members of the great Busto-Aranda clan. José María de Irizar was the son of a Basque merchant, Lucas de Irizar. Manuel de Otero was the brother of Pedro Luciano, and Ventura Carrasco the manager of the Valenciana. Manuel García de Zeballos was a Montañés. The merchant-aviadores similarly formed a small homogeneous group. Apart from the two Valenciana partners, there were four Montañés merchant houses belonging to Septién, Pérez Marañón, Bustamante, and Revuelta. Whereas Martín de Septién backed eight substantial refiners, Pérez Marañón and Revuelta supported a large number of petty enterprises. Somewhat less important were the two Basque firms owned by Compains and Alamán (Arechederreta's heir). Irizar figures here also—his father having at times associated with Arechederreta.

The chart reveals the marked degree of autonomy that existed between the two sectors of the industry. About half of the ore produced was sold on the open market to refiners. This lack of vertical integration was more pronounced than the chart would suggest since all three of the Valenciana partners owned refining mills to handle their share of the mine's ore.

Much of Guanajuato's stability can be ascribed to the development of an independent refining sector.

Unfortunately, not much is known about Guanajuato's refining mills. Most were situated along the riverbanks in the village of Marfil. The largest formed considerable industrial enterprises although none were built on the scale of the establishments constructed by the Count of Regla at Real del Monte or the Fagoagas at Sombrerete. In 1780 the treasury estimated that the town possessed 50 large and medium-sized mills and another 300 of the smaller variety called *zangarreros*, these being little more than occasional sheds worth a few thousand pesos. By 1803 a certain degree of concentration had occurred since in that year the larger mills numbered 75 and the smaller 200.[1] By then, the largest, the Salgado, had 42 arrastres.[2] Total refining capacity also rose during the period—from 1,164 arrastres in 1760 to 1,866 in 1803.[3]

Like all the industry, Guanajuato refiners benefited from the reduction in the price of mercury introduced by Gálvez. The range of ore worth refining was extended considerably. Whereas in the 1720s the treasury asserted that ore which contained less than $1\frac{1}{4}$ ounces of silver per hundredweight could not be profitably refined, by 1793 that proportion had dropped to $\frac{3}{4}$ ounce of silver per hundredweight.[4] But here as elsewhere, the most important effect was to increase the profits that could be made upon medium-grade ore. The proportion of silver separated by amalgamation as compared to that smelted rose from two-thirds in the 1740s to about seven-ninths by the close of the century[5] (see figure 3).

In addition to the reduction in costs the refiners were helped by a fall in the discount rate charged by aviadores. Whereas prior to 1770 the local price for silver paid by aviadores was 56 rls. and 52 rls. a mark for amalgamated and smelted silver respectively, by the 1790s their prices had risen to 58 and 56 rls. Indeed some merchants paid their refiners the full rate current on the open market of 59 rls.[6] This change in prices could easily provoke misunderstandings. At the turn of the century, one

1 AHH, 204/15, Guanajuato treasury to Domingo Valcárcel, 22 November 1780; AGI, Mexico 1622, Iturrigaray to Soler, 27 July 1804.

2 AGN, Minería 221, Guanajuato treasury report, 21 June 1797; Ward, *Mexico in 1827*, II, 434.

3 AGI, Mexico 2251, Guanajuato mining deputation to viceroy, 12 September 1760; Humboldt, *Ensayo político*, p. 357.

4 Villaseñor y Sánchez, *Respuesta*, pp. 68, 82–3, 102–3; Humboldt, *Ensayo político*, p. 381.

5 AGI, Mexico 2122, Guanajuato treasury accounts, 1742–44; Humboldt, *Ensayo político*, pp. 346, 372.

6 AHGP, Minas, 6 August 1785; AHGP, Cabildo, 4 May 1809; AGN, Minería 76/18, Guanajuato deputation to mining court, 20 September 1791.

Francisco Aguilar, a refiner, transferred his account from Juan Vicente Alamán to José María Irizar. In three years he received about 260,000 ps. and produced some 18,000 marks of amalgamated silver and 20,000 marks of smelted silver. After striking the balance, Irizar declared that Aguilar

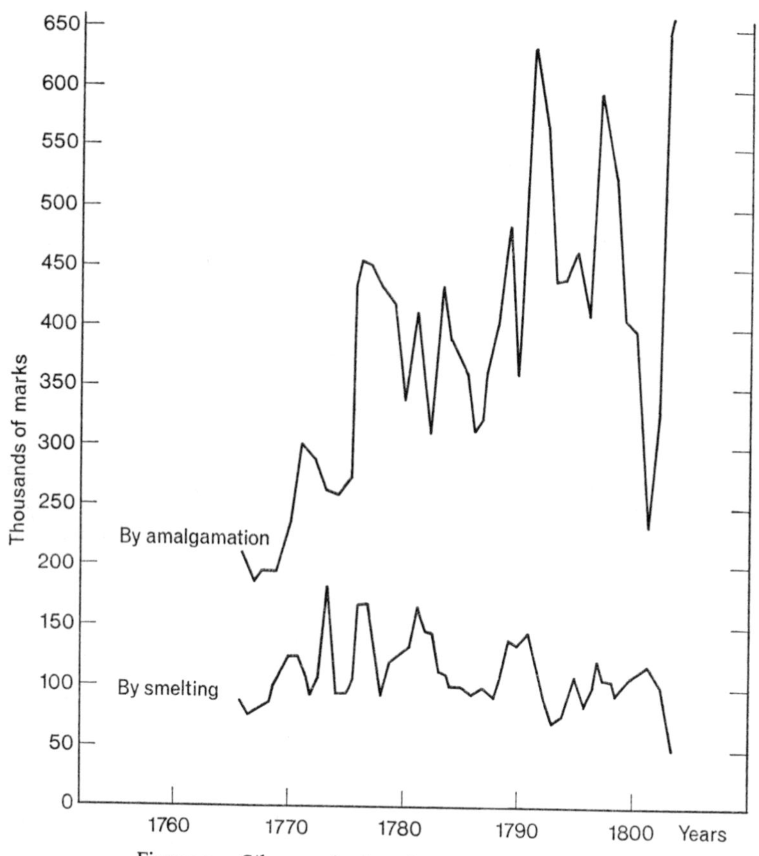

Figure 3 *Silver production of Guanajuato, 1766–1803.*

owed him 13,000 ps. It was only then that the refiner discovered that Irizar was paying 56 and 52 rls. a mark respectively instead of the new rate of 58 and 56 rls.[1]

The fall in discount rates naturally reduced the profits of the aviadores. There is evidence to suggest that several established houses began to withdraw from this business. Some, especially during the 1780s, purchased

[1] AHG, Minería, undated, unnumbered, legajo *c.* 1804–5.

refining mills. Others, at a somewhat later date, simply issued loans at 5 per cent interest. The Irizar brothers, for example, preferred to employ their capital in this fashion. By 1808 two leading refiners owed about 70,000 and 90,000 ps. respectively to the Irizars and to the Oteros, in each case the debt resulting from loans at 5 per cent rather than from overdrawing on an avío account.[1]

Although refining profits undoubtedly increased, the system of weekly sales of ore could easily favour the miner. Here it is necessary to consider the precise mode of purchase. By the end of the century most mines held weekly auctions. The refiners assembled at the pithead, inspected by hand the different classes of ore, and then whispered their bids to the miner in charge. The highest bid obtained the ore.[2] Prices varied from season to season and from year to year. But information as to any trend is almost totally lacking. Nevertheless, a few fragments, which we shall present on a later page, indicate that by 1788 prices for ore at the Valenciana were beginning to rise. Furthermore, at a later date, in 1798, the manager of the Salgado mill declared that refiners were buying poor quality ore from the Valenciana with what he called 'great daring' by which he presumably meant they stood to make a loss.[3] Possibly then by the 1790s the balance of profit which had already shifted from the aviador to the refiner was moving in favour of the miner. Certainly this hypothesis would explain the adoption of weekly sales of ore by mines such as the Mellado and the Tepeyac, which were renovated at this time. It would further account for the movement of mercantile capital first into refining and then into mining. Whatever the case, and evidence is so sparse as to prove nothing, the creation of this complex structure of silver production helped to free the miner from his old dependence upon merchant-aviadores and silver banks.

V

To render the structure of Guanajuato's mining industry fully comprehensible we must examine the Valenciana more closely. For that great mine, according to certain estimates drawn up by its general manager, produced some two-thirds of all silver refined in Guanajuato. These estimates printed by Humboldt, show that in the four-and-a-half years, January 1787 to June 1791, the Valenciana produced 1,737,052 marks of

[1] AHGP, Cabildo, 13 January 1808, Fernando de la Concha owed Pedro Otero 91,789 ps.; 15 July 1808, Bartolomé Villaseñor owed the Irizar brothers 69,482 ps.

[2] J. R. Poinsett, *Notas sobre México, 1822* (Mexico, 1950), p. 227.

[3] FV, 3, Manuel de Villamor to Rul, 3 October 1798.

silver out of the total 2,569,081 marks registered in the treasury. Elsewhere, Humboldt himself assumed that the mine regularly produced some 360,000 marks out of the 551,319 annually presented in the treasury; that is to say, for about 30 years, from 1780 to 1810, the Valenciana accounted for between 60 and 70 per cent of the total.[1] For the years 1788–1810, precise figures are available as to the current value of the Valenciana's output, costs of operation, and profits (see table 45).[2]

Table 45 *Valenciana production, costs, and profits, 1788–1810.* (In pesos)

Year	Production	Costs	Profits
1788	1,571,216	429,159	1,142,057
1789	1,633,459	448,131	1,185,328
1790	1,499,939	454,523	1,045,416
1791	1,639,085	733,321	905,764
1792	1,049,753	757,173	292,580
1793	1,042,876	738,354	304,522
1794	1,282,042	799,328	482,714
1795	1,696,640	815,817	880,823
1796	1,315,425	832,347	483,078
1797	2,128,439	878,789	1,249,650
1798	1,724,437	890,735	833,702
1799	1,584,393	915,438	668,955
1800	1,480,933	977,314	503,619
1801	1,393,438	991,981	401,457
1802	1,229,631	944,309	285,322
1803	1,232,045	937,931	294,114
1804	1,185,265	941,121	244,144
1805	1,113,756	946,346	167,410
1806	1,040,632	914,662	125,970
1807	1,191,582	1,019,781	171,801
1808	1,523,815	1,205,924	317,891
1809	1,385,611	1,204,333	181,278
Total	30,944,412	18,776,827	12,167,585

This scheme, it must be emphasised, indicates the value of ore sold and the cost of production. We must suppose that the term 'sold' includes that amount of mineral which was distributed to the partners of the mine. Their

[1] Humboldt, *Ensayo político*, pp. 353–6.

[2] This list is taken from Pedro L. Monroy, 'Las minas de Guanajuato, memoria histórico-descriptiva de este distrito minero', *Anales del ministerio de fomento de la república mexicana* x (1888) pp. 69–740. The list we print occurs on pp. 101–2; the same scheme was printed by Ward, *Mexico in 1827*, II, 140, with minor differences. The grand totals contain trifling errors of computation.

ore was priced at the current market rate and strict account was kept by the mine's general manager. Presumably they provided enough cash to meet operating costs.[1] But the mine's profits were based upon a nominal scale which presupposed that the partners paid the going rate for their ore. Whatever the method of bookkeeping, all the partners operated refining mills to handle their share of ore. But these mills, which in all did not number more than twelve, certainly did not possess sufficient capacity to refine all the Valenciana's vast product.

Information as to the movement of prices on the weekly sales is difficult to obtain. But tables 46 and 47 provide some indication of possible trends.[2]

Table 46 *Total estimated production of the Valenciana, 1774–86, as valued before refining.*

Types of Metal	Loads	Average value (pesos)	Total value (pesos)
Metal	320	350	112,000
Polvillos	8,911	175	1,559,325
Jabones	4,740	70	331,800
Apolvillados	212,840	21	4,469,640
Limosnas de iglesia	245	7	1,715
Partidos de barreteros	32,506	5	162,530
Ordinarios	263,805	3·5	1,055,220
Granza	22,282	7	155,974
Tierras apolvilladas	21,140	7	147,980
Tierras ordinarias	54,660	3·5	197,310
Granzón	17,698	3·5	61,945
Total	639,127		8,255,439
Sold for all 24 shares			1,590,995
Total			9,846,434
Costs of production			4,697,766
Profits			5,148,668

A simple comparison of these two tables reveals that prices were moving upwards, and that in addition they varied according to the season of the year. Secondly, it seems that the range of ore was falling in value, i.e. proportionally more low-grade mineral was listed in 1788 than in the earlier period. This trend, however, was reversed for at least one year, 1791, for which Humboldt found evidence to suggest that the more

[1] See Poinsett, *Notas*, p. 223.

[2] AHGP, Presos, 5 November 1807; for year 1788 see AGN, Minería 114/4, report of José Gómez Campos, November 1789.

valuable ores accounted for two-thirds of the product. He also indicated the expected silver content of certain classes of mineral (see table 48).[1]

To take the category, *apolvillados*, it appears that in 1788 refiners paid 36 to 42 ps. for a load of ore expected to yield 238 pesos of silver. On the

Table 47 *Production of Valenciana for six months of 1788.*

Type of metal	January to March: Quantity in loads (3·5 cwt.)	Average price: pesos	rls.	Product (pesos)	July to September: Quantity in loads (3·5 cwt.)	Average price: pesos	rls.	Product (pesos)
Polvillos (in cwt. only)	75	60		4,500	355	92	2	30,903
Jabones (loads)	50	80		4,045	233	109	5	25,605
Apolvillados	414	36		14,904	1,866	41	7·5	78,255
Tierras de jabones					259	25		6,485
Blancos	9,192	8		73,536	11,400	9	4	108,300
Partidos	1,188	5	3	6,385	696	5	3	3,741
Tierras de limpia, maduros	3,219	4	6	15,290	4,656	4	6	22,116
Granza de Dolores					2,940	4	3·5	13,046
Total				118,661				288,453
Sold for all 24 shares				37,385				78,053
Total				156,046				366,506
Costs				111,679				106,802
Profits				44,366				259,704

Table 48 *Production of Valenciana, 1791: types and value of ore produced.*

Proportion		Average silver content per cwt.
$\frac{5}{1000}$	polvillos, jabones	22 marks, 3 ozs.
$\frac{28}{1000}$	apolvillados	9 marks, 3 ozs.
$\frac{152}{1000}$	blanco y bueno	3 marks, 1 oz.
$\frac{815}{1000}$	granzas, tierras ordinarias, etc.	3 ozs.

other hand they paid $4\frac{1}{2}$ ps. for a load of inferior ore called *granza* or *tierras ordinarias* which was expected to yield little more than 11–12 pesos of silver. The proportional difference is striking.

The mine capable of sustaining the world's greatest silver industry was no mere pit in the ground. Rather it was an underground city, composed

[1] Humboldt, *Ensayo político*, pp. 353–6.

of a multitude of worktunnels about four to five yards in diameter which followed the lode at all depths and in all directions. Prior to 1786 ore, once cut, was brought to the surface via three great shafts serviced by whims.[1] These were:

	Cost of construction
1. Square shaft of San Antonio, 188 yards deep, serviced by 4 whims	396,000 ps.
2. Square shaft of Santo Cristo de Burgos 125 yards deep, serviced by 4 whims	95,000 ps.
3. Hexagonal shaft of Nuestra Señora de Guadalupe, 290 yards deep, serviced by 6 whims	700,000 ps.

This million peso capital investment in shafts probably amounted to over 25 per cent of the operating costs from 1774 until 1786. But the Valenciana's efficient and rapid exploitation soon drove the work tunnels beneath the levels reached by these shafts. In 1803 Humboldt found the tunnels to be 125 yards below the foot of the nearest shaft, a situation which threatened to raise the cost of porterage to the point where production would cease to be profitable. But by then work had already begun on a new shaft, the San José, cut in octagonal form, for eight whims, with a diameter of 11 yards. Projected at an estimated expense of a million pesos, by 1810 it had been driven over 600 yards through the living rock.[2] Such a shaft represented a capital installation upon a scale rarely associated with non-industrial societies. In all, the partners of the Valenciana invested over two million pesos in what Mexican miners were accustomed to call 'dead works'. Their reward was a consistent income for a period of over forty years.

Both in the construction of shafts and for daily production, labour formed the chief item of cost. In the first epoch of the Valenciana this expense was reduced by the grant of partidos. But in the 1790s, a new manager, José Quijano, a Montañés, decided to abolish this system, replacing it by an increased daily wage of 8–9 rls. for the pick and blast men. Naturally, he then was obliged to supply them with gunpowder, candles and picks, hitherto purchased from their partidos. If the causes of this decision remain obscure, its results were clear and immediate. Out of a thousand men who worked underground, only three hundred accepted the new arrangement.[3] Costs rose dramatically from 454,000 ps. in 1790 to 733,000 ps. in the following year. Moreover, production, as measured by the sale of ore, fell from 1,639,000 ps. in 1791 to 1,042,000 ps. in 1792. Profits, in consequence, also moved downwards, from over a million pesos to

[1] Humboldt, *Ensayo político*, p. 353.

[2] *Ibid.*, p. 354; Ward, *Mexico in 1827*, II, 440.

[3] AGN, Minería 114/4, report of Francisco Pallares, 5 May 1791.

292,580 ps. Admittedly this dramatic fall proved to be only a temporary adjustment: by 1795 profits once again approached the million peso mark. But expenses remained at a high level and indeed, as the mine grew deeper, slowly increased.

The termination of the partidos provoked a labour shortage of such gravity as to drive the Valenciana management to employ press-gang methods of recruitment. This custom was of course perfectly legal, being expressly mentioned in the new mining code of 1783. Nevertheless, its introduction led the regidor, José Hernández Chico, to complain to the viceroy.[1] He protested that 'night and day agents of the magistrate, called collectors or whipmen, patrol the streets for the Valenciana mine'. Fights were common since they often seized domestic servants and artisans; it had become dangerous for men of these classes to walk in the streets. Yet, he claimed, 'there is at present a surplus of useful and profitable mining labour'. Only the lack of a share of ore deterred workers from entering the Valenciana.

A visitor to the town in 1790 confirmed that the cessation of partidos had caused a massive desertion. He found that only five hundred men descended the mine each shift instead of the eight hundred that were required. The same visitor, Francisco Mourelle, a well-known Spanish naval captain, wrote an interesting description of working conditions within the mine.[2] He was shocked by the heavy loads carried by the porters, protesting at 'this degradation of rational beings to a state inferior to that of beasts'. Even a mule only bore a load of 350 pounds whereas some of these porters would carry 450 pounds, climbing up steps and ladders. He stopped a boy aged ten and found that by midday in four trips he had carried up 600 pounds of ore. In all, Mourelle was horrified with what he saw. 'The caverns of Vulcan are hardly a fit symbol of these infernal tunnels.' He also stated that many persons were forced against their will to work in the Valenciana. Theft was common and upon leaving the mine each worker was subjected to a disgusting personal examination. He commented:

> Many times I have heard that they were reduced to this condition by the abolition of the partidos and the continual lowering of their wages. It is very common to draft men down the mine, making use of the magistrate's authority. For who, unless driven by the hope of riches, would seek to work in the many places where it is

[1] AGN, Minería 94/7, José Hernández Chico to viceroy, 8 December 1790.

[2] BN (Mexico) MSS 454 (1791), ff. 15–60.

necessary to cool one's shoulders with cubes of ice, and where the steam is suffocating?[1]

All our evidence points to a decisive fall in both the earnings and status of the mine-workers of Guanajuato. Prior to the Gálvez Visitation they had acted as the virtual partners of the owners. But, then, first in the Rayas, and later in the Valenciana, they were reduced to the status of day wage-earners and subjected to a vigorous discipline. Moreover, as most mines and especially the Valenciana, grew deeper, the conditions of work deteriorated since the temperature rose the further down one went. Nevertheless, too black a picture should not be painted. The mine-workers still constituted a sort of labour aristocracy. A notion of their earnings can be gathered from a scheme drawn up in 1803 by the intendant Riaño (table 49).[2]

Table 49 *Work force and wage scale of the Valenciana, c. 1803.* (An extracted summary)

Classification of workers	Number	Wage scale (reales/day)
General manager, Asst. managers	4	
Foremen, skilled miners, artisans all on weekly wage	203	
Pick and blast men (barrenadores and piquiadores)	684	10
Porters (tenateros)	680	5–8
Peons	83	4–3
Water-wheel men (norieros)	64	5
Whim-minders (malacateros)	111	6
Maintenance and construction workers (faeneros)	180	4
Receivers of metal (despachadores)	91	5–6
Women to separate, classify ore (pepenadoras)	720	3
Crushers and packers (quebradores, cajoneros)	377	4
Miscellaneous on daily wage	135	4–6
Total number of workers	3,332	

The pick and blast men, always the highest paid workers, received 10 rls. a day, i.e. about 375 ps. a year. The porters were paid by commission, but could expect to reach up to 8 rls. By contrast the other workers only made the standard 4 rls. We may compare these earnings with the rates current in other occupations. In agriculture a peon on a hacienda obtained between 1 and 2 rls. a day; on the other hand, he could usually expect allowances of food or a plot of land.[3] In Guanajuato peons working on the construc-

[1] BN (Mexico) MSS 454 (1791), ff. 31–2.

[2] Silva Herzog, *Documentos*, pp. 75–8.

[3] Gibson, *The Aztecs*, pp. 250–1.

tion of the municipal granary collected 3 rls. a day; the pickmen building a short road to the village of Santa Ana were paid 5 rls. A skilled mine-worker, therefore, could expect to earn at least double the wage paid to a worker of comparable skill outside the industry. It should be noted that the Valenciana's rate was slightly higher than that of other mines. In the Rayas the pick and blast men only received 8 rls. a day, rather than 10 rls.[1]

The most striking feature of the Valenciana's labour force, however, lies in its size and composition. The mine required over 3,332 persons to produce 720,000 cwt. of ore.[2] But only a quarter of these men actually worked at the lode-face, cutting and blasting ore. Simple porterage from the work tunnels to the foot of the shafts absorbed another quarter. Once hauled to the pithead, the ore had then to be broken up, sorted into categories by value, and packed. In addition, the mine had to be kept drained, its shafts maintained, its whims serviced. The Valenciana employed a small army of workers, most of whom were engaged not so much in mining but in carrying, sorting, and packing the vast quantity of mineral produced. The deeper and the more extensive the work tunnels the greater the logistical expense. Moreover, as the quality of ore declined the proportion of labour costs increased since a greater amount of mineral had to be cut to produce the same value of silver.

Labour was of course by far the highest cost, comprising at least 75 per cent of the total. Yet other items were not inconsiderable, since Humboldt calculated that the mine consumed 160,000 pounds of gunpowder each year and 150,000 pounds of steel for its picks.[3] But it was the mounting expense in labour that prompted the construction of the new San José shaft. Even so, by 1808 operating costs had risen to just over 1,200,000 ps. a year. The very efficiency of the Valenciana's exploitation had driven it to a point not reached by other Mexican mines in three hundred years of production. By 1810 the mine had already cut most of the ore worth refining.

VI

In some years the Valenciana yielded more than a million pesos profit to its owners. What use did they make of such vast sums? In the first place, they did not neglect their religious obligations. They and their workers subscribed over 391,000 pesos to build the magnificent San Cayetano

[1] AHG, Haciendas, Cuentas 1770. These wages relate to the year 1804.
[2] Silva Herzog, *Documentos*, pp. 79–81.
[3] Humboldt, *Ensayo político*, pp. 353–6.

Church, an edifice which still numbers among the chief glories of Mexican churrigueresque architecture. They donated another 30,720 pesos to restore the exquisite façade of the San Diego Church in Guanajuato itself.[1]

But this subscription apart, the Valenciana's two principal shareholders mainly reinvested their profits in the mining industry of Guanajuato. The guiding spirit here was Antonio de Obregón, whose eminent services as a taxpayer were rewarded by grant of the title of Count of Valenciana. As early as 1780 the treasury noted: 'The Count of Valenciana is the particular upholder of all this industry, since he has distributed hundreds of thousands of pesos among many miners and refiners simply to foster his *patria* and foment mining for the benefit of the King and the public.'[2] This lavish outlay of cash soon caused Obregón to dominate a large section of the local industry. In 1788 his estate registered 158,266 marks at the treasury, no less than 38 per cent of all silver presented.[3]

At his death in 1786 Obregón bequeathed an estate worth 1,549,564 ps., a sum which by 1791, the year of its division among his heirs, had increased in value to over four million pesos. Leaving aside the cash in current use for the operating costs of the refining mills, we can extract from the Obregón inheritance the items shown in table 50.[4]

Table 50 *Principal items of the Obregón estate, c. 1791.* (In pesos)

Plate	68,000
Cash	719,809
Avíos	370,172
Credits advanced (good)	929,791
Credits advanced (bad)	468,533
Value of the Barreda, Flores and Salgado refining mills	265,038
Haciendas	300,740
Houses	113,365

The great accumulation of specie no doubt reflected the executors' desire not to make further investments before apportioning the inheritance. The most striking feature of the estate was the total 1,768,496 ps. issued out in loans, good and bad, and in avíos to a wide circle of local merchants, miners and refiners. The loans carried the customary 5 per cent interest,

[1] AHGP, Presos, 5 November 1807.
[2] AHH, 204/15, Guanajuato treasury to Domingo Valcárcel, 22 November 1780.
[3] AGI, Mexico 1795, Guanajuato treasury report, 27 October 1795.
[4] AHGP, Cabildo, 19 August 1793.

whereas the avíos of course implied the contractual delivery of silver at a discount. Numbered among the chief debtors were these persons:

	pesos
Juan de Villamor	74,429
Ignacio de Obregón	63,645
Manuel Portu	74,171
Fernando de Miera	30,354
Juan Vicente Alamán	20,000
Manuel Ramón de Goya	300,000

Part of the loans to these men sprang from fraud. A son-in-law of the defunct Count claimed that Juan de Villamor had 'abused his power as executor and manager [of the Obregón estate] taking for himself and distributing among various individuals more than 500,000 ps.; he consented and tolerated that Manuel Ramón de Goya should dissipate another 300,000 ps'. Goya, the Mexico City merchant who acted as an agent for Obregón, had misappropriated the consignments of silver he handled and invested the proceeds in the Zacatecas mines of Marcelo de Anza.[1] Ignacio de Obregón used his loans to finance the purchase and development of the Purísima mine in Catorce from which he made a vast fortune. But in general most of these loans and avíos supported Guanajuato refiners and miners. That is their importance. Without such a plenteous disbursement of cash the local refining industry probably could not have handled all the ore of the Valenciana, or alternatively, would have called upon Mexico City merchants to provide the necessary capital.

Much the same investment policy was followed by Pedro Luciano de Otero, the other chief shareholder in the Valenciana. The inventory of his estate, taken in 1788, the year of his death, revealed the main items shown in table 51.[2]

After Otero's death his estate was directed for his children by his brother, Manuel Antonio de Otero, a mine-mad individual, who proceeded to squander the vast profits then accruing from the Valenciana. By 1791 Otero had invested 340,452 ps. in mines belonging to himself and a further 40,026 in the San Bruno and San Refugio. In addition, he advanced as avíos 434,193 ps. to some 19 refiners and miners. In that year, however, Otero's widow acting under the guidance of her new husband, José Antonio del Mazo, obtained a division of the inheritance. The management of her share and that of her three young sons passed to Mazo. It was

[1] AGN, Vínculos 216/10, Dowager Countess to Revillagigedo, 7 June 1793. AHGP, Cabildo, 25 October 1791, 1 December 1792.

[2] AGN, Tierras 679, inventory, 31 October 1788.

only then that the full extent of Otero's prodigality was revealed. For example, in the five weeks, 20 September to 20 October 1790, he had supplied 39,843 ps. to a string of nine mines which between them only produced 20,843 ps., leaving Otero with a 19,000 ps. loss. In the same five weeks he advanced 74,794 ps. to some 17 refiners, received back in silver 31,644 ps., and so lost 43,150 ps. This latter loss was cumulative: for

Table 51 *Estate of Pedro Luciano de Otero, October 1788.*

	pesos
The Escalera, San Agustín and Cuevas refining mills	161,552
Silver being refined	366,300
Haciendas of San José del Comedero, Santa Guadalupe de las Cuevas, Atotoniquillo	245,664
Houses	114,433
3 shops and stock	73,961
Avíos to refiners	122,155
Credits advanced, good	147,170
Credits advanced, doubtful and bad	136,620
Invested in mines of San Bruno, San Refugio, Remedios	159,775
In mines of Manuel de Otero	32,395
Smaller items	315,703
	1,875,728

when the balance of accounts was struck in May 1791 Mazo found that over a period of two-and-a-half years beginning in November 1788 the same 17 men had run up debts of 487,882 ps.[1]

It is now possible to calculate in what direction the Valenciana's vast profits were expended during this first period up to the years 1791–3. In the first place, a great mass of capital was reinvested in the mining industry, nearly all of it in Guanajuato itself. A simple addition of their joint investment yields the following sum:

	pesos
Avíos to refiners	926,521
Credits advanced, good and bad	1,682,136
Invested in mines	572,648
	3,181,305

By contrast, the capital placed in land did not amount to more than 600,000 ps. Even the value of the seven refining mills owned by the two

1 AGN, Minería 141/1, report 29 October 1790; AGN, Minería 20/6, oidor Anda to viceroy, 21 March 1792.

families did not total more than 460,000 ps. and this sum was only double the value of their joint urban property—some 227,000 ps. Clearly, then, Guanajuato's prosperity rested not just upon the Valenciana's mineral production but also upon this lavish disbursement of credit and capital.

During the 20 years 1790–1810, all the older mines of Guanajuato were restored to production. In part, these renovations were promoted by the shareholders of the Valenciana, in part by the entrance of merchant capital into actual mining, with only the Rayas forming a partial exception to this rule. Of the Valenciana partners, the Oteros were the most active. Manuel Antonio de Otero inherited a fifth of his brother's estate and the portion left by his eldest nephew, who had entered the priesthood. He owned $5\frac{8}{9}$ shares of the Valenciana. During the 1790s he invested heavily in the restoration of the Sirena mine, the same property which had virtually bankrupted Lorenzo de Incháurregui in the 1750s. He also helped to finance the development of La Luz, a new discovery which was to yield magnificent profits during the 1840s. In general, it appears that Otero continued to squander his money in a variety of mines without any marked degree of success. He held shares in the Valenciana, the Sirena, the San Bernardino, the San Nicolás, the Purísima Concepción in Villapando, the San Agustín in Real del Monte, and the Purísima in Catorce. By 1802 when he took an inventory of his possessions he reckoned his fortune at 1,245,000 ps. Debts and credits balanced quite evenly, since he had lent 350,000 ps. and had borrowed 320,000 ps.[1]

In contrast to Otero, José Antonio del Mazo carefully avoided all direct mining investments. Instead, he preferred to issue loans at 5 per cent interest and to improve the refining mills and the haciendas left by Pedro Luciano de Otero. He avoided acting as an aviador. This preference would seem to indicate (for Mazo was a shrewd and cautious businessman) that an annual 5 per cent return upon capital without risk equalled the profits to be had from the aviador contracts. Whatever the case, by 1799 he had 327,877 ps. distributed in loans to a large number of individuals.[2] At about this time a correspondent noted: 'Friend Mazo is one of those who does most business in Guanajuato and if God gives him a long life he will gobble up all the city.'[3]

[1] AHGP, Cabildo, 27 April 1807. In 1797 Otero tried to register a claim to a vast stretch of land on the Michoacán coast in the jurisdiction of Coalcomán and Coahuayana. See AGN, Tierras 1283, Otero's first claim, 14 July 1797; he abandoned the project 20 April 1807; for an attack on his plan see BN (Madrid) MSS 18739, report of Bishop of Michoacán, 8 February 1805.

[2] AHG, Bienes Difuntos, September 1800.

[3] FV, 4, Francisco Alonso Terán to Diego Rul, 11 August 1798.

Mazo died in 1805 leaving most of his fortune to his wards, the two surviving Otero sons, Pedro and Mariano. In the following year they divided their inheritance, which comprised the items listed in table 52.[1]

Table 52 *Otero estate in 1806.*

	pesos
Hacienda de Cuevas	180,931
Hacienda de Atotoniquillo	140,830
Hacienda de Comedero	101,721
Hacienda de Mendoza	28,242
	451,726
Refining mills:	
Dolores	79,282
San Agustín	54,433
Barrera	38,205
San Juan Nepomuceno	28,204
San Ignacio	27,106
Purísima	15,758
	242,988
Loans at 5 per cent	316,969
Houses	205,094
Value of $2\frac{8}{9}$ Valenciana shares, held from Manuel de Otero	193,078
Debts of Manuel de Otero	139,078
Other loans	159,775
Shops	116,817
Silver bar and cash	114,550
Avíos	42,604
Smaller items	99,348
	2,082,027

Once again we may comment upon the relatively small amount invested in land—its value being here overstated since the Cuevas hacienda comprised a refining mill as well as an agricultural estate. The section loans contained one very large item, some 89,000 ps. to Fernando de la Concha, a leading refiner. For the rest the inventory reveals a pattern of continuing reinvestment in the Guanajuato mining industry if, by this time, in the cautious form of loans at 5 per cent interest.

In contrast to the Oteros, both Obregón's sons-in-law, Antonio Pérez Gálvez and Diego Rul, purchased titles of nobility and chains of haciendas. A balance sheet drawn up by the Count of Pérez Gálvez on 31 December

[1] AHGP, Cabildo, 19 July 1806.

1798 (see table 53) gives a clear picture of this policy. In 1793 his wife had inherited 3⅓ shares in the Valenciana and 597,215 ps. distributed in cash, avíos, loans, a house and the Flores refining mill.[1]

Table 53 *Estate of Antonio Pérez Gálvez, 1798.*

	pesos
3⅚ shares in Valenciana at 100,000 pesos each	383,333
Flores refining mills with stock	175,121
San Pedro Mill (rented with stock)	51,336
Santa Ana furnace with stock	15,955
Guanamé hacienda, grain stock	485,068
Its cash and loans advanced	91,467
San Pedro de Mezquite hacienda with stock	326,787
Its cash and loans advanced	31,945
José del Copal hacienda	163,976
Its cash and credit advanced	16,410
General loans advanced	281,870
Cash	17,167
Stock of warehouse	2,221
Textile workshop in Acámbaro in partnership	11,131
Mercury mine in Real de los Pitahayas, with Count of Valenciana	14,859
House in Guanajuato	30,000
Personal plate and jewellery	40,000
Smaller items	8,031
Total	2,146,677

More than half of this fortune was invested in haciendas, at least two of which lay at a considerable distance from Guanajuato. Guanamé was situated in the intendancy of Zacatecas and San Pedro del Mezquite in San Luis Potosí. Nor did Pérez Gálvez rest content with these properties since by 1810 he had bought the haciendas of San Agustín del Vergel in Zacatecas, San Juan Nepomuceno de las Norias in Durango, Soledad in New León, and San Francisco de Potosí in New Santander. By then he also owned 4½ shares in the Valenciana, 5 in the Mellado-Fraustro mine, and three refining mills.[2]

Equally anxious to become a great landowner was his brother-in-law, Diego Rul, Count of Casa Rul, who on inheriting at marriage the same amount of money as Pérez Gálvez bought the three great haciendas of San Jacinto de Ciénega Grande, Cieneguilla and Santa Rita de Tetillas, all within the Zacatecas intendancy. At one time Jesuit property, they had

[1] *Libro manual del conde de Pérez Gálvez*, balance taken 31 December 1798. This book is in the possession of Ingeniero Tiburcio Alvarez, Guanajuato.

[2] AHG, Insurgencia 1812–14, 6 February 1814; AHGP, Cabildo, 19 December 1808.

been purchased by the Count of Regla, whose son sold them to Rul. In 1803, after heavy improvement, he valued the Cieneguilla at 240,035 ps. and the Ciénega Grande at 275,452; the great hacienda of Tetillas, located in the Nieve district, he reckoned to be worth 784,560 ps., although from this value he had subtracted the 100,000 ps. mortgage it bore. This hacienda comprised 169 *sitios de granado mayor*, i.e. 169 square leagues.[1]

Rul, a man of taste as well as wealth, commissioned a house to be built in Guanajuato of which Humboldt wrote that 'one could be proud of it in the best streets of Paris or Naples'.[2] Its construction cost 112,410 ps., the architect, possibly the well-known neo-classic Eduardo Tresguerras, receiving a commission of 6,800 ps. Rul possessed two refining mills, the Salgado worth 151,389 ps. and the Sacramonte worth 57,581. He also bought 12 shares in the Mellado-Fraustro mine.

The huge land purchases of both these men followed a deliberate and probably wise policy. After all, one day the Valenciana was sure to be abandoned as the quality of its ore fell and the level of its costs rose. Only the land could offer permanent security. Moreover, both Rul and Pérez Gálvez aspired to establish noble families. It is noteworthy that the haciendas they bought all lay to the north. Equally significant was the fact that Rul acquired his estates from the second Count of Regla: the cycle of mining fortunes was often very rapid.

Although Pérez Gálvez and Rul invested the greater part of their capital in land, they did finance the renovation of the Mellado. This ancient and still potentially rich mine had lain waterlogged since the 1750s. In 1804 its shareholders, who lacked the capital necessary to drain it, finally agreed to amalgamate with the adjoining Fraustro mine, an unfruitful property of the Obregón family. In return, the three counts—Valenciana, Pérez Gálvez and Casa Rul—promised to supply some 40,000 ps. for the development of both mines. Diego Rul took an especial interest in the enterprise, buying out several of the lesser shareholders, so that he soon held 12 out of the Mellado's total 32 shares.[3] By 1808 the three brothers-in-law had spent the stipulated 40,000 ps. without much return, although the bulk of the costs were met out of weekly sales of ore. Part of the difficulty sprang from the wretched condition of the Mellado. After a visit to the mine, Rul's business manager, José Joaquín Peláez, exclaimed: 'It is painful to see how badly worked are these mines, whose owners in order to profit from them have acted like savages who to eat fruit cut

[1] AGI, Mexico 1795, valuations on 1802–3.

[2] Humboldt, *Ensayo político*, p. 343.

[3] AHGP, Cabildo, 12 November 1804.

down the tree.'[1] By this time the descendants of the original owners possessed but fractional shareholdings. The descendants of the last Marquis of San Clemente, for example, owned but $\frac{24}{60}$ of a share in the mine which had once made their family wealthy. One José Ignacio de Busto, the holder of half a share, proved unable to pay the 103 ps. costs levied upon it, and so to avoid debt had to sell it to the Count of Valenciana.[2] Whether this final development of the Mellado produced much silver we do not know. But it certainly revealed the destitution of the Busto and Aranda families.

VII

The Mellado, however, was the only ancient mine restored by the second generation of Valenciana partners. The way was thus left clear for the entrance of mercantile capital. The major instance concerned the Tepeyac mine, a relatively small property adjoining the Valenciana. First registered anew in 1787 by Juan de Revuelta and Manuel Cobo García, two Montañés merchant-aviadores, three years later the mine still remained largely flooded. It was then, in 1790, that Francisco de Septién y Arce, the guardian and heir of the great fortune left by Martín de Septién, took the last step in his journey from merchant-aviador to miner via refining. He bought eight shares in the Tepeyac in partnership with Manuel García de Zeballos and Andrés Sagaz Herrera.[3] This investment does not appear to have met with any great success. Evidence is fragmentary. Mourelle stated that its first sale of ore took place in 1790.[4] We have reference to weekly sales of ore worth 2,000 ps. during March 1798. But in his will, drawn up in November 1799, Septién stated that the mine was by then unproductive, having struck base metal.[5] The Tepeyac continued to be worked and was later managed by Angel de la Riva who married the daughter of García de Zeballos. In general, however, this entrance of an old merchant house into mining did not yield Septién the Valenciana-like profits for which he must have pined.

The second merchant-aviador firm to enter more directly into productive enterprise belonged to Juan Vicente Alamán, a former cajero of Gabriel de Arechederreta, a man who like Septién y Arce made his fortune by marriage to his former employer's widow. In 1789 Alamán, after having acted as an aviador to some ten refiners, rented his own mill. To

1 FV, 5, Peláez to Rul, 6 December 1805.

2 AHGP, Minas, 9 November 1808.

3 AHGP, Minas, 8 March 1790, 10 June 1791.

4 BN (Mexico) MSS 454 (1391), f. 38.

5 AHGP, Presos, 4 November 1799; FV, 3, Alonso García Candamo to Rul, 16 March 1798.

finance this new undertaking he borrowed 30,000 ps. from his friend, the dowager Countess of Valenciana.[1] Not content to remain a refiner, or possibly desirous of obtaining a cheaper source of ore, Alamán in conjunction with his brother Tomás and brother-in-law Salvador de Rétegui, decided to initiate once again the renovation of the Cata. All three men possessed small shareholdings in this mine by reason of their marriages with females of Busto descent. Moreover, during the early 1790s an attempt to drain the mine had only failed by reason of insufficient capital. Once again, evidence is too sparse to ascertain the outcome of this final restoration. In 1808, the year of Alamán's death, he had already advanced at least 52,000 ps. without return.[2] The interest here is to be found in the decade in which these merchants decided to enter the industry off which they had lived at a distance. It was during the 1780s when they first made the transition into refining to be shortly followed by investment in mining.

The fate of one other great mine of Guanajuato remains to be described —the Rayas. Flooded since 1780, no attempt was made to drain it until 1799. In 1790 Mourelle inspected the mine and found it worked by no more than 30 *buscones* and their 50 peons; the main shaft lay waterlogged for over 100 yards out of its 280 yards depth. He declared that the mine required a new shaft, but added that 'an invincible obstacle to this necessary work is the diversity and lack of fortune of the partners'.[3] In fact, however, the second Marquis of San Juan de Rayas owned 13 out of the 24 shares of the mine: the rest were held by the three grand-daughters of a sister of the first marquis.

By 1803 when Humboldt visited Guanajuato, the mine had been restored. Each week it sold ore worth 8,000–15,000 ps. with costs of no more than 4,000 ps.[4] To produce what possibly amounted to 790,000 ps. worth of ore a year the mine employed 560 men of whom, as in the case of the Valenciana, barely a quarter were engaged in actually working the lode.[5] The mine was still relatively shallow, but in 1805 work began on a new shaft, cut in octagonal form with a diameter of 13½ yards, which by 1810 had reached a depth of 318 yards.[6]

But with what capital and management was the Rayas restored after nearly two decades of neglect? In the first place, a vigorous Basque

1 AGN, Intendencias 79, Amat to Revillagigedo, 2 December 1784; AHGP, Cabildo 2 May 1789, 24 January 1791, and 3 April 1793.

2 AHGP, Minas, 19 June 1806, 3 December 1806, and 23 July 1808.

3 BN (Mexico) MSS 454 (1391), ff. 40–1.

4 Humboldt, *Ensayo político*, p. 354.

5 Silva Herzog, *Documentos*, pp. 79–81.

6 Ward, *Mexico in 1827*, II, 450.

manager, Francisco Iriarte, was installed to administer the mine, aided by a German expert, Francisco Fischer.[1] Then the second Marquis of San Juan de Rayas, José Mariano de Sardaneta, applied to the Valladolid diocesan court, and in 1798 received a loan of 80,000 ps. For this great sum he offered as mortgage the string of haciendas that his father had purchased, two refining mills, an inn and the family home in Guanajuato, the property in all being valued at about 420,000 ps., from which had to be discounted previous Church mortgages of 80,000 ps.[2] This new loan, granted by the enlightened Manuel Abad y Queipo, director of the diocesan fund, was undoubtedly sufficient to pay for the first stage of renovation. In addition the other partners also raised cash, one man selling a refining mill for 25,000 ps., and another borrowing 18,000 ps. from José Antonio del Mazo. These sums, combined with the weekly produce that the mine sold at the pithead to the independent refiners, must have been enough to generate sufficient surplus to finance the cutting of the new magnificent central shaft of 1805.[3] Ward stated that in the four years 1799–1803 the Rayas had yielded 400,000 ps. profit.[4]

Sardaneta encountered a serious problem in 1806 when the ecclesiastical consolidation junta demanded the payment of the Church mortgages with which his estates were charged—a total of 154,000 ps. He protested, in vain, that the new shaft would cost half a million pesos, and the Rayas had again struck water; he was obliged to pay, 12,000 ps. at once, and the remainder in eleven annual installments.[5] However, Sardaneta, elected in 1806 as administratoi-general of the mining court, used his position to recoup his losses. Despite the court's indebtedness he secretly borrowed from its funds 84,000 ps. for which he offered his Irapuato hacienda as security, and furthermore appropriated the court's income to 'repay' Antonio Bassoco, the Mexico City merchant, another 163,000 ps. which Bassoco had formerly lent to him under the court's alleged guarantee. By 1808 he had thus succeeded in taking 247,000 ps. from the court, with the destination, we may presume, of investment in his mine.[6]

The sources of the capital used to restore the Rayas do not fall into any normal pattern. First, the exceptional factor of Church funds, a

[1] AGN, Minería 225, Marquis of San Juan de Rayas, 21 September 1801; FV, 5, Peláez to Rul, 6 December 1805.

[2] ACM, 433, loan approved by Abad y Queipo, 29 November 1798.

[3] AHGP, Cabildo, 24 March 1800; 13 July 1795; 8 May 1800.

[4] Ward, *Mexico in 1827*, II, 449–50.

[5] AMM, 143, case heard 1 September 1806; see also AGN, Consolidación 5, Valladolid diocesan payments, 18 February 1808.

[6] AGI, Mexico 2254, Fausto de Elhuyar to Lizana, 17 December 1809.

source open only to those miners who owned property to offer as security. Then the loan from the merchant-capitalist Antonio Bassoco. And finally the secret redirection of mining court funds into what was, after all, their legitimate purpose. The Church, a merchant financier, the mining court, a small amount from the Otero estate, and the weekly sales of ore—all these contributed to finance the renovation of the Rayas, a renovation, we may note, which enjoyed far greater success than the operations undertaken in the Cata, the Sirena and the Mellado.

VIII

By 1809 all the great mines of Guanajuato were at work. The town's industry still retained its position as the leading producer in New Spain, with an output of 5,220,000 ps. of silver, a good fifth of total mintage for that year. As we have now amply demonstrated, the capacity to regularly produce these huge amounts of silver rested upon a highly complex structure of industrial production. What the Bajío was to New Spain, so was Guanajuato to the mining industry—highly significant, but not necessarily typical. But then, as should be by now obvious, the typical Mexican mining camp did not exist: the industry was too old, the stages of its development in different camps and different regions too diverse for any common pattern to emerge. In Guanajuato it was the Valenciana's peculiar and continuous success which generated and sustained the industry's individual structure. It was the Valenciana which freed the town from the dominance of the Mexico City mercantile capital which was so noticeable in the first half of the century. This is not to say that Guanajuato's industry and the Valenciana itself did not experience and benefit from the same factors that accounted for the Mexican mining industry's prosperity after 1767—the reduction in costs, the higher profits and the greater availability of capital. But ultimately the discovery and, equally important, the efficient exploitation of the Valenciana, added a new dimension and perspective to the play of these factors. They operated in a more propitious terrain than was to be encountered elsewhere. Not, of course, that these assertions can be proved. Could the Valenciana have been developed so successfully before the 1760s? Here is a question for future mining historians.

CHAPTER 9

THE ÉLITE

There is no certain or statistical way of isolating the members of Guanajuato's social élite from the broad mass of the population. The racial and occupational categories which can be extracted from the 1792 census are insufficiently refined for such a purpose. True, it can be argued that all three hundred peninsular Spaniards then resident in the town should be defined as at least *potential* members of the élite. But according to what criteria are we to distinguish the potential from the actual, or, more concretely, a petty tradesman from a Septién? And in the case of the creoles the difficulty is even worse. Rather than attempting to manipulate such rough and ready statistics it is preferable to concentrate our attention upon a more restricted group of individuals, i.e. the very wealthy and the office-holders.

The problem of selection here becomes important. How can we obtain a representative sample of Guanajuato's upper élite? What is the best method of studying this group? Fortunately, a relatively simple solution can be found by comparing the economic élite with the political élite, defining that latter group as those persons who composed the town council, the merchant and mining deputations and, to a lesser extent, the officers of the militia. The most cursory examination reveals that these two élites were virtually identical. The possession of public office closely followed the distribution of wealth.

With our group roughly identified, how can we come to a closer definition? Here the paucity of available evidence greatly restricts the inquiry. For example, was there any rivalry between creole and gachupín, any jealousy between long-established families and the new rich; any tension between the élite and the populace? Alas, our material does not yield answers to such questions. On the whole, the most promising line of approach has been to study families—to find out when they came to the New World, whom they married, and what occupations they pursued. Certain families immediately chose themselves. No analysis of the town's élite could be complete without a close examination of the great miners and merchants—the Busto and Aranda, the Sardaneta, the Obregón and Otero, the Septién and the Pérez Marañón. These genealogical exercises soon disclosed some fascinating patterns. In many cases the division between gachupín and creole was soon resolved into little more than a distinction of generations: creole lawyers were often the sons of gachupín merchants and gachupín merchants were equally often the sons-in-law of creole miners. Our method, it must be emphasised, is overwhelmingly descriptive; but the sample is sufficiently generous as to include most members of Guanajuato's upper élite and therefore some convincing general arguments can be extracted from it. In order to make full sense of the exercises that follow, the reader is advised to consult the genealogical charts in the appendices.

I

It is convenient to begin with the Bustos since the family, in addition to being both wealthy and numerous, comes close to being the paradigm case from which all other creole genealogies in Guanajuato can be construed. Its first member to arrive in the New World, one Pedro de Busto, settled in León during the latter half of the sixteenth century. It was his grandson, Francisco de Busto y Jerez, who became a silver miner in Guanajuato, renovating the Mellado and gathering together a considerable fortune. His children, two sons and a daughter, built upon his work: they maintained the Mellado, and developed the Cata. His eldest son, Francisco Matías, the Marquis of San Clemente, was the first miner in Guanajuato to obtain such a title of nobility.[1] His daughter, Josefa, married an Extremeño, the merchant-aviador Manuel de Aranda y Saavedra.[2]

The Marquis begot ten children—six daughters and four sons. Of his sons two entered the priesthood; another, Juan Alejo, pursued a brief but unsuccessful career as a miner; the eldest, Francisco Cristóbal, inherited his father's title and retired to León where he ended his days in relative poverty since he did not receive much more property than any other heir. His son, Pedro de Busto y Peredo, the third Marquis, was obliged to renounce the title since he could not afford to pay the special tax levied on the nobility.[3] Pedro provided a piquant comment on family decline when he informed his mother of his intention to marry his mistress, a mulatto servant girl. The indignant dowager marchioness appealed to the magistrates to prevent this unequal match.[4] In little more than one generation, therefore, the Busto sank into social obscurity following the ruin of the Cata and the Mellado and the division of the first Marquis' estate.

[1] Ortega y Pérez Gallardo, *Historia genealógica*, I, *Marqués de San Clemente*; see also Lohman Villena, *Los americanos en las órdenes nobiliarias*, I, 12.

[2] AHGP, Cabildo, 30 August 1730.

[3] AGN, Vínculos 152/3, f. 134.

[4] AHL, Caja 1786/17, appeal heard 25 October 1786.

If the family continued to figure in Guanajuato it was through the female line. For all six daughters of the first Marquis married peninsular Spaniards—two chose Extremeños, Antonio Jacinto Diez Madroñero and Gonzalo de Aranda, both nephews and cajeros of Manuel de Aranda y Saavedra; the remaining four preferred Basques. For the most part their husbands relied upon their wives' dowries and the backing of the first Marquis to start their business careers.[1] This pattern of matrimony also prevailed among their children. Juan José Compains and Francisco Azpilcueta, both also Basques, inherited the business of their fathers-in-law.[2] In some cases the pattern repeated itself in the third generation. Gabriel de Arechederreta and Juan Vicente Alamán married a granddaughter of Antonio Jacinto Diez Madroñero. The latter's son, Lucas Alamán, the distinguished nineteenth-century historian and statesman, thus possessed a decidedly curious genealogy.[3] Although on his mother's side he could claim an American descent that stretched back to the sixteenth century, for the last three generations that ancestry had been mediated through successive unions with immigrant peninsulars. Alamán had to go to his great-grandfather—to the Marquis of San Clemente himself—before he could find an American Spaniard among his male ancestors.

The Arandas underwent much the same phenomenon. All three of Josefa's daughters married Basques, although what happened to their descendants is less clear.[4] The careers of her seven sons is similarly hard to trace. One joined the priesthood; another settled in Spain; Juan Ignacio became a miner. But only Ramón Luis did particularly well; he won the hand of an heiress, who owned estates in Silao, and ran a successful mine, the San Ramón which he finally sold to the Valenciana. Much against his wishes, however, his only daughter married an immigrant, one Juan

[1] Gregoria married Francisco de Mendizábal, a Basque: AHGP, Minas, 6 August 1785; María Manuela married Domingo de Alegría from Biscay: AHGP, Cabildo, 7 July 1736; Ana Gertrudis married Lorenzo de Olazábal from Guipuzcoa: AGN, Minería 158/3, last will, 18 September 1773; Josefa married Antonio Jacinto Diez Madroñero from Extremadura: AHG, Bienes Difuntos 1761–79, last will, 16 November 1779; Francisca Anastasia married Gonzalo de Aranda y Saavedra from Extremadura: AHG, Bienes Difuntos 1761–79, will, 14 September 1779; María Josefa married first Francisco de Ochoa, and later Domingo de Aribe from Navarre: AHGP, Presos, 24 August 1806, bound in 1803 volume.

[2] Compains, from Navarre, married María Josefa de Alegría, his second wife was María Josefa de Ochoa: AHG, Bienes Difuntos 1785; AHGP, Cabildo, 1 May 1786. Azpilcueta, from Navarre, married María de Olazábal: AGN, Minería 158/2, will, 21 April 1794.

[3] Lohman Villena, *Los americanos en las órdenes nobiliarias*, II, 271–72. Alamán, *Documentos diversos* (4 vols.; Mexico, 1947), IV, 11.

[4] María Rafaela married Juan Antonio Quintana from Biscay: AHG, Bienes Difuntos 1742–61, settlement, 27 July 1756. María Antonia married José Antonio Mendizábal from Biscay: AGN, Vínculos 144/1, lawsuit, 11 October 1751. Ana Francisca married Francisco Alipasolo, also a Basque.

López.[1] Finally we may note that at least two of the four daughters of Andrés de Busto, the first Marquis' brother, also chose peninsular Spaniards. Bernardo Fernández de Riaño thus inherited part of Andrés' mining interests.[2]

Here then, in the seemingly arid study of genealogy, some salient features of creole society can be discerned. The Busto family experienced an almost Sabine seizure of its females. No less than eleven of the thirteen daughters of the first Marquis, of Andrés, and of Josefa, married peninsular Spaniards. The importance of these alliances for the immigrants cannot be overestimated: many based their business careers upon their wife's dowry. In this particular case, of course, the failure of both the Cata and Mellado slowly led several into bankruptcy, but this does not detract from the broad implications of the marriage pattern. In effect it appears that a large proportion of creole women of good family were reserved for gachupines.

At the same time we can also detect a certain withdrawal from society of the creole sons: some followed their brothers-in-law into the bankruptcy caused by mining failures. But in addition, three out of the eleven sons of the first Marquis, Josefa and Andrés entered the priesthood. And in the next generation a full nine grandsons followed the same celibate career. When in 1767 the Jesuits were expelled from New Spain, no less than five Busto grandsons sailed for Italy.[3] If this propensity for the Church among creole sons is combined with the marriage preferences of creole daughters then once again the peculiarly favourable position of the immigrant Spaniards becomes manifest.

But not all families possessed the paradigm characteristics of the Bustos. The Sardanetas, blessed with a certain infertility, outlived the century. In the first instance, however, they showed almost exactly the same pattern. As in the case of the Bustos, they could trace their arrival in New Spain back to the late sixteenth century. It was a grandson of the first settler, José de Sardanata, who acquired the Rayas and assured the family's social survival. He belonged to that critical second generation; he numbered a priest and a lawyer among his brothers; both he and his brother Pedro

[1] Ramón married Ana Josefa de Laris y Olavarría, of Silao. See ACM, 617, 27 February 1788; AGI, Mexico 1732, protest to audiencia, 12 October 1781.

[2] Andrea married Bernardo Fernández de Riaño, from Rioja: AHGP, Minas, May 1784; Antonia married Francisco de Iguirátegui from Guipuzcoa: AHGP, Cabildo, 26 February 1736.

[3] For these priests consult the family genealogy. The five Jesuits were Francisco and José de Alegría, Manuel and Pedro Arenas, and Francisco de Iguirátegui. See Cuevas, ed., *Tesoros documentales*, pp. 234–6, 258.

took their chance at silver mining. Of his four daughters two married peninsular Spaniards; one son entered the Jesuit order and the other became the first Marquis of San Juan de Rayas. But here the parallels with the Bustos, hitherto so exact, ended. By some genetic quirk only three grandchildren issued from his five married children, and one of these in turn was infertile.[1] This lack of descendants proved to be a blessing in disguise since it prevented the excessive subdivision of the family estate. The second Marquis inherited shares in the Rayas and the property of his aunts as well as of his father.

The Sardanetas, therefore, constituted a striking exception to the general rule of family decline among the creole élite. They weathered the usual shipwreck of mining fortunes. Yet it must be pointed out that their resilience sprang from the skill and enterprise of José de Sardaneta. After all, we hear little of the descendants of his brothers. In later years the Rayas employed several Sardanetas as foremen; whether theirs was a legitimate descent we do not know. One curious occurrence may be mentioned. During the 1790s the Rayas was managed for a brief period by one Melchor de Sardaneta, an immigrant from Guipuzcoa, who claimed to be a distant relative of the Marquis.[2] In general the family's survival rested upon the possession of an exceptionally good mine, the Rayas, and upon the peculiar infertility of José de Sardaneta's descendants.

By a striking coincidence almost too perfect for verisimilitude, both the principal shareholders in the Valenciana, Antonio de Obregón and Pedro Luciano de Otero, belonged to the same generation of settlement as the two other great Guanajuato miners, Francisco de Busto y Jerez and José de Sardaneta. Both were grandsons of Spanish immigrants. During the 1680s, Obregón's grandfather left the small hamlet of Llerana in the mountains of Santander to establish himself in León, where he quickly became a municipal magistrate and a prominent member of its society.[3] This position was inherited and maintained by his children and grandchildren. Antonio de Obregón y Alcocer, the only son of his father's first marriage, was not therefore the ignorant fiddle player of legend. He received an education to the level of the baccalaureate and in March 1742 applied to the Valladolid diocesan authorities for the first tonsure and admittance into the four lesser clerical orders.[4] But he did not pursue these sacerdotal ambitions;

[1] Ortega y Pérez Gallardo, *Historia genealógica*, I, *Marqués de San Juan de Rayas*; AHGP, Cabildo, 1 December 1730, 2 November 1786; AHGP, Presos, 12 May 1746; AGN, Vínculos 171/2, 12 March 1782.

[2] AHGP, Cabildo, 1 March 1806, he was a native of Oñate in Guipuzcoa.

[3] AGI, Mexico 1795, here is to be found the entire Obregón genealogy.

[4] Antonio Obregón was baptised in San Francisco de Pénjamo, 24 June 1722, but reared in

instead he sought his fortune in the silver mines of Guanajuato. At first he found little more than a wife: in her will she declared that when they married 'neither of us had any money'.[1] And in 1760 Obregón ceded eight shares of his mine, then called Animas, to Pedro Luciano de Otero for no more than 400 pesos.[2]

Once recognised as a wealthy man, Obregón soon figured as a town councillor, a municipal magistrate, interim alcalde mayor, and Count of Valenciana. No doors were barred to a silver millionaire. But then, socially speaking, Obregón belonged by origin to the creole élite even if during his younger days he was penniless. Moreover he was distantly related to the Bustos; his paternal grandmother was the daughter of Ana de Busto, the sister of the grandfather of the first Marquis of San Clemente! Obregón's wife was also the grand-daughter of a peninsular Spaniard. Her mother's first marriage had been to a Sardaneta.[3] It is interesting commentary upon provincial society at this time that his wife could not read nor write.[4]

After Obregón's death his vast fortune soon attracted the usual swarm of immigrant fortune hunters. His eldest daughter, María Gertrudis, was courted by one Antonio Pérez Gálvez, a Malagueño, the son, his enemies alleged, of a carpenter, who traded upon his distant relation to the Gálvez family. He was the close friend of Francisco Fernández de Córdova, a fellow Malagueño and superintendent of the mint, who later married a grand-daughter of the Marquis of Jaral. Despite these auspicious connexions, he did not impress the dowager Countess of Valenciana. She forbade the union, appealed to the Council of the Indies to prevent it, and tried to persuade her daughter to marry Manuel García de Quintana, the Montañés whose Septién wife had died. Apprehensive that his beloved one and her fortune might escape him, Pérez Gálvez convinced María Gertrudis to elope—to Guanajuato's only decent inn, where the same night they were discovered. Shortly after this event their relations were sanctified by the Church.[5] Pérez Gálvez soon acquired more than sufficient means to purchase the title of count and several large haciendas. He survived the wars of Independence, and lived to have dealings with the British mining companies, whose manager, not impressed by his commercial rectitude,

León. See ACM, 743, Episcopal approval for his application, 6 March 1742. His half-brothers, the Obregón y Arce, continued to play an important role in the life of León.

1 AHG, Bienes Difuntos 1801–5, the will of Countess of Valenciana, 20 October 1798.

2 AHGP, Minas, 15 September 1760, 24 September 1760.

3 See the bulky genealogy in AGI, Mexico 1795.

4 AGN, Vínculos 216/10, Countess to Revillagigedo, 7 June 1793.

5 AGI, Mexico 1777, Dowager Countess' complaint to Council of the Indies, 22 December 1790; on the elopement see AGI, Mexico 1893, Revillagigedo to Alcudia, 30 June 1794.

described him in the following terms: 'This Count Gálvez was an Andalusian shoemaker ... by his intriguing spirit, he contrived to marry the daughter of Obregón, Count of Valenciana, and exchanged his lapstone for a coronet.'[1] This English opinion was shared by his brother-in-law, the young Count of Valenciana, who in a letter to Viceroy Revillagigedo, complained: 'We do not agree either in our character or our ways of thinking ... mine is very reserved, taciturn and opposed to all plots, labyrinths and entanglements, but Pérez Gálvez's character is all the contrary.'[2] He was affronted with the scandal and then hurt by intrigues within the family.

Obregón's other daughter, María Ignacia, also married a Malagueño, but the alliance did not meet with any opposition. Her husband, Diego Rul, came from a good family; he was educated; he already possessed a trading firm in Salamanca worth 40,000 ps.[3] A man of advanced tastes as his magnificient neo-classic mansion indicated, he befriended the gifted mathematics lecturer in Guanajuato's college, José Antonio de Rojas. When the young man fled to the United States after being accused of heresy and freethinking he stopped for a time in Rul's hacienda in Aguascalientes. Rul himself was denounced to the Inquisition by an embittered creole lawyer, Lic. Vicente Figueroa, who claimed that Rul owned forbidden books and that in conversation he had affirmed that Jesus Christ 'was a good and a just man, but not God'. But these charges were dismissed.[4] Whatever the case, Rul clearly belonged to that small group of enlightened Spaniards, men such as the intendant, Riaño, who then lived in Guanajuato.

If Obregón's two sons-in-law displayed both energy and talent in the acquisition of wealth and public honours, his own son, the second Count of Valenciana, did little to distinguish himself. He neither accepted local office nor approached the viceregal court. While still a minor, he wasted over 41,000 ps. in two years on personal expenses and lent out another 51,000 in business loans. This extravagance prompted his alarmed mother to complain to the viceroy, who ordered an inquiry into the management of Obregón's estate. Ironically enough, his letter was read out to the Countess by the unsuspecting young Count, who later described the scene in these terms: 'I am not capable of expressing to Your Excellency [the Viceroy] the shock given to me in the very act of reading, since it

[1] James, *Remarks on the Mines*, p. 32.

[2] AGN, Vínculos 216/10, Count to Revillagigedo, 8 July 1793.

[3] AGI, Mexico 1795, contains a statement of his ancestry and property.

[4] For Rojas see AGN, Inquisición 1357, f. 158. For the accusation see AGN, Inquisición 1434/3, f. 96, report by Lic. José Vicente Figueroa, 30 January 1807.

occurred so suddenly and unaware, especially since the very mother who gave me birth had treated me with so little concern in making public my concerns.'[1]

On the other hand, his half-brother, Ignacio de Obregón, who was, if we accept his enemies' accusations, the first Count's illegitimate son, displayed both business sense and social aspiration. He had settled in Guanajuato as a child where 'in the company of my father señor don Antonio de Obregón y Alcocer . . . I followed the honourable career of mining'.[2] Later, however, he returned to live in León, to serve as a regidor and municipal magistrate, and to work in Catorce where in partnership with the Basque miner Francisco Miguel de Aguirre he developed the highly successful Purísima mine. From his mining profits Obregón purchased a chain of haciendas in León and Pénjamo so that when Ward visited Mexico his family numbered among the chief landowners of the area.[3] In later years Obregón established his residence in Mexico City and became a member of the mining court and an intimate of Viceroy Iturrigaray, a clear proof that in Mexico wealth could outweigh accusations of illegitimacy. His creole social ambitions received severe condemnation from Diego Rul's peninsular business manager, José Joaquín Peláez, who wrote to his employer:

> I do not doubt that Obregón will remain at the doors, and that is the only benefit he has got from living in Mexico City and neglecting his business. What a pity, compadre, and what blindness to strive to ruin oneself by this mania for cutting a figure, which, well considered, is despicable. How much better it would be to live in León and be there the first. That crowd of empty-headed flatterers just rush to fleece the fools from the north.[4]

The last great mining family to be considered, the Oteros, afford further corroboration for the patterns of behaviour already observed. Pedro Luciano de Otero was the grandson of an immigrant from Castile who had settled in San Luis Potosí. Two of his brothers, José Joaquín and Agustín, entered the priesthood.[5] He himself set up a small shop in the Rayas mining village. His success he owed to his brother Manuel Antonio, to whom he bequeathed a fifth of his entire estate, 'in consideration of his being for many years the manager of all my fortune and business'.[6] In a

[1] AGN, Vínculos 216/10, Count to Revillagigedo, 8 July 1793.

[2] AGN, Minería 152/10, Ignacio Obregón's statement, 1 June 1801. See also AGI, Mexico 2246, testimonials to Obregón, presented 28 January 1803. Obregón grew very indignant at accusations of his illegitimacy, yet never stated who his mother was.

[3] Ward, *Mexico in 1827*, II, 152, 502.

[4] FV, 5, Peláez to Rul, 25 October 1805.

[5] AGN, Vínculos 282/2, statement of ancestry, 21 February 1809.

[6] AHGP, Cabildo, 29 October 1788.

subsequent lawsuit a witness stated that 'against the will and excuses of his brother, Manuel continued to supply the Valenciana'. And Pedro himself was alleged to have said: 'All that I have I owe to my brother Manuel, since without him I would have had nothing.'[1]

In these circumstances it was only natural that Manuel should continue to direct the estate after Pedro's death, the more especially since the eldest son, the only child of Pedro's first matrimony had joined the Church. Manuel and his brother's widow acted as guardians of the three sons of the second marriage. But within three years his control of most of this vast fortune was wrested from him by an immigrant Spaniard, one José Antonio del Mazo, who had married Pedro de Otero's widow. The contrast between the two men is so striking as to demand closer inspection.

A favourable description of Manuel de Otero, given by the judge Juan Francisco Anda, declared him to be 'without vices or defect other than an extraordinary propensity for the excavation and working of mines, in which he has spent the greater part of his possessions'.[2] And, we may add, a good portion of his wards' inheritance. His nephew, Mariano de Otero, provided a somewhat different picture:

> Don Manuel fell from an inferior post as his brother's assistant to be a muleteer by which he supported himself for nine years, without more property than a mule, a *machete* and the rough clothes of that condition and when don Pedro bettered his fortunes, he summoned don Manuel to his side, who then suddenly began to enjoy the pleasures of abundance without more curb than the repressed desires of his former misery. . . . He abandoned himself to the thirst of gold.[3]

The social vista uncovered by this description is intriguing. Clearly the Oteros lived on the margin of the respectable classes. The employment possibilities for an impoverished and relatively uneducated creole were remarkably limited. We can note that despite his great wealth Manuel de Otero never became a municipal magistrate or a town councillor.

By comparison the social background of Otero's supplanter, José Antonio del Mazo, was more explicit and distinguished. His family had acted for generations as regidores in the valley of Meruelo in Santander; he himself had farmed the pulque tax for the Tula district, and later served as the excise official in the same area.[4] In addition his connexions were

[1] AGN, Tierras 678, f. 146.

[2] AGN, Minería 20/6, Anda to Revillagigedo, 21 March 1792.

[3] AGN, Tierras 678, ff. 265–6, report of Lic. Oláez, 25 September 1810.

[4] Fermín de Sojo y Lomba, *Ilustraciones a la historia de la M.N. y S.L. Merindad de Trasmiera* (2 vols.; Madrid, 1931), II, 360, 438; also *Prueba de hidalguía* of José Antonio del Mazo y Munar, *real cédula*, 14 May 1778 (a bound mss. volume in the possession of Señor Manuel Leal, Guanajuato).

excellent; one nephew, Anselmo de Viernia y Mazo, acted as *asesor general* to the Santa Fé viceroyalty and another, Nicolás, was a brigadier in the army. His wealth enabled him to give employment to another nephew, Modesto de Villa, to whom he entrusted the management of a refining mill.[1] His prosperity attracted other relatives, since on one occasion he was to be found proposing for advancement 'three young men recently come from Spain and recommended by relatives'.[2] Evidently a man of intelligence as well as enterprise, he possessed an extensive library that comprised 106 titles. In his will he left a legacy of 8,500 ps. for the establishment of schools in Meruelo besides other sums for members of his family still resident in the valley.[3]

II

The astonishing regularity with which immigrants snapped up mining heiresses should not obscure the fact that most peninsular Spaniards in Guanajuato started off their business life as cajeros, and made their fortunes, if at all, through trade. Merchants comprised a substantial part of the town's élite. In the years after 1770 the two most important mercantile families were the Pérez Marañón and the Septién. That both were from Santander was not fortuitous since the 1793 census revealed that Montañeses formed by far the largest provincial group among the immigrant community. Moreover, the 1781 mercury distribution indicated that the most important merchant-aviadores came from the same region. More surprising is the fact that both the families in question took their origin from the small village of Llerana in Vallecarriedo in Santander, the same place from which Antonio de Obregón's grandfather had taken leave in the previous century.

It is the history of the Septién family which best reveals both the pattern of peninsular immigration and the formation of a creole élite. No less than four generations of Septién settled in the Bajío: the perspective is therefore considerably more extensive than for our other lineages. The first immigrants of whom we have notice were two brothers, Agustín and Manuel de Septién y Montero, who sometime in the second quarter of the eighteenth century settled in Guanajuato and León respectively. Agustín proved to be the more successful merchant; he also married an heiress, the daughter of José de Austri, regidor *alférez real* of León. By the time Agustín died he had accumulated a fortune of over 200,000 ps., for the

[1] AHG, Bienes Difuntos 1801–5, will, 18 March 1805.

[2] AHGP, Cabildo, 21 March 1804.

[3] See above, note 1; also Sojo y Lomba, *Ilustraciones*, p. 438.

most part invested in a group of small haciendas. In Guanajuato he purchased the office of regidor *fiel ejecutor*, a post which remained in the family for the rest of the century.[1]

At the age of eighteen, Agustín's eldest son, Pedro Antonio de Septién Montero y Austri, became alcalde ordinario of León, but following his marriage he transferred his residence to Querétaro, where for over 37 years he served as regidor *alférez real*, an office he inherited from his wife's father, Pedro de Primo y Jordán. He played an important role in Querétaro's public life, escorting the Jesuits to Veracruz in 1767, and promoting the establishment of a royal tobacco factory in the town. In the five-year period 1796–1801 he acted as the subdelegate of Celaya and Salvatierra, a lucrative office that carried with it an income of over 3,000 ps.[2] Pedro survived long enough to be accused in 1808 of being an advocate of independence; the charge he was able to rebut, although he admitted his advocacy of a Mexican provincial junta similar to those formed in the Peninsula.[3]

Both of his brothers also took office, José Domingo as regidor *alguacil mayor* in Querétaro and José Ildefonso as regidor of León. The latter appears to have lived off his inherited estates: in 1787 he was obliged to increase the mortgage on his San Nicolás hacienda from 5,000 ps. to 14,000 ps.; yet the property was only valued at 25,400 ps. Nor did he pay off the new mortgage within the stipulated five years since in 1807 it still carried the full 14,000 ps.[4]

As was to be expected in such a family, Septién's sister María married a gachupín, Bernabé de Bustamante, a native of Toranzo in the Santander mountains, who acted both as merchant and aviador in Guanajuato. A leading member of its Montañés community, he was apparently a cultivated individual who owned a considerable library. His tastes rather than his occupation were evidently inherited by his sons, José María, Miguel, and Benignio, since all three taught as professors in Guanajuato's college. José María became a well-known natural scientist in the years following Independence.[5] Pedro de Septién had another gachupín brother-in-law. Antonio de Septién y Castillo married his wife's sister María Gertrudis Primo y Jordán. This Septién, a distant relative, represented the second

[1] AHGP, Cabildo, 21 February 1750, 5 February 1772, and 13 February 1744.

[2] See the testimonials to Septién's public service in AGI, Mexico 1790, Marquina to Caballero, 26 June 1802.

[3] AGN, Historia 49/43, accusation made 26 September 1808. Septién also published a small devotional work. See Beristáin, *Biblioteca*, IV, 334.

[4] ACM, 617, 25 June 1787; AGN, Consolidación 5, 25 February 1807.

[5] AGI, Mexico 1795, in a section devoted to Obregón family; also Romero, *Noticias*, p. 170.

stage of immigration from the village of Llerana, since his home town was San Vicente de la Barquera, situated on the coast of Santander, where his father had been regidor. His grandfather was registered as a householder in Llerana. In Querétaro, his chosen home, he served as regidor, engaged in commerce and invested in land.[1] It may be noticed in passing that the grandfather of their wives, Juan de Primo y Jordán, had also come from Santander.[2]

Curiously enough, the second generation of Septién to settle in the Bajío reproduced almost exactly the pattern established by the Querétaro branch of the family. This time three brothers immigrated, Martín, Francisco and Juan Fernando, the sons of Bernardo de Septién y Montero, the brother of Agustín and of Manuel, who had remained at home in Spain. A brief glance at Bernardo's background will not be misplaced, since it will permit a comparison between the Peninsula background and the subsequent career of his children. Information can be obtained from the invaluable *catastro* or census prepared in 1752 by the Marquis of Ensenada.

Bernardo de Septién lived in the hamlet of Llerana, situated in the valley of Carriedo not far from Santander. In 1752 the village contained 72 householders (*vecinos*) of whom 39 were listed as farmers and 30 as widows: all without exception were counted as hidalgos.[3] Most dwelt in their farmhouses scattered across the valley, since the actual village itself possessed little more than ten houses. Bernardo de Septién was described in the *catastro* as a farmer by occupation and an hidalgo in rank. His four sons were all absent; three had gone to the Indies, and the other was a priest—'a friar of the Trinidad Calzada'. Clearly a farmer of some substance, he kept two servants, who lived in a separate house, also his property, situated some ten paces away from his own dwelling place. He possessed a yoke of oxen, three cows with calves, fourteen sheep and one goat. His property, located in separate tracts throughout the valley, comprised arable and pasture lands as well as vegetable gardens.[4] A brief comparison with the listed property of other householders would suggest that he belonged to the richer group within the valley; and unlike many his land was not burdened with any mortgage. The picture emerges of the prosperous peasant, whose children emigrated not through dire necessity

[1] CV, Sala de Hijosdalgo 1145/9, certification, 15 January 1733, where Septién is described as a merchant of Querétaro; see also Martínez Cossío, *Los caballeros*, pp. 269–70.

[2] AGI, Mexico 1790, Marquina to Caballero, 26 June 1802.

[3] Tomás Maza Solano, *Nobleza, hidalguía, profesiones y oficios en la montaña segun los padrones del catastro del Marqués de la Ensenada* (4 vols.; Santander, 1953–61), I, nos. 4970–5066.

[4] APS, Catastro del Marqués de Ensenada, 475, Libro Llerana, f. 79, 17 May 1752.

(although the inheritance clearly could not maintain all four brothers in comfort) but out of a desire to participate in the new-found wealth of their two uncles. There was, after all, a marked difference between a yoke of oxen, three cows and fourteen sheep, and the 200,000 pesos accumulated by their uncle Agustín.

In part their aspirations were justified. Martín de Septién became the leading merchant in Guanajuato, the owner of an estate worth over 600,000 ps. His wealth and position strengthened the entire Montañés community in Guanajuato and clearly acted as a magnet for further immigration from Vallecarriedo. Septién recruited his cajeros from among his compatriots and as an aviador chose to back mainly Montañés refiners. For example, he employed Martín de la Riva, a native of Vallecarriedo, as his cajero, and financed Martín's brother Pedro as a refiner. A third brother Angel entered mining. These immigrants were by no means the *polizones* of popular imagination. Septién's chief manager, Manuel García de Quintana, another native of Vallecarriedo, came from very much the same class as José Antonio del Mazo or Diego Rul. His father was a lawyer, his brother a Carmelite priest. Similarly the de la Rivas had another brother who was a 'doctor', presumably a priest.[1] It must not be thought that family connexions alone sufficed to create a fortune. Neither of Martín's two brothers did particularly well. Francisco lost money in the bankruptcy of his father-in-law, the regidor Agustín de la Torre, and it appears lived largely off the proceeds of his post as regidor *fiel ejecutor*, an office he inherited from his uncle Agustín.[2]

Francisco de Septién y Montero had four daughters and two sons. At least two, possibly three, of these girls found Montañés husbands, one choosing García de Quintana, Martín's cajero.[3] His eldest son, José María de Septién, qualified as a lawyer, married María Pérez Marañón, a daughter of the Montañés merchant, who brought him a small inheritance; and after his father's death, became regidor *fiel ejecutor*, an office which he later claimed yielded an income of 2,000 ps. a year.[4] His financial future was assured when in 1805 his own daughter María Josefa married Pedro de Otero (the younger), a shareholder in the Valenciana.[5] José María de Septién found himself in exactly the same position as his second cousin, Pedro Antonio de Septién of Querétaro. Both of these first generation creoles took municipal office and public affairs for their career; both were

[1] For Quintana, AHGP, Cabildo, 18 September 1787; for de la Riva, AHGP, Cabildo, 3 September 1786.

[2] AHGP, Cabildo, 13 January 1783.

[3] AHGP, Cabildo, 21 November 1808.

[4] AHGP, Cabildo, 17 August 1793; AHG, Insurgencia 1812–14, 25 January 1814.

[5] AHGP, Cabildo, 14 May 1805.

confronted with the inevitable gachupín brothers-in-law who made great fortunes in trade and mining. Little evidence, however, survives as to their feelings about this curious social situation.

The third generation of Septién to settle in Guanajuato was represented by Francisco de Septién y Arce, a native of Llerana, who became the cajero of his distant uncle Martín de Septién. He possessed other close relatives in Guanajuato, since his maternal uncle, Francisco de Escalada y la Flor had settled in Guanajuato earlier in the century; his daughter married Juan Vicente Alamán. With such connexions, Septién y Arce could hardly fail to do well, but he scored a magnificent coup when he won the hand of Martín de Septién's young widow and so inherited all his uncle's vast wealth. His three sons founded the third branch of the Septién family resident in the Bajío.[1]

After three generations of immigration one might have surmised that enough was enough. In fact, yet another three brothers arrived from the Peninsula—Bartolomé, Baltazar and Martín de Septién y Arce, 'nephews' as always of their predecessor, who entered, respectively, refining, ranching in Silao, and the priesthood. But their careers suffered an abrupt termination in 1810 when the insurgents killed Bartolomé and Baltazar.[2] Martín, protected by his cloth, escaped with a few bruises.

That the pattern observable among the Septién was not uncommon can be demonstrated from the case of the Pérez Marañón. Members of this family lived in the same village of Llerana. In the 1752 *catastro*, Francisco Pérez Marañón, by occupation a farmer and in rank an hidalgo, was listed as owning a yoke of oxen, and three cows with calves. He held less land than Bernardo de Septién, his property was charged with a small mortgage, and he employed but one servant-woman. By that year two sons, José and Joaquín, had already emigrated to the Indies; his remaining son Manuel was was soon to join them.[3] Evidently his status as an hidalgo was not secure since during his absence from the valley a census taken in 1758 omitted to include him in this class. He was therefore obliged to rectify the error in the Valladolid Chancery court.[4]

Of the three migrant brothers, Joaquín and Manuel died in modest economic circumstances. José, however, who lived to bury both of them

1 Septién had three sons, José Migel, José Francisco, and José María. See AHGP, Presos, 4 November 1799.

2 For Bartolomé see AHGP, Cabildo, 11 January 1809, 9 September 1809; for Baltazar see AGI, Mexico 1686, Iturrigaray to Caballero, 26 April 1806; for Martín see Alamán, *Historia*, I, 277. Also AHGP, Cabildo, 31 August 1811.

3 APS, Catastro del Marqués de Ensenada, 475, Libro Llerana, ff. 158–60, 22 May 1752.

4 CV, Sala de Hijosdalgo 1123/54, 19 May 1760; 1164/36, 30 September 1783.

and their nephew Francisco, prospered far beyond the dreams of Llerana.[1] As in the case of Martín de Septién, his success attracted other members of his family to join him in Guanajuato. One nephew, Francisco, came from his home village. Then two more distant 'nephews', natives of valleys other than Vallecarriedo, also migrated. Felipe acted as his cajero and Agustín Pérez Marañón borrowed 12,000 ps. from his uncle to begin what proved to be a solid business career.[2]

In contrast to these nephews, none of José Pérez Marañón's sons showed any desire to enter business. Fernando, the eldest and most distinguished, qualified as a lawyer, obtaining the honorary position of vice-rector of the College of Lawyers of Mexico. In Guanajuato he purchased the office of regidor *alférez real* and soon emerged as the effective leader of the town council. Impressed by his legal talent, the intendant Riaño frequently employed him as his counsel in public affairs and litigation and indeed recommended his appointment as the official legal lieutenant and assessor of the intendancy.[3] Presumably such institutional labours did not offer much pecuniary reward, however, since Pérez Marañón still maintained his father's firm, installing a Gallego to manage it.[4]

The three remaining brothers all avoided commerce. Antonio joined the Church; Marcos served as a minor official in the postal service.[5] Alonso became the manager of the tobacco monopoly in Salamanca; he also bought a small hacienda there worth 10,000 ps.[6] These first generation creole sons thus chose the classic colonial professions: the Church, the law and the fiscal bureaucracy. As for their sisters, one married a Basque merchant and the other a creole lawyer, Lic. José Mariá de Septién.[7]

Other creole lineages show much the same pattern. Bernardo Fernández de Riaño, the prominent miner, begot four sons. Of these, one became a lawyer who served on Guanajuato's town council; another entered the priesthood; a third died young; and the fourth plunged into silver mining, there to fall into debt to the tune of 23,000 ps.[8] Their Liceaga

1 AHGP, Cabildo, 29 September 1750, 20 December 1790; AHG, Bienes Difuntos 1784–8, 28 June 1785.

2 For Felipe, AHGP, Cabildo, 4 April 1797; for Agustín, AHG, Actas de Cabildo, January 1792.

3 AHG, Actas de Cabildo, November 1792; AGI, Mexico 1893, Iturrigaray to Caballero, 26 November 1804.

4 AHGP, Cabildo, 15 February 1798.

5 AHGP, Cabildo, 17 August 1793.

6 ACM, 433, 15 September 1798; AMM, 150, 8 October 1806.

7 AHGP, Cabildo, 9 September 1801.

8 AHGP, Minas, May 1784; AHGP, Cabildo, 14 July 1790, 6 October 1803; AMM, 150, 13 September 1806.

cousins followed a similar line. Their father, José de Liceaga, appears to have been a fairly prosperous miner; he also figured as a member of the town council.[1] But by 1774 the treasury noted that his son's mine, the Chichindarito, was only worked by buscones.[2] His eldest son, Tomás de Liceaga, played a leading role in the suppression of the 1767 revolt. Gálvez rewarded him with the post of lieutenant-colonel of the newly levied Príncipe regiment of militia.[3] In 1776, no doubt to remedy his parlous financial position, he accepted the salaried position of deputy-general in the mining court. When he expired three years later his affairs were in such bad order that his family had to borrow 700 ps. to bury him.[4] His brother, Ramón Luis, succeeded him as deputy-general, yet despite a 14-year tenure (1779–93) he also died in debt. The court granted a special subvention of 300 ps. in order to provide him with a decent burial.[5] The third Liceaga brother, Manuel Esteban, became administrator of the municipal granary, a job with an annual salary of 700 ps.[6] His widow, left with a large family and few resources, married a wealthy gachupín, Juan de Villamor, the former manager of the Obregón estate.[7] After 1810, her son, José María de Liceaga, emerged as a well-known insurgent leader. In the course of one debt-burdened generation the family passed from active loyalty to open rebellion.[8]

Enough evidence has been presented for us to form a reliable impression of the composition of Guanajuato's upper élite. Its most noticeable feature was the almost continuous upward pressure exerted by the peninsular Spaniards. Each generation they obtained a good share of the economic and civic prizes. Their creole sons inherited their wealth and in many cases, although not invariably, wasted it. Generally speaking, those second generation creoles who did figure in eighteenth-century Guanajuato achieved their prominence not so much as the result of inheritance as through their own efforts in silver mining. Guanajuato's élite was almost entirely composed of recent arrivals, new rich, gachupín merchants and creole miners. Yet the Americans who moved upwards were usually men with connexions, men from families on the point of losing their 'respectability', men who entered silver mining to remake their fortunes

[1] AGN, Minería 5/1, testimonies of ancestry, 10 October 1738.
[2] AGN, Minería 11/1, treasury officials to Bucareli, 3 February 1774.
[3] Priestley, *José de Gálvez*, p. 225.
[4] AGN, Minería 113/1, meeting of creditors, 25 November 1779.
[5] AGN, Minería 52/12, mining court to viceroy, 27 June 1792.
[6] AHG, Actas de Cabildo, January 1784.
[7] AHGP, Cabildo, 30 January 1787, 21 November 1807.
[8] Liceaga's mother, María Josefa, in company with her son was imprisoned for disloyalty to the Crown: AHGP, Cabildo, 18 September 1811 and 8 October 1811.

and to regain a lost social status. Similarly those immigrants who joined the élite usually enjoyed the advantage of extensive family backing. Clearly the role of individual talent must not be underestimated: in both mining and commerce neither the best connexions nor backing could save a person who did not possess energy or enterprise from falling into debt.

In many respects it is misleading to divide this élite into its European and American components. To do so cuts many families into two. But then that, presumably, was also the effect of the wars of independence, especially in their first stage. The enmity between the two branches of the Spanish nation often took the form of a revolt of sons against their fathers, a quarrel between brothers-in-law and cousins. Unfortunately, no evidence is yet available as to what depths of feeling this irritation and hostility touched in Guanajuato. The closest statement we have is the public vindication issued by the largely creole cabildo after the massacre of several hundred peninsular Spaniards by Hidalgo's insurgent forces. The author of this pamphlet, Lic. José María de Septién y Montero, wrote:

> Those abominable distinctions of creoles and gachupines . . . have never been made among the noble, cultivated and distinguished people of this city . . . the Europeans were our relatives, they were married to our daughters or sisters, they were our good friends and we did business with them. Our interests and wealth were mixed with theirs and indeed depended upon them absolutely. In their misfortune we were all involved.

Septién wrote on behalf of the town council, but there seems no reason to doubt that he expressed his own sentiments, and possibly the sentiments of most men of his generation and social position.[1] In Guanajuato at least very few members of the town's élite, young or old, joined Hidalgo or the rebellion; most rallied to the Crown.

III

The membership of such bodies as the town council, the merchant and mining deputations and to a lesser extent the commissioned ranks of the militia reflected with remarkable precision the current balance of wealth and prestige within Guanajuato's élite. An Obregón, newly enriched, could buy a seat on the town council as well as a title of nobility. A Busto, once impoverished, soon disappeared from such bodies. The political élite, therefore, was almost identical with the economic élite. To prove this assertion we shall examine the membership of the town council, the militia

[1] *Pública vindicación del ilustre ayuntamiento de Guanajuato* . . . (Mexico, 1811), pp. 12, 25–6. For Septién's authorship see: José María Liceaga, *Adiciones y rectificaciones a la historia de México por don Lucas Alamán* (2 vols.; Mexico, 1944), I, 81.

and the merchant and mining deputations. Our evidence, it must be emphasised, essentially relates to the period following the Gálvez Visitation.

The records of the town council (the *cabildo*) began in 1777 when it possessed some 15 councillors, permanent and temporary alike.[1] For the most part these regidores obtained their posts from the Crown by simple purchase. Occupants, however, enjoyed the right to bequeath or to sell their offices, the Crown merely demanding the usual purchase fee. A slight modification to this system occurred during the 1760s when the Crown decreed that a certain number of regidores should be elected. But whereas in the Peninsula these *regidores honorarios* were elected by popular suffrage, in Guanajuato they were chosen by the town council itself.[2] Every year the cabildo selected the two alcaldes ordinarios, the municipal magistrates, one *procurador general del común* who served as the guardian and representative of popular interests, and two regidores honorarios, these last for a two-year period, so that at any one time, the cabildo contained four of these elected councillors. The nucleus of the ayuntamiento was composed of five members whose offices entailed especial responsibilities—the *alférez real*, the *alcalde provincial*, the *alguacil mayor*, the *depositario general*, and the *fiel ejecutor*. In addition a varying number of regidores *capitularios* completed the cabildo's permanent membership. A brief enumeration of the responsibilities and prices of these offices will be useful for future students of municipal government, if not for the general reader.

The *alférez real* acted as the cabildo's president in the absence of the intendant and, as the senior member for most of the century 'by privilege of his office', proposed the names from which the alcaldes ordinarios were nominated; thus in 1778 the alférez real advanced two candidates for the senior post and three for the junior from which the council was obliged to choose.[3] After 1780 this custom was terminated when the cabildo, despite protests, resumed its right to select whom it pleased.[4] For most of the century this post was held by the Bluet Iguiño family until financial ruin drove them to sell out in the 1780s to the Sardanetas; in 1792 the second Marquis sold it for 750 ps. to Lic. Fernando Pérez Marañón, who retained the office until 1810.[5]

[1] Marmolejo, *Efemérides*, I, 190; II, 50.

[2] For Peninsula practice see: A. Desdevises de Dézert, *L'Espagne de l'Ancien Regime: Les Institutions* (Paris, 1899), pp. 185–6.

[3] AHG, Actas de Cabildo, 1 January 1778.

[4] AGI, Mexico 2240, Guanajuato mining deputation to viceroy, 14 January 1783.

[5] AHG, Actas de Cabildo 1792; AGI, Mexico 2126, 21 July 1792.

The *alcalde provincial*, theoretically in charge of the rural police, had no real function, hence the price of his post, like that of the alférez real, was low—in 1788 no more than 700 ps. For many years the first Marquis of San Juan de Rayas occupied this office; from 1788 to 1810 it was owned by Bernardo Chico Valdés, a Castilian refiner and merchant.[1] The *alguacil mayor* acted as the town's chief constable, supervised the town's prisons and apparently derived a handsome commission from these duties. In 1791 it was purchased for 1,165 ps. by Vicente Regil, a creole refiner, a creature of the Otero family: in 1805 Mariano de Otero acquired it for 3,500 ps.[2] Another valuable office was the *depositario general*, who administered all intestate inheritances in the first instance, a task from which, no doubt, a certain return could accrue. It was held by two generations of the Pérez Marañón family from the 1760s onwards, and its value was reckoned at 2,000 ps.[3] The *fiel ejecutor*'s duties consisted in checking the weights and measures used in the town's shops, and inspecting the markets; apparently this task brought in a good income since its incumbent in 1812 estimated that he obtained 2,000 ps. a year in commissions. Its value was placed at 1,000 ps. and the office was occupied by three generations of the Septién family from at least the 1740s onwards.[4]

In addition to these posts the cabildo also included a handful of permanent regidores, who varied in number from two to five according to the year. By the 1790s the current prices paid for these posts ranged from 500 to 600 ps. Clearly only those offices that provided an income received a valuation above 750 ps.

Table 54 indicates the composition of the Guanajuato cabildo in the later eighteenth century: the three years 1778, 1793, and 1809 have been selected to demonstrate both the changes and relative stability in its composition.

For the most part the names are familiar. Nearly every important merchant house or mining enterprise possessed a member serving on the city council. This was especially the case in 1778. For example, to take once more the 1781 mercury distribution as our yardstick of importance, we find that with the one exception of Ramón de Aranda all the chief miners, and seven out of nine leading aviadores were represented that year. The

[1] AHG, Actas de Cabildo, 1 January 1788.

[2] For the duties of the office see Constantine Bayle, *Los cabildos seculares en la América Española* (Madrid, 1952), pp. 189–95. AGI, Mexico 2125, 9 December 1790; AHG, Actas de Cabildo, 14 January 1805.

[3] AGI, Mexico 2126, 27 August 1792.

[4] Bayle, *Los cabildos seculares*, pp. 207–24; AHG, Insurgencia 1812–14, statement, 25 January 1814.

Table 54 *Composition of Guanajuato's Ayuntamiento, 1778, 1793, 1809.*

1778

Alférez real
Joaquín Bluet Iguiño (creole)

Alcalde provincial
Marquis San Juan de Rayas (creole)

Alguacil mayor
Manuel Güemes de la Concha (?)

Depositario-general
José Pérez Marañón (Montañés)

Fiel ejecutor
Francisco de Septién y Montero (Montañés)

Regidores capitulares
Gabriel de Arechederreta (Basque)
Juan José Compains (Basque)
José Hernández Chico (Castilian)
Miguel de Rivera y Llorente (creole)
Antonio de Obregón y Alcocer (creole)
Felipe Fernández de Riaño (creole)

Regidores honorarios
Juan Alejo de Busto (creole)
José María de Irizar (creole)
Ramón de Liceaga (creole)
Pedro de Clavería (creole)

Alcaldes ordinarios
Pedro Sereno de Cobarrubias (creole)
Pedro Luciano de Otero (creole)

Procurador general
Francisco de Azpilcueta (Basque)

1793

Alférez real
Fernando Pérez Marañón (creole)

Alcalde provincial
Bernardo Chico Valdés (Castilian)

Alguacil mayor
Vicente Regil (creole)

Depositario general
Agustín Pérez Marañón (Montañés)

Fiel ejecutor
José María de Septién y Montero (creole)

Regidores capitulares
José Hernández Chico (Castilian)
Martín Coronel y Jorganes (creole)
Recently resigned:
Juan Vicente Alamán (Basque)
Felipe Fernández de Riaño (creole)
Miguel de Rivera Llorente (creole)

Table 54 (cont.)

Regidores honorarios
Francisco de Septién y Montero (Montañés)
Francisco Azpilcueta (Basque)
Francisco de Septién y Arce (Montañés)
Julián Lavín (Castilian)

Alcaldes ordinarios
Manuel García de Zeballos (Montañés)
Pedro Félix de Quijano (Montañés)

Procurador-general
José Antonio del Mazo (Montañés)

1809

Alférez real
Fernando Pérez Marañón (creole)

Alcalde provincial
Bernardo Chico Valdés (Castilian)

Alguacil mayor
Mariano de Otero (creole)

Fiel ejecutor
José María de Septién y Montero (creole)

Regidores capitulares
Martín Coronel y Jorganes (creole)
Pedro de Otero (creole)
Rafael López de Miera (creole)
Francisco de Septién y Arce (creole)
Agustín Pérez Marañón (Montañés)

Regidores honorarios
Joaquín Aguiar (?)
Carlos Montes de Oca (creole)
Juan Antonio Ginori (Canaries)
Miguel Chico Valdés (creole)

Alcaldes ordinarios
Francisco de Iriarte (Basque)
José María de Septién y Montero (creole)

Procurador-general
Pedro Cobo (peninsular)

Totals	*1778*	*1793*	*1809*
Peninsulars	6	11	5
Creoles	11	6	10
Unknown	1		1
	18	17	16

past still had a voice. A son of the Marquis of San Clemente retained a seat and no less than six men were listed who had married into, or were descended from, the Busto-Aranda connexion.

By 1792–3, a marked change in the council's composition had occurred. In the first place the deaths of the two first Valenciana partners and the first Marquis of San Juan de Rayas left a certain vacuum into which stepped an entire group of Montañeses and their creole sons. Peninsular Spaniards enjoyed a clear majority. Whether this seizure of control was fortuitous or planned, it certainly reflected the peculiar predominance of Montañeses within Guanajuato's immigrant and mercantile community. By then the old Basque group which had married into the Bustos was dwindling in importance.

By 1809 the balance of numbers had swung back in favour of the creoles. By this time the Septién family was entirely embodied by its creole members. A significant feature was the withdrawal of the titled aristocracy. None of the three Counts of Valenciana, Pérez Gálvez or Casa Rul sought municipal office. Similarly, although his father had always served as a councillor, the second Marquis of San Juan de Rayas sold his office and did not seek election. On the other hand, both the young Otero brothers bought posts on the council, a sign perhaps of their lesser prestige. By this year not a single member of the Busto-Aranda clan remained.

This brief study of the cabildo proves beyond doubt that purchase of office did not detract from the council's representative character. To the contrary: the sale and purchase of these posts acted as a remarkably good index of their possessor's economic standing. Guanajuato's cabildo represented the rich and the powerful.

Loss of power to influence the city council could be damaging, particularly for families in social decline. An interesting example of this danger occurred when in 1781 Manuel García de Zeballos, the *procurador general del común*, pointed out that much land surrounding the city and bordering the river previously used by refining mills was now occupied by mine workers. The ostensible owners, the former refiners, did not have valid legal titles, yet they collected a rent from all the occupants of these lands.[1] In 1790 after this protest was reiterated by Agustín Pérez Marañón, *procurador general* for that year, the cabildo took the matter to the Mexican audiencia and obtained a viceregal decree depriving the so-called owners of their rights to rent. According to mining law, lands adjacent to the city counted as common ground to which the workers as miners enjoyed free access. Now the dispossessed nearly all belonged to families prominent at an earlier period but which by 1790 had experienced a marked social decline.[2] These were the Bustos, Aranda, Diez Madroñero, Fernández de

[1] AGN, Minería 37/1, protest by García de Zeballos, 8 October 1781.

[2] AGN, Minería 37/1, Pérez Marañón to viceroy, 2 June 1790.

Riaño, Uribarren, the Count of San Pedro del Alamo, and the Sardaneta. Clearly the group of Montañeses who seized power in the Guanajuato cabildo in no way felt obliged to respect the interests of such families.

Another important, if less reliable, index of élite membership was rank in the militia. But since such commissions often entailed onerous duties, by no means all the rich cared to join the local regiments. This was especially the case in the first years after the Gálvez Visitation when only the post of colonel of the Príncipe regiment appeared to attract well-known Guanajuato figures. These were Tomás de Liceaga, Simón Eugenio de Arroyo y Sardaneta, also a creole and a shareholder in the Rayas mine; and Alfonso Bravo González, a peninsular who married into the Sardaneta family.[1]

Table 55 *Guanajuato infantry battalion officers in 1800.*

Rank	Name	Origin
Lieut.-colonel	Manuel García de Quintana	Montañés
Captain	Augusto González del Campillo	Montañés
	Angel de la Riva	Montañés
	Ignacio de la Lama	Montañés
	José Manuel Pezuela	creole
Lieutenant	Manuel de Escalera	creole
	Andrés Antonio Pelayo	Montañés
	Francisco Bustamante	Montañés
	Juan Gómez	Montañés
Sub-lieutenant	José María Trujillo	Andaluz
	Juan Manuel del Río	Montañés
	Gerónimo Gómez	Montañés
	José Manuel Bustamante	creole
	New Sub-lieutenants in 1804	
	Joaquín Lavín	Montañés
	José María de Bustamante y Septién	creole
	Manuel Pérez Marañón	creole
	Mariano de Sein	creole

During the 1790s, however, when Revillagigedo disbanded the old regiment and Branciforte raised two new forces, several wealthy Guanajuato miners purchased commissions. A list of the officers in the town's infantry battalion (table 55) indicates some of this change.[2]

The composition reflected that unexplained Montañés 'take-over'

[1] AGI, Mexico 1387, Mayorga to Gálvez, 27 May 1780.

[2] AGS, Guerra Moderna 7276, record sheets of Guanajuato Battalion officers for 1800; AGN, Guerra 121 A, Guanajuato Battalion, December 1804.

which occurred during the 1790s in nearly all the town's major institutions. García de Quintana was of course the old manager of Martín de Septién, by now a wealthy refiner. Angel de la Riva directed the Tepeyac mine for Septién y Arce and García de Zeballos; González del Campillo and Pezuela were both shareholders in the Rayas.

In addition both the Counts of Pérez Gálvez and Casa Rul became colonels of newly levied militia regiments, a privilege for which they had to pay at least 40,000 ps.[1] Membership of these forces extended beyond Guanajuato so that for the most part the names of their officers are unfamiliar. But the first lieutenant-colonel of the new Príncipe cavalry regiment, raised by Pérez Gálvez, was Francisco de Septién y Arce. When he died in 1799 he was succeeded by yet another Montañés, José Gaspar Quijano, a landowner in Silao.

Table 56 *Origin of officers of the Bajío militia regiments,* c. *1800.*

	Guanajuato		Príncipe		Reina		Celaya		Valladolid		Totals		
Officers	P	C	P	C	P	C	P	C	P	C	P	C	GT
Colonels			1			1	1		1		3	1	4
Lieut.-colonels	1		1			1	1		1		4	1	5
Captains	3	2	6	4	3	3	3	6	4	6	19	21	40
Lieutenants	4		6	6	6	4	6	4	7	1	29	15	44
Sub-lieutenants	2	1					6	2	2	9			
and Ensigns			4	7	4	8					18	27	45
Reg. adjutants	1		1	1	2		1		2		7	1	8
Reg. lieutenants	2		2		2		3	1		3	9	4	13

KEY: P = peninsular; C = creole; GT = grand total.

In general, whether by plan or chance, peninsular Spaniards formed the majority of officers in the Guanajuato militia. In 1804 seven out of the Príncipe's eight captains were peninsulars.[2] Among the lieutenants and ensigns this predominance was less marked. However, not all the forces in the intendancy followed the same pattern. In the Reina cavalry regiment, recruited in the district of San Miguel, the colonel, the lieutenant-colonel, and half the captains were creoles. In the regiment at Celaya, only three captains out of nine were peninsulars. These differences of recruitment are presented in a scheme in table 56.[3]

There is no evidence that the viceroy deliberately favoured peninsular

[1] AGI, Estado 23, Branciforte to Alcudia, 30 August 1795.

[2] AGN, Guerra 242 A, Príncipe officers record sheets, 1804.

[3] Compiled from record sheets of officers of these regiments in AGS, Guerra Moderna 7276.

Spaniards; rather, the immigrants were more avid for honours, more able to raise the necessary purchase fee. It is striking that neither the young Count of Valenciana nor the second Marquis of San Juan de Rayas made any attempt to obtain military rank. Here, however, we enter the problem of individual psychology. The Count's half-brother Ignacio de Obregón, the wealthy miner of Catorce, did in fact buy himself a colonelcy.[1] Whatever the case, the table shows that a rough parity between creoles and peninsulars was maintained at the rank of captain, but that among the lieutenants and below the creoles easily predominated.

Two institutions of considerable importance for the élite remain to be described—the mining and merchant deputations. The former merits an entire chapter; the latter can be dismissed in a few words. The reason for this discrepancy lies in their respective powers. Whereas the mining deputation exercised a private jurisdiction, its mercantile counterpart only acted as the agent of the Mexico City consulado; it did not itself constitute a court. The only occasions at which the merchant deputation emerged from obscurity was when it defended its members from what it considered to be the exactions of the miners.

In 1781, the mining deputation, directed by the Count of Valenciana, at the time the town's interim magistrate, decreed that the four remaining grains of the old seigniorage real (of which eight grains had been granted to the mining court) should be paid to the Crown as a war donation for a period of five years. The two merchant deputies, José Pérez Marañón (a Montañés) and Juan José Compains (a Basque) strongly protested against this unilateral imposition, especially since, as they claimed, 'the introducers of these metals (into the treasury) have not been and are not miners, but are in great measure merchants and aviadores'.[2] They reluctantly agreed to pay the charge, but only for the war's duration. This antagonism between these two groups began to subside during the 1780s as the merchants invested more directly in the industry. And in 1791 the merchants amicably assented to the imposition of a duty of 2 grains per mark designed to provide revenue for the mining deputation. It was then stated that 'in reality the two bodies of miners and merchants have come to be united in this mining community by reasons of the bonds and dependence they have on each other'.[3]

The merchant deputation also experienced a Montañés 'take-over'

[1] In 1797 he organised the new regiment of Dragoons of Galicia, paying 30,000 ps. in costs. See AGS, Guerra Moderna 7276.

[2] AGN, Minería 18/9, merchant deputation protest, 7 May 1781.

[3] AGI, Mexico 2248 mining deputation, 14 September 1791.

when at the 1788 January general meeting it terminated the old practice of dividing the electors into two parties of Basques and Montañeses; instead 'it was resolved by the joint agreement of Montañeses and Basques that henceforward they should choose eight electors without division into parties'. The point of this resolution was made clear at the subsequent election when the meeting chose six Montañés electors.[1] However, in all fairness, it should be pointed out that both the existing deputies, José Pérez Marañón and Juan José Compains, and the new deputies chosen by the electors, Francisco de Septién y Arce and Juan Vicente Alamán, represented the two provincial groups. They also, of course, owned the leading merchant-aviador houses in Guanajuato. Once again, in a distinct context, the same names occur. At different times a man such as Francisco de Septién y Arce served as alcalde ordinario, regidor honorario, mining elector and deputy, and lieutenant-colonel in the militia. Juan Vicente Alamán, the militia rank apart, paralleled most of these honours. The circle of elective office-holding was limited, yet clearly important for those who sought these posts. For some of the reasons as to why such offices might be important we must examine the history of the mining deputation in these years. It was there that Guanajuato's élite met to engage in political battle.

[1] AHGP, Cabildo, 11 January 1788.

CHAPTER 10

THE DEPUTATION

When Domingo Valcárcel, the aged oidor and superintendent of the mercury monopoly, learned of Gálvez's scheme to create a mining court and guild with its own private jurisdiction over all litigation arising out of the industry, he wrote a strong letter of protest to the Crown, attacking the new regime in all its central points. He predicted that the public election of local deputies would provoke disorders and factions, and that the justice they would mete out would be distorted by the influence of family and business relationship. The net result would be 'notorious monstrosities'.[1] As an example of what he feared, Valcárcel cited a case from Guanajuato where Tomás de Liceaga, the newly elected deputy-general of the mining court, had conspired with the town's alcalde mayor to retain possession of a mine while only working it for a few days every four months. Upon appeal, the audiencia had reprimanded Liceaga, ordering him to work it properly or cede it to the new claimant. With the concession of the *fuero*, however, the audiencia would be debarred from all intervention. Valcárcel was also pained to see the reduction in 'the power and authority of this audiencia', which the fuero entailed.[2]

In many respects these predictions were amply fulfilled. Under the new code of 1783 the mining deputations were endowed with extensive jurisdiction over the settlement and arbitration of disputed claims to ownership, the correct demarcation of adjoining mines, rival registrations of deserted shafts, underground fights between the workers of neighbouring enterprises and the relations between owners and their employees. In a word, the deputations henceforth exercised power over property; an unfriendly decree on their part could easily ruin a miner. Small wonder, then, to find that their elections soon became the scene of bitter intrigue. In Guanajuato this was particularly the case because there a junta of seven electors nominated the deputies and this junta, chosen by free vote of all registered miners, stayed in office for four years. It was this body, rather than the deputies, which governed the town's industry and to which election was most eagerly sought. In many ways it was the most powerful institution in Guanajuato.

[1] AGI, Mexico 2240, Domingo Valcárcel to Crown, 29 August 1777.

[2] AGI, Mexico 1728, judgment of alcalde mayor, 28 February 1775.

Given these circumstances it should come as no surprise to discover that the 1783 general meeting was peculiarly acrimonious. By then the Valenciana partners, Antonio de Obregón and Pedro Luciano de Otero, had largely gained control of the junta. At the 1779 meeting Obregón, his mine manager, Buenaventura José Carrasco, and his protegé, Lic. Felipe Fernández de Riaño, the lawyer son of the owner of the San Lorenzo, were all elected along with the Marquis of San Juan de Rayas, and two Basques, Juan José Compains and Francisco Azpilcueta, who had married into the old Busto-Aranda connexion.[1] This control was now challenged by a group of Montañés merchants and refiners acting in conjunction with José Hernández Chico, the quarrelsome director of the postal service. Their reasons for this attack were several. In the first place, they resented the mining deputation's unilateral imposition of a duty on all silver entering the treasury. On the first occasion, in 1775, it amounted to $1\frac{1}{2}$ grains in every mark, but in 1781 the deputation, led by the Count of Valenciana, decreed the collection of 4 grains ($\frac{1}{3}$ real) for a period of five years as a war donation to the Crown.[2] In the second place, the mercury distribution of 1781, in which the Valenciana partners emerged as the chief recipients, provoked much controversy and accusations of corruption. On this opportunity Hernández Chico, himself fined for illegal sale of mercury, denounced Obregón and Otero to the viceroy alleging bribery of the treasury officials.[3] Finally, this was the time when merchants everywhere were making more direct investments in mining. After the death of Martín de Septién, the two managers of his vast enterprise, Francisco de Septién y Arce and Manuel García de Quintana, both purchased refining mills and shares in small mines.[4] To protect their position in the industry they formed an alliance with Hernández Chico and moved rapidly to acquire institutional power.

The upshot is best described by the two outgoing deputies, Pedro Luciano de Otero and Felipe Fernández de Riaño. 'Many of those who came that night [12 January 1783] brought their ballot-papers prepared, with their votes written in and the names of the persons whom they picked for election already listed. . . . This resulted in the choice of don

[1] See Appendix V for the junta's membership throughout this period, taken mainly from a lengthy *expediente* in AGI, Mexico 2243.

[2] AGN, Minería 113/1, merchant deputation protest, 18 August 1778; also AGN, Minería 18/9, merchant deputation's protest, 7 May 1781.

[3] See the lengthy *expedientes* in AHN, Consejos 20701; also AGI, Mexico, 2209, Revillagigedo to Lerena, 27 August 1790.

[4] AHGP, Minas, 7 December 1799; AHGP, Cabildo, 24 December 1782; AHGP, Minas, 9 January 1783.

Manuel García de Quintana and don Francisco de Septién y Arce as electors although as merchants of the town they had been quite distant from all mining activities.' Furthermore, the town's notary certified that whereas the deputation had summoned 48 registered miners (of whom 14 did not come) the meeting was attended by 62 persons.[1] Certainly the Valenciana partners had reason for disquiet, since all the new electors were peninsular Spaniards, with no less than four being Montañeses. Moreover, the very next day, the new junta, ignoring the previous custom whereby the outgoing deputies provided names from whom their successors were to be picked, chose Francisco de Septién and José Hernández Chico as the new deputies. The accountant of the local treasury attributed the initiative in these tactics to Hernández Chico whom he claimed 'has seduced don Francisco de Septién and the various other Europeans who were chosen as electors . . . these unsavoury manoeuvres are the cause of this city being full of hatred and ill-will'.[2] Faced with this coup, Fernández de Riaño and Otero appealed to the mining court and to the viceroy. The Count of Valenciana complained to Gálvez himself, suggesting that to avoid future disputes the mining court or the viceroy should nominate the deputies. But whereas Viceroy Mayorga intervened to suspend the elections, Gálvez replied to the effect that the new mining code should be fully observed.[3] The creole miners had to wait, therefore, until 1787, when they swept the board installing as electors both the Otero brothers, and two Fernández de Riaño; the only peninsular Spaniard was Juan de Villamor, manager of the Obregón estate.

The swing of the electoral pendulum was in part determined by the definition of the constituency. The 1783 ordinances prescribed that refiners should only cast half the vote given to miners. At the 1787 meeting this rule was enforced, and since the Montañés party was strongest in refining it lost the election.[4] But three years later Francisco de Septién y Arce quietly secured a resolution to grant refiners full voting rights.[5] The outcome was that in 1791 four Montañeses were chosen as electors, three of them, Manuel García de Zeballos. Andrés Sagaz y Herrera and Septién y Arce, being shareholders in the Tepeyac mine.[6] By this time of course

[1] AGI, Mexico 2240, Pedro Luciano de Otero and Felipe Fernández de Riaño to viceroy, 14 January 1783.

[2] AGI, Mexico 2981, accountant to Gálvez, 18 June 1783.

[3] AGI, Mexico 2240, Count of Valenciana to Gálvez, 16 July 1783.

[4] AGI, Mexico 1849, deputation report, 10 October 1787.

[5] AGN, Minería 128/3, complaint of miner, Juan Antonio Ferrón to viceroy, 20 October 1790.

[6] AGI, Mexico 1549, junta general, 8 February 1791.

the original Valenciana partners had died leaving only the somewhat unbalanced Manuel de Otero to deal with this new situation.

Just how important it was to control the junta became clear during the years 1790–2, when a fierce dispute broke out over the underground demarcation of the adjoining Camargo and Sirena mines. The case was all the more serious because the principal shareholders of the opposing sides were José Hernández Chico and Manuel Antonio de Otero. Now the exact sequence of events is lost in the welter of accusation and counter-accusation. Apparently fighting broke out between the workers of the two men, with the eventual result of both mines being left flooded. Hernández Chico claimed that after the Camargo had struck rich the Sirena workmen invaded the property. Otero asserted that his opponent, taking advantage of the Camargo's higher position, had deliberately used his waterwheels to flood the Sirena.[1] The rights and wrongs of the case remain obscure. All we can be sure of is that the fine art of judicial lying, so prevalent in eighteenth-century Mexico, here reached a rare peak.

The true interest of the dispute, however, lies in the conflict of jurisdictions that it provoked, a conflict which revealed with great precision the new balance of power and influence established by the Bourbon reforms. It all started, as Valcárcel predicted, with an obvious miscarriage of justice. The 1791 junta of electors nominated Hernández Chico as one of the two deputies for that year. Two months afterward, in March 1791, he proceeded to imprison one of the lesser shareholders in the Sirena for denouncing to the deputation his conduct as owner of the Camargo. Otero immediately protested to Viceroy Revillagigedo, who at the advice of the Crown attorney referred the matter back to the interim intendant José de Soriano, ordering him to form a local appeal court to re-try the case. But this solution proved impossible since no one could be found willing to serve on such a body. Subjected to reiterated appeals from Otero and irritated by Hernández Chico's manoeuvres, Revillagigedo then made the mistake of consulting with Francisco Javier de Gamboa, regent of the audiencia. The aged jurist, never an advocate of the new fuero, counselled viceregal intervention. He asseverated that in Guanajuato 'all take turns at being judge, and all are bound by ties of blood, friendship, interest and business.... It is impossible to obtain peace without the viceregal authority of your Excellency ... exercising the supreme political and executive power in order to sustain and give authority to justice and to ensure that boldness and audacity do not prevail'. The viceroy then commissioned the

[1] AGI, Mexico 1557, Revillagigedo to Gardoqui, 31 March 1793. The entire case is to be found within this *legajo*.

oidor Juan Francisco Anda, then visiting Guanajuato, to act as his delegate and settle the matter. All further appeals could only be heard by the viceroy himself.

Far from accepting this decree, the Guanajuato junta calmly informed the viceroy that he had no right to invade the private jurisdiction of the deputation. Highly annoyed by this resistance, led apparently by Manuel García de Zeballos, in that year both a municipal magistrate and an elector, Revillagigedo instructed the intendant to reprimand the junta for 'their spirit of insubordination and lack of respect for my superior resolutions . . . they are animated by a spirit of faction and sedition'.[1] Not one whit abashed by this viceregal reproof, however, the two deputies, Hernández Chico and Lic. Martín Coronel, and the four Montañés electors, in a statement prepared for them by the Mexico City lawyer Lic. Francisco Primo Verdad y Ramos, respectfully defended the mining fuero, and stated their incomprehension of the judicial grounds which justified Revillagigedo's intervention, since 'His Majesty prohibits them [the viceroys] by repeated laws from taking cognizance of lawsuits between parties'. They justified their resistance to his decrees by a citation of the medieval *Leyes de Partida* of Alfonso X, which laid down that it was quite possible that the King himself, although 'the Oracle of Justice . . . might despatch letters and privileges not only against written and arbitrary law but even against the natural law which is born within us and which does not depend on discourse: in which case it is quite legitimate for the subject not to obey until further inquiry is made. . . . *No deben cumplir ça no han fuerza*'. They enjoined Revillagigedo to 'regard how the very legislator of the kingdom permits his vassals, in a certain manner, to judge his sovereign resolutions'.[2] Moreover, the viceroy had slandered respectable citizens, accusing them of sedition for doing little more than defending the jurisdiction granted them by the Crown.

Revillagigedo's reaction was swift. He imprisoned the junta's Mexico City agent, confiscated the papers of the case, and requested the audiencia not to accept any appeals since the matter belonged to the sphere of executive government rather than to that of justice. But then the affair took a more grave aspect. For the audiencia, led presumably by Gamboa as regent, now decided to admit the appeal and ordered the government notaries to remit the confiscated papers. The court, it should be noted, enjoyed the right to inspect all legal documents arising out of viceregal measures which

[1] AGI, Mexico 1547, Revillagigedo to Gardoqui, 1 May 1792.

[2] AGI, Mexico 1557, Guanajuato mining junta to Revillagigedo, 3 May 1792. Ironically enough, Otero's lawyer was Miguel Domínguez, later Corregidor of Querétaro.

affected private interests. But in this instance Revillagigedo refused to comply with their request asserting that he had acted as captain-general, in an attempt to maintain public order, and hence the audiencia could not take cognisance of the case. Then, after the customary ritual of three applications and refusals had taken place, both parties wrote to Madrid to protest each other's conduct.

Meanwhile the viceroy heard disquietening rumours that the new intendant, Juan Antonio de Riaño, favoured his Montañés compatriots. He therefore sent a letter of reproach inquiring why Riaño had not calmed the quarrel. The intendant, who in part owed his appointment to Revillagigedo's recommendation, immediately replied defending his record. He had persuaded the Obregón family not to intervene, but so far Otero had proved to be obdurate. As for the Montañeses they 'possess unequivocal proofs of my way of thinking, and it would be a palpable stupidity if they flatter themselves that I am capable of such prostitution as to sacrifice to the call of *paisanaje* [compatriotism] that which is owed to justice'.[1] Moreover, in another month, by June 1792, he reported that the long-suffering oidor Anda had finally worked out a compromise whereby Hernández Chico agreed to cede the Camargo to Otero in return for 100,000 ps.

This was not the end of the matter, however, since the Guanajuato junta persisted in their grievance and petitioned the Crown for redress against the viceroy's invasion of their fuero. Sure enough, in November 1792, Madrid decided in their favour and despatched a royal decree to Revillagigedo couched in sharp admonitory terms:

> You should not have taken cognisance of a mining lawsuit . . . the defect of jurisdiction annuls in the legal sphere all the measures both of Your Excellency and your delegate . . . none of the reasons advanced at all justify the manner in which Your Excellency took cognisance and proceeded to treat with such indecorous expressions judges who possessed a private jurisdiction and who belonged to the most respected class of subjects. . . . Your Excellency should be convinced that it is absolutely forbidden for him to introduce himself into any similar cases of miners and mining.

In addition the audiencia was also reproached for its interference in a mining case.[2] The actual settlement effected by Anda was allowed to stand in order to avoid any further disorders. Naturally the contents of this decree soon became public since, as a later informant noted, 'even though it was private the deputation divulged the news, distributing copies of the triumph obtained over the resolutions of . . . the Count of Revillagigedo'.[3]

[1] AGN, Minería 23/2, Revillagigedo to Riaño, 8 November 1792.

[2] AGI, Mexico 2244, *real orden* to Revillagigedo, 8 November 1792.

[3] AGI, Mexico 2247, Lic. José Vicente Figueroa to Viceroy Azanza, 26 April 1800.

The exuberance of the Montañés party was all the more pronounced because they had also succeeded in stripping Otero of his guardianship of his nephews' vast inheritance. Here again, they made skilful use of jurisdictional rights. In 1792 the oidor Anda was commissioned by the audiencia to settle the dispute between Manuel Antonio de Otero and José Antonio del Mazo, the Montañés husband of his brother's widow, over the guardianship of the dead man's sons and their estate. After Anda found in favour of Otero, Mazo gave notice of an appeal to the audiencia. Incensed by this manoeuvre, Anda ordered Mazo to cede possession of the children to their uncle, and upon meeting resistance, instructed a lieutenant of the *sala del crimen*, the audiencia's lower court, to surround Mazo's house to secure the young Oteros. But then the senior municipal magistrate, Manuel García de Zeballos, declared the lieutenant's credentials to be invalid and promptly arrested all his men.[1] The commandant of the militia, Manuel García de Quintana, refused Anda's plea to intervene. The outwitted oidor complained to Revillagigedo of 'the shameful outrage I have suffered in this city where I have had the most despised role a man can have'.[2] In response to these laments the audiencia promptly summoned García de Zeballos to Mexico City and fined him 200 ps. for his obstruction. As in the other case, he appealed to Madrid where the Council of the Indies quashed the sentence, declaring that once an appeal had been lodged with the audencia Anda should have taken no further cognisance of the case and hence García de Zeballos' intervention was perfectly justifiable.[3]

While these Guanajuato intrigues and quarrels reached their climax during the summer months of 1792, in Mexico City and Madrid the fate of the central mining court was the subject of animated discussion. Gamboa, observing the fiasco of the finance bank, favoured outright abolition. But Revillagigedo, after listening to several other opinions, recommended its revival and indeed proposed that in the future it should act as court of appeal from the judgments of the deputations. In this way 'if these remain entirely subordinate to the mining court it will be possible to dictate opportune measures to forestall or stop and punish those abuses which they commit'.[4] This suggestion was adopted by the Council of State which considered the matter, and in February 1793 a new constitution for the mining guild was framed in which the local appeal courts

[1] AGI, Mexico 1719, representation of Francisco Javier del Mazo to the Council of the Indies, 31 July 1793.

[2] AGI, Mexico 1457, Anda to Revillagigedo, 20 April 1792.

[3] AGI, Mexico 1779, fiscal of Council, 23 September 1793.

[4] AGI, Mexico 2238, Revillagigedo to Lerena, 13 January 1791.

were abolished and replaced by the central mining court resident in Mexico City.[1]

The prospect of being subjected to the judicial review of the mining court thoroughly alarmed Guanajuato's junta of electors. For they had already quarrelled with the permanent director-general, Fausto de Elhuyar, and indeed on every occasion had blocked the court's attempts to intervene in their affairs. When Elhuyar visited the town in 1788 to assist Professor Fischer test the Born method of amalgamation, the local deputation had immediately demanded that he submit to a public comparison of the costs of the new method with the old patio process. They later derisively commented: 'The director and the professors have made repeated tests of the German method, and have extracted less silver and consumed more mercury than is the custom with the usual method.'[2] And again: 'Experience has proved that the German process cannot be applied to America. Perhaps it can be attributed to the fact that those who wish to set themselves up as masters here have not learned it very well or possibly American miners know more mineralogy and metallurgy than the Germans.' In a later protest to Madrid against the mining court's pretensions, the deputation's agent inveighed against 'a certain pretended enlightenment and despotism', and requested that 'those employed in the court should recognise that they depend upon, or spring from, the mining community and are supported at the latter's expense'.[3]

Elhuyar, needless to say, took an entirely different view of the matter. In a long memorandum he roundly pronounced the deputations to be inefficient, ignorant and corrupt: 'Breeding or education are not to be expected among these people.' His remedy was even more drastic than that of Revillagigedo. He proposed to augment the powers of the administrator-general, give this position to a permanent official and unite it to the superintendency of the mint.[4] In a word, the peninsular technocrat wished to subject the Mexican mining industry to someone rather like himself, capable of governing it for the increased profit of the Crown.

For the plans of both sides to the controversy, therefore, the outcome of the mining court's elections, to be held in December 1793, was decisive. At stake was the control of the court, since the posts of administrator-general and all three deputies-general were up for election. In consequence

1 See Howe, *The Mining Guild*, Chapter 3; AGI, Mexico 2238, Council of State, 25 January 1793.
2 AGI, Mexico 1560, Revillagigedo to Gardoqui, 30 November 1793.
3 AGI, Mexico 2238, Francisco Javier del Mazo, 30 September 1792.
4 AGI, Mexico 2243, Elhuyar to Aparici, 30 July 1791.

the general meetings proved remarkably stormy.[1] Guanajuato's delegate, Francisco de Septién y Arce, denounced the court's mismanagement of the finance bank and demanded a public presentation of its accounts. He laid down the doctrine that in money matters the court should hold itself responsible to the general meetings of deputation delegates. In his view it constituted little more than the elected executive of the mining community and hence true authority lay with the representative assembly. Finally, he proposed the exclusion of the merchant-aviadores who acted as the delegates for the smaller mining camps and insisted that all candidates for office should have fulfilled the obligatory ten years' mining practice.[2] None of all this pleased Elhuyar, who pointed out that in fact finance was the court's especial responsibility. Moreover, the general meetings, far from having a deciding vote, were convoked simply to elect officers and to approve the general summary of accounts. He protested that Septién wished 'to make the general meeting both judge and attorney of the court, which instead it ought to respect as its head'.[3]

This controversy became particularly sharp when, in the words of one observer, 'the delegate from Guanajuato in conjunction with some others ceaselessly tried to arrange that members of their own faction should be elected as administrator-general and as deputies-general. But another party having been formed to oppose Guanajuato's, the elections were made according to one or the other'.[4] In fact, Septién had made a pact with Fermín de Azpezechea, the representative of the Zacatecas deputation; he also secured the backing of Catorce. In the first instance this provincial alliance succeeded. The only surviving deputy-general, the merchant Antonio Barroso, installed by the viceroy in 1786, was firmly ejected from his place. Then Manuel García de Zeballos was elected as administrator-general. This surprising choice clearly shocked the other party into greater activity since in the upshot the first two elected deputies-general, José Manuel Valcárcel and Juan Manuel Guiles, both residents of Mexico City, narrowly defeated rival candidates from Zacatecas and Catorce. The third deputy-general was José Mariano de Fagoaga, manager of his family's great enterprise at Sombrerete.

This last nomination gives us the clue as to the composition of the other party that had been organised to oppose Septién and Azpezechea. It sprang from a union of Elhuyar with the merchant-capitalists and finance houses

1 AGI, Mexico 2246, December 1793. Here are to be found the bulky records of the sessions.
2 AGN, Minería 167/10, various petitions, 3 February 1794.
3 AGN, Minería 30/7, mining court to Gardoqui, 28 February 1794 (signed by Elhuyar, Guiles and Valcárcel).
4 AGI, Mexico 2244, San Luis Potosí delegate to Gardoqui, 27 January 1794.

of Mexico city led by the Fagoagas. There was nothing surprising in this: Elhuyar knew the Fagoagas quite well from the days when they had welcomed him to Sombrerete to test the Born method of amalgamation. The Marquis of Apartado had frequently acted as an advisor to the court. Moreover, fairly recently the territory of the Vetagrande mine in Zacatecas, of which the Fagoagas with Bassoco were the chief shareholders, had been invaded by Azpezechea and his associates. Since the latter controlled the local deputation only the mining court could reverse any decisions which might permit Azpezechea to register several unworked Vetagrande shafts.[1] Thus it was highly important to the Fagoagas to defeat the alliance of the Guanajuato and Zacatecas deputations. Sure enough, in the following year, Azpezechea renounced his designs upon the Vetagrande, and instead took over the Quebradilla from the grandchildren of José de la Borda.

The 1793 elections can best be described as a prelude to the nineteenth century. Possibly for the first time the representatives of the provinces travelled to Mexico City to seize control of a central governing body, until then led by persons radicated in the capital. Moreover, these provincial miners and refiners were fighting the influx of Mexico City almaceneros into the industry and, of course, that one great family, the Fagoagas, which had for so long dominated entire sections of Mexican mining. It must be emphasised, however, that this dispute did not follow any simple line of merchants against miners, or peninsulars against creoles. Septién himself was a merchant turned miner. In many ways what the Fagoagas were to New Spain at large, the Septién were to the Bajío. All the parties concerned, moreover, were born in Europe. What we find here, then, is an open struggle for power between a group of Guanajuato Montañeses acting in collaboration with the Basques of Zacatecas against the almaceneros and the Fagoagas of Mexico City.

One last question arises: power for what? And here, alas, our story lacks a denouement. Nothing much happened after the election of Manuel García de Zeballos as administrator-general. What then were the motives that led a group of Montañeses to try to seize control first of the institutions of Guanajuato and then of the mining court itself? In these years they came to dominate the militia battalion, the town council, the merchant and the mining deputations. Two great victories were scored over Manuel Antonio de Otero: Hernández Chico received 100,000 ps. for the Camargo and Mazo obtained the guardianship of his step-children's estate. But what was there in all this for Francisco Septién y Arce? Here one cannot refrain from speculation. He along with García de Zeballos

[1] AGN, Minería 107, Vetagrande company to viceroy, undated, at the end of 1792.

and a third Montañés, Andrés Sagaz y Herrera, took over the Tepeyac mine in 1790, the year before all three became electors on the mining junta. Now the Tepeyac, a relatively small property, adjoined the Valenciana. May not the possibility exist, therefore, that behind these institutional manoeuvres there lay a concealed plan to invade the Valenciana's rich section of the lode? Possibly . . . but without proof we should not slander the reputations of the dead. Certainly, however, Antonio Pérez Gálvez, the abductor of the eldest Obregón daughter, hinted as much when, in a letter written to Revillagigedo on the eve of the 1793 December elections, he asserted that the Guanajuato junta and deputation was led by one group of men, united by ties of blood, marriage and partnership. He said that these men opened shafts next to mines which had struck rich and then stole the best ore underground, their control of the deputation preventing any judicial redress.[1] However, since Pérez Gálvez's rival for the hand of the Obregón heiress was the Montañés García de Quintana, he clearly had no cause to like this group; in no sense was he a reliable witness. And there we must leave the matter. The Tepeyac never did very well, the Valenciana was not taken over or attacked. All that we are left with is a series of accusations and hints. Whatever the case, most of these men died within the next ten years, their position then being assumed by their creole sons.

[1] AGI, Mexico 1561, Antonio Pérez Gálvez to Revillagigedo, 29 November 1793. See also the appeals of Petra Alcántara Muñoz who accused the Tepeyac partners of stealing her mines' ore: AGI, Mexico 1594, Azanza to Soler, 27 December 1799; AGI, Mexico 2246, Council of the Indies, 12 May 1803.

EPILOGUE

The concluding act in the Bourbon revolution in government was the consolidation or amortisation decree of December 1804. Driven by the threat of impending bankruptcy, the Crown demanded that all ecclesiastical funds should be paid into the royal treasury, which henceforth would be responsible for the payment of the 5 per cent interest on the deposited principal.[1] Now these funds amounted to over forty million pesos and for the most part took the form of mortgages and loans secured upon agrarian and, to a lesser extent, urban property.[2] The new law, therefore, constituted a direct assault upon the economic interests of most land-owners and a good few merchants and miners. Everyone who had borrowed money from the Church was required to redeem their loans in instalments spanning a period of not more than ten years. Many landowners found it difficult to meet their obligations; a few had their estates seized and auctioned. Moreover, as so many haciendas appeared simultaneously on a market where at best demand was sluggish, land prices tumbled, with the consequence that the proportional value of the remaining fixed charges increased. By the end of 1808 this savage capital levy had squeezed over twelve million pesos from the purses of the propertied classes.[3]

The Marquis of San Miguel de Aguayo, for example, was expected to find no less than 450,000 ps. Gabriel de Yermo, a Basque sugar planter, had to pay some 200,000 ps. The Mexican consulado and the mining court which in part had financed their various projects with ecclesiastical funds now had to redeem these debts. The miners of Guanajuato suffered as much as anyone. The estates of the Marquis of San Juan de Rayas bore a cumulative debt of 154,000 ps., raised to finance the renovation of the Rayas mine. He was obliged to pay off this huge sum in yearly instalments of 12,000 ps.[4] Similarly, the Fernández de Riaño children had to find the 23,000 ps. which, over forty years before, their father, Bernardo, had spent on the San Lorenzo mine. Ramón de Aranda's widow could not redeem the 50,000 ps. with which her property was burdened, so the junta

[1] R. Flores Caballero, 'La consolidación de vales reales en la economía, la sociedad y la política novohispanas', *Historia Mexicana*, 18 (1969), 3, pp. 334–78.

[2] Mora, *Obras sueltas*, escritos de Abad y Queipo, pp. 231–3.

[3] Sociedad mexicana de geografía y estadística, *Boletín*, 2nd series, 1 (1869), pp. 486–95. The total collected from the Church in these years was 12½ million pesos.

[4] AMM, 153, 2 May 1807.

ordered the auction of one of her haciendas.[1] The house of María Josefa de Busto, charged with a 4,000 ps. mortgage was also embargoed.[2] In the nearby town of San Miguel el Grande several families had fallen heavily into debt. The Lanzagortas, for example, owed 61,950 ps. and the Sautos 34,200. The sons of Domingo Narciso de Allende had to pay annual instalments of 1,500 ps. to redeem their 18,000 ps. mortgage.[3] And in the congregation of Dolores the parish priest, Miguel Hidalgo y Costilla was unable to find the 7,000 ps. charged upon his small hacienda.[4] His estate, therefore, was embargoed and rented out; he did not regain possession of his property until the early months of 1810. Amortisation, without doubt, predisposed the colony to revolution, and was resented by creole and gachupín alike.

When in 1808, therefore, news reached New Spain of the French invasion of the Peninsula and the enforced abdication of the Bourbon dynasty, the accumulated tensions generated during forty years of economic reform and social change all exploded. Bourbon Mexico began to dissolve into its component parts. A stronger viceroy might well have averted some of the incipient chaos, but in the upshot José de Iturrigaray, a creature of Manuel Godoy, proved to be as vacillating as he was venal. He had already offended the somewhat puritanical members of the consulado by his extravagant mode of life and his cultivation of the creole aristocracy.[5] Now he endangered their interests by summoning a series of public juntas to discuss the vexed question of sovereignty. Immediately, the creoles led by the ayuntamiento of Mexico City and by the alcalde del crimen, Jacobo de Villaurrutia, seized the opportunity to demand the convocation of a national, representative assembly to assist the viceroy govern the country. Faced with this clear challenge to the traditional form of government, the old institutions which the Bourbon statesmen had so laboured to diminish in power, now staged an aggressive reaction. The audiencia conspired with the archbishop and the consulado, effected the seizure and resignation of Iturrigaray and installed their own nominee, an aged and impecunious Basque soldier, as viceroy.[6] In the audiencia the leaders were Guillermo de Aguirre y Viana, the nephew of that Count of

[1] AMM, 150, 13 September 1806; AHGP, Cabildo, 21 July 1807.

[2] AMM, 147, 4 August 1806.

[3] For Lanzagorta and Sauto see AGN, Consolidación 5, 9 March 1807, and 2 October 1807; for Allende see AMM, 154, 18 January 1807.

[4] AMM, 153, 2 May 1807, cost of case declared, 19 February 1810.

[5] Among his intimate friends were the Marquis of San Juan de Rayas and Ignacio Obregón, at this time, respectively, the administrator-general and deputy-general of the mining court. See Alamán, *Historia*, I, 153.

[6] *Ibid.*, I, 114–53.

Tepa who had opposed the creation of intendancies, and Miguel de Bataller, the son of a former judge in the same court.[1] The consulado faction was led by Gabriel de Yermo, a sugar planter, the nephew and uncle of priors of this bastion of the gachupín almaceneros.[2] Both he and Aguirre were Basques, whose nation's traditional liberties the government of Manuel de Godoy had recently attacked.[3] No doubt, Antonio Bassoco, by this time the acknowledged head of the community in New Spain, was cognisant of their plans; he came from the same valley as Yermo. The 1808 *coup d'état* possessed a twofold significance. It was both a manoeuvre of old Habsburg bodies acting to protect their prerogatives and also a determined stand made by Mexico's true aristocracy, the gachupín immigration, in defence of their position in colonial society.

Conservatives, however, may start revolutions, but they rarely finish them. The political situation in the two years following Iturrigaray's overthrow remained uneasy and explosive, the peninsulars unduly triumphant, the creoles resentful and conspiratorial. This malaise was deepened by popular unrest caused by successive bad harvests. In Guanajuato, in September 1809, after a summer of scarce rainfall, the intendant reported that maize already cost over 20 rls. a fanega, a figure more than double the normal price. At the same time in the central Mexican intendancy, 30 out of 41 districts gave notice of bad harvests; in some areas prices quadrupled.[4]

Such price levels were ruinous for the mining industry, since refining mills could no longer afford to feed and maintain their mules. By 1810 in Guanajuato only 1,200 arrastres out of a total 1,700 were at work, a decline which 'sprang from the terrible drought of that year and still more from that of the preceding year'.[5] Unemployment followed closely upon drought. As the Guanajuato cabildo stated: the mine-workers 'have suffered all the effects of the hunger and sickness of this calamitous year. They, who pour out their life in streams of sweat, were the first to find their efforts rendered fruitless by the extreme decadence at which the mines have arrived'.[6]

Clearly, the combination of a weak government in Mexico City and a

[1] For Aguirre see BN (Madrid) MSS 20417, recommendation of the Count of Tepa to Crown, 24 July 1798, that Aguirre should be promoted to the Council of the Indies; see also AGI, Mexico 1889, Aguirre to Crown, 8 August 1797. For Bataller see AGI, Mexico 1540, Branciforte to Llaguno, 3 June 1795, petition of the elder Bataller's widow, for her son Miguel's advancement.

[2] For Yermo see Alamán, *Historia*, I, 156–7.

[3] Carr, *Spain, 1808–1939*, pp. 63–4.

[4] AGN, Intendencias 73, Riaño to viceroy, 25 August, 11 September 1809.

[5] AGN, Minería 192/1, Guanajuato mining deputation to viceroy, 8 November 1816.

[6] AHG, Insurgencia 1810–11, Cabildo to Riaño, 22 September 1810.

hungry multitude in the provinces offered a propitious situation for creole conspirators. And it was in the towns of the Bajío, in a region whose recent prosperity, based upon mines, textiles and agriculture, had liberated it from the financial control of Mexico City capital, that the first open rebellion against viceregal government occurred. In September 1810 a group of militia officers in San Miguel el Grande, led by the parish priest of Dolores, Miguel Hidalgo y Costilla, unfurled the banner of Our Lady of Guadalupe, called upon the peasantry to revolt, and marched upon Guanajuato.[1]

There, upon the approach of the insurgent forces, the intendant, Juan Antonio de Riaño, suspicious of popular loyalty, withdrew into the newly completed Alhóndiga de Granaditas, the fortress-like municipal granary. He took with him the contents of the treasury and the local battalion of militia. The bulk of the town's peninsular community also accompanied him.[2] By contrast few of the creole élite joined him. The Ayuntamiento, led by Fernando Pérez Marañón, besought Riaño to defend the entire town; they assured him of popular support.[3]

In fact, the intendant's worst fears were confirmed: the masses joined Hidalgo; indeed, the Valenciana's manager, Casimiro Chovell, the Mining College's choice pupil, organised his workers into a regiment. It was these mine-workers as much as the Indians of Dolores who were most active in the siege of the granary. Riaño's decision to guard the treasury's bullion proved to be mistaken, since, as a later account put it, 'the knowledge that so much treasure lay shut up within served to incite the masses of the town and the crowd of Indians to attack the granary with greater fury'.[4] Within a few hours, Riaño was dead, and the granary taken.

After the capture the populace perpetrated an indiscriminate massacre of the peninsulars who continued to resist. Moreover, those prisoners who were taken, were later killed in cold blood just before the entrance of royalist troops into the town. In all at least three hundred peninsular Spaniards—merchants, miners and officials—lost their lives during the siege and the two subsequent massacres.[5] The Alhóndiga de Granaditas, the project of an enlightened governor, erected to ensure a cheap supply of

[1] See Liceaga, *Adiciones y rectificaciones*, I, 16–66.

[2] A group of peninsulars, including Tomás de Alamán, uncle of the future historian; Joaquín Antonio de Iramátegui, brother-in-law of the Pérez Marañón, and Bernardo Chico Valdés, stayed at home, and later swore 'fidelity, obedience and submission to the American nation'. See AHG, Insurgencia, 1810–11, 8 October 1810. The Count of Pérez Gálvez and Pedro de la Riva fled to Acapulco; see Liceaga, *Adiciones y rectificaciones*, I, 79.

[3] See *Pública vindicación*, pp. 19–20.

[4] AGN, Minería 192/1, Guanajuato deputation, 8 November 1816.

[5] Alamán, *Historia*, II, 39–47.

grain for the people of Guanajuato, in effect became the mausoleum of Spain's colonial empire, and the birthplace of an independent Mexico. The memory of these massacres forbade any comfortable accommodation between creoles and gachupines, who, henceforward, became no longer quarrelling cousins, but watchful suspicious foes.

The rebellion of 1810 possessed a peculiar fratricidal quality that made the Guanajuato slaughter all the more shocking. For all three rebel captains of San Miguel, Ignacio Allende, Juan Aldama and Mariano Abasolo, were first-generation creoles, the sons of Basque immigrants. Allende's father owned a shop and a small hacienda; Abasolo's father had rented the tobacco monopoly in Dolores; Aldama's progenitor had served as the manager of an obraje owned by the wealthy Canal family.[1] In a word, all three men belonged to that managerial, commercial immigrant class for which no precise English equivalent can be found. Their creole sons became captains in the militia and entered the ayuntamiento. But this local hegemony they had to share with a fresh wave of gachupín cousins and rivals. On the other hand, Hidalgo came from an older creole family, that reached back on his mother's side to the sixteenth century. His father acted as the manager of a large hacienda in the isolated district of Pénjamo. Two of the sons, Manuel and Miguel, entered the priesthood, a third took up law. This was the lesser creole class, that survived only by rural retreat or entrance into the professions, especially the priesthood.

In Guanajuato only two creoles of any note joined the rebels. José María Chico, a younger son of the regidor Bernardo Chico Valdés, a newly qualified lawyer already in debt to his elder brother to the tune of 5,000 ps., was a first-generation creole like the San Miguel group, who became Hidalgo's minister of justice.[2] On the other hand, José María de Liceaga was the nephew of Tomás de Liceaga who had helped Gálvez to suppress the 1767 revolt; by descent he was connected to the Busto family.[3] His father had acted as the manager of the municipal granary, a lesser functionary. These two men apart, the creole élite of Guanajuato chose to remain neutral in the struggle between Hidalgo and Riaño. But once the town was recaptured by royalist forces they rallied to the Crown. Ironically enough, in many cases, these neutral American Spaniards were the residuary beneficiaries of the rebellion. Fernando Pérez Marañón

[1] Juan Martineña, *Documentos*, p. 83; Alamán, *Historia*, I, 228–30.

[2] AHGP, Presos, 21 August 1810; José María Chico was 24 in 1810. See AHGP, Presos, 13 July 1803. After the recapture of Guanajuato, Bernardo Chico Valdés made his peace with the Crown by a gift of 35,000 ps. AGI, Mexico 2127, Cuentas de Caja, 1810.

[3] AHGP, Cabildo, 30 January 1787, 21 November 1807, 18 September 1811, 8 October 1811.

refused to serve under Hidalgo and in reward for his loyalty and in recognition of his capacity, the viceroy appointed him intendant.[1] Similarly Lic. Martín Coronel, another creole lawyer, became his legal lieutenant. In the treasury also, American subordinates received promotion. Pérez Marañón, who remained in office until 1821, was of course like Chico or Allende a first-generation creole, born of a merchant father.

The reasons why some men desired independence whereas others supported the Crown followed no fixed pattern. Agustín de Iturbide, a creole who based his military career upon a ruthless suppression of the insurgency, came from much the same social background as Allende; he was the son of a Basque merchant. On the other hand, certain geographical concentrations soon became evident. In San Luis Potosí, Félix Calleja, rather like his Peruvian counterpart Juan Manuel de Goyeneche, used his family connexions to rally the great landowners to the royalist cause.[2] He also counted upon the silver sent in by the gachupín owners of the Quebradilla mine in Zacatecas.[3] With this backing he soon created a small army, largely officered by creoles. His success restricted Hidalgo and Allende to the near north—to the intendancies of Guanajuato, Michoacán and Guadalajara—where all the militia regiments joined the rebellion. In the ensuing civil war they were defeated by a combination of Calleja's brigade from San Luis Potosí with the regular and militia regiments of Mexico and Puebla led by Manuel de Flon. Creoles of course fought on both sides. Calleja later complained about the passivity of the peninsular merchants who refused to enlist in his army.[4] At the same time, however, they denigrated the very men who were defending them and anxiously awaited the arrival of regular troops from Spain. The Peruvian judge, Manuel de la Bodega, commented: 'In the language of some Europeans, rebel and American have become synonymous.'[5] During the ensuing years, creoles were promoted to high civil and military office upon an unprecedented scale and yet at the same time were distrusted as never before. Naturally this situation could not last. It was these royalist conservatives who finally achieved New Spain's independence. The civil war of 1810–21 completed the militarisation of political power already started by

1 Liceaga, *Adiciones y rectificaciones*, I, 168.

2 AGI, Mexico 2345, Calleja to Crown, 12 January 1818; by marriage he was cousin to the powerful Rincón Gallardo family.

3 Alamán, *Historia*, I, 293. These were Fermín de Azpezechea, Bernardo de Iriarte and Julián Penmartin.

4 Bustamante, *Cuadro histórico*, I, 133.

5 AGI, Indiferente General 42, Manuel de la Bodega to Miguel de Lardizábal y Uribe, 27 October 1814.

the Bourbons. The 1821 *coup d'état* was organised by a colonial army largely raised to suppress the insurgency and supported by a conservative Church desirous of freeing itself from the control of a civil authority which had become too liberal. It was to take the new Mexican state more than a generation to regain control over these forces of reaction.

In 1814 several prominent officials expressed their views about the causes of the rebellion. The former judge of the Mexican audiencia, Ciriaco González Carbajal (one of 1808 conspirators) traced its origins back to the expulsion of the Jesuits. That order, he claimed, had inculcated attitudes of loyalty to the Crown among the creole élite with the result that 'in their time the name Spaniard was not so hated as it had been since'. The vacuum in education left by their departure was but poorly filled by badly trained American-born teachers who infected the young with their own anti-peninsular sentiments.[1] Equally revealing were the comments of Miguel de Lardizábal y Uribe, a scion of a distinguished Mexican family and in that year a Minister of the Crown. He perceived a social distinction between the rebels and royalists. The old aristocracy, many of whom descended from the conquistadors, had remained faithful to the monarchy. It was rather the progeny of immigrant 'shopkeepers, barbers, tailors, and polizones' who had caused all the trouble. 'The creole children of such people, that is to say, of low and common folk, are the authors and sustainers of the insurrection.'[2] In effect, both men, therefore, saw the rebellion as the direct outcome of the new Bourbon régime initiated by José de Gálvez.

The rebels themselves were slow to formulate any declaration of their principles. Three years passed before a national congress pronounced independence to be the goal of their movement. At the emotional level, however, the masses at once coined a slogan which best expressed what they were fighting for: 'Long live Our Lady of Guadalupe! Death to the gachupines!' Their leaders, although pandering to popular taste by allowing most accessible European throats to be cut, put the matter somewhat differently. They simply wished to be masters in their own house, to govern New Spain free from all foreign interference. They also desired to terminate that system whereby peninsular Spaniards, generation by generation, came to Mexico not merely to rule the colony, but also to dominate the commanding heights of its economy and society. In a word, they deeply resented that pattern of gachupín immigration which we

[1] AGI, Mexico 1158, Ciriaco González Carbajal to Miguel de Lardizábal y Uribe, 21 June 1814.

[2] AGI, Indiferente General 42, Miguel de Lardizábal y Uribe, 29 October 1814.

have laboured to define. Their sentiments were given classic expression in a proclamation issued by Father Hidalgo at Guadalajara. He attacked the gachupines in terms which Montezuma's ambassador may well have used when describing his first encounter with Cortés. He denounced them as 'unnatural men, who have broken the closest bonds of blood, abandoning their fathers, brothers, wives and their own children . . . to cross immense oceans, exposing themselves to hunger, nakedness and danger to life. The force behind all their toil is sordid avarice . . . they are only Catholics through policy, their true god is money'.[1]

[1] Printed in Alamán, *Historia*, II, 391–3.

APPENDIX 1

Select genealogy of the Fagoaga family connexion [1]

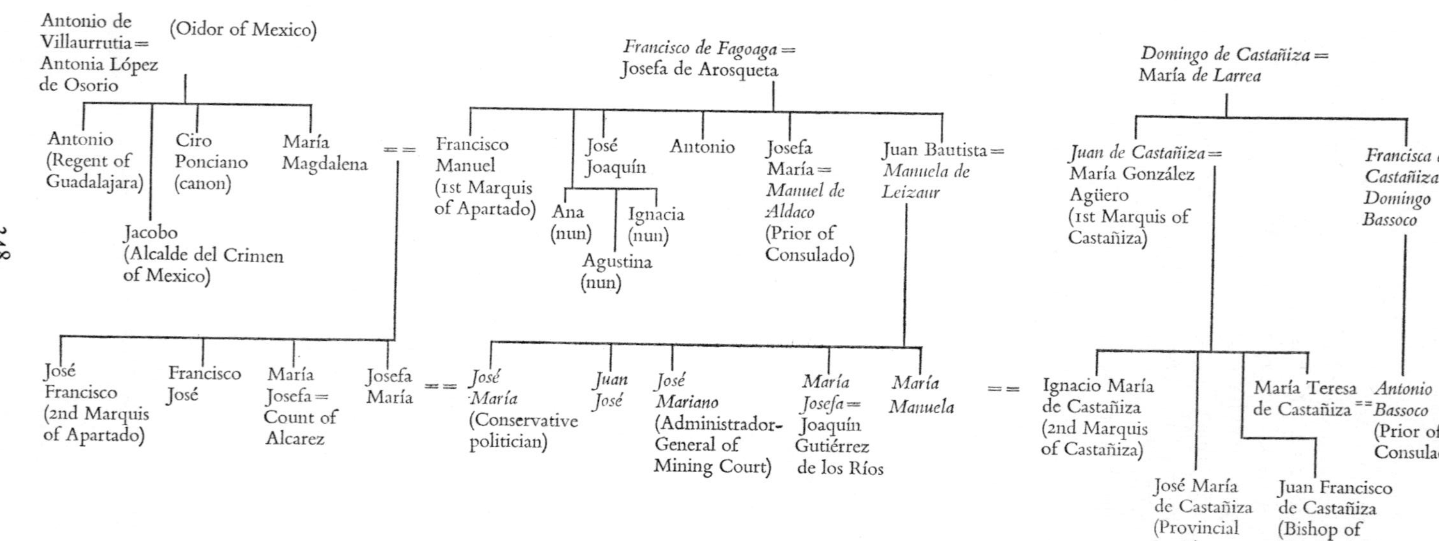

[1] Names italicised are peninsular Spaniards, others American-born.

Select genealogies of the Busto and Aranda families [1]

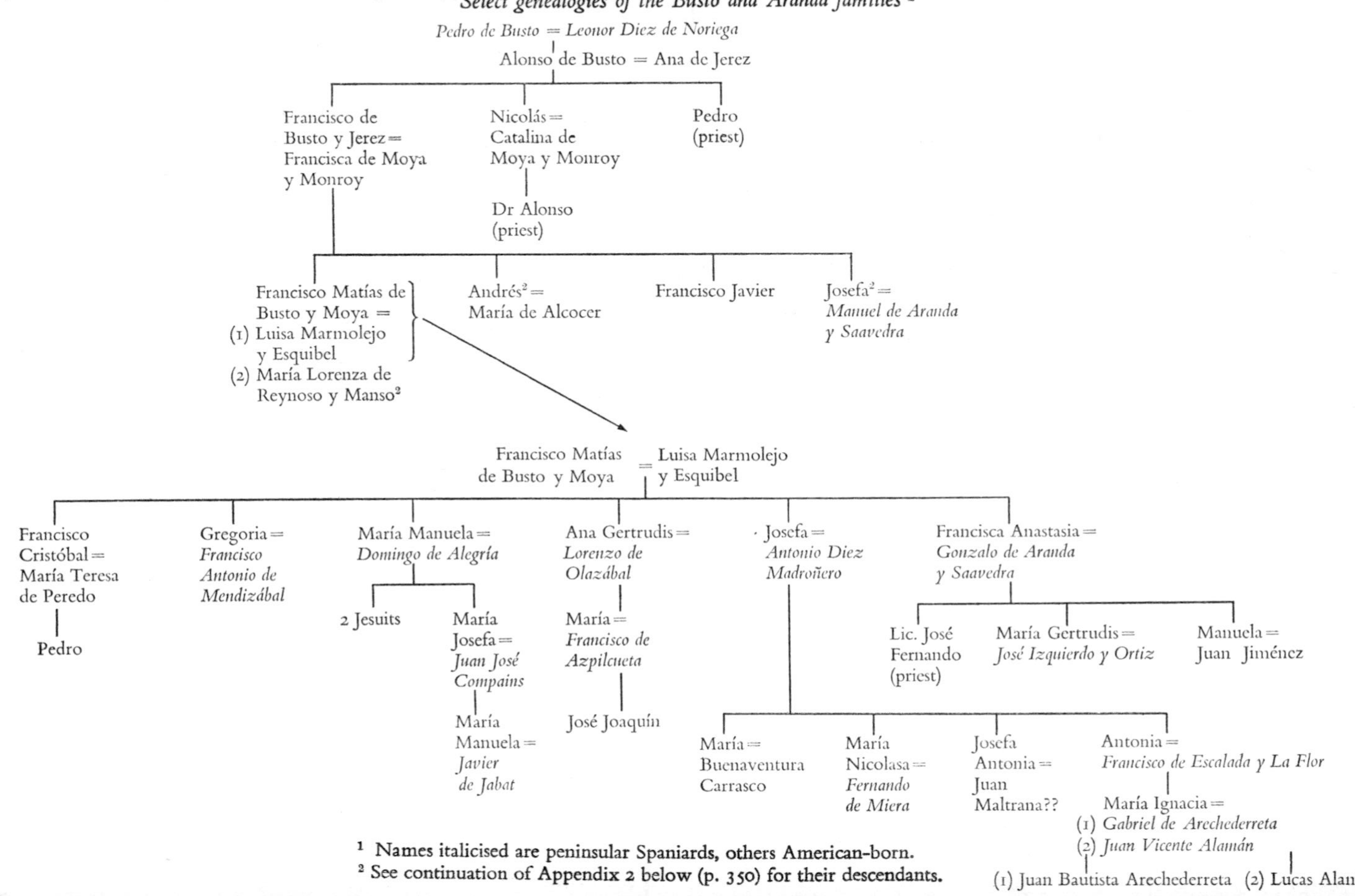

[1] Names italicised are peninsular Spaniards, others American-born.
[2] See continuation of Appendix 2 below (p. 350) for their descendants.

(APPENDIX 2—*contd.*)

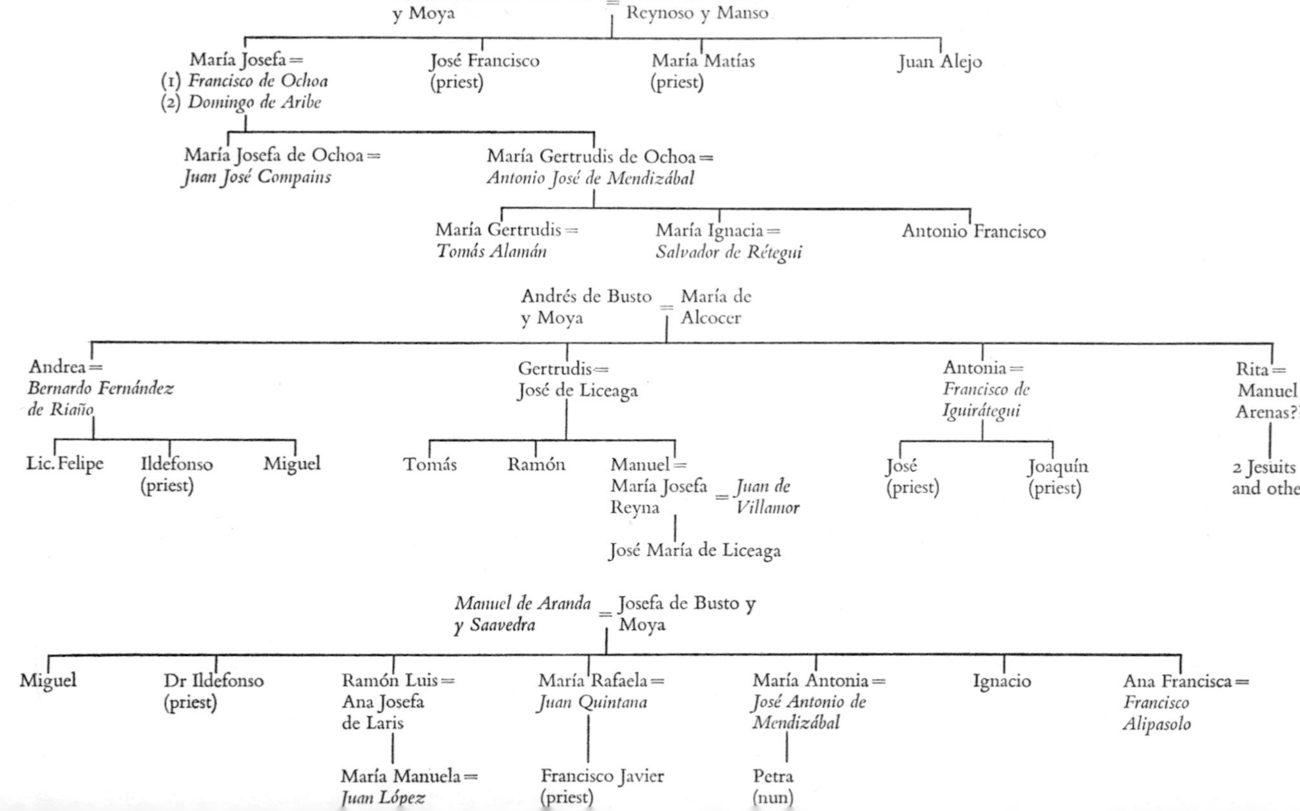

APPENDIX 3

Select genealogy of the Sardaneta family [1]

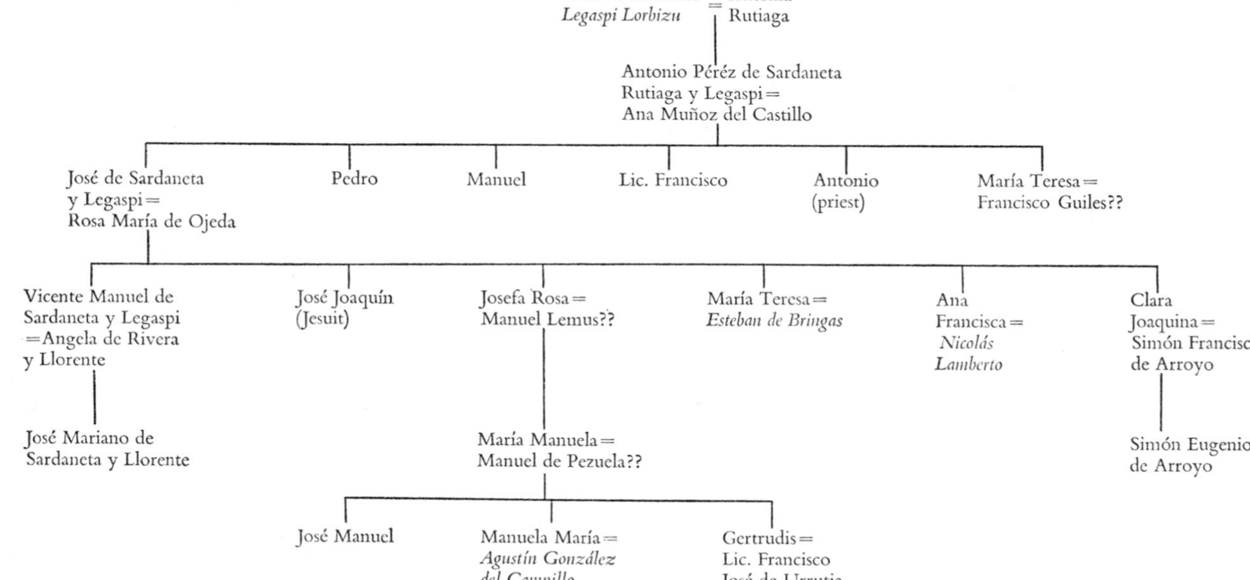

[1] **Names italicised are peninsular Spaniards, others American-born.**

N

APPENDIX 4

Select genealogy of the Septién family [1]

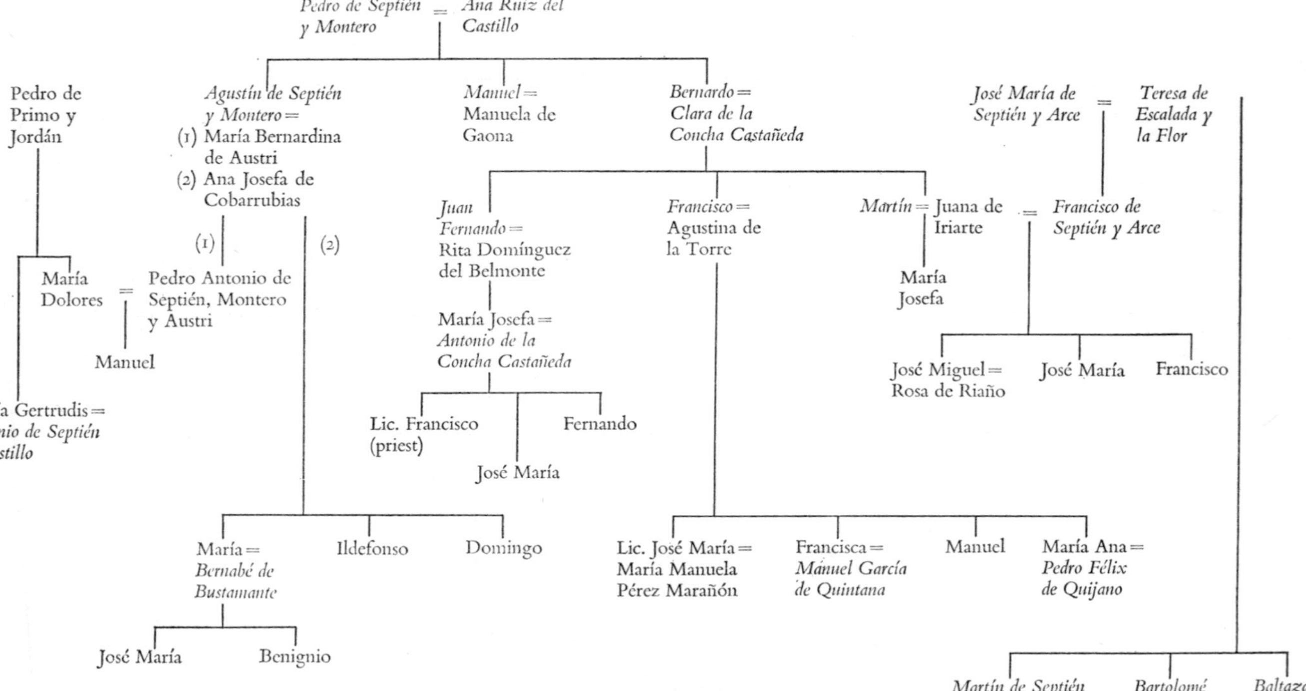

[1] Names italicised are peninsular Spaniards, others American-born.

APPENDIX 5

The Junta of Electors and Mining Deputation of Guanajuato, 1751–1808

February 1751	
Electors	
Antonio Jacinto Diez Madroñero	Extremeño
Lorenzo de Incháurregui	Basque
Juan Antonio Quintana	Basque
Gonzalo de Aranda y Saavedra	Extremeño
Vicente Manuel de Sardaneta	Creole
Augusto Gallartu	?
Andrés de Regil	?
Francisco Javier de Uribarren	?
Previous Deputies	
Antonio Jacinto Diez Madroñero	Extremeño
Francisco Javier de Uribarren	?
New Deputies	
Esteban de Bringas	Andaluz
Ignacio de Uribarren	Basque
September 1771	
Electors	
Juan José Compains	Basque
Bernardo Fernández de Riaño	Castilian
Lucas de Irizar	Basque
Domingo de Aribe	Basque
Tomás de Liceaga	Creole
Juan José Iguirátegui	Creole
Juan Ignacio de Aranda	Creole
Previous Deputies	
Antonio Jacinto Diez Madroñero	Extremeño
Marquis of San Juan de Rayas	Creole
New Deputies	
Fernando Antonio de Miera	Montañés
Gabriel de Arechederreta	Basque
April 1775	
Electors	
José Hernández Chico	Castilian
Domingo de Aribe	Basque
Juan José Compains	Basque
José González del Peral	Montañés
Antonio de Obregón	Creole
Tomás de Liceaga	Creole
Pedro Luciano de Otero	Creole

Previous Deputy	
José González del Peral	Montañés
New Deputy	
Domingo de Aribe	Basque
February 1779	
Electors	
Juan José Compains	Basque
Francisco Azpilcueta	Basque
Domingo Presa	Basque
Count of Valenciana	Creole
Ventura José Carrasco	Creole
Lic. Felipe Fernández de Riaño	Creole
Marquis of San Juan de Rayas	Creole
Previous Deputies	
José Hernández Chico	Castilian
Domingo de Aribe	Basque
New Deputies	
Lic. Felipe Fernández de Riaño	Creole
José María de Irizar	Creole
January 1783	
Electors	
José Hernández Chico	Castilian
Domingo de Aribe	Basque
Manuel García de Quintana	Montañés
José Campero	Montañés
Juan Revuelta	Montañés
Manuel García de Zeballos	Montañés
Antonio José de Mendizábal	Basque
Previous Deputies	
Pedro Luciano de Otero	Creole
Lic. Felipe Fernández de Riaño	Creole
New Deputies	
José Hernández Chico	Castilian
Francisco de Septién y Arce	Montañés
February 1787	
Electors	
Juan de Villamor	Castilian
Gervasio de Irizar	Creole
Lic. Martín Coronel	Creole
Pedro Luciano de Otero	Creole
Manuel Antonio de Otero	Creole
Lic. Felipe Fernández de Riaño	Creole
Miguel Fernández de Riaño	Creole
Previous Deputies	
Domingo de Aribe	Basque
Francisco de Septién y Arce	Montañés

New Deputies

Manuel García de Zeballos	Montañés
Lic. Felipe Fernández de Riaño	Creole

February 1791

Electors

Manuel García de Zeballos	Montañés
Andrés Sagaz y Herrera	Montañés
Francisco de Septién y Arce	Montañés
José Quijano	Montañés
Juan Bautista de Incháurregui	Creole
José María de Irizar	Creole
Marquis of San Juan de Rayas	Creole
Juan Vicente Regil	Creole

Previous Deputies

Domingo de Aribe	Basque
Miguel Fernández de Riaño	Creole

Past Deputies

José Hernández Chico	Castilian
Lic. Martín Coronel	Creole

November 1793

Electors

Manuel Fernando de Portu	Peninsular
Juan de Villamor	Castilian
Gervasio de Irizar	Creole
Manuel García de Zeballos	Montañés
Marquis of San Juan de Rayas	Creole
Lic. José María de Septién y Montero	Creole
Juan Vicente Regil	Creole

New Deputies

Andrés Sagaz y Herrera	Montañés
Lic. Martín Coronel	Creole

November 1796

Electors

Domingo de Aribe	Basque
Juan Vicente Alamán	Basque
José Antonio del Mazo	Montañés
Martín de le Riva	Montañés
Pedro Félix Quijano	Montañés
José Campero de Montero	Montañés
Manuel Antonio de Otero	Creole

New Deputies

León de Sein	Basque
Juan de Villamor	Castilian

Appendix 5

December 1799

Electors	
Juan Vicente Alamán	Basque
Tomás Alamán	Basque
Fernando de la Concha	Montañés
Andrés Sagaz y Herrera	Montañés
Francisco de Septién y Arce	Montañés
Pedro de Bustamante y Tagle	Creole
Marquis of San Juan de Rayas	Creole
Deputies	
Martín de la Riva	Montañés
Gervasio de Irizar	Creole

November 1802

Electors	
Manuel Fernando de Portu	Peninsular
Count of Pérez Gálvez	Malagueño
José Miguel Carrica	Basque
José Antonio del Mazo	Montañés
Pedro de la Riva	Montañés
Pedro Félix Quijano	Montañés
Lic. José María de Septién y Montero	Creole
José María Hernández Chico	Creole
Deputies	
Juan Vicente Alamán	Basque
Agustín Pérez Marañón	Montañés

November 1808

Electors	
Juan Vicente Alamán (dead)	Basque
Sebastián Sorondo	Basque
Modesto de Villa	Montañés
Joaquín Gutiérrez de Mercadillo	Montañés
Pedro de Otero	Creole
José Miguel de Septién y Arce	Creole
Joaquín de Aguiar	?
Deputies	
Francisco de Iriarte	Basque
Martín de la Riva	Montañés

Merchant Junta of Electors and Deputies

January 1788

Electors	
Juan de Villamor	Castilian
Juan Vicente Alamán	Basque
Bernabé de Bustamante	Montañés
Fernando Mazorra	Montañés
Andrés Sagaz y Herrera	Montañés

Francisco de Septién y Arce	Montañés
Agustín Pérez Marañón	Montañés
Gervasio de Irizar	Creole
Previous Deputies	
Juan José Compains	Basque
José Pérez Marañón	Montañés
New Deputies	
Juan Vicente Alamán	Basque
Francisco de Septién y Arce	Montañés

BIBLIOGRAPHY

A. PRIMARY SOURCES

(MSS cited in Notes)

SPAIN

AGI—Archivo General de Indias

Audiencia de Guadalajara, legajos 203, 477–8.

Audiencia de Lima, legajo 1119.

Audiencia de México, legajos 1045–6, 1127, 1129–30, 1133, 1136, 1138–40, 1143, 1158, 1196, 1317, 1365, 1367, 1369–70, 1377–8, 1380, 1382, 1387–8, 1390–1, 1394, 1396–8, 1400, 1403–5, 1416, 1418, 1420–1, 1426–7, 1448, 1454, 1457, 1461, 1463, 1509–11, 1513, 1515, 1521–2, 1525, 1528, 1531–3, 1540–2, 1544–5, 1547–5, 1547–9, 1554–5, 1557, 1560–1, 1568, 1571–3, 1577, 1579–81, 1587, 1594, 1608, 1614, 1617, 1619–20, 1622–3, 1630, 1632–4, 1645, 1660, 1686, 1719, 1724, 1728, 1730, 1732, 1743, 1745, 1750–3, 1762, 1765, 1768–9, 1772, 1775, 1777, 1779–80, 1783–4, 1786, 1790, 1795, 1804, 1809, 1811–12, 1815, 1817, 1849, 1856–9, 1862–3, 1866–8, 1870–2, 1876, 1878–9, 1883, 1887, 1889–90. 1893, 1895, 1960, 1973–6, 2018, 2026, 2032, 2119–20, 2122, 2125–7, 2200, 2202–3, 2205–9, 2212–14, 2235, 2238, 2240–8, 2251, 2254–6, 2345, 2356, 2379, 2504–5, 2512, 2811, 2981, 2990.

Estado, legajos 20, 23, 41, 42.

Indiferente General, legajos 42, 1713.

AGS—Archivo General de Simancas

Guerra Moderna, legajos 7015, 7275–7.

AHN—Archivo Histórico Nacional

Consejo de Indias, legajos 20688, 20701, 20727, 20728.

APS—Archivo Provincial de Santander

Catastro, volume 475.

Consulado, legajo 2.

BN (Madrid) Biblioteca Nacional

MSS volumes, 2929, 17618, 18636, 18739, 20417.

BRP—Biblioteca del Real Palacio

MSS volumes 2815, 2816, 2824.

CV—Cancillería de Valladolid

Sala de Hijosdalgo, legajos 1123, 1145.

GREAT BRITAIN

BM—British Museum

Additional MSS volumes 17557, 20999.

Egerton MSS volume 517.

Bibliography

MEXICO

ACM—Archivo Casa Morelos

Legajos, 433, 598, 617, 688, 743.

AGN—Archivo General de la Nación

Civil, volumes 142, 161, 189, 256.
Consolidación, volume 5.
Consulado, volumes 44, 123.
Guerra, volumes 121A, 242A, 5B.
Historia, volumes 44, 49, 130, 503, 523.
Inquisición, volumes 1384, 1434.
Intendencias, volumes 8, 17, 48, 64, 73, 79.
Minería, volumes 5, 11, 18, 20, 23, 25–8, 30, 37, 40, 45–6, 50–2, 56, 58, 75–6, 80, 82, 87, 94, 97, 106–8, 110, 111, 113–15, 120, 128, 137–8, 141, 148, 151, 152, 158, 167, 180, 192, 193, 202, 211, 216, 221, 225.
Padrones, volumes 30–3.
Subdelegados, volume 2.
Tierras, volumes 678, 679, 1283.
Vínculos, volumes 6–8, 10, 25, 106, 123, 144, 150, 152, 158, 171, 174, 176, 213–14, 216, 282.

AHG—Archivo Histórico de Guanajuato

Actas de Cabildo, volumes for years 1778–1810.
Alhóndiga, one legajo.
Bienes de Difuntos, legajos for years 1742–61, 1761–79, 1784–8, 1795–9, 1801–5.
Insurgencia, legajos for years, 1767, 1810–11, 1812–14.
Protocolos de Cabildo, yearly volumes, 1730, 1736, 1744, 1750, 1770, 1772, 1776, 1782, 1783, 1786–1811.
Protocolos de Minas, volumes for years 1760, 1780, 1783–5, 1790, 1799, 1806, 1808.
Protocolos de Presos, yearly volumes, 1746, 1755, 1799, 1803, 1806, 1807, 1810.

AHH—Archivo Histórico de Hacienda

Legajo 204.

AHL—Archivo Histórico de León

Legajo for year 1786.

AMM—Archivo Municipal de Morelia

Legajos, 143, 147, 150, 153–4.

AMZ—Archivo Municipal de Zacatecas

Legajo 23.

BN (Mexico) Biblioteca Nacional

MSS volumes 1187, 1374, 1380, 1385, 1388, 1391, 1396, 1405, 1535, 1791.

FV—Fundación Valenciana

legajos 3–5.

Private MSS—Libro manual del Conde de Pérez Gálvez; prueba de hidalguía de José Antonio del Mazo.

B. BIBLIOGRAPHICAL AIDS AND GUIDES TO ARCHIVES

Aguilar y Santillán, Rafael, 'Bibliografía geológica y minera de México', *Boletín del Instituto geológico de México*, x–xv (1898–1901).

Bermúdez Plata, Cristóbal, *Archivo general de Indias, catálogo de documentos de la sección novena*, I (Seville, 1949).

Gayangos, Pascual de, *Catalogue of the Manuscripts in the Spanish Language in the British Museum* (4 vols.; London, the Trustees, 1875–93).

Gómez Cañedo, Lino, *Los archivos de la historia de América. Período colonial español* (2 vols.; Mexico, 1961).

Gómez Molleda, D., *Bibliográfica histórica española, 1950–54* (Madrid, 1955).

González Palencia, Angel, *Un extracto de los documentos del Consejo de Indias conservados en la sección de Consejos del archivo Histórico Nacional* (Madrid, 1920).

Guía del archivo histórico de Hacienda, siglos XVI–XIX (Secretaría de hacienda y crédito público; Mexico, 1940).

Handbook of Latin American Studies (Harvard University Press, 1936–50, University of Florida Press, 1951).

Humphreys, R. A., *Latin American History, A guide to the literature in English* (Oxford, 1958).

Indice histórico español (Universidad de Barcelona, Centro de estudios históricos internacionales, Barcelona, 1953–).

Jones, C. K., *A Bibliography of Latin American Bibliographies* (2nd ed.; Washington, 1942).

Paz, Julián, *Catálogo de manuscritos de América existentes en la Biblioteca Nacional* (Madrid, 1933).

Peña y Cámara, José María de la, *El archivo general de Indias de Sevilla, guía del visitante* (Seville, 1958).

Rubio Mañé, Ignacio, 'El archivo de la nación', *Revista de Historia de América*, IX (1940), pp. 63–169.

Sánchez Alonso, Benito, *Fuentes de la historia española e hispano-americano* (3rd ed., 3 vols.; Madrid, 1952).

Títulos de Indias, Catálogo XX del archivo general de Simancas (Valladolid, 1954).

Zavala, Silvio, 'Catálogo de los fondos del centro de documentación del museo nacional de historia en el castillo de Chapultepec', *Memorias de la academia mexicana de la historia*, XII (1953), pp. 177–244.

C. PRINTED DOCUMENTS AND CONTEMPORARY WORKS

Abad y Queipo, Manuel, '*Los escritos . . .*', printed in José María Luis de Mora, *Obras sueltas* (Mexico, 1963).

Ajofrín, Francisco de, *Diario del viaje que hizo a la América en el siglo XVIII* (2 vols.; Mexico, 1964).

Alamán, Lucas, *Documentos diversos* (4 vols.; Mexico, 1947).

Historia de Méjico (5 vols.; Mexico, 1942).

Bibliography

Alzate Ramírez, José Antonio, *Gacetas de literatura de México* (4 vols.; Puebla, 1831).

Amat y Junient, Manuel de, *Memoria de gobierno*, edición y estudio preliminar de Vicente Rodríguez Casado y Florentino Pérez Embid (Seville, 1947).

Beleña, Eusebio Buenaventura, *Recopilación sumaria de todos los autos acordados de la real audiencia y sala del crimen de esta Nueva España* (2 vols.; Mexico, 1787).

Berghes, Carlos de, *Descripción de la serranía de Zacatecas formada por I. A. Bustamante* (Mexico, 1834).

Beristáin de Sousa, José Mariano, *Biblioteca hispano-americana septentrional* (3rd ed., 5 vols.; Mexico, 1947).

Bustamente, Carlos María de, *Cuadro histórico de la revolución mexicana* (3 vols.; Mexico, 1961).

Campillo y Cosío, José del, *Nuevo sistema de gobierno económico para la América* (Madrid, 1789).

Cañete y Domínguez, Pedro Vicente, *Guía histórica, geográfica, física, política, civil y legal del gobierno e intendencia de la provincia de Potosí* (Potosí, 1952).

Castañiza González de Agüero, Juan Francisco, *Relación del reestablecimiento de la sagrada compañía de Jesus en el reyno de Nueva España* (Mexico, 1816).

Castelazo, José Rodrigo de, *Manifiesto de la riqueza de la negociación de minas conocidas por la Veta Vizcaína* (Mexico, 1820).

Cavo, Andrés, *Los tres siglos de México durante el gobierno español hasta la entrada del ejército trigarante. Publicada con notas y suplemento por Carlos María de Bustamante* (3 vols.; Jalapa, 1870).

Chávez Orozco, Luis, ed., *El comercio exterior y su influjo en la economía de Nueva España en 1793* (Mexico, 1960).

ed., *Conflicto de trabajo con los mineros de Real del Monte, año de 1766* (Mexico, 1960).

Colección de documentos para la historia del comercis exterior de México (Mexico, 1959).

Croix, Marqués de, *Instrucción ... que deja a su sucesor Antonio María de Bucareli*, prólogo y notas de Norman F. Martin (Mexico, 1960).

Cuevas, Mariano, ed., *Tesoros documentales de México siglo XVIII: Priego, Zelis, Clavijero* (Mexico, 1944).

Díaz del Castillo, Bernal, *Historia verdadera de la conquista de la Nueva España*, introducción y notas de Joaquín Ramírez Cabañas (Mexico, 1960).

Dictamen de la comisión especial nombrada para informar sobre el importante ramo de minería (Mexico, 1821).

Diez de Bracamonte, Juan, *Por la justicia ...* (Mexico, 1699).

Discurso sobre el testamento de la señora María Teresa Castañiza de Bassoco (Mexico, 1830).

Discurso sobre la minería en este imperio (Mexico, 1822).

Elhuyar, Fausto de, *Indagaciones sobre la amonedación en la Nueva España (Madrid*, 1818).

Fabry, José Antonio, *Compendiosa demonstración de los crecidos adelantamientos que pudiera lograr la real hacienda ... mediante la rebaja en el precio del azogue, que se consume para el laborío de las minas de este reyno* (Mexico, 1743).

Fonseca, Fabián de and Carlos de Urrutia, *Historia general de Real Hacienda escrita por órden del virrey, conde de Revillagigedo* (6 vols.; Mexico, 1845–53).

Funes, Gregorio, *Ensayo de la historia civil de Buenos Aires, Tucumán y Paraguay* (2 vols.; Buenos Aires, 1856).

Gálvez, José de, *Informe general. . . . al excelentísimo señor virrey d. frey Antonio Bucareli y Ursúa* (Mexico, 1867).

Gamboa, Francisco Javier de, *Comentarios a las ordenanzas de minas dedicados al cathólico rey, nuestro señor don Carlos III* (Madrid, 1761).

Commentaries on the mining ordinances of Spain: dedicated to his Catholic Majesty, Charles III. By Don Francisco Xavier de Gamboa . . ., trans. from the original Spanish by Richard Heathfield (2 vols.; London, 1830).

Garcés y Eguía, José, *Nueva teórica y práctica del beneficio de los metales* (Mexico, 1802).

Gemelli Carreri, G. F., *Viaje a la Nueva España* (2 vols.; Mexico, 1955).

González de Cossío, Francisco, ed. *Gacetas de México* (3 vols.; 1944–50).

Gómez de Cervantes, Gonzalo, *La vida económica y social de Nueva España al finalizar el siglo XVI*, prólogo y notas de Alberto María Carreño (Mexico, 1944).

Granados y Gálvez, Fr. José Joaquín, *Tardes americanas* (Mexico, 1778).

Guijo, Gregorio M., *Diario 1648–1684* (2 vols.; Mexico, 1953).

Guridi Alcocer, José Miguel, *Censor extraordinario* (Cadiz, 1812).

Hall, Basil. *Extracts from a Journal written on the coasts of Chili, Peru and Mexico in the years 1820, 1821, 1822* (2 vols.; Edinburgh, 1824).

Hawks, Henry, 'A Relation of the Commodities of Nova Hispania, and the Manners of the Inhabitants', Richard Hakluyt, *Voyages* (8 vols.; London; Everyman, 1962).

Hernández y Dávalos, Juan, *Colección de documentos para la historia de la guerra de independencia de México de 1808 a 1821* (6 vols.; Mexico, 1877–82).

Holland, Lady Elizabeth, *The Spanish Journal* (London, 1910).

Humboldt von, Alexander, *Ensayo político sobre el reino de la Nueva España*, ed. Juan A. Ortega y Medina (Mexico, 1966).

Humboldt von, Alexander and Aimé Bonpland, *Personal Narrative of Travels to the Equinoctial Regions of America during the years 1799–1804* (3 vols.; London, 1870).

Instrucciones que los virreyes de Nueva España dejaron a sus sucesores (Mexico, 1867); second, enlarged edition (2 vols.; Mexico, 1873).

James, Edward, *Remarks on the Mines, Management, Ores etc. of the District of Guanaxuato belonging to the Anglo-Mexican Mining Association* (London, 1827).

Jáuregui, José María de, *Discurso en que se manifiesta que deben bajarse los réditos a proporción del quebranto que hayan sufrido en la insurreción los bienes y giros de los deudores* (Mexico, 1820).

Jovellanos en la real academia de la historia (Madrid, 1911).

Juan, Jorge and Antonio de Ulloa, *Noticias secretas de América* (2 vols.; Madrid, 1918).

Lassaga, Lucas de and Joaquín Velásquez de León, *Representación que a nombre de la minería de esta Nueva España, hacen al rey* (Mexico, 1774).

Lerdo de Tejada, Ignacio, *Discurso que en la profesa solemne del cuarto voto* (Mexico, 1816).

Lerdo de Tejada, Miguel, *El comercio esterior de México* (Mexico, 1853).

Liceaga, José María, *Adiciones y rectificaciones a la historia de México por don Lucas Alamán* (2 vols.; Mexico, 1944).

López de Gómara, Francisco, *Cortés, The Life of the Conqueror by His Secretary*, trans. and ed. Lesley Byrd Simpson (Berkeley and Los Angeles, 1966).

López de Cancelada, Juan, *Ruina de la Nueva España* (Cadiz, 1811).

El Telégrafo Americano (Cadiz, 1812).

Maniau Torquemada, Joaquín, *Compendio de la historia de la Real Hacienda escrita en el año de 1794* (Mexico, 1914).

Martineña, Juan Martín de Juan, *Verdadero origen, carácter, causas, resortes, fines y progresos de la revolución de Nueva España* (Mexico, 1810).

Mier, Fray Servando Teresa de, *Memorias* (2 vols.; Mexico, 1946).

Mora, José María Luis de, *Méjico y sus revoluciones* (3 vols.; Mexico, 1950).

Obras sueltas (Mexico, 1963).

Moreno y Castro, Juan, *Arte ó nuevo modo de beneficiar los metales de oro y plata* (Mexico, 1758).

Morfi, Fray Agustín de, *Viaje de Indias y diario del Nuevo México*, ed. Vito Alessio Robles (Mexico, 1935).

Mota y Escobar, Alonso de la, *Descripción geográfica de los reynos de Nueva Galicia, Nueva Vizcaya y Nuevo León*, introducción por Joaquín Ramírez Cabañas (Mexico, 1940).

Navarro y Noriega, Fernando, *Memoria sobre la población del reino de la Nueva España* (Mexico, 1954).

Novísima recopilación de las leyes de España (6 vols.; Madrid, 1805–26).

Observaciones sobre el acuerdo de la cámara de senadores . . . relativo a la testamentaría de la señora doña María Teresa Castañiza de Bassoco (Mexico, 1830).

Osores, Félix, *Noticias bio-bibliográficas de alumnos distinguidos de San Pedro y San Pablo y San Ildefonso de México* (2 vols.; Mexico, 1908.)

Paz, Melchor, *Guerra separatista, rebeliones de indios en Sur América, la sublevación de Tupac Amaru* ed., Luis Antonio Eguiguren (2 vols.; Lima, 1952).

Poinsett, J. R., *Notas sobre México, 1822* (Mexico, 1950).

Pública vindicación del ilustre ayuntamiento de Guanajuato. . . . (Mexico, 1811).

Quirós, José María, *Memoria de estatuto. Idea de la riqueza que daban la masa circulante de Nueva España sus naturales producciones en los años de tranquilidad a su abatimiento en las presentes conmociones* (Veracruz, 1817).

Ramírez, José María, *Elegía a la muerte del padre José María Castañiza, provincial de la compañía de Jesús de México* (Guadalajara, 1817).

Ramos Arizpe, Miguel, *Memoria sobre el estado de las provincias internas de oriente presentada a las Cortes de Cádiz*, Noticia biográfica y notas por Vito Alessio Robles (Mexico, 1932).

Rasgo breve de la grandeza guanajuatense, generoso desempeño con que celebró la regocijada dedicación del suntuoso templo de la sagrada compañía, que a sus expensas erigió . . . (Puebla, 1767).

Representaciones del real tribunal de minería a favor de su importante cuerpo y declaración del excmo. señor virrey de estos reinos (Mexico, 1781).

Revillagigedo, Conde de, Juan Vicente Güemes, Pacheco, Padilla y Horcasitas, *Instrucción reservada que . . . dió a su sucesor en el mando el Marqués de Branciforte sobre el gobierno de este continente en el tiempo que fue su virrey* (Mexico, 1831).

Rivera Bernárdez, Joseph de, Conde de Santiago de la Laguna, *Descripción muy breve de la muy noble y leal ciudad de Zacatecas* (Mexico, 1732).

Sarria, Francisco Javier de, *Ensayo de metalurgia* (Mexico, 1784).

Sierra, Luis María de la, *Memoria sobre el estado de comercio que publica la real junta de Santander* (Santander, 1833).

Silva Herzog, Jesús, *Colección de documentos*, III. *Relaciones estadísticas de Nueva España a principios del siglo XIX* (Mexico, 1944).

Sonneschmid, Frederick, *Tratado de amalgamación de Nueva España* (Paris, Mexico, 1825).

United Mexican Mining Association, *Reports* (London, 1827–9).

Ustáriz, Gerónimo de, *Theórica y práctica de comercio y de marina* (2nd ed.; Madrid, 1755).

Velasco Ceballos, Rómulo, ed., *La administración de d. Frey Antonio María de Bucareli y Ursúa* (2 vols.; Mexico, 1936).

Villaroel, Hipólito, *Enfermedades políticas que padecen la capital de esta Nueva España* (Mexico, 1830).

Villaseñor y Sánchez, José Antonio de, *Respuesta que . . . a favor de la real hacienda en que defiende no ser el precio del azogue, el que da motivo a que no se costean las minas de cortas leyes* (Mexico, 1742).

Theatro americano, descripción general de los reynos y provincias de la Nueva España y sus jurisdicciones (2 vols.; Mexico, 1746–8).

Wall, Bernardo, *Proyecto económico* (Madrid, 1779).

Ward, H. G. *Mexico in 1827* (2 vols.; London, 1828).

Ximénez y Frías, José Antonio, *El fénix de los mineros ricos de la América. Fúnebre presentación en el día . . . en que se celebró el sufragio de honras del caballero José de la Borda* (Mexico, 1779).

Zaragoza, J. ed., *Castellanos y vascongados* (Madrid, 1876).

Zavala, Lorenzo de, *Ensayo histórico de las revoluciones de Nueva España* (2 vols.; Paris, Mexico, 1831).

Zelaa e Hidalgo, José María, *Glorias de Querétaro* (Mexico, 1803).

D. SECONDARY WORKS

Aguirre Beltrán, Gonzalo, *La población negra de México, 1519–1810. Estudio etno-histórico* (México, 1946).

Alessio Robles, Vito, *Coahuila y Texas en la época colonial* (Mexico, 1938).

Arcila Farías, Eduardo, *El siglo ilustrado en América, reformas económicas del siglo XVIII en Nueva España* (Caracas, 1955).

Artola, Miguel, 'Campillo y las reformas de Carlos III', *Revista de Indias*, 50 (1952), pp. 685–714.

Bibliography

Ashton, T. S. and Joseph Sykes, *The Coal Industry of the Eighteenth Century* (Manchester, 1964).

Bailyn, Bernard, *The New England Merchants in the Seventeenth Century* (2nd ed.; New York, 1964).

Bargalló, Modesto, *La amalgamación de los minerales de plata en Hispano-américa colonial* (Mexico, 1969).

La minería y la metalurgia en la América española durante la época colonial (Mexico and Buenos Aires, 1955).

Barger, Harold and Samuel H. Schurr, *The Mining Industries 1899–1939. A Study of Output, Employment and Productivity* (New York, 1944).

Barreda y Ferrer de la Vega, Fernando, *Aportación al estudio de la historia económica de la montaña* (Santander, 1957).

Bayle, Constantine, *Los cabildos seculares en la América española* (Madrid, 1952).

Bazant, Jan, 'Evolución de la industria textil poblana (1554–1845)', *Historia Mexicana*, 13 (1964), pp. 473–516.

Bernstein, Henry, 'A Provincial Library in Colonial Mexico', *Hispanic American Historical Review*, 26 (1946), pp. 162–83.

Berthe, Jean Pierre, 'Las minas de oro del Marqués del Valle en Tehuantepec 1540–1547', *Historia Mexicana*, 7 (1958), pp. 122–31.

'Xochimancas, les travaux et les jours dans une hacienda sucrière de Nouvelle-Espagne au XVIII siècle'. *Jahrbuch für Geschichte ... Lateinamerikas*, Band 3 (Köln, 1966).

Bobb, Bernard, *The Viceregency of Antonio María Bucareli, 1771–79* (Austin, 1962).

Borah, Woodrow, 'America as Model: The Demographic Impact of European Expansion upon the Non-European World', *Congreso Nacional de Americanistas* (Mexico, 1962), pp. 379–87.

Early Colonial Trade and Navigation between Mexico and Peru (Berkeley and Los Angeles, 1954).

'Un gobierno provincial de frontera en San Luis Potosí, 1612–20', *Historia Mexicana*, 13 (1964), pp. 532–50.

New Spain's Century of Depression (Berkeley and Los Angeles, 1951).

'Race and Class in Mexico', *The Pacific Historical Review*, 22 (1954), No. 4, pp. 331–42.

Borah, Woodrow and Sherburne F. Cook, *The Aboriginal Population of Central Mexico on the Eve of the Spanish Conquest* (Berkeley and Los Angeles, 1963).

Price Trends of Some Basic Commodities in Central Mexico, 1531–1570 (Berkeley and Los Angeles, 1958).

Brading, D. A., 'La minería de la plata en el siglo XVIII: El caso Bolaños', *Historia Mexicana*, 18 (1969), pp. 317–33.

Braudel, Fernand, *El mediterráneo y el mundo mediterráneo en la época de Felipe II* (2 vols.; México City and Buenos Aires, 1953).

Burkart, Juan, 'Memoria de la explotación de las minas de Pachuca y Real del Monte', *Anales de la minería* (Mexico, 1861).

Calderón de la Barca, Frances, *Life in Mexico* (London; Everyman ed., 1960).

Bibliography

Calderón Quijano, José Antonio, *El banco de San Carlos y las comunidades de indios de Nueva España* (Seville, 1963).

Carr, Raymond, *Spain, 1808–1939* (Oxford, 1966).

Chaunu, H. and P., *Séville et l'Atlantique (1504–1650)* (8 vols.; Paris, 1955–9).

Chevalier, Francois, *La formación de los grandes latifundios en México* (Mexico, 1956).

Clayburn La Force, Jr., James, *The Development of the Spanish Textile Industry 1750–1800* (Berkeley and Los Angeles, 1965).

Cook, Sherburne F., 'The Incidence and Significance of Disease among the Aztecs and Related Tribes', *Hispanic American Historical Review*, 26 (1946), pp. 320–31.

Cook, Sherburne F. and Woodrow Borah, *The Indian Population of Central Mexico 1531–1610* (Berkeley and Los Angeles, 1960).

'Quelle fut la stratification sociale au Centre du Mexique durant la première moitié du XVIe siècle?' *Annales*, 18 (1963), pp. 233–5.

Cook, Sherburne F. and Lesley Byrd Simpson, *The Population of Central Mexico in the Sixteenth Century* (Berkeley and Los Angeles, 1948).

Desdevises de Dézert, A., *L'Espagne de l'Ancien Regime: Les Institutions* (Paris, 1899).

Domínguez Ortiz, Antonio, *La sociedad española en el siglo XVIII* (Madrid, 1955).

Edwards Vives, Alberto, *La fronda aristocrática* (Santiago de Chile, 1952).

Esquivel Obregón, Toribio, *Biografía de d. Francisco Javier de Gamboa* (Mexico, 1941).

Eyzaguirre, Jaime, *Ideario y ruta de la emancipación chilena* (Santiago de Chile, 1957).

Farriss, N. M., *Crown and Clergy in Colonial Mexico, 1759–1821* (London, 1968).

Fisher, Lillian Estelle, *The Intendant System in Spanish America* (Berkeley, 1929).

Flores Caballero, Romeo, 'La consolidación de vales reales en la economía, la sociedad y la política novohispanas', *Historia Mexicana*, 18 (1969), pp. 334–78.

Florescano, Enrique, *Precios del maíz y crisis agrícolas en México 1708–1810* (Mexico, 1969).

García Caraffa, Alberto and Arturo, *Enciclopedia heráldica y genealógica hispano-americana*, (Madrid, 1919).

Gerhard, Peter, *México en 1742* (Mexico, 1962).

Gibson, Charles, *The Aztecs under Spanish Rule* (Stanford, 1964).

González Cancino y Aguirre, Francisco, 'Santillana del Mar en el año de 1753', *Altamira*, 2 (1934), pp. 73–178.

Guthrie, Chester L., 'Colonial Economy, Trade, Industry and Labor in the Seventeenth Century', *Revista de Historia de América*, 7 (December, 1939), pp. 103–34.

Hagen, Everett E., *On the Theory of Social Change* (Homewood, Ill., 1962).

Hammond, George P., *Juan de Oñate and the Founding of New Mexico* (Santa Fe, N.M., 1927).

Hamilton, Earl J., *American Treasure and the Price Revolution in Spain 1501–1650* (Cambridge, Mass., 1939).

Haring, C. H., *The Spanish Empire in America* (New York, 1963).

Heckscher, Eli F., *Mercantilism* (2 vols.; London, 1934).

Herr, Richard, *The Eighteenth Century Revolution in Spain* (Princeton, 1958).

Hoskins, W. G., *Provincial England* (London, 1963).
'The Elizabethan Merchants of Exeter', in *Elizabethan Government and Society: Essays presented to Sir John Neale*, ed. S. T. Bindoff, et al. (London, 1961).
Howe, Walter, *The Mining Guild of New Spain and its Tribunal General 1770–1821* (Cambridge, Mass., 1949).
Jiménez Moreno, Wigberto, *Estudios de historia colonial* (Mexico, 1958).
Lohman Villena, Guillermo, *Los americanos en las órdenes nobiliarias 1529–1900* (2 vols.; Madrid, 1947).
Lynch, John, *Spain under the Habsburgs* (2 vols.; Oxford, 1964–9).
Spanish Colonial Administration (London, 1958).
Macalister, Lyle N., *The fuero militar in New Spain 1764–1800* (Gainesville, Fla., 1957).
Mariscal Romero, María Pilar, *Los bancos de rescate de plata* (Seville, 1964).
Marmolejo, Lucio, *Efemérides guanajuatenses* (4 vols.; Guanajuato, 1884).
Martínez Cosío, Leopoldo, *Los caballeros de las órdenes militares de México* (Mexico, 1946).
Matilla Tascón, A., *Historia de las minas de Almadén* (Madrid, 1958).
Maza Solano, Tomás, *Nobleza, hidalguía, profesiones y oficios en la montaña segun los padrones del catastro del Marqués de la Ensenada* (4 vols.; Santander, 1953–61).
Mecham, J. Lloyd, *Francisco de Ibarra and Nueva Vizcaya* (Durham, N.C., 1927).
Mendizábal, Miguel Othón de, *Obras completas* (6 vols.; Mexico, 1946–7).
Minchinton, Walter E., 'The Merchants in England in the Eighteenth Century', in *Explorations in Enterprise*, ed. Hugh G. J. Aitken (Cambridge, Mass., 1965).
Miranda, José, 'La población indígena de México en el siglo XVII', *Historia Mexicana*, 12 (1963), pp. 182–9.
Morse, Richard M., 'Some Characteristics of Latin American Urban History', *The American Historical Review*, 63 (January, 1962), pp. 317–38.
Motten, Clement G., *Mexican Silver and the Enlightenment* (Philadelphia, 1950).
Navarro García, Luis, *Intendencias de Indias* (Seville, 1959).
Neasham, V. Audrey, 'Spain's Emigrants to the New World', *Hispanic American Historical Review*, 19 (1939), pp. 146–60.
Nieto y Carvellas, Rafael, *Los Villaurrutias* (Habana, 1952).
Obregón, Jr., Gonzalo, *El real colegio de San Ignacio de México* (Mexico, 1949).
Orozco, Rafael, *La industria minera de México, distrito de Guanajuato* (Mexico, 1921).
Ortega y Pérez Gallardo, Ricardo, *Historia genealógica de las familias más antiguas de México* (3 vols.; Mexico, 1908–10).
Otero, Mariano, *Obras* (2 vols.; ed. Jesús Reyes Heroles; Mexico, 1967).
Ots Capdequí, José María, *Historia de América: instituciones* (Barcelona and Madrid, 1959).
Otte, Enrique, 'Los mercaderes vizcaínos Sancho Ortiz de Urrutia y Juan de Urrutia', *Boletín Histórico Fundación Boulton*, 6 (1964), pp. 3–32.
Palacio Atard, Vicente, *Areche y Guirior, observaciones sobre el fracaso de una visita* (Seville, 1946).
El comercio de Castilla y el puerto de Santander en el siglo XVIII (Madrid, 1960).

Palmer, R. R., *The Age of the Democratic Revolution* (Princeton, 1959).

Parry, J. H., *The Audiencia of New Galicia in the Sixteenth Century* (Cambridge, 1948).

The Spanish Seaborne Empire (London, 1966).

Pimentel, Francisco, *La economía política aplicada a la propiedad territorial en México* (Mexico, 1866).

Postan, M. M. ed., *The Cambridge Economic History of Europe*, I. *The Agrarian Life of the Middle Ages* (2nd ed.; Cambridge, 1966).

Potash, Robert A., *El banco de avío de México, 1821–1846* (Mexico, 1959).

Priestley, Herbert Ingram, *José de Gálvez, Visitor-General of New Spain (1765–71)* (Berkeley, 1916).

Probert, Alan, 'Bartolomé de Medina: The Patio Process and the Sixteenth Century Silver Crisis', *Journal of the West*, 8 (January 1969), pp. 90–124.

Ramírez, Santiago, *Noticia histórica de la riqueza minera de México* (Mexico, 1884).

Raso, José Antonio del, *Notas estadísticas del departamento de Querétaro, año de 1845* (Mexico, 1846).

Real Díaz, José Joaquín, *Las ferias de Jalapa* (Seville, 1959).

Romero, José Guadalupe, *Noticias para formar la historia y la estadística del obispado de Michoacán* (Mexico, 1862).

Rosenzweig, Fernando, 'La economía novo-hispánica al comenzar el siglo XIX', *Ciencias Políticas y Sociales*, 9 (1963), pp. 455–93.

Rowe, John, *Cornwall in the Age of the Industrial Revolution* (Liverpool, 1953).

Rubio Mañé, Ignacio J., *Gente de España en la ciudad de México año de 1689* (Mexico, 1966).

'Síntesis histórica de la vida del II conde de Revillagigedo, virrey de Nueva España', *Anuario de estudios americanos*, VI (Seville, 1949).

Sarmiento, Domingo de, *Conflicto y armonía de las razas en América* (2 vols.; Buenos Aires, 1953).

Shafer, Robert Jones, *The Economic Societies in the Spanish World, 1763–1821* (Syracuse, N.Y., 1958).

Sierra Justo, *Evolución política del pueblo mexicano* (Mexico, 1957).

Juárez, su obra y su tiempo (Mexico, 1956).

Simpson, Lesley Byrd, *Exploitation of Land in Central Mexico in the Sixteenth Century* (Berkeley and Los Angeles, 1952).

Smith, Robert, 'The Institution of the Consulado in New Spain', *Hispanic American Historical Review*, 24 (1944), pp. 61–83.

'Sales Tax in New Spain, 1575–1770', *Hispanic American Historical Review*, 28 (1948), pp. 2–37.

Sojo y Lomba, Fermín de, *Ilustraciones a la historia de la M.N. y S.L. Merindad de Trasmiera* (2 vols.; Madrid, 1931).

Lierganes (Madrid, 1936).

Soraluce y Zubizarreta, Nicolás de, *Real sociedad bascongada de los Amigos del País* (San Sebastian, 1880).

St Clair Duport, Henri, *De la Production des Metaux Precieux au Mexique* (Paris, 1843).

Stone, Lawrence, *The Crisis of the Aristocracy, 1558–1641* (Oxford, 1965).
Toussaint, Manuel, *Don José de la Borda restituída a España* (Mexico, 1933).
Tasco (Mexico, 1931).
Tovar Velarde, Jorge, 'La audiencia de Lima 1705–1707. Dos años de gobierno criollo en el Perú', *Revista de Historia*, 23 (Lima, 1957–8).
Velásquez, María del Carmen, *El estado de guerra en Nueva España 1760–1800* (Mexico, 1958).
Vicuña Mackenna, Benjamín, *Los orígenes de las familias chilenas* (3 vols.; Santiago de Chile, 1903).
Vidal, Salvador, *Señor Francisco García Salinas, 'Tata Pachito'* (Zacatecas, 1962).
Vilar, Pierre, *La Catalogne dans l' Espagne Moderne* (3 vols.; Paris, 1962).
West, Robert C., *The Mining Community in Northern New Spain: The Parral Mining District* (Berkeley and Los Angeles, 1949).
Whitaker, Arthur, 'The Elhuyar Mining Mission and the Enlightenment', *Hispanic American Historical Review*, 31 (1951), pp. 558–83.
Wolf, Eric R., 'The Mexican Bajío in the 18th century: An Analysis of Cultural Integration', *Synoptic Studies of Mexican Culture*, ed. Munro S. Edmundson (New Orleans, 1957).
Wolf, Eric R. and Sidney W. Mintz, 'Haciendas and Plantations in Middle America and the Antilles', *Social and Economic Studies*, 6 (1957), pp. 380–412.
Zavala, Silvio, 'Orígenes coloniales del peonaje en México', *El Trimestre Económico*, 10 (1943–4), pp. 711–48.

MAP 1. New Spain: Political divisions

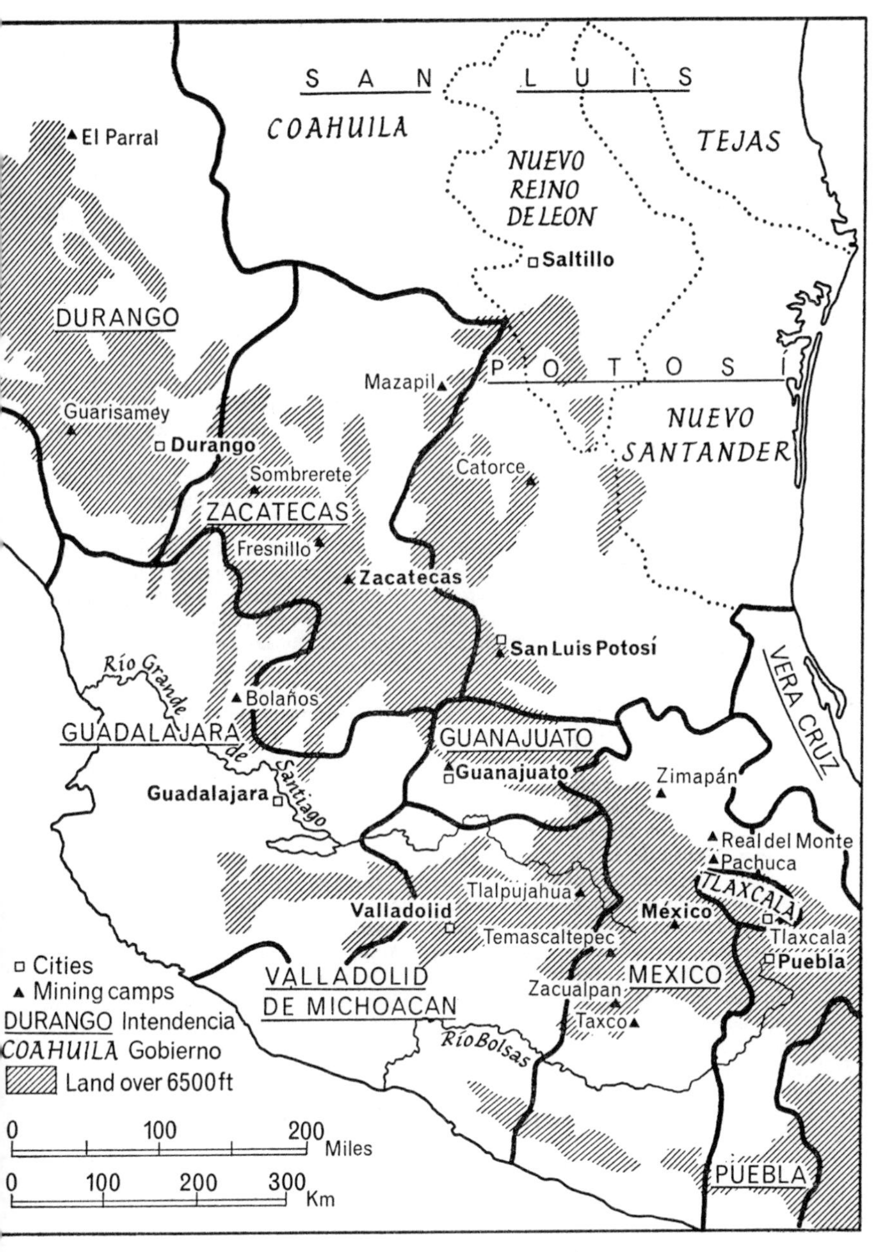

MAP 2. Central New Spain: Mining Camps

INDEX

Index